MW01627646

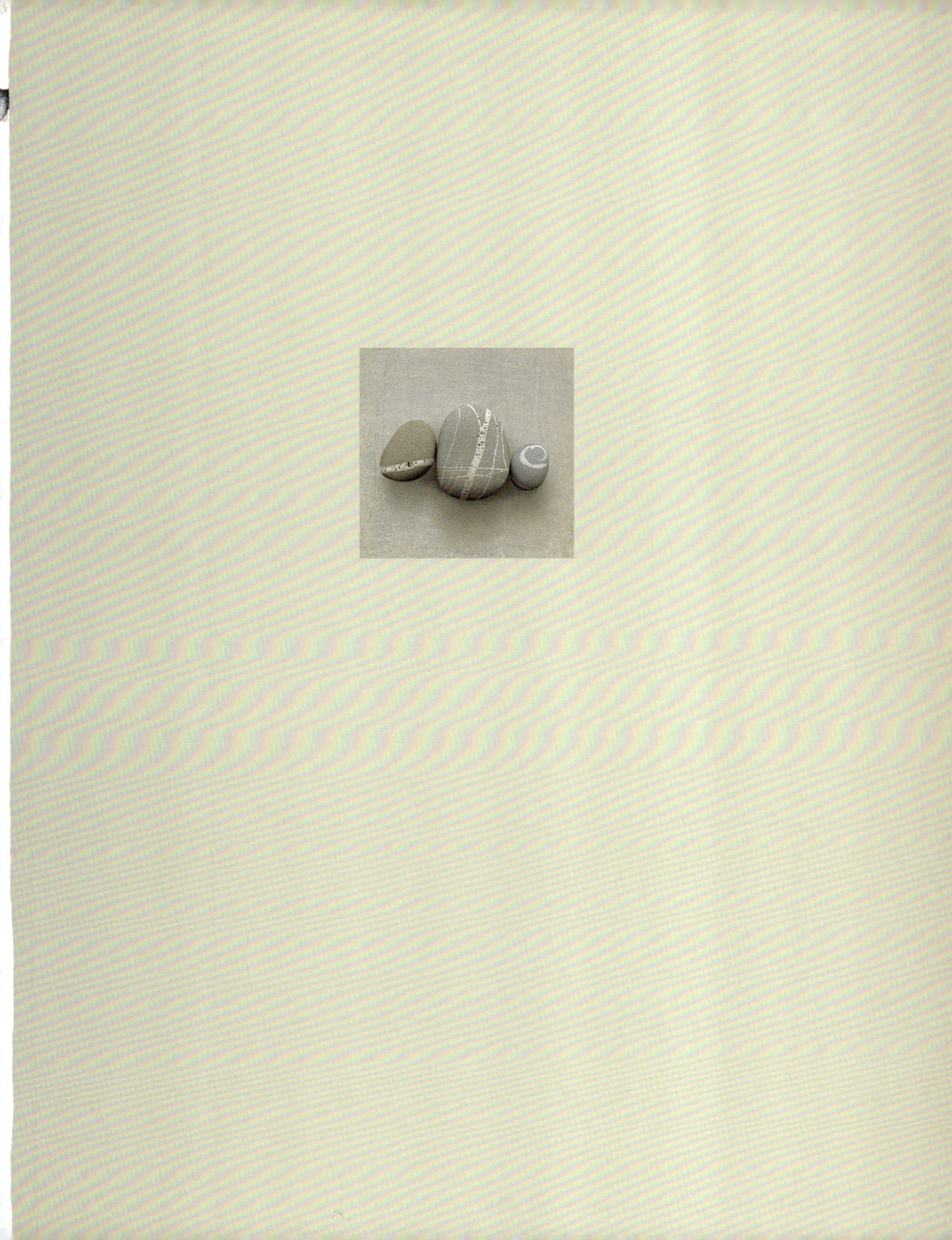

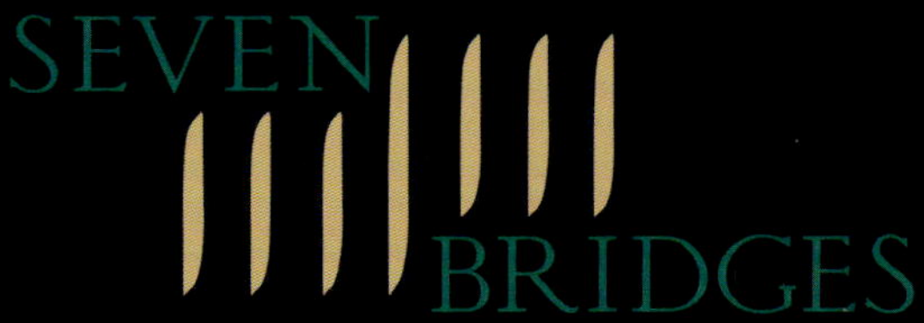

This book has been published with the generous support of Seven Bridges Foundation, established by Richard and Molly McKenzie for the exhibition and preservation of works of art in a natural setting. The foundation houses a unique collection of modern and contemporary representational art in its Gallery building and on landscaped grounds. The Gallery, completed in 1994, presently holds over 200 paintings by Odd Nerdrum, Richard Maury, Alan Magee, Will Wilson, Christian Vincent, William Beckman, Gregory Gillespie, Steven Assael, Chester Arnold and others. Sculptures by Henry Schiowitz, Cynthia Schaefer, Michael Bergt, Eric Goulder, Sean Henry and others are installed on the grounds. Seven Bridges Foundation is located in Greenwich, Connecticut and is open, by appointment, to museum groups, scholars, artists and students.

ALAN MAGEE

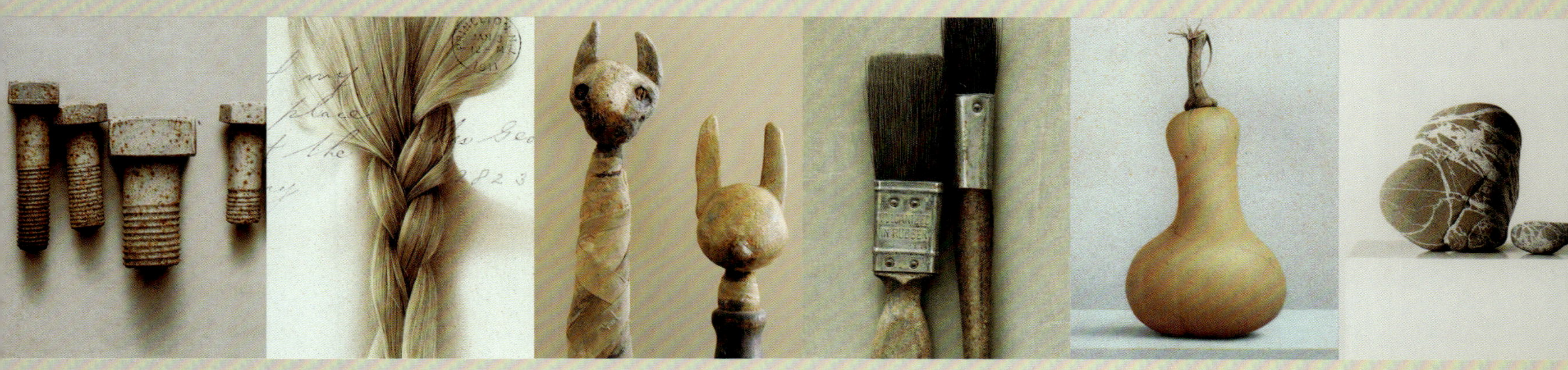

Alphabet • Parable • Knot • Luftpost • An Exact Anatomy of Man • Natural History • Rhyme • A First Seminary • Polestar • Pact

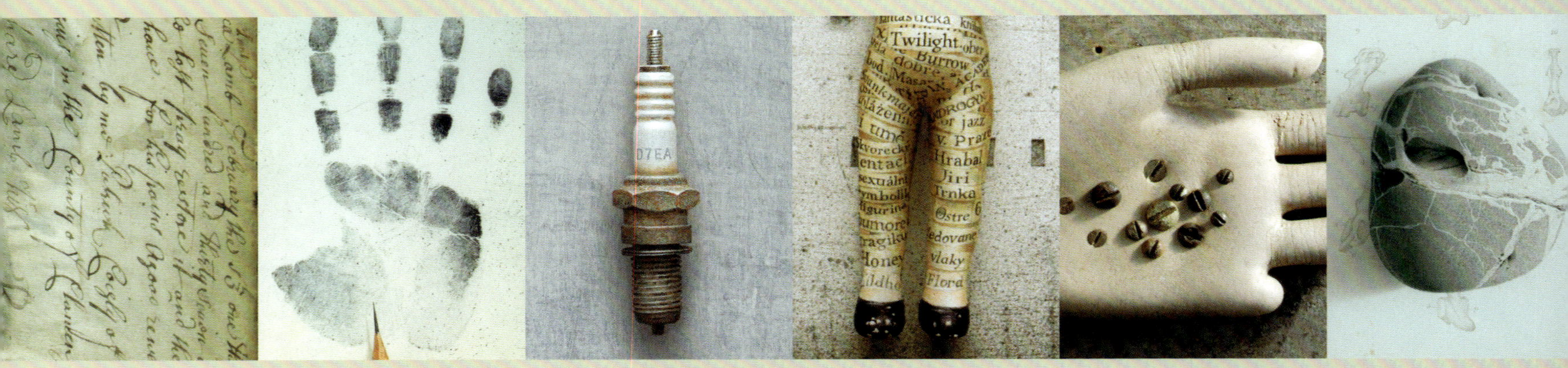

Catena • School Figures • Selbstbildnis • Heartland • Collected Letters • Samizdat • Pocket Guide • Knowledge • Palimpsestos

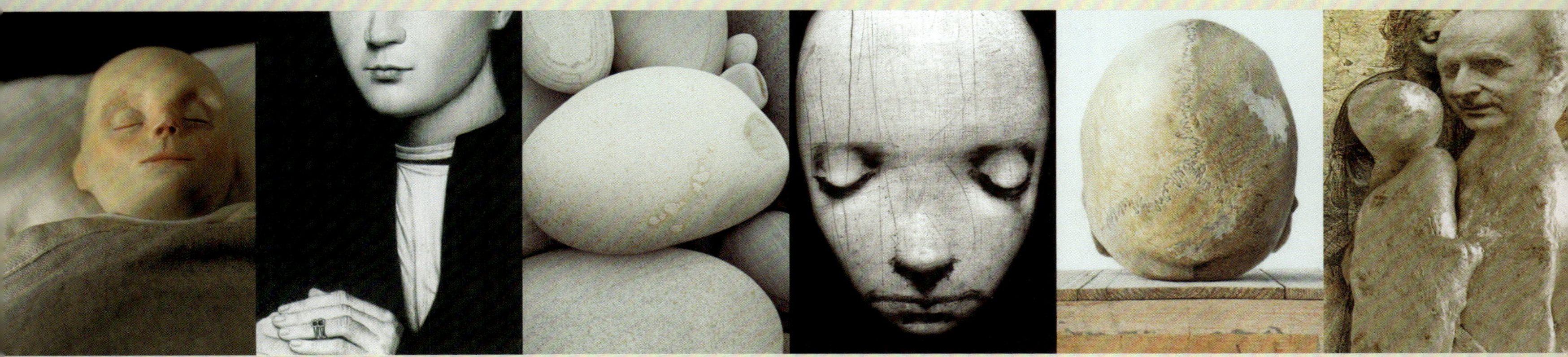

Couplet • Solaris • The Lost Memling • Moonlight • Numen • From an Anthology of Childhood • Coda • Evidence • Earthwork

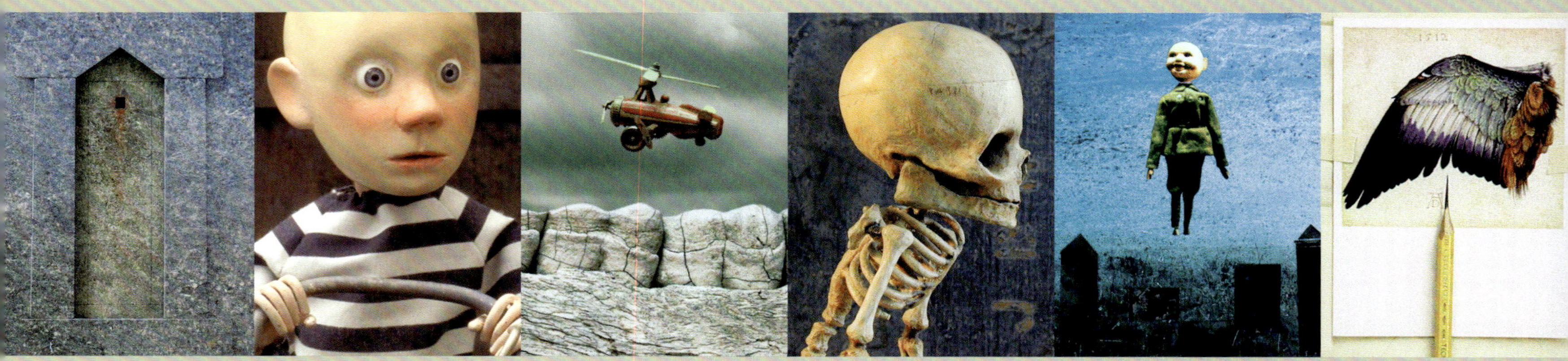

Inlet • Colonnade • The Ruins at Glanum • Mesa Blanca • The Anatomist's Notebook • Steps • The Lamb • Mitteleuropa • Wind

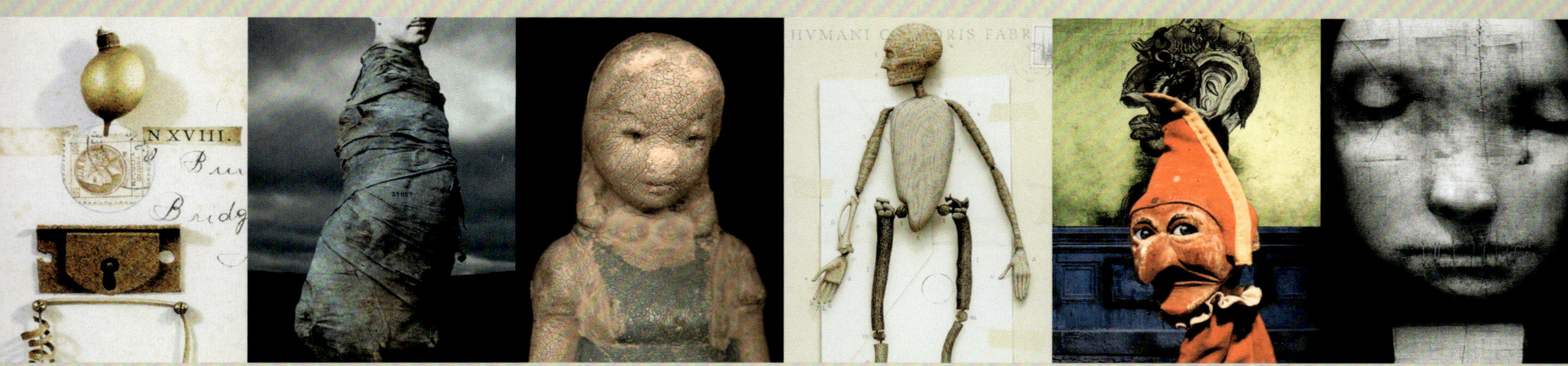

Domus • Silence • Memoir • Going Over • The Hemispheres • Number 22 Alchemist's Street • Burrow • Silence • The Animals

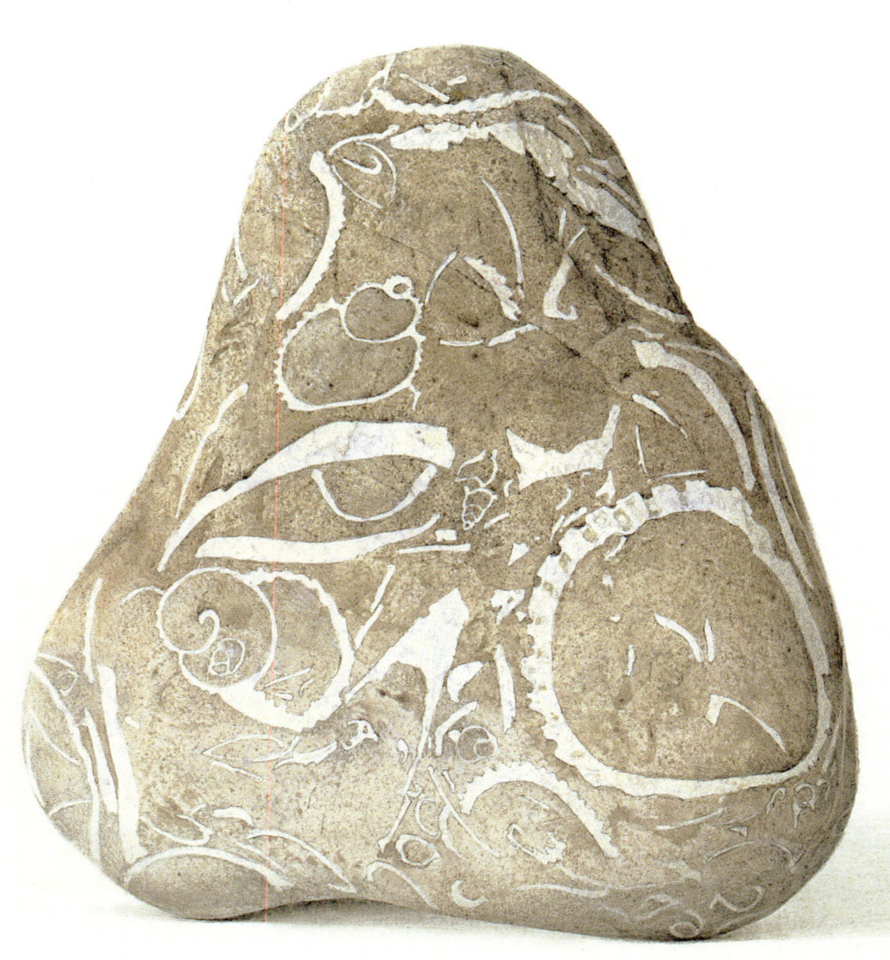

ALAN MAGEE

PAINTINGS
SCULPTURE
GRAPHICS

CONVERSATION WITH

BARRY LOPEZ

APPRECIATION BY

JONATHAN WEINER

FOREWORD BY

RICHARD V. WEST

PUBLISHED BY

FORUM GALLERY

NEW YORK · LOS ANGELES

Alan Magee: Paintings, Sculpture, Graphics was published by Forum Gallery on the occasion of the Alan Magee retrospective exhibition of the same title, organized by the Farnsworth Art Museum, Rockland, Maine.

James A. Michener Art Museum Bucks County, Pennsylvania October 25, 2003 to January 26, 2004

Farnsworth Art Museum Rockland, Maine April 11 to July 5, 2004

The Museum of Texas Tech University Lubbock, Texas September 5 to November 28, 2004

Frye Art Museum Seattle, Washington January 15 to March 15, 2005

Cover: *Convergence*, 2001, acrylic and oil on panel, 50 x 40"

Opening illustration: *Proverb* (detail), 2000 acrylic and oil on panel, 10 x 8"

Frontispiece: *Ghost* (detail), 1982, watercolor, 15.5 x 19.5"

ISBN 0-9675826-6-0

Printed in China

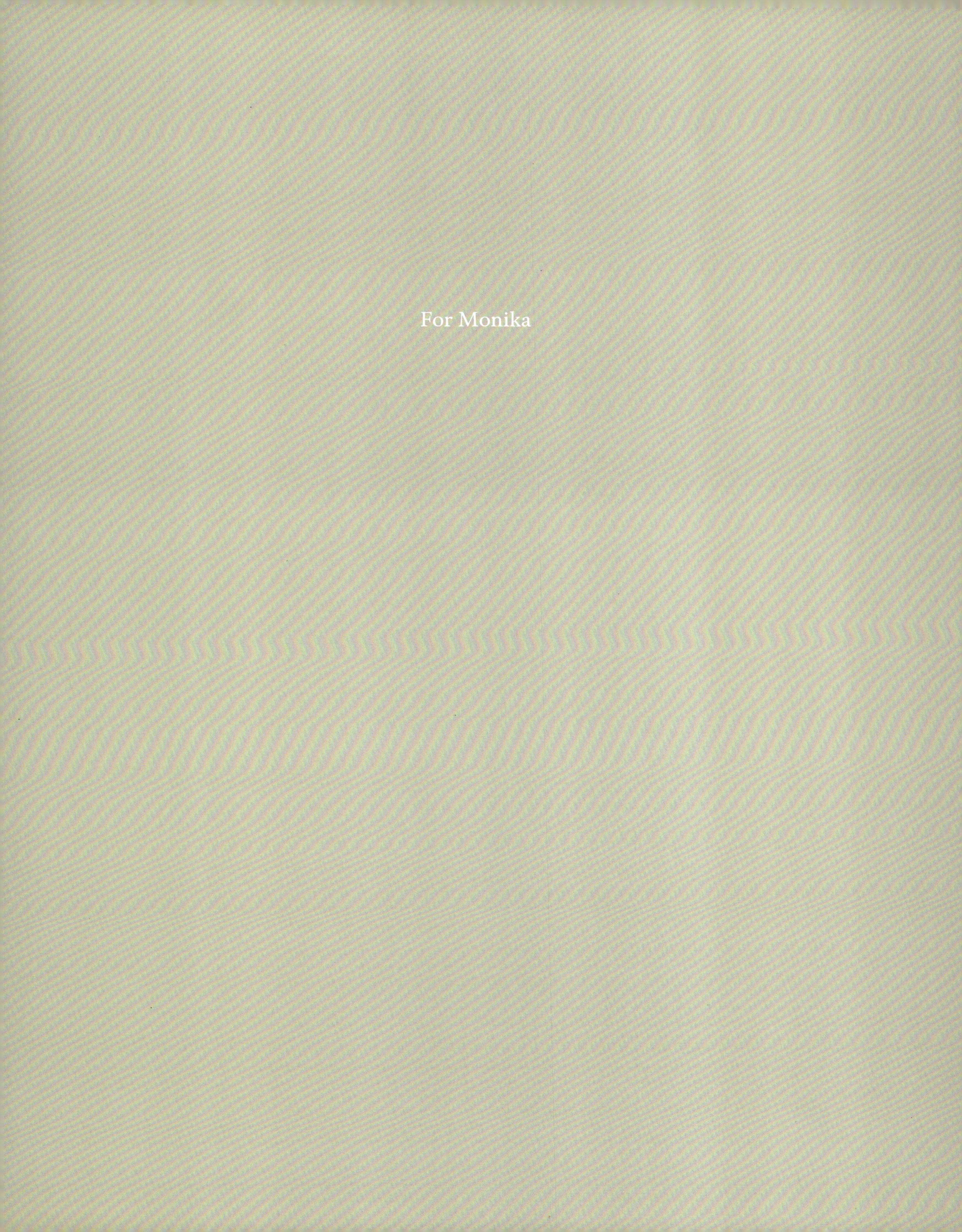

For Monika

Art does not lie down on the bed that is made for it; it runs away as soon as one says its name; it loves to go incognito. Its best moments are when it forgets what it is called.

JEAN DUBUFFET

CONTENTS

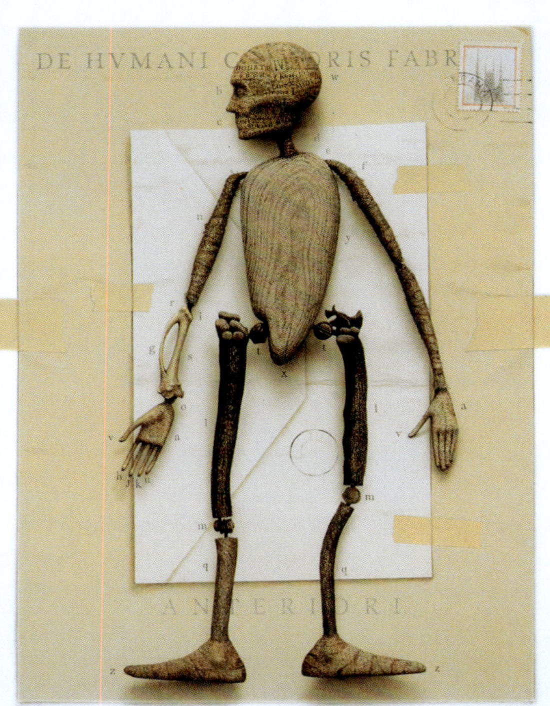

An Exact Anatomy of Man (detail), [illegible], watercolor and graphite on paper, [illegible]

AN EXACT ANATOMY OF ALAN MAGEE BY RICHARD WEST

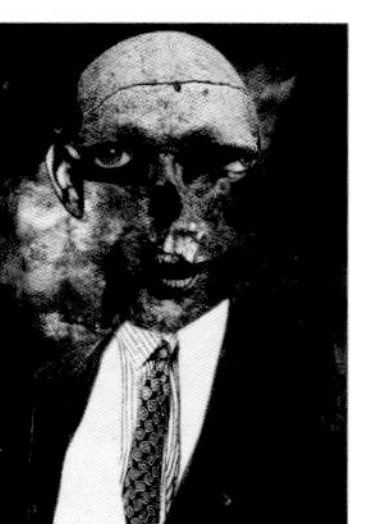

Mystery. A grotesque, curiously likable marionette confronts you. Its head, not quite a skull, resembles an ancient phrenological bust. Swathed in tantalizing strips of text, the head is turned in one direction. What is it saying?

The body consists of a beautifully worn, heart-shaped piece of driftwood; the limbs are sticks and bone, wrapped wire, and two delicately carved hands—the hands of an artist. What do they do?

The legs are meticulously jointed with wire, screws, and nuts, so that the figure—temporarily lifeless on a bed of anonymous correspondence—can come to life again, when needed. Where will it go?

The various points of the little puppet-man, every perturbation, every finger, are painstakingly catalogued on a list long since vanished. Why is it gone?

Another mystery. A postage stamp is affixed to a sheet that is not really an envelope, but the remnant of a discarded anatomy text. The twin-spired image on the stamp shimmers in a Saint Vitus dance, pinned down by a postmark: PRAHA. How did the page get here?

And another mystery. Is this an illusion, or the illusion of an illusion? In itself, illusionism is an ancient visual trick, admired from the time of the Greeks and enshrined in American art through the wonders performed by Harnett, Peto, and Haberle in the 19th century. Although it is unlikely that we will ever see birds fooled into pecking at the little puppet the way they supposedly pecked at Zeuxis's grapes, the point of *trompe l'oeil* (fool the eye) painting is, nevertheless, that possibility: momentary belief followed by the pleasurable *frisson* of being fooled.

The beauty of Alan Magee's puppet—and by extension, all of his work in one way or another—is that while the eye is being *trompe*'d, the mind is being trumped. His images are not, in fact, illusions of things that are there, but projections of ideas given form through objects. The idea hovers behind the illusions, a *doppelgänger* that simultaneously shapes and is shaped by the constellation of objects that seem to be, but aren't.

If we are to construct an exact anatomy of the artist, it is this mystery of duality that has to be plumbed. For example, Magee not only creates images of puppets, he constructs actual puppets as well. Except that the terms "puppet" or "marionette" are misnomers for most of the ominously puzzling three-dimensional beings that emerge from the collision of found objects with the artist's active imagination. The results can be chilling, as in *Dissent* (Page 179); ominous, as in *Der Dichter* (Page 176); or downright unnerving, as in *Twins* (Page 168). As disconcerting as some of these contructs are, they are absolutely necessary to Magee's expression of the animé that quickens his forms. This underlying vitality can be found everywhere in his work, from the realist renditions of power drills with writhing power cords looping around them to the face-like apparitions that emerge from the smoky backgrounds of dreams in the artist's haunting series of monotypes.

A final mystery. How has Alan Magee gotten in touch with the ghosts of Dada and Surrealism and transformed them into his very own language? In his eerie ability to turn elusive concatenations of inert elements into living objects, the artist seemingly pays homage to the surreal dolls of Hans Belmer and the bone constructions of Max Ernst. Magee himself has frequently mentioned his admiration for the collages of Hannah Höch, one of the supreme collagists of Weimar Germany. The shadow of John Heartfield, the other great collagist of this period, can also be discerned. Magee's achievement has been to meld the ideas of the past with his own formidable technique and artistic ethos to create something quite unique, at once beautiful and dangerous. *Disinformation* says it all: *caveat pictor*. Nothing is what it seems. All the beautifully rendered clues, the compelling constructions, the illusionistic serenity, are not the end products of his work but rather the entry points into the mysterious worlds that have attracted artists for centuries.

Richard V. West, Director, Frye Art Museum, Seattle

Disinformation, 1988, monotype collage, 7 x 5"

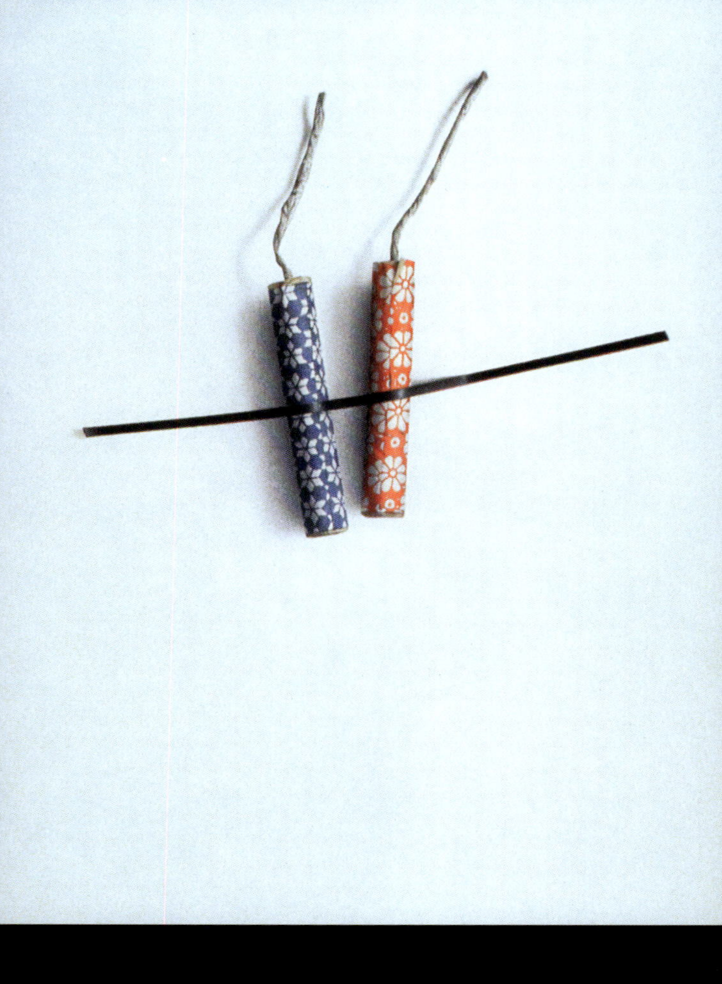

Two Firecrackers (detail), 1981, watercolor and graphite, 15 ½ x [illegible]"

ALAN MAGEE: AN APPRECIATION BY JONATHAN WEINER

Alan Magee was born in 1947 in Newtown, Pennsylvania. His father, Dick, owned an Esso station at Washington Crossing. His mother, Rena, was passionate about drawing. She had grown up on a farm in the small town of Trevose, where between the ages of six and 16 she had made hundreds of drawings of fashionable women: women in made-up faces, women in fancy dresses, long illustrated comic-book-style tales of the cosmopolitan world—an escape from her strict Baptist parents and her life on the farm. She used to say, "On a day that I couldn't draw, I felt that I couldn't breath." Her father drew too. He had taken night classes, but he couldn't keep it up—after a day of farm labor his hands were too tired. Rena used to take envelopes from the kindling box, open them, and sketch one of her High Society sophisticates. Then, as often as not, her mother—Alan's grandmother—would recycle the envelopes. They went right back into the kindling box. She did not want to give her daughter any worldly notions.

Rena taught her own children to read and write long before they went to school, and she encouraged Alan to draw as soon as he could hold a pencil. There were no museums nearby, and the art world was as far away as the sophisticated life had been for his mother. But he found his own influences. His realist painting, some of the finest realist work in America, celebrates objects from his childhood, including the cairn of a few pebbles on a beach, firecrackers like the ones that he and his friends smuggled up from the South for the Fourth of July, and also old power drills, wrenches, and half-assembled engines like the ones in his father's service station at Washington Crossing. To all of these, even to his own paintbrushes, he brings a childhood love of objects, a child's eye for the miraculous, and an adult's sense of joy and loss. He presents each nail, bolt, and paint-tube in a style so clear, so apparently straightforward and style-less, that he makes the artist's work seem very close to the craftsman's, and celebrates both at once.

Magee's fantastic flights from realism, which are equally remarkable, trace back to Newtown also: to the night at the age of 10 when he happened to watch a late show called "Shock Theater" on TV. The show's announcer and host was a Philadelphia botanist named John Zacherley, who, as Roland, "The Cool Ghoul," in macabre makeup, was introducing reruns of 1930s horror films. The movie that night was James Whale's *Frankenstein*. From the enormous uneasy excitement of the first scenes, it was a revelation—a world away from his classes at Newtown Joint Elementary School and the art that he knew from the readers and textbooks of the late '50s, the Eisenhower years. On "Shock Theatre" he watched Todd Browning's atmospheric *Dracula*, with Bela Lugosi; *The Werewolf of London*, starring Henry Hull; and *The Mummy*, with Boris Karloff as the ancient Egyptian restored to life. In their sets, gestures, and lighting those '30s horror films played with the German Expressionist styles of the '20s. Of course, a 10-year-old knows nothing about any of that. But horror movies gave him a world of strange, mysterious ideas, which he folded back into drawing. They opened up worlds and styles that he would later explore in his vivid and often frightening studies of the tragedies of Eastern Europe, and of global politics—some of the most worldly, otherworldly, and unclassifiable art I know.

As a writer with an interest in science and nature, I feel the strongest sense of personal connection with Alan Magee's work. In his realist paintings—the work that he does on the day shift, so to speak—he accomplishes what writers try to do in creative, or literary, nonfiction. This kind of writing (Richard Rhodes calls it verity) uses all the tools of the novelist and the journalist to paint portraits of the way things are. And what Magee does when he takes off on his fantastic flights from realism—the work he does on the night shift—reminds me of the magic realism of Gabriel Garcia Marquez, Isaac Bashevis Singer, and the greatest master of the form, Franz Kafka. But like the best work in any medium, Magee's paintings seem to exist outside all schools. Partly, perhaps, because he grew up in small towns, not cities, his paintings are not about art, about trends or theories, but about the beauty and magic of the thing seen, and the things unseen beyond it.

In the 1960s, Magee went to the Tyler School of Art, and then the Philadelphia College of Art (PCA), now the University of the Arts. At the time, realistic art was down and out. Painting from life was supposed to be dead. His interest in drafting figures and portraits landed him by default in PCA's illustration department. At first this felt like a kind of banishment. (He had applied to the fine arts department.) But the banishment turned out to be a wonderful experience for him. In those classes he met some gifted students, including the Quay Brothers, who later became extraordinary filmmakers, and also the late Richard Amsel, who was so skilled as a draftsman and illustrator that he began drawing art for Hollywood and Broadway while he was still a student, working on his mother's dining-room table. Magee graduated in 1969 and soon he too was in demand as an illustrator in New York. He did high-profile assignments for *Time*, *Playboy*, the *Atlantic Monthly*, *The New York Times*, and the city's paperback houses. His work won him many prizes, including the American Book Award for a collection of surrealist work by the Czech writer John Sladek. Magee feels that back in the '70s, illustrators enjoyed more freedom than they do now. The big corporate and commercial publishing agendas have changed the nature of the job. He got his first taste of what the multinational takeovers would mean for publishing when he was working on a doomed cover illustration for Bernard Malamud's novel *The Fixer*. The publisher's sales team told him to avoid any references to jails, Jewish toughs, and hard luck—the themes of the book. They asked him to paint something like the movie poster for *Fiddler on the Roof*.

By the late 1970s, Magee was phasing out his illustration work, and painting the first of his gemlike studies of things as they are. It may seem strange to talk about the supernatural in the presence of these realist paintings, which seem so completely natural, but from the beginning his best work reached a level where we have to believe that an element of magic comes into it. He leads us to contemplate and celebrate the object before us in ways we have forgotten. He makes a common thing like a pebble, a drill, a braid, a gourd, or an envelope speak to our own secret passions, agitations, and preoccupations. His craftsmanship is so fine that many of his paintings compare with the greatest works of *trompe l'oeil*. But that term suggests trickery. Here the technique has a serious purpose, an involvement with the way things are, and we feel as we look at them that we share in the visual communion.

In one early review, the art critic Theodore Wolff wrote in *The Christian Science Monitor*: "His best paintings can stand beside the best modernist art produced since World War II, in much the same way that the best modernists can stand beside the good art of the past. Viewing Magee's paintings I had the same feeling of being in the presence of something truly vital that I had in the mid 1940s standing before the early abstract canvases of Jackson Pollock and Clifford Still. In both cases I felt that a page from art history was in the process of being turned."

Magee invites us to stare at a utilitarian object like an envelope, and as we look it begins to assert and reveal itself. In ordinary life, of course, an envelope comes and goes. Its wrinkles, frayed corners, stamps, and postmarks never have time to reveal themselves to us. In one of Magee's paintings, contemplated so respectfully, the envelope itself becomes a letter to us, and however exotic the stamps and postmarks, it reaches us. A dozen years ago, in an essay about Magee's work, Barry Lopez wrote that "if art is merely decorative or entertaining, or even just aesthetically brilliant, if it does not elicit hope or a sense of the sacred, if it does not speak to our fear and confusion, or to the capacities for memory and passion that imbue us with our humanity, then the artist has only sent us a letter that requires no answer." Alan Magee's envelopes say so much so well that we do not quite know how to reply, but we always feel that they require an answer.

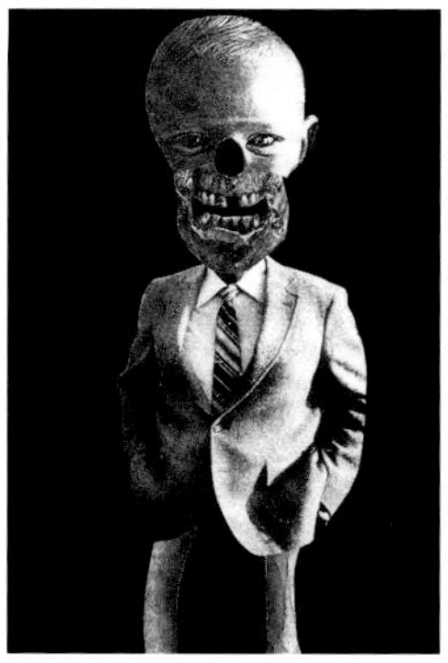

Sometimes he puts stones on pedestals, as if to say, These are wonderful, too. The pebbles that we took back with us from the beach, which lost their shine when they dried and got thrown away in the flowerbeds: here they are again. They are worth keeping. More often, Magee paints large fields of pebbles and stones. These have become his best-known subjects. What is it about these wonderful stones? When we look at them, our eyes want to register them as absolutely real. At the same time, in the subtle order and pleasure and peace we feel, we know that the artist has shaped and brought them to order, like Bach with notes of music, or like science or literature with their underlying patterns. We feel gratitude for the mind that found the order for us—saw the patterns and brought us to see them. Again and again as we stare, the stones seem to fall back into the realm of perfect reality. The experience is something like seeing the bed of a tidal pool clearly for a moment beneath wavering water. But each time, we reject the illusion. We don't want the stones alone, we want Magee's representation of the stones, because we know that we are building something with the artist. It is almost as if, together, we are restoring some sort of meaning to the world.

Magee's paintings of stones feel something like an invitation to put ourselves back together, and at the same time to leave ourselves entirely behind. "I don't know what I may seem to the world," Isaac Newton said, "but, as to myself, I seem to have been only like a boy playing on the sea-shore, and diverting myself in now and then finding a smoother pebble or a prettier shell than ordinary, whilst the great ocean of truth lay all undiscovered before me." In a pebble we can see something of cosmic action in space and time. Just as spark plugs and rusty nails are private loves of Alan Magee's, for most of us pebbles are private objects, among those secret things that we feel are absolutely special to us. They have been personal revelations ever since we were children, when a stroll on a beach could sometimes lead us to moods as shattering as the Revelation of Saint John the Divine: "To him that overcometh will I give to eat of the hidden manna, and will give him a white stone, and in the stone a new name written, which no man knoweth saving he that receiveth it." Magee's stone paintings, especially when we can sit and contemplate the original canvases, most of which are huge, restore us to those feelings that have come to all of us on the beach in our best moments. The thoughts that we are afraid to speak aloud, because they sound so simple, are the thoughts we come back to all our lives, because in the end these are the outer limits of what we can think. These are our shores.

In 1983, when Magee had been painting full-time for a few years, his first New York dealer, George Staempfli, organized a one-person show for him in Paris at the Foire Internationale d'Art Contemporain (FIAC). It was his first trip to Europe, and after the show he and his wife, Monika Magee, made trips into France and Italy. Something about the encrusted facades, the chipped patinas, the patched and the repatched walls in the hill towns of Tuscany made him feel that he had to start over as a painter. He decided that he had a problem with realism. Realistic paintings could be beautiful and contemplative, he thought, but they offered a limited emotional range. He was anguished about the troubles of El Salvador and Nicaragua at that time, and he did not see how he could express those political concerns with his pictures of pebbles, paintbrushes, and pears. He felt that he could not do what he needed to do. The frustration of this impasse came to him in the image of a door, a sealed door of stone. "One has to trust these images, whether one understands them or not, if they have power," he says. Again and again he painted mystical stone doors. To me this series has always looked like a riddle about death. What is the one door through which we cannot pass, but will have to pass? The door that always stands closed in front of us, as sealed as the face of a cliff, but through which each of us must go?

The door was a passage in a sense. Magee passed through it somehow into strange interior explorations. I think of this episode in his career as something like Piranesi's turn from his architectural engravings of Roman ruins to his series of *Carcieri Invenzione*, the Imaginary Prisons. When Magee turned from the outer to the inner world, his drawings and paintings became as dark as anything in Piranesi's prisons, with a touch of the paperback book illustrator about them, and more than a hint of Bela Lugosi and Boris Karloff. Magee drew corporate animals, Wall Street beasts of the Reagan era, and party spokesmen who seemed to stare out from solitary confinement or the fifth circle of Hell. He drew children torturing insects, and two boys hanging a dog: nightmare children as political metaphors, sketched in a very simple, elemental style. When Magee gave slide talks during those years, audiences were appalled by some of those pictures. Many people seemed to feel that he was advocating what he drew. Much of the work was too harsh to show.

Cost of Sales, 1988, collage, 10 x 8"

Through his wife, Monika, who was born in Essen, Germany, Magee had also become concerned with Eastern Europe, and the Holocaust, which was "the exemplary event" of modern history, as Primo Levi says in *The Drowned and the Saved*. It loomed like a negative spire above the landscape of the 20th century. Magee found himself in sympathy with the terror of the future that European artists had experienced before World War II. Those artists took him even deeper into the darkness, and again Magee produced exemplary objects. There is so much in his work from this period, including *Trauerarbeit*, the work of mourning, a term that he borrowed from the work of the German psychologists Alexander and Margarete Mitscherlich. By *Trauerarbeit* the Mitscherlichs meant the human processes that allow us to mourn: the repetition, reiteration, rehashing, the going over things again and again. We can either allow all those processes to happen by instinct, or we can block them. But when we inflict or suffer harm and try to brush it off, the harm comes back to haunt us.

Magee's most disturbing images, the monotypes, the most remarkable series he made in his dark period, were acts of *Trauerarbeit*. He made them by rolling black ink on a zinc etching plate, then rubbing away some of the ink with a paper towel until a face emerged. He made or discovered these faces in the summer and fall of 1990, as America moved into the Gulf War. These images of future anxiety were inspired by the work of the German Expressionists he had come to love, particularly the collages made by Hannah Höch between the wars, many of which were as prophetic as Kafka's *The Penal Colony*. Somehow the great German artists absorbed the temper of their time and by working ferociously created images and stories that seem now uncannily predictive of the death camps and gulags to come. With Magee's monotypes too we feel we are in the presence of fear and grief that's anchored in the way things are and the way things will be.

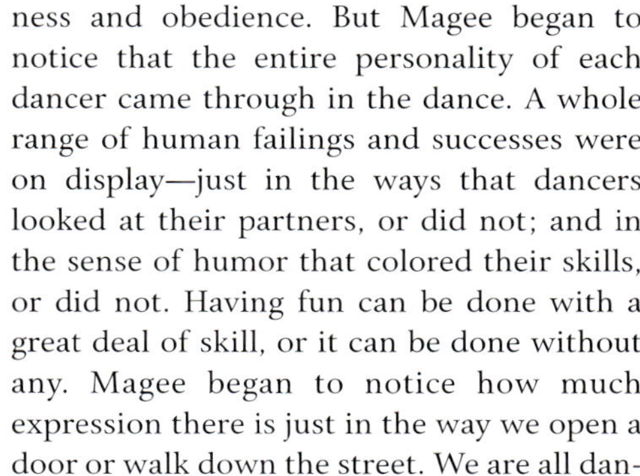

In a sense, these gray faces are as realistic as anything Magee has ever done, whether we see their suffering as political or purely existential. Take the monotype that Magee titled *Archive*, for instance. The face is sort of library, a repository of frail hope, sadness, and disappointment, pain and resilience. *Archive* bears scarred and awful records of the hardest parts of life, records that most faces keep hidden.

To me, *Archive* evokes those four-in-the-morning moods when the self reproaches itself, rummaging through its private archive of compromises made in cowardice, in fear of the dark; when the ego sees itself as a sad thing stitched, patched, and repatched against darkness, against disgrace and silence; when the soul feels that it could reveal its face to no one, because that secret archive is too harsh to show.

Another of Magee's monotypes, *Schistos*, has this same put-upon, put-together look. The mouth is a guarded slit, shut tight. The eyes are hapless, weak, sensitive, hurt, watchful, and set wide apart, suggesting mystical tendencies. The monotype *Wound*, in which we seem to see the face of every victim of the last hundred years, and the next hundred, is almost unbearable to look at.

Oliver Sacks, in a preface to *Awakenings*, says that we find our greatest disturbances of mind and heart in medicine, "[I]n the study of our most complex sufferings and disorders of being; for we are here compelled to scrutinize the deepest, darkest, and most fearful parts of ourselves, the parts we all strive to deny or not-see. The thoughts which are most difficult to grasp or express are those which touch on this forbidden region and reawaken in us our strongest denials and our most profound intuitions." That is where Magee goes with his monotypes, and after one quick glance, many people simply refuse to follow him. Magee himself told a reporter once, "I think of the word *contraindication*. There are some people who absolutely can't use them."

In a profoundly intuitive way, Magee worked through his feelings and sympathies for the victims of war through these monotypes, and he arrived at last at a kind of peace. "When you make things this way it's not a reasoned or an intellectual act at all," he says. "Your body just keeps wanting to make them, until the body is satisfied."

For years, Magee thought he would never return to realist painting. It was too mute and obedient a medium. He found his way back to it while dancing with Monika. The two of them had fallen in love with Latin swing, and they went to Swing Festivals in Boston and New York, where they danced side by side with some of the greatest swing dancers in the world. Of all the arts, the rules of dance would seem to make it the ultimate for muteness and obedience. But Magee began to notice that the entire personality of each dancer came through in the dance. A whole range of human failings and successes were on display—just in the ways that dancers looked at their partners, or did not; and in the sense of humor that colored their skills, or did not. Having fun can be done with a great deal of skill, or it can be done without any. Magee began to notice how much expression there is just in the way we open a door or walk down the street. We are all dangerously transparent. If swing dancers, in their somewhat circumscribed and limited art form, radiate so much personality, then surely realist painters can too. If dancers express themselves so fully, he thought, then realist painters must follow the same cosmic rules. They had to, even without knowing it.

So Magee returned to realism. He made several colorful monotypes of pears in 1992 and '93, images that he associates with this change of heart. He also went back to the stones, which some people had misunderstood as simple *trompe l'oeil*. He was after something more than that, and he decided now that he had abandoned them prematurely. He went back to large canvases of stones seen in the serenity and power of daylight. He began painting envelopes, paintbrushes, and power drills again, objects that were made to be useful and showed the marks of use.

When describing action, Homer and Virgil often pause to linger lovingly over tools, weapons, and bowls. These are at once the trophies and the symbols of the action. They represent the pleasures of civilization and of life itself. They tell the whole story. Classicists have a name for that kind of stop-the-action passage: *ekphrasis*. (One of Magee's accomplished friends, Michael Putnam, the chairman of the Classics department at Brown University, has even written a book about it.) From the beginning, Magee's well-used, well-worn artifacts have always looked as if they were part of an epic. It is as if we were viewing them from an emotional height, so to speak, or from a great dis-

Little Fugue, 1979, acrylic on canvas, 38 x 40"

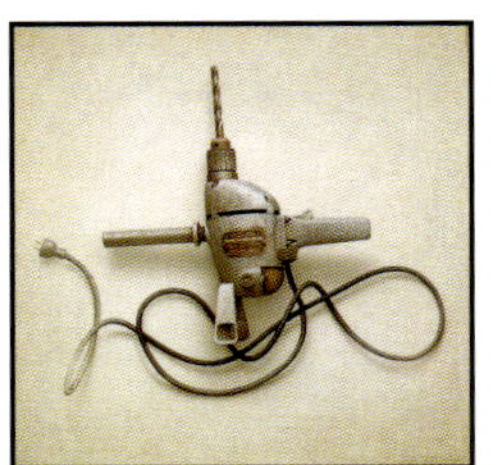

tance in time—as if our age were already as far in the past as Rome, Troy, or the caves are from us today. And in returning to realism, Magee brought to this world of epic objects, more than before, an element of *Trauerarbeit*, the work of mourning. He was painting a world that was rusting away and vanishing, a world of work that was very different from the digital abstract world of computer code in which we live now. He was recording a whole realm of relics that he had grown up with, machine tools that smelled of oil and had a certain weight, with their heavy cast-metal casings. They were part of an earlier period of industrialization. They looked different and felt different, and they were going away. The weights of these things had become fixed in his memory. He had worked with them as a kid, and when he looked at them now he felt the weight of them as a part of what he had retained, along with the smell of the oil. For Magee, even spark plugs now had some of the eternal poignance of those stones on the beach.

In his paintings, a drill is a beautiful totem like an African mask. It is a symbol almost as powerful as a crucifix. Because it looks like a mask, symbol, emblem, it invites us to wonder what it stands for. We note the solidity of the thing, which casts soft shadows, though the drill bit looks sharp enough to cut. The drill has been laid in the center of the picture for us to contemplate, and the cord, by fading out, enforces our attention by sending our eyes back toward the center again and again. The drill says, among other things: this was fine work. And there is something of the pain and the weight of work, the crucifixion of it there too. In its blankness, we can see almost anything we want of our feelings about work and the way things are. The tool seems to speak to us very specifically of many things. It seems to speak straight to our hearts, and we will never know everything it says.

One of the images in this book is titled *Going Over*. In his notes, Magee explains that this was a phrase that Franz Kafka used "in describing the point at which a work of otherwise realistic fiction passes into the realm of the dream, or the impossible. Kafka felt that this shift, to be effective, should be subtle and that the dreamlike elements must not overpower the entire work." Somehow in his best realist work Magee goes over, and in his best surreal work he comes back.

Alan and Monika Magee now live in the small town of Cushing, Maine. In person, Alan is mild-mannered, soft-spoken, and unassuming. It is only after some space of conversation that one begins to be aware of his brilliance and range. Sometimes when I talk to him, I remember a critic's line about Bill Moyers: he dazzles gradually. He takes his responsibilities as an artist seriously. Sometimes when he is with friends and a little wine or Jameson, his responsibility and solemnity dissolve into a gentle Irish deviltry.

I admire his unpretentious sense of art and craft. Not long ago, when he painted his magnificent *Stone Triptych* for the Maine State House, he took the canvas (which is about 6 x 8') to a local auto body shop. He had arranged to varnish it there. When he brought it in, the guys in the shop dropped everything they were doing and came over. There was a long silence while they took it in. While Alan did the varnishing, they studied it from a distance and from very close up. They knew a lot about the practical side of what he was doing, because they were painters and maskers too. They understood the airbrushes and the paint spatters, because those are techniques they use every day, with the same masking tape and spray guns. They admired, and then they kibitzed. They stared at the stones from inches away and said, "Wow, cool." "Yeah, I see how you did this."

Since realistic painting is still less than prestigious in the art world, Alan's rededication to it includes a willingness to be somewhat obscure. In this, he is like another American original who moved to Maine, E.B. White, who wrote in the foreword to one of his essay collections that the essayist has to give up hope of a Nobel Prize, but is comforted by the sight of Michel de Montaigne's ratty old mantle hanging in the back of his closet. For Magee, as for White, the work does not get easier as he approaches the status of a master. I once asked him about this and he quoted a Russian novelist: "The distance between the idea and the finished work is traveled on the knees." In this book we can see the whole path so far. His erudition (never academic, always passionate, enthusiastic, or contemplative) shines through every painting, as it does in the notes he has placed in the back of this book. His personal pantheon includes Adolph Menzel, a great artist of 19th century Berlin, and a favorite draftsman of Magee's; the 18th century anatomist Bernard Siegfried Albinus; the filmmakers Carl Theodor Dreyer, Jan Švankmajer, and the Quay Brothers; the photographers Emmet Gowin and Frederick Sommer; the writers Walter Benjamin, Franz Kafka, Wilfred Owen; the painters Hannah Höch and Antonio Lopez-Garcia; and the old Flemish master Hans Memling, who, Magee writes in one note, "produced some of the most beautifully designed and finely crafted portraits of the Northern European Renaissance. His best work projects a sense of transcendent calm and clarity unique among the paintings of his day." In his entry for *The Lost Memling*, Magee explains, he re-creates a missing Memling portrait (documented only through a remaining black and white catalog photograph) that was stolen from the Uffizi during the Nazi evacuation of Italy in 1944.

After the attack of September 11, 2001, Magee painted a set of paintbrushes. Then he painted two small panels: one of a row of firecrackers, one of two small stones. Next he painted a very complicated open paint box, and after that a large cairn. The painting of the brushes he called *Résumé*. When we talked on the phone, he told me that he felt the futility that everyone felt after the tragedy. He felt awful that all he could do was paint. But I told him that I was glad he was working. I thought that for a painter like Magee to continue working just then was precisely what we needed for civilization to continue. In another time, the event would have thrown him into dark flights from realism, but now the realism felt right, even essential, to him. Later I wrote Alan a note to say how much I liked *Résumé* and another, older painting. He wrote back, "You were right. Focusing on small occasions for beauty does seem appropriate somehow. I am pleased that you liked *A First Seminary*. The title comes from a line in Spenser: 'There is a first seminary, of all things according to their kynds.'"

Emblem, 2000, acrylic on panel, 30 x 30"

A CONVERSATION BETWEEN BARRY LOPEZ AND ALAN MAGEE

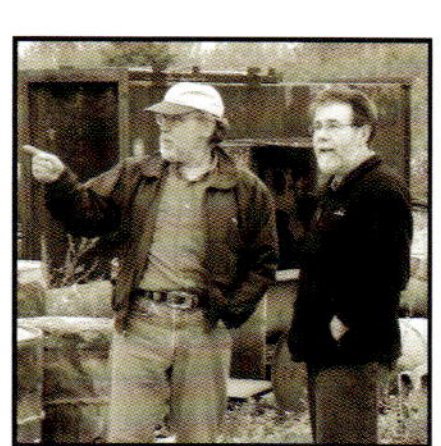

LOPEZ: I want to begin by asking you about something. You extended an invitation to me to talk about common ground, ground we share as a writer and as an artist. How can you explain the integrity of your individual artistic vision in the light of the close working relationships you have with myself and other writers, with photographers and artists?

MAGEE: I came across your work many years ago in Santa Barbara, looking for something to read at the bookstore in town, and found that narrow, gray-covered copy of *Winter Count*. I took it to the hotel, read a few of the stories, and immediately felt that I had discovered someone whose work, though in a different field, was very close to mine. In getting to know you, I've come to realize that what I had felt intuitively in the stories hinted at a much larger field of correspondences with you. There must exist some kind of ambient, collective response to the world we live in—guiding people with inclinations such as ours to very similar conclusions. Although we express it in vastly different ways, that particular strain of understanding is clearly identifiable when we run across it.

So, how can I understand and explain the singularity of my work within this community of people, like you, with whom I seem to share so much? I don't think this sense of concord with others erodes the edges of our singular visions. For me it is only an encouragement. It's an affirmation and a reassurance, even though each of our efforts must be made in private.

LOPEZ: I've felt the same, informing energy in your work. You weren't doing something I wanted to do, but because you were doing what you were doing so well, I understood better, and felt propelled to a greater degree, in what I wanted to do.

It's occurred to me, from long-term contact with Native people, and from wondering about our positions as intermediaries, in the popular sense, between the so-called real world and the metaphysical world—this is space traditionally filled in hunting cultures by a shaman—that your colleagues and mine, these dancers, photographers, and painters, all participate in that personage of the shaman. I don't mean, at all, to promote the idea that what we're doing is somehow greater than what other human beings do. It's just that our calling is to move in this ground between the reification and the imagination. So I long ago began to feel, as a writer, a sense of companionship with men and women in traditional societies who were acting in this intermediary role, and it occurred to me then that one of the reasons, in a society like ours that separates that role into so many disciplines, that we gravitate toward each other is because we recognize this, that our roles are similar. There's never really a question of overriding someone else's artistic vision. You'll always have your own artistic vision. But this thing plays directly, of course, into the insecurities some of us feel as writers and artists about originality.

MAGEE: I'm glad that you mention your associations with Native people, and also your longstanding identification with the solitary, focused life of the visionary. In that regard I love your story "The Orrery" in *Winter Count*. The story is based so firmly in reality, the description of landscape, stones, the barren, lonely topography, everything in it is clear and attentively observed. Then, at a certain point, the story passes over into a kind of magic. This is what I felt was so wonderful—that your story wasn't *steeped* in magic, but that the magic sprang naturally out of reality, sprang, in this case, from a person who was intimately observing, paying a kind of fierce attention to the landscape.

LOPEZ: Didn't you once say this about Kafka?

MAGEE: That's right. Kafka used the term "going over." Many of Kafka's stories are in the vein of what we are talking about. They are not saturated in unreality. They are stories with real buildings, chairs, and doors. "Going over" describes the delicate transition into a dream-like state within a narrative.

LOPEZ: Right.

MAGEE: In working with realist painting I feel the need to pursue a related path. I don't know if it's always going to be successful, but I hope to bring observation to the point where it can go over, where somebody looking at that drawn version of a real thing feels that the drawing has invited them into another realm, and I don't know a better way of doing that than passing thoroughly through the solid ground of real experience.

LOPEZ: We have known each other for 15 years or more, and we quite quickly began what is for us now a friendship-long discussion of what should probably be called politics: how we feel about our work, our reflections on the political realities we confront. Both of us have been profoundly anguished and disturbed by U.S. embroilment in the Middle East, and we've wondered what we could do in response as writers and artists, not by writing pamphlets as it were, but by making our work a reflection of this concern. When I look at your work—and actually this is something that you stimulated in me. I found the words for it when you sent me this article by Hillman.

MAGEE: About beauty?

LOPEZ: Yes. What I was going to say—I've got to back up here and start over. If a painter makes a photorealistic representation of a rusted bolt on a surface of some sort, that's not engaging for me unless I am immediately aware that the bolt "opened up" to

Photo of Barry Lopez and Alan Magee by Monika Magee

the painter, that there was a reciprocal relationship. In that case, which is where I see your work, the painter invites you to become deeply engaged with what is real. You see that "the real" is not a surface but a depth. I think what we're asking is for the viewer or reader to look more closely, to go more deeply; and a frustration for us about our country at the moment is that the nation acts as though it isn't very deeply informed. In a general sense, your painting asks a person to stay deep or to go deep across the range of their life. I think I'm trying to do the same—when somebody calls me a magical realist, I'm a little bit perplexed because if you really engage in an intimate way with the real world you go that deep into reality. You're not in some kind of magical landscape divorced from reality. The place you are is integral with reality.

MAGEE: That's right. The magic isn't a concoction.

LOPEZ: Yes, it's not a concoction.

MAGEE: And when you talk about the idea of work having political implications, I think it all does, whether it's a statement of complicity or dissent, it all has a political dimension. For me this goes back at least as early as art school, when I began to understand how the art world functions, how the world of contemporary art works. I found this insular, self-reflexive world an essentially inhospitable place to do what I wanted to do. The practice of observation, attentiveness, praise, even beauty, was pretty much excluded from contemporary "fine" art as it was taught during my school years. Because these same elements were so attractive to me—were the reason for art—I understood that I had to rough out a framework in which I *could* operate. I felt that I had to step out of that particular art-maze in which we, as young artists, were expected to remain. And that consciousness has stayed with me until now. I don't think it's so much a taste for dissent, or contention, but a great discomfort in conforming to molds that feel unhealthy and inappropriate. So, I knew and understood that this was political, yet invisibly so, from the very beginning. As you live, the recognition of how political your actions really are becomes very clear.

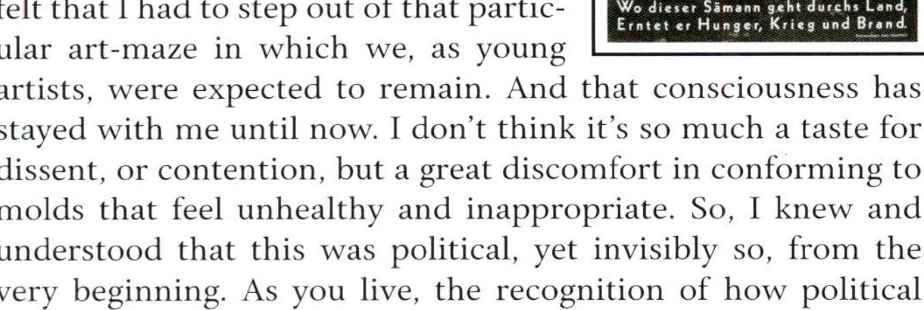

LOPEZ: So let me ask a question about Borges and Neruda. If you have an obligation to the society of which you are a part, what *is* that obligation to society for an artist or a writer? One of the things that fascinate me about the difference between Borges and Neruda is that Neruda was seen as a political activist. There was no question about his opposition to Pinochet, for example. But with Borges, a man politically inactive by comparison, you still have such a politics behind it that you make a mistake, I think, in saying he did not stand up against what was wrong. The thought is a comfort to me because I don't feel compelled to make public pronouncements about what I think is wrong in my country, though, at this point, things seem so dire I may change that. Maybe I could ask you to speak to this question, which for young artists just stepping into art school is so terrifically difficult, and that is: How can I develop myself as an artist, be true to the discoveries of my own artistic vision, and still do this strange thing which is to be an active, caring, moral member of U.S. society, living out an experiment in democracy?

MAGEE: I find myself living more in the Borges camp, working with ideas that have political implications, yet don't shout politics. What this means to me is that our work develops out of an understanding of the avenues of our greatest effectiveness. I'm probably more effective working through the sensitivity, the heart of a particular viewer than through waging a political argument with him. Nevertheless, I have done work that creeps into those argumentative realms as well, but in doing so I think it's only been to lead me back to work that has more to do with the quiet, inner lives of people.

In speaking to younger artists about these things, about the question of just where on that scale between activism and poetry one's work finally ought to fall, I don't believe this question can be answered in the abstract. It can only be answered through the sensibilities, and inclinations, the genius of that particular artist. I often advise young artists to find out something about history, literature, biology, or natural history—study something other than painting, and let the painting spring from an interest in the world. Then, as the artist's sense of the world shapes his work, its social and political usefulness will follow naturally—will find their appropriate place. The photographer Frederick Sommer said, "I can forgive ignorance in anyone—except an artist." Like you, I've often wondered if I should be more overtly political in my work, and have the things I care about more explicitly spelled out. Yet, tying an image to a particular issue or moment would actually contradict some of my essential reasons for working.

Particular events in recent American history are terribly disturbing—the mirror-image tragedies that took place in El Salvador and Nicaragua, for example. I never released anything for public view that was focused on those particular problems. Yet the kind of regret that wells up out of witnessing events like these finds its way into work that is, I hope, more generally useful to people. It goes back to what you were saying about simply encouraging and fostering attentiveness in the world. This requires us to restate our belief, not widely held, that attentiveness and the recognition of beauty *does* have an ethical component to it. I think that this is what James Hillman, in his essay "The Practice of Beauty" was getting at. If beauty were only an amenity, a kind of gloss over life to give us a few moments of pleasure, then it probably would have been correctly put aside—banished from contemporary art. But I think what people of our generation might be trying to dig out, or resurrect, is the idea that beauty, and the perception of it, is informative and life-changing in a way that we can't let slip away.

LOPEZ: I feel exactly the same way, and that continuum you describe, between activism and poetry, has been a difficult one for me because I've felt defensive. With what was happening in El Salvador or Nicaragua or recently in Peru with the sterilization of Native peoples—why aren't I at the barricades? I have to tell myself that even though I am not seen, I am there; and the work I'm trying to do means having to stay at a distance, to try to keep alive a fire that's been burning since Cro-Magnon time. I believe traditional peoples have a profound sense of this need—that the act of making something beautiful sustains us. I would say that beauty is not a quality of life, but a condition for the existence of life. Life cannot exist without beauty, and to the extent that we destroy beauty we are destroying something that makes life possible. So, my small pinpoint of work in the world is to try to keep alive a sense of beauty and of engagement. It

John Heartfield, *Die Saat des Todes (The Seeds of Death)*, 1937, and Hannah Höch, *Der Melancholiker (The Melancholic)*, 1925

transcends the coming and going of nations, the United States of America included. My love for my country is great, but it's a love of people and landscape in North America rather than this political abstraction that is constantly finding reasons to intimidate people, to go to war, and to stuff its economic system down the throats of communities that have no way to protect themselves. I am, as you know, and you are too, infuriated and embarrassed that this country's corporate mob, over which we have no control, carries our flag to places it doesn't belong, and doesn't even ask if they can raise it, they just do, and they take down the other community's flag and say ours is better—no different from the Spanish in the 16th century or the English in the 17th, 18th, and 19th centuries.

MAGEE: There is no doubt that behind every action of ours, yours and mine, there is at least the consciousness of these things ongoing. Sometimes I recognize that this bedrock cultural uneasiness that I feel is a kind of armature over which layers of clay are placed to cover the structure, but nevertheless this armature gives shape to the object being formed.

This reminds me of an example from the art of Weimar era Germany. Think of the political photomontages of John Heartfield, for example, how explicit they were in shouting to Germans about the dangerous rise of the Nazis. These startling images were seen primarily as covers for the socialist magazine *A-I-Z* and as posters on the streets of Berlin. But around the same time in Berlin, more quietly, the artist Hannah Höch was making collages that were disturbingly beautiful, many of them not at all politically discernible. Viewed from where we sit today, the clarity with which she seemed to see what was going on, and in fact, to predict the coming tragedy in Europe, is uncannily prescient. When you remember what was happening in the years that followed the making of those little collages (they date from 1922-1926) you see that what she made was about as clear a prophecy as you could imagine. This example may be an indication that we have to allow ourselves to do what we do. Allow the sense of political dread and anxiety caused by events in the world—let them exist in the body, and then work.

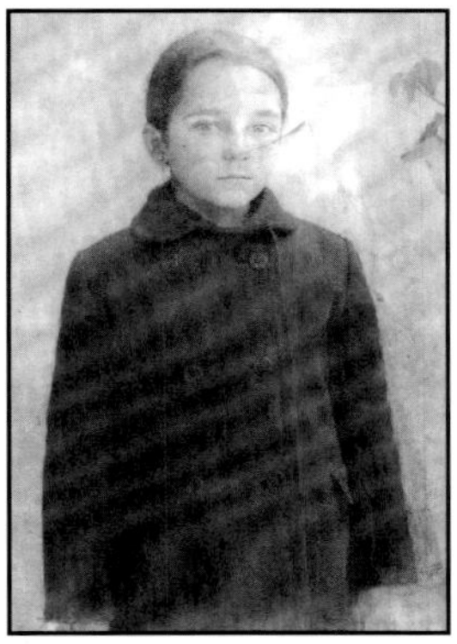

LOPEZ: And use your profession as an artist or writer to make sure the clay that covers the armature is engaging, to use all our technical skills. For some reason this is reminding me, because I know it's important to both of us, about issues of humility. So much of my awareness of what it means to write has grown out of contact with Native peoples that I'm ill at ease in the celebrity-driven world, some dimensions of it, of American literature. I have no patience with the idea that we are all writing the same thing, or that the writer or the artist is a person of no consequence. I believe in individual artistic vision, but I'm troubled sometimes by how that drive to distinguish yourself as an artist or a writer can draw you away from something that your body knows, that there is a *community* of artists and writers, and that we have social responsibilities which go back many thousands of years. We are in some sense—I don't mean to be too grandiose or simplistic, but we are the enemies of forgetting. You said to me once, you know, "No matter how dire the political situation, if you can get the information in front of people they will do the right thing." The problem is that in a society like ours which is awash in information, there are too few narrative structures in which to arrange that information; or the information you receive is so shallow it's hard to locate anything in it with depth—a book with depth, a painting, or something like that. So we must be conscious ourselves, not to be seduced somehow into producing facile work. I'm always suspicious of a piece of mine that comes too quickly. Is this something that's been generating for six or eight or 10 years and I haven't been aware of it? Or is it, really, only a witty remark, something that just pops into your head, and you think it's profound when it's really just part of the flotsam and jetsam, you know, not really worth remembering. But I think, to go back, we are, in the high sense of collegiality, the collective enemies of forgetting. We know that it is in our human nature to forget how to behave, to forget what works, to forget what's important. We're against that in our work. I said to someone once, "You don't, as an adult, read a work of fiction and discover something that you didn't know. What happens is, you are reminded of something that you have forgotten."

MAGEE: Jon Weiner sent me a wonderful paraphrase from Proust a while back: "Everything has already been said, but since nobody pays attention, it has to be repeated every morning."

So, I suppose that's why we keep reshaping these ideas continually, trying them out with different materials, different narratives, but we keep repeating some essential story that we know shouldn't be forgotten.

Among the many things that you've said, one thing that caught my attention is that we have to talk about our work with a certain reserve and discretion. What helps me here is talking about the work of *other* artists, and showing my appreciation, in a public way, for the importance of what they've achieved.

When you were speaking I was reminded of the work of the painter Antonio Lopez-Garcia. I wish his work was better known, but I believe that people who need it will find their way to it. Though you're not likely to stumble across a Lopez-Garcia in the contemporary wings of the major art museums of today. Nevertheless, Lopez-Garcia is working and doing wonderful things. My wife, Monika, ordered a book of Lopez-Garcia's work through a local bookstore, and when it came in the bookseller said, "I had no idea anything this wonderful was out there."—just one example of a book passing through someone's hands, and offering a revelation of what contemporary art *could* be. When you look at a Lopez-Garcia painting you sense that the artist is manifestly *not* looking over his shoulder at what other artists are doing. He seems so focused on his relationship with his work and with the subject of his work that there is no room for this kind of intrusion—the worry over how his paintings might fit into art world discourse.

It's easy to forget about these good things. The distractions are relentless, but I find that within this constellation of art that I value there exists a sustenance, an energy that helps me keep going. I look at the films made by the Quay Brothers, who were schoolmates of mine in Philadelphia. Their work, too, has that quality of unassailable singularity. Their work isn't a matter of adapting cleverly to the art-climate, it's a fixation so complete that makes no concessions to the culture. Again, you end up with something of extraordinary value. But we've reached a point in art where the look over the shoulder has become the norm. Students are trained to examine current criticism as if it were a stream of traffic, and to find a way to slide gently into that stream as if merging onto a freeway. We see evidence of this all around us and we certainly don't need to single out any

Antonio Lopez-Garcia, *Maria*, 1972

specific examples.

LOPEZ: Yes. I've often wondered how to answer a young person who asks: Should I take my work into an environment where criticism and theory fills the air—like an academic environment or a urban environment—or should I remove myself from society and listen to this weak, imperfect voice of mine that is trying to come to life? It's different, it is so different for every person, and there are perils at both ends of that spectrum. If you work in urban environments or academic environments, without realizing it you may feel too much the desire to be loved, and so produce work likely to be critically acclaimed. Then you're plagued by the doubt that what you are doing is merely fashionable rather than substantive. At the other end of the spectrum, you know, living at a remove from the arenas of theory, of accolade, and criticism, you can run into long periods of self-doubt because nobody is talking to you. When the list of writers or painters is posted, it goes up on the city wall and it's always local people, you know. When you live out of town, it's not a judgment against your work not to be listed, it's just you don't turn up often enough in people's living rooms to have them remember you. So I think that there are difficulties at both ends, and it's your individual temperament that leads you to seek an art school, for example, to mature in or an MFA program in creative writing. For other people, those are the wrong places. They need to take their work elsewhere.

I feel that way about my own work. Whatever it is that I've been able to do, I've done partly because I'm so far out of town. For example, my childhood sense of the possibility of a conversation with wild animals was never compromised to the extent that it might have been had I stayed too long in an urban environment, where such a thing in an adult might be seen as an affectation or as daft. Where I live now, in rural Oregon, I am literally a pitched stone away from the lives of mountain lions, bears and salmon. Salmon spawn in the river right in front of the house. Mink, elk, bobcats, and beaver, they are all right there near the house. It doesn't strike me in any way as strange that I would be involved in conversations with these parallel cultures. Because I continue to do this at 57, and have done so under the tutelage of different Native peoples, I feel that I'm holding on to something that I wish my culture hadn't thrown away. If I lived in an environment where I was dealing with critics emphasizing the "important" themes and styles in American literature, I never would have … maybe I'm not a strong enough man not to have been intimidated by all that. I didn't want acceptance so much that I would give up something that is part of my lifework.

MAGEE: It seems to me that even with the issue of strength put aside, we can't help but absorb and affirm our surroundings. And, in an odd way, our temperament places us.

Even so, while I live in a rural place as you do, I'm not sure there isn't an element in my temperament that wouldn't thrive in a city like London, for example. That would be my fantasy—just to be in that enormous playground of museums, theater, shops, music, and, yes, pubs. Yet, when it comes down to work, and really understanding the requirements of my process, I recognize that I do have to stay here.

Rural environments are so central to what we both do. I wonder about Samuel Johnson's notion, for example, that the intellect withers in a rural setting, that without the continual quipping and the constant exercise of wit the ability to think critically will atrophy. On the other hand, some of the people that you've written about in your fiction and nonfiction stand as clear examples of the opposite view. Your wise, monastic characters develop understandings that would be impossible in urban settings, simply because the distractions wouldn't let an individual go that deep. He or she would be cut short by another art exhibition, play, article, or critique, or yet another slant on an aesthetic argument. I don't know that I'm here to sort out or debate arguments, but maybe just to do the work that is most perfectly suited to my inclinations and abilities—so I continue to live and work here.

LOPEZ: I'm more interested in illumination than in solution. Solution can bring fame in certain arenas—mathematics, for example. What I want though is to put more light in poorly lit areas. I gravitate, as you do, toward a milieu in which I feel I can get that conversation going pretty quickly. I can do it in the woods, and that is why I choose to live there. I would choose Paris instead of London, I think, but you know, some people assume if you live in a rural area you have something against the city. That's not it at all. Your work requires that you stay in the places where you're fed. I love to come back east, to go to New York. Debra and I were in Paris this summer, and I was so stimulated there that when I got home—it's unusual for me—I wrote a story right away about a man living in Paris, a carpenter who takes to visiting cemeteries. There are so many value judgments made about artists and writers that have to do with popularity, and condemnation is always hovering around people who are not doing the fashionable things. It leads young people, I think, to exaggerate certain aspects of their work or their character in order to stand out in a reaction against fashion. But a reaction against fashion is part of the same syndrome. The thing is to not involve yourself with issues of fashion.

I think of a remark you made once. You quoted someone to the effect that if in the middle of your life as a painter you decide to become a sculptor, you'd better get another name. You know, you have an example of this in your own life, where a lot of people want you to paint stones for the rest of your life. They don't want you to work with these *Archive* faces. I find the same thing in my work. If I happen to write about some dimension of human experience that doesn't directly involve "nature"—sexual trauma, say—some people ask, "Well, why don't you just keep writing about the Arctic or about wolves?"

What was that quote?

MAGEE: I believe I was talking to you about the Berlin journalist Kurt Tucholsky. He wrote political articles in the 1930s imploring Berliners to take the Nazis seriously, he wrote poems, even a novel. Right from the start he was savvy with regard to human perceptions about artists; he gave himself five different names just to avoid grief over his literary diversity. Very smart. He said, "I am the five fingers of a single hand."

That would have been a better way for me to start out too, given the diverse things that have come to interest me.

I don't know about the solution to this problem. The dogma of the "signature style" in contemporary art is so entrenched that the alternative to it, creative diversity, cannot be comprehended by many. If you are Alan Magee and you paint stones, why are you now doing something that appears to us so drastically different? So I'm forced to understand that we're working in a culture with a very distorted notion of creativity. Artists have so thoroughly shaped themselves to cultural expectations that going back to a more natural way of working can be bewildering to people.

I don't know if the kind of diversity that I enjoy would be appropriate for everybody, but it's very appropriate for me. The particular painting or monotype is, just as you've explained, only a metaphysical handle for some greater concept or insight. We cannot help finding a number of ways of looking at these larger issues.

The problem with staying with the same thing year after year is that it tends to evolve—if you are not careful—into a parody of what you had done at the outset; whereas at the beginning it was a genuine and fresh statement—a discovery.

LOPEZ: Yes. I think what we're talking about, in some way, is marketing, and the intrusions of commerce in the world of art, some of which are so subtle we don't know that we've responded to them until long after the fact. Again, to me, it is essential to your real value, your long-lasting value to society, to hold your distance, to try to achieve an overview of the large patterns rather than the smaller, more transitory patterns in the spatial and temporal framework of your society. Open up a weekly magazine and you see all the minutia of the moment there, the small patterns. What I watch for is work by people who see a larger pattern, who can, for example see the United States in terms of the British Empire; not necessarily to condemn it or to hold yourself apart, but to be able to point sharply to the lessons of history. So, the contemporary books that are most valuable to me are those written by women and men who have this great overview of what's going on and who are trying to articulate the things that we should hold on to. Not because they believe these things are intrinsically better than something else, but because in the long record of humanity, the last 50,000 years, say, this is the stuff that works.

• • •

I've been thinking recently, I know you and I have talked about this, about the loss of languages. With English now we're seeing the evolution of a language that can be understood by many, but which many can't use to communicate anything very deep. I know of situations in Europe today where someone from France and someone from Germany, instead of one asking the other to speak French or German, both will agree to speak English—a show of respect for the complexity of each other's idiom. Yet their command of English is such that they can't go very deep with each other.

Ours is a society in which, in order to keep up with the rate of change, the speed that's valued purely for velocity, it's not easy to linger. It goes a little bit against the grain now to linger and go deep with a thought or deep with a sonata, or to sit on a beach and watch the tide go out. We say, "I watched the tide go out," but that could be, say, five seconds in the planet's interaction with the moon. If you say you watched the tide go in and out, shouldn't that mean a longer time? I think there's a general sense in popular culture that to linger, to consider over a long period of time is to waste—where do we even get this idea of waste?—waste time. Again, I think some of what you're doing or of what I'm doing is an iteration of the value of becoming intimate with a stone or a clevis pin or a skull or, in my case, with some individual living in the desert who has become so intimate with that world he enters the realm of magical realism. So, if you are saying, as we did earlier, that in general our work is a reaction against forgetting, it certainly, in the beginning of the 21st century, is a plea for the wisdom of lingering. Because without that lingering there is no intimacy, and with no intimacy you get a superficial language, superficial art, superficial reputation, on and on.

MAGEE: We've been talking a little bit about the loss of languages, and among them might be the practice of representational painting. Though it has been much maligned in the 20th century, it remains a potentially rich language, with many untapped uses for people.

During my school years, students were advised to pick up painting, to quote certain teachers, where Picasso left off. Which means, we weren't expected to start at our own beginnings, but at some hypothetical point where the ideology of modernism had taken us. There's probably nothing wrong with that, if taking that express lane to a desired destination was a student's strong inclination.

Representational painting appeals to me, in part, precisely *because* of the time involvement required, and because it does require going back to the beginning to a very basic process of looking, and understanding, and studying, and being confronted with my failures, and then trying again. This takes the artist through a learning process that is actually going to work if he engages with it. He ends up, in the best circumstances, with something that might convey this quality of attention to somebody else. It brings a viewer back to a place where he or she can see that the notion of "wasted time," is a false, misleading concept. A painting might offer the viewer a glimmer that: yes, this is something that I also know, but it's been such a long time since I've thought about it or talked to anybody about it. This may be why art works better for some people than an encounter with the original phenomenon in nature. Didn't Browning say this in his poem "Lippo Lippi," that art is sometimes "better for us" than nature? It can act as a hand given to another as a reminder of what's available. That gift of attention can only be offered when the artist has worked through the process the long way around: from beginning to end, not by starting where someone else left off.

LOPEZ: Yes, well, that's the disease behind the notion of progress. I'm certain we could go back 10,000 years and if we could overcome the very obvious problem of language, find people just as sensitive to complexity as we are today. The idea that human beings get smarter or better, whatever those terms mean, over hundreds of years, I think is just naïve. The things we truly value—various forms of fidelity, the capacity for grace, the ability to forgive—how can we possibly say that today people have more of this capability than they did 500, or 1,000, or 5,000 years ago? I'm so resistant to the idea that art—I mean it seems silly to say that art "improves" over time.

MAGEE: I often think about the extraordinary quality of sources that I draw on from the past, and I have a difficult time finding correspondences from today that measure up to them. We have a friend who teaches Classics at Brown—not only their historical value—but their ongoing relevance. He presents them as great examples of outstanding insight and advice about universal human experiences.

I love the *Essays* by Emerson, and I used to wonder if there was something specific to that period in the mid-19th century wherein readers were able to grasp Emerson's almost cosmic understanding of human beings and their role on Earth. It's as if he understood the world from a post-Apollo moon landing viewpoint. He could comprehend this planet, isolated in deep space, and see as well the spiritual lay of the land, grasp humanity's place in this enormous field of nature. I would wonder, is this because the reading public, his audience, was so keen? But I think he probably had a small audience, just as such flashes of brilliance do today.

It is rare during any period that these outstanding insights show up. Nevertheless, there is this long historical stream of them. It breaks your heart to see them ignored. There was another phrase very popular during and after my art school years: "Nothing is important before Warhol." Sure, let's just throw everything away—everything in human history.

It's a great loss when we only look at this cultural moment and imagine that this is the culmination, believing that we can take it all from right here, right off this plate of pop culture, thinking it will provide everything we really need.

Some of my paintings contain tributes to art from the past. I work these things in simply to be clear about what I value.

LOPEZ: There is a way in which scientific thinking, thinking posited on obsolescence, has overtaken the arts. It's true in science that a certain discovery can make a previous way of putting this information together obsolete. In other words, in science's terms the old way is wrong or incomplete, and here's a better way to do it. That thinking has crept into the arts, but it's not in any way true. A modern painting can't make an ancient painting obsolete. Art is the long-term struggle of human beings with a relatively small set of ideas: What is the relationship of the individual to God? What is the relationship of the individual to the state? You know, relatively few ideas; and we keep coming at them, century after century, because they are important to our sense of being. If the idiom of another era or another geographical region speaks to you in modern times as an artist, why should you feel in any way self-conscious about immersing yourself in it or trying to call attention to it? Your supposition has to be that there are other people like you who would revel in what you discovered in 14th century England, or 21st century Gambia, you know, contemporary iron work in Gambia or something like that. So, I'm in agreement with you, and I often find the efforts in American literature to—do you know this phrase of Ezra Pound's to "make it new"? I think in some way people misread that to mean if it's not Warholish then it's not relevant. I think what Pound really meant was to take the things we know and make them fresh by exploring them in a modern idiom.

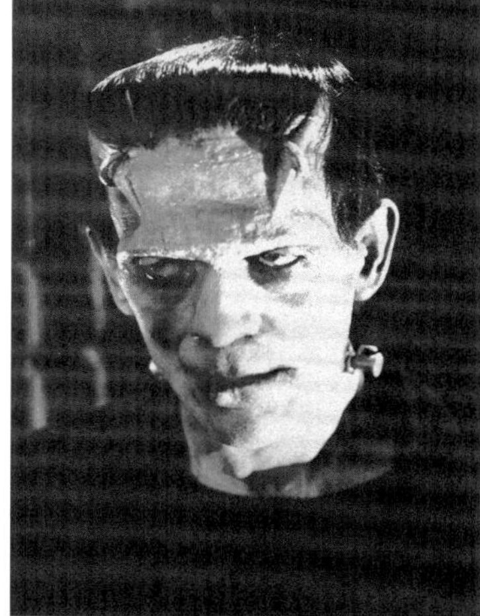

MAGEE: I'm sure he did. And he wasn't the only writer to give this particular advice. Tolstoy said the same thing. But Tolstoy didn't mean—any more than Pound—that novelty for its own sake should be the goal. It is so easy for this trivial interpretation to take hold because it's the easy one, obviously. It's not so easy to really make something new; then you've got a serious challenge. Tolstoy said that art charted the progress of humanity. As he put it, the "progress of human spiritual development." The art that was "genuine" and pertinent to any period, according to Tolstoy, was that leading edge of comprehension as people progressed in their humanity, their kindness. I agree with that. But that makes art an enormous challenge and, today, suggesting that *use* of art would be too presumptuous an idea to profess in art-world circles.

Yet if we don't embrace art on that level, or at least recognize that this is the prime challenge, then we will simply shy away from it and leave art as the thin entertainment that much of it has become. The phrase "Arts and Entertainment" tells everything about where we are.

LOPEZ: There's some conventional wisdom, folklore maybe, that the poem is a superior form of writing to the novel, and that the novel is superior to a collection of short stories, and that the short story is superior to the essay. You know, this is the ladder. In most areas of human life I find myself suspicious about both hierarchy and the notion of progress, that the new thing is automatically the better thing. What I've found in my own life is that while I've always wanted to write short stories, I never saw anything that, using my sort of language and ideas and sense of scale, would work as a novel. That's no longer true. At the age of 57 I've now outlined a novel I'd like to approach. But I don't see myself "progressing" from the short story to the novel. It's just that my sense of space and time and their interrelatedness has shifted such that I can now see how to make a story work in the space and time of a novel rather than the 10 or 20 pages of a short story. So in an individual artistic or literary life, I would accept that you can become more technically skilled, and you can refine the ideas that you have, and you can even discover something new and refine that. But I can't see this as a way of "making progress."

You were quoting someone once, saying that the only way that we could really appreciate our earlier work would be to execute it again as an adult rather than go back and work with it in the form in which we first created it. I've never had trouble believing my earlier work was naïve or technically flawed, that its scaffolding showed or something like that, but I don't feel any need to go back and erase that. It's all part of what that work is. But, in the Borgesian sense, I'd love to create a character, a writer, who writes a short story at the age of 17, and then sets himself the task of writing the same story again at 27, 37, 47, 57, all the way through, and the book would be the same story told six or eight different times through the decades of a writer's life. The reader would have the advantage of knowing that each time it was going to be a completely different story even though it involved the same character doing the same things.

MAGEE: That is interesting. And, yes, I feel that I'm covering the same ground in a very different way than I did earlier on. I often feel as if I have hold of this very large fabric and I keep folding it in different configurations. When we become more able and more facile, of course there is the responsibility of putting on the brakes so that craft will not start to coast on its own. There has to be an element of the struggle or the unknown in the work, because technique can start to run ahead of us.

That quotation you mentioned just now was from the Polish writer Bruno Schulz. This will have to be a paraphrase, but he said: "If we want to experience the thrill of those first books we read as children, we have to rewrite them from memory, as adults." I see that I have been trying to do that. But for me those "books" were films and custom cars. These are hot sources from early on. We can never quite shake free of them, and we keep making our own versions even as the exact memories of the originals fade. If we were to open those books again the simplicity of them would be quite astonishing—how little it takes to get us started.

For me James Whale's 1930 film *Frankenstein* was a window, a perfect antidote to the environment of my early elementary school which was in every way conservative and concocted to look extremely benign. Discovering the 1930s horror films shown on late night television when I was about 10 appeared to be an invitation from another world. I had a friend, Robin Hunt,

Boris Karloff (in pre-production experimental make-up) as the monster in James Whale's *Frankenstein*, 1930 who would watch these movies with me. We recognized that there was something, even though we had no language for it, something powerfully true for us within those films that we weren't being told about, and not just the horrors and monsters, but a nether-realm that we were being sheltered from. I see this force that we felt as the temptation to creativity—the invitation to just floor it, go ahead and make things from the contents of our own minds.

LOPEZ: One of the things that intrigue me about what you've just said is how often serious art grows out of a relationship with popular culture. If you tell someone that you have a classical education what it means is that not only were you exposed to Epictatus, for example, or Thucydides, but that you might have even read that work in Latin or Greek, that you were exposed to Aristotelian philosophers and to Plato's *Republic* and to Socratic dialog. That leads some people to believe that serious art can only come out of formal education, and that an exposure to the classics—certain books, certain films now, seeing a Brancusi, standing before Bernini's altar at St. Peter's—you need all of these things in order to become a serious artist. Well, sure, they can speak to you. I remember at the Vatican Museum with Agesander's statue, touching Laocoön's leg and finding a marble surface that appeared smooth to my eye felt completely muscled beneath. I'll never forget that, the charge of that moment as a 17-year-old boy. But I can also remember moments when I saw birds lifting off the water in such a way that it made my hair stand on end—and the impact of comic book art or something like that from your childhood. We've been talking, in a way to try to be reassuring and encouraging to a generation of writers and artists younger than we are about self-consciousness, about the ways people try to imply that you are unsophisticated for one reason or another. If you live in the country, if you don't live in the city, then you're unsophisticated. If you draw your inspiration from popular art then you can't be a serious artist. Some young people, I think, when they get into certain academic environments are afraid to follow their impulses because they think of them as inappropriate or not profound enough. It's the world that's profound, and our interpretations of it are sometimes less so. So I'm glad that you've talked about Roth, for example, as an influence because some people wonder how somebody who was considered a popular artist could have influenced you or excited you.

MAGEE: This is a perfect example; Ed Roth was an inspiration to 15-year-old boys in my generation. He was a shameless eccentric who was also a brilliant artist in the design and the execution of fantastic cars. Roth could also draw. He did airbrushed paintings on sweatshirts for his fans at car shows. That was another influence for me, just watching him draw with the airbrush. I thought that was absolutely marvelous. But Roth also presented an example of a way to live completely differently. He was certainly one of those pre-'60s originals whose example corresponded to the emergence of the Beat writers in San Francisco—the first stirrings of the counterculture. Roth's art was so "low" that it was beneath art world consideration, but he was very conscious of what he was doing. Now his cars and designs turn up in museums, and are acknowledged by art writers like Dave Hickey.

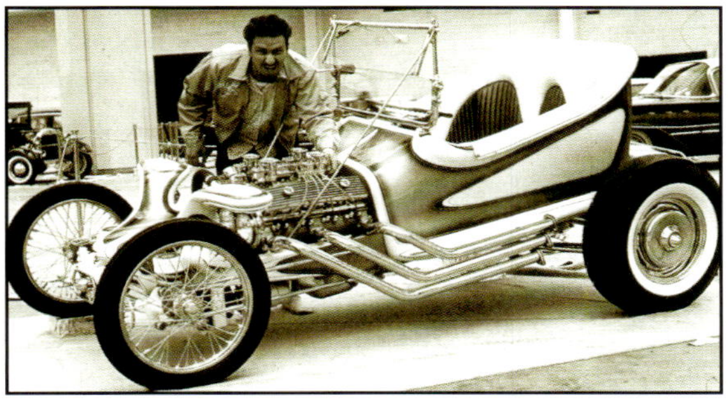

LOPEZ: When I was in college at Notre Dame I got a very good, a very rigorous education, but it wasn't enough. So I'd take off and go to West Virginia, for example, to spend long weekends with a man I'd gotten to know who had "only an eighth grade education." But I learned as much from him on that farm as I learned in some of my classes. And I think for me that fixed a belief I had had as a child. I grew up in an agricultural environment in California. I was self-conscious about those roots when I came to New York and entered, at the age of 11, a Jesuit prep school, a radically different intellectual environment. As I grew older, I knew I didn't completely trust either environment. Physical labor, tasks that were all about using your hands, would occupy me for a while and then I'd want to read a book. Then after a period of reading I'd want to be back at physical work again. My whole adult life has evolved like that. A lot of characters I've created in short stories have been people who were intellectually active, who had histories of reading and inquiring into ideas, but whose everyday life was that of a carpenter, or a gardener, or something. These people, for me as a writer, are very authentic. That doesn't mean other types of people, of course, are not, but that's where I find the roots of authentic existence. And it's made me feel very supportive of the idea that a teacher can be somebody who's not certified by any kind of institution. I feel as indebted to such people as I do to university teachers. Again, this goes back to the idea of what it means to be sophisticated. Why can't a person living in a small-scale human environment, a rural environment, have as profound an appreciation of how the music of Arvo Pärt is related to the music of Bach as a person who is living in Chicago or Mexico City? I think we lose so much because we believe that people who are not formally educated don't have much to say. Or that because they might be inarticulate, we shouldn't spend time waiting for them to say what they mean.

I went back once and looked at some scrapbooks I kept as a boy when I was five, six and seven years old. I learned two things: one, because you're not trying to invent yourself as a young child, you are just tearing out these ads in *Life* magazine that really speak to you. You paste them in the book. You're not trying to create an image of yourself to induce people to say something complimentary. It's all gut reaction. So when you go back to that material there are no lies in it. Second, I found that these images from popular magazines were of things I later addressed myself to as an adult. One image in particular I remember was an amphibious plane, a PBM Navy Mariner, sitting on the water in Antarctica, a large amphibious plane with penguins standing there on the ice. To this day I am fascinated with, and involved with, specialized aircraft in remote settings—and six trips now to Antarctica. So I see in the scrapbook the adumbrations of what I addressed myself to as an adult writer. I gravitated as a boy toward images of Native American life, and in the scrapbook it's all kind of simplistic, I guess you would say, just these images of Hopi people at a ceremony or a Lakota man up on a horse. But, 15 or 20 years later, I became actively involved in those situations, looking much deeper into them, into the racism, the imperialism, than I could have as a child. Still, as a child I recognized the image as something I wanted to immerse myself in. When I was growing up, people

Ed Roth with *The Outlaw*, c. 1957

would say, "Don't get involved with Native people, they're pagans." Or, "They're unsophisticated." Or, "Humanity has progressed so much, these people have been left in a backwater." As a young adult I believed not only has society not "progressed"—we were in Vietnam, still ruthlessly enforcing our economy on other nations, still sending out missionaries as cultural shock troops—but that the very people I was told to ignore, because they supposedly had nothing to offer, were the people who gave me through the tradition of storytelling more than I could get out of my own culture about what it has meant historically to be a storyteller. So it's so important to emphasize the tremendous impact of all of this childhood stuff.

MAGEE: And for that reason I think it's so important that an education not systematically break the fingers of the developing personality, but to recognize qualities that are already there and need only time and encouragement. What you've just described, having your future life foretold in the pictures you chose as a child, could sound a little like prophetic magic. But I've had exactly the same experience. Things that I drew as a child explicitly predicted the interests and life that I would live later. This seems perfectly sound, that we are already formed and inclined toward what is ours. And it makes perfect sense that, in each case, we found much of what we needed on the periphery, outside of school.

LOPEZ: Yes. Yes.

MAGEE: So much of what's been valuable to me over the years has come from the uncertified route. Though we value opportunities to go to Europe and to be close enough to touch a magnificent and esteemed work of art, we recognize also that the ingredients that go into meaningful work, for us, have to be a mixture of the high and the low—the masterpiece and the found object with no pretense to art. So what we end up with is a synthesis of both, and as you say, a healthy mistrust for either one in its "pure" form. What we're talking about is the insistence of walking about on level, open ground and a refusal to acknowledge the maze of fences that specialists like to construct for us. We have to pass easily between this field and that one, that's a requirement for the kind of work that you and I value. And neither of us would say that we were elevating the low, because we recognize that it's already elevated.

• • •

About our early years and the influences that we recognized as our own—I am interested in how we disengaged from those influences once we learned the essential lessons in them.

If we hear someone play the violin incredibly well, our first response might be that we have to get a violin. Of course, later we recognize that this desire is guiding us, not to become musicians, but to a dedication to our own talents.

So gradually I was able to learn, and I'm still learning, that the things I am drawn to must stand as examples rather than as temptations to enter fields that are not mine. Seeing extraordinary films, and feeling the uneasy attraction that I have to moving imagery, has made me want to make films. I had to learn to separate the fascination with the form from its more valuable, archetypal example.

LOPEZ: I can identify with many of the things that you've said, and they actually help me sort out what has happened to me. When I was young I made the mistake of thinking I wanted to do exactly what somebody else was doing. What they had made was intrinsically exciting to me. How did they get this out of their head onto a piece of paper or onto a piece of celluloid? Technique? That was one answer. But the real mystery is how to turn what you feel into something that can be sensed, you know, seen. I'm sure that's what pulled me into photography when I was 19. I was not so much interested in photographing an object as I was in the set of relationships among colors and textures and line—*that* was deeply stimulating to me. It didn't have to be anything. It was just this translation I wanted. Early on, I thought the same way you might have, you know, "If I love this violin I have to learn to play the violin." But, really, what you're attracted to is a phenomenon: somebody *felt* something, and then they made it available to another human being by getting it out of their internal landscape. Later, once you've recognized what your forte is, you can address that strange thing inside you in terms of the technical skills you've gained as a painter, a dancer, whatever.

When I finished *Arctic Dreams* in the mid-'80s I became so distracted by the attention I was getting that for a while I flirted with the idea of not speaking again. I didn't want to be involved in all of these interviews—What was my meaning? What were my politics? I couldn't make any connection between what those things were and what I wanted to do. So for a period of time—a couple of months, not much longer than that—I was determined to work in large outdoor sculptural forms. That's where I was going to exercise the impulse that up until then I felt had been located in writing and photography. Now I would say that when I see you paint it doesn't make me want to be a painter; I love this contact with you because of the hunger and dedication in your work. I would like to believe it is akin to the hunger and dedication that I feel, and that when I stumble and lose my focus I can imagine that you've gone through similar stumbling periods, and that this will pass and we'll go on. So, when you're young, you're attracted to people who have accomplished that magic thing of getting the interior landscape outside of themselves, and you can mistake their forms of expression for your forms. Then you discover your form and your alliance with other artists is not one of wanting to imitate their work, but, rather, getting in step with the dedication with which they approach their work.

Where I am in my work now, I feel a somewhat mischievous impulse to confuse issues of authorship. I like the idea of making something where the question of who made it becomes irrelevant and the real question becomes: Does this help? Does this theatrical performance, does this combination of images and language, this pulling together of the work of two or three people, does this help us as a culture? The question of exactly who drew this particular line, you know ... I think there must be that sense of mischievousness in many artists. You do recognize your own work, but the point of the work is not what you did, the point of the work is the work.

MAGEE: You've touched on a lot that I've been thinking about. Of course, imitation is a very natural thing, and probably one of the appropriate ways for young people to learn. We see heroes that are bigger than life, and their heightened stature makes us stand on tiptoes to try to measure up to them. We gather our hero's energy and eventually harness it to our own inclinations. Another thing that you talked about was collaboration. Of course, you and I have talked a good deal about working together and have made plans for projects in the future. This is a very natural part of what we've always done, even while working alone. I feel that I've been collaborating with you since I picked up that first book of yours. There's no doubt in my mind that this kind of unacknowledged collaboration sends out infinite roots from artist to artist.

Whenever I give a talk to students, I try to bring in a dozen or so examples of artists that I look at very seriously. It conveys not only the idea that there are artists out there that these students might not know, but that every artist has roots into the ground which reach across to other trees. We are not just standing there drawing it all out of the air. This is an extremely important part of the creative process, how we're linked to other people.

A recent experience reinforced this. I had written a short piece for the glossary in this book about the Quay Brothers and how I had met them as fellow students at the Philadelphia College of Art. At the end of this paragraph I wanted to mention the Quays' influence on contemporary film—which, in my view, has been enormous. I asked them if might I mention a well-known filmmaker as having been particularly taken with their work and whose films show their influence. They wrote back asking me not to mention this. The Quay Brothers see their own work as being influenced by many sources, and feeling that debt to their personal canon of masters, they didn't want to be publicly credited with having a been a singular influence on another filmmaker's work.

This is the ongoing collaboration. When we get together to organize a joint project, we're only formalizing something which is happening in our minds and in our work all the time.

LOPEZ: It's interesting for a writer like me who works in both fiction and nonfiction. I'm expected to have an acknowledgements section in a work of nonfiction, but in fiction that's not supposed to be necessary. There is some prohibition here—that to give a lot of credit in the front of a novel or a collection of short stories somehow suggests that the creative act in literature has been compromised, or is more in the realm of nonfiction. I can't explain it very well, but it makes sense to me to thank everyone by name in a work of nonfiction and it also makes sense to me to say something like that in fiction. You know, you and I were talking this morning about a short story that is sort of turning over in my head, and it all got triggered because you and Monika thought we should go to see this particular house and visit this particular person. So, it makes sense to say, "This story happened because Alan and Monika Magee decided one day we should go and visit a friend of theirs." But we don't do that. I think our wrestling with it, our worry about the propriety of it suggests an undercurrent, which is there all the time in your work: Yes, the work is yours, but you are always dependent on other people not only for technical assistance—how to get the thing done more simply, more elegantly—but also for the inspirations, the stimulations. You have a conversation with some person, nothing much seems to happen, but every time you talk to this person something pops up for you as an artist, and you make a couple of notes about it. It's very murky business, how we all help each other, how we inform each other's work. For a period of time—and now I've started doing it again—whenever I would give a reading I would first read the poetry of colleagues. What I was trying to say was, "I'm part of a community of women and men who write, and here's work that I admire. Let's be clear that we're all here in this room tonight out of respect for what happens to us when we hear a story, and let me tell you I'd feel more comfortable if the focus were not on me, but on this pattern that I've made, because I've had the life-long instruction, and love, and companionship of my friends, some of whom are writers and artists, some of whom are farmers or people who work in the woods. These people in some invisible way helped me make this story."

And here's something else. You took me yesterday to the Dragon Cement Plant, which for 20 years has been a visual stimulation and inspiration for you. I'd never been there, but when we got there I wanted to stay for a long time. I recalled, walking around together, the excitement I felt earlier in my life as a photographer. I wanted so much to photograph this place. What's that all about? What do you think that is all about?

MAGEE: Well, what springs immediately to mind from what you've just said was how Cartier-Bresson, after a long career in photography, decided to sit down with a sketchbook and draw expressive line drawings of his friends. I think that's marvelous.

That cement plant *is* extraordinary, and I think we both get very charged up in an environment like that. I can understand how the process of photography calls out to you again in that setting. I think that at a particular stage in life, when we feel like we've worked enough in the chosen field, that it might be time to do a little of something else. I would like to think at the end that I had tried everything that I thought was appropriate to try.

LOPEZ: So isn't it just as legitimate to say—if I am a painter and I have something to say and there's no history of this in my discipline—isn't it just as legitimate to try and infuse the discipline with a technique that broadens the capacity of that medium for expression? I sometimes felt when I was working as both a photographer and a writer that I had to allow commercial uses, money-making issues, some place in my writing life—I had to make a living—but with photography I never allowed commercial issues any play. I'd go and photograph with no thought at all about how those photographs would fill the needs of my stock agency, for example. I just wanted to photograph. Now, 20 years after putting my cameras down to turn entirely to writing, here is something that so rarely happens for me. You said, "I'd like to take you to a place that's very stimulating for me, and we'll just kind of walk around and pick up things, and point things out to each other." I thought: Things are going on here visually at the cement plant that I've written about. I want to make language that will carry these images into a person's head; but I also felt keenly the urge to photograph. So I think both of us might have a yearning expressed through our collaborators, to find forms of expression that get us outside the areas where we have chosen to work.

You're a painter who has confused people because you won't stay in a box, and there is something of that in my work too. What we're interested in is this exploration. The tradition of realism in painting serves you to a certain point, then you're out wandering in places where academic critics don't want you to be, or commercial art appraisers don't want you to be, because you're an object to them rather than a human being. You're not going to quit at the point of commercial success, but continue to go on, even if it means you'll have less commercial success.

MAGEE: Your urge to photograph certainly brings you back to a medium that you've practiced before and enjoyed and loved, and the instinct to return to it is not so strange on that level. But in addition to this, we seem to share a healthy instinct to bring a part of the work into a place where professional constraints

Quay Brothers, *The Street of Crocodiles (animation frames)*, 1986

are not in force—where we can shake a part of the work free from any kind of business. Of course, professionalism catches up to you quickly.

We recognize the need to find a space, metaphorical or real, to practice our work that's free from any of the professional constraints that apply to the work we are doing publicly. In fact, this was such a strong tendency in me that when I wanted to wind down the illustration work that I was doing in the 1970s, I set up a separate studio on the main street of Camden, a few blocks from where we lived. I felt it very important not to bring any reminders of illustration into that studio. I brought in other materials and tools so that there was no cross-contamination—a kosher environment.

LOPEZ: There is a correspondence for me with a story. A book is a living thing for me and I treat it like a living thing. I'm concerned about light and air, for example, around a manuscript. I would never put anything on top of a manuscript. When I'm writing a book, I always find a way to rearrange the house or rearrange one of my workrooms so the book has a place, a room in which no other book has ever come to life. I guess after a while I will have to add rooms to the house or something to make it work, but this is a curious thing, the way you feel the physical nature of the manuscript or the painting. I remember that studio in Camden and your effort to break away from illustration and become more thoroughly immersed in something that wasn't commercially defined, which was your painting. I guess I've gone through similar things. What it makes me want to ask you is something like: Why did you want to make the shift from illustration into painting? Were you aware of things you couldn't act on when you were an illustrator, and then you just got into this situation where you could do the work? Or was it a shift in what you wanted to do with your talent?

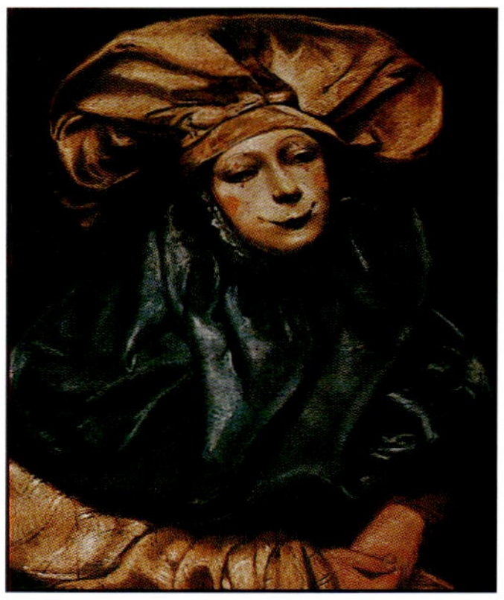

MAGEE: I think all of those things were connected to it. With illustration, I felt like I was on a moving train and kept glimpsing things out the window that I needed to see in more detail. I wanted to get off the train and walk around and spend a year or more, maybe the rest of my life, investigating this amazing industrial ruin, desert landscape, or stone beach.

LOPEZ: Yeah.

MAGEE: The illustration process kept bringing me in contact with writers, with ideas, with visual discoveries that were fascinating, but the profession requires you to put each experience down when you are finished with it and go on to another. I had the sense that this was no way to develop a philosophical point of view that would hold. I was looking for a practice where style, subject, the entire field of investigation could be stable—a process that I could spend time with.

Illustration was that moving train, and I came into contact with things that I would never have found on my own. Fortunately I was in a position to be given really wonderful writers to illustrate because I had a somewhat surreal style, and I was given nearly complete freedom to illustrate these great books as I saw fit.

Finally, the work of writers like Graham Greene, and Bernard Malamud (two writers whose books I was illustrating in series) presented an example of art for me that I couldn't deny. Those books exemplified an art that sprang out of life itself. This is what the illustrator cannot do because the subjects always shift and because the subjects aren't of the artist's choosing. Graham Greene in particular was the catalyst for me. Reading and illustrating a number of his books, and observing the way his hardened, street-wise characters and seedy, Third World backdrops were the framework for an unflinching spirituality in his novels, I realized there was something fundamental that I needed to learn from this writer.

So, I had to wind the illustration work down, of course, but there was a practical problem: how to make a transition into another field of art and continue to make a living. Because I was young and innocent I underestimated the difficulties of those problems; and for that reason—because of my innocence—it all worked out.

However, I think there *are* serious problems when you try to accomplish that particular shift. Fine arts professionals use the word "illustration" to describe a realm of art that is scorned in critical circles. But, as I said, in my case it worked out quite well.

LOPEZ: Yes it did. I wonder about illustration. You know people condescend to it as a discipline. But isn't that partly because people view it as a response to somebody else's work rather than as something self-generated?

MAGEE: I suppose it is. But, if we accept that, we get into the great difficulty weighing the achievement of all the extraordinary historic art that was done "for hire" like the work of the contemporary illustrator. All the great work commissioned by the Church, the great civic and private paintings and sculpture of the Renaissance, would have to be reckoned with if we dismissed art that is not self-generated. The paradox becomes obvious the minute we try to condemn illustration on those grounds.

I left illustration, not because I didn't respect it as a field, but because my aptitudes didn't lie there. I needed freedom to generate good work, rather than to respond beautifully and elegantly to any challenge—that wasn't my strength. I have enormous respect for illustrators who, time after time, *can* respond to those challenges and come up with something inventive, technically beautiful, and also conceptually perfect for the subject. I knew illustrators who did that. The illustrators Alan Cober and John Collier did it admirably throughout their illustration careers and I respect them as much as I do any gallery artist. You asked about illustration and the reason it doesn't enjoy the same kind of respect culturally as what we call the fine arts, and I've always had questions about the usefulness of that term. It's clear to anybody who practices either of these professions responsibly that there's no difference in the nature of the two kinds of artists—their skills, their level of engagement or their dedication. I think the fine art/commercial photographers of today are teaching us that individual artists can function in both of these realms as long as there is some kind of guiding ethic in which that artist is working. Just because one's skills are "for sale" doesn't mean that they are for sale to anybody for any reason. We are wise enough to apply our work to practical as well as poetic ends.

LOPEZ: I'm much more comfortable with that idea as a writer. For example, writers like Ursula Le Guin or Philip Dick have been kept in the margins in some sense as literary writers because of the form they've chosen to work in. In another country, where our rather extraordinary North American investment in reason and "the real" doesn't hold sway, those two writers

John Collier, *Clown*, 1978 (client: Push Pin Graphic, art director: Seymour Chwast)

might be appreciated in a different way. They would have been more welcome in the literary community. I think, though, people like to feel some pressure to define themselves within the high arts or to operate with those kinds of distinctions around. You used a word a little bit ago—spiritual, the spiritual nature of someone's endeavor in their work. We've said James Hillman has articulated some issues for us that are very important. For example, if you want to talk about suppressed topics, anathema topics today, beauty is certainly a concept people are very uncomfortable discussing in public. Spirituality is as well. When you bring spirituality in, the discussion often turns to pop culture, or it gets thoroughly confused with religion. But I'm curious what you might speculate about the spiritual nature of your work. Are you comfortable at all with that phrase?

MAGEE: I would be, I suppose, if the word hadn't been so thoroughly misused, popularized, and applied to so many things to which I wouldn't want to attach my name. But yes, I am comfortable with it in the quiet conversation between a couple of friends or within my own work. I think when you talk about beauty it becomes inseparable with the realm of spirit.

Early on, after the illustration years, taking the time to draw objects the way I wanted, spending great lengths of time observing, applying that observation back into a drawing, it became curious to me how the beauty of a thing reveals itself with attention. Attention and beauty are so closely linked.

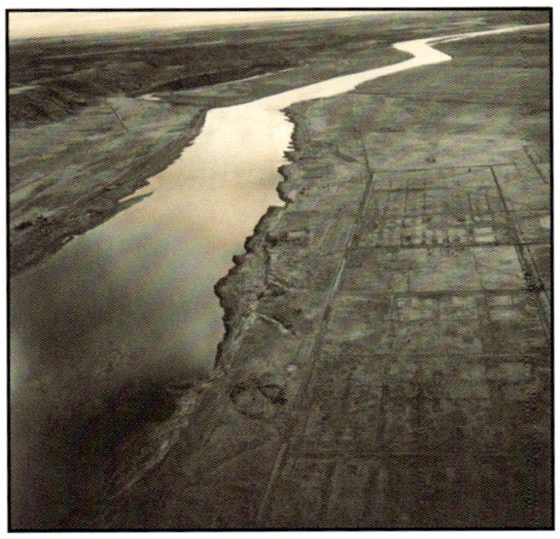

Further, there seems to be a kind of spiritual/ethical dimension to all of this. So many of the problems that we seem to be bumping our heads against constantly, that we are struggling with interpersonally and internationally, are related to a failure of appreciation. If it's true that with some kind of attention the quality of beauty is almost a guarantee, then the perception of ugliness or repugnance are certainly linked to a failure of attention. If it is true that with heightened attention places, objects, and people reveal themselves as singularly beautiful, then surely the inverse of this must govern our dismissals and our hatreds of the unfamiliar. It is not such a reach to come to these conclusions if you draw and paint.

Recently you and I ran across an essay by James Hillman, "The Practice of Beauty," where he was saying more or less the same thing, that we have impoverished ourselves by banishing beauty. But why did our culture do that? I can only report that in the visual arts, from the time I was in art school, it was made clear that beauty was equated with triviality. If something was beautiful it wasn't considered to be engaged; it had nothing to do with the serious struggles and anxieties of our culture. Awareness required us to honor what was harsh, condemning, ironic, and cold. Hillman suggests that without a component of beauty, religion, for example, becomes a rigid and unpleasant set of dogmatic structures.

So then, what we may be saying is that beauty may be the energy source for the spirit, the place within the mind where sympathy, concordance, kindness are born and regenerated. What else do we tap into to energize our instincts for any kind of spiritual understanding of things? We have to start with what we are given.

The German theological scholar, Rudolf Otto, was saying something similar. In his book from 1923 called *The Idea of the Holy*, he explained that religion consists of both the "numinous," and a system of ethics. He wrote about the stimulus for spirituality coming from a "world awe" that, in religions, is coupled with codes of right behavior. Those two ingredients combined make a religion. This understanding had value for me as a painter. A painter works with world awe too, and knows that some notion of social responsibility has to inform his work. The great works of Rembrandt radiate with this kind of dual understanding. And you and I have recognized this duality in Emmet Gowin's marvelous aerial photographs.

LOPEZ: I was thinking that maybe John Berger gave both of us this thought, that maybe we stumbled onto it with him. And that is that, in a representation of the real world, what makes a painting different from a mechanical reproduction of that world is the conversation between the object and the painter. The painter is fully engaged here, at both the material and spiritual levels, engaged with the stone on the beach or whatever it might be. You told me something once about painting stones, that if all you were interested in was the realistic reproduction of a set of stones on a beach you could be done with the painting in a matter of a couple of days or something. But you could also look at the painting and see while it was acceptable as an accurate representation of a stretch of beach it had none of the quality that would make it a painting, and that it might take you weeks of going in, say, and completely dismantling a part of the painting that had one stone in it and turning it into six stones to get it right, using an intuitive sense of the references the stones had to have to each other. Berger's idea that the artist, even in representational painting, is in a deep conversation is, I think, an expression of this idea that you are trying to engage that part of the world you are recording that most accentuates, makes most plain, its spirituality. In other words, a person looking at a painting of stones of yours on a museum wall might say in effect, "I never noticed that before." Well, it's not the arrangement of stones they didn't notice, but that the painter, you in particular, put something into the painting in terms of line, and color, and texture, that excited a sense of the spiritual dimension of ordinary life, which a person might not pick up on the beach because the quality of the numinous might not be so apparent.

You make the numinous more apparent in your representation of ordinary things. Something that most people would throw in a junk pile, a drill for example, becomes riveting in your paintings because it, too, has this numinous quality. It's a reflection of the inventive power of human beings and their incredible ability to manipulate materials to make electric armatures, and drill bits, and to apply paints that adhere to metal then wear off over time as the hand moves over them. All of that stuff that makes it much more than just a drill is what makes your paintings come to life.

Another thing that I think of about beauty is that if somebody asks me what I'm trying to do, and I want to give them a succinct answer I won't attempt to talk as I often do about the Paleolithic roots of story, its therapeutic dimension, pattern, the Bach cello suites—all these things I bring in to explain how a story works. What I say is, "I'm trying to make something beautiful." Period. What that word beauty means to me here is: intimate with you, coherent within itself, and an approximation

Emmet Gowin, *Old Hanford City Site and the Columbia River, Hanford Nuclear Reservation, Near Richland, Washington*, 1986

of the face of God. For me, with my upbringing, the way I imagine the Great Spirit, the Overriding Spirit, is absolute seamlessness. It is so coherent there is no place where a seam can develop and incoherence thereby become apparent. What beauty is finally to me is an unimaginable coherence. A thing so fully integrated that you merge with it and lose the terrible sense of loneliness and identity that separates you from the world. The numinous feels like an invitation and you long for it. I think people long all the time, all their lives in their dreams and in their waking hours, to be included. Part of the power of art to me is that in a particular painting with a particular artist you feel that sense of inclusion in the world. You feel the ignition of your imagination where before it had just been smoldering. So you look at a painting of stones and you walk out the door of the gallery and you're thinking how much you love your wife. Somebody might ask, "Well, how are these connected?" They're connected because you came to life again in the presence of the painting, forms that spoke directly to you of the numinous as a result of this miracle of painting.

MAGEE: I couldn't agree with you more. I think this *is* the latent possibility of art. This is what happens in literature, and painting, and great architecture, in anything that we make when we are attached to these incredible seamless patterns that you have mentioned. Experiencing the power of these patterns in nature, even in their most unassuming manifestations, is an experience of being renewed—reset to begin the work again.

No matter how satisfied I might feel when I'm finished with a painting of beach stones, when I go back to Pemaquid beach I realize how far off the mark anything I could paint would be, when measured against this magnificent reality. It immediately seizes me with its riveting quiet. It is beyond argument.

So this sends you back to work, whether it be at painting stones or anything else. But you return to work aware of this gap, which is always a challenge and an exhilarating tension, realizing that the world is good company. You travel along behind it and make what you can, guided and informed by it.

• • •

LOPEZ: I think there are also some things that you could talk about with students that would be very unsettling for them. For example, people often assume if you have a certain sort of commercial success, or artistic or critical success, that you can then put the car on cruise control and that's it for the rest of your life. But, in fact, any artist or writer who is honest will say the times of self doubt, or loss of self confidence, continue until your life is over, especially if you are determined not to stop in one place and be happy with what you have. You know, you discover a kind of formula, for example, and you go back to it again, and again, and again.

I remember thinking once that for many writers the act of creating the story is not completed until you hear from the reader. I believe that there is a component in a literary or artistic personality that, to put it in stark terms, makes us want to be loved. The creation of the work is in this sense a request to be recognized, and if you do a certain kind of work and there is a tremendous response to it, there is always a temptation to want to do that same work again in order to get the reinforcement. What you have to recognize as an artist or writer is that you can't do this or your work will fade. What you have to do is keep pushing on with your first small handful of questions; if there's no public response, you can't say, "Okay I'm going to stop." You have to keep pushing through, and maybe you'll get somewhere where there will be a public response. I'm surprised sometimes that some young people believe that once you have a few stories published in well-known magazines then the rest of your life poses no great difficulty, you just keep turning pieces out and people publish them, and if the quality of the work falls off your name still carries you. That can happen, but you hope it doesn't. I know I go through periods when I wonder: Am I fooling myself? Is this work really good? I've got this other work behind me, I've got a certain reputation, am I still measuring up here? You know, all of that stuff, at least for me, is always there. Is the work still any good?

MAGEE: As uncomfortable as it is to live like this I think this is the only way to go. It is habitual for me, too, to ask if this work measures up, is it any good, does it simply spring out of momentum that I've created earlier or does it have an engine of its own? Is it powered in some distinct way by its own energy?

LOPEZ: Yes. Yes.

MAGEE: I think there is no other way to live. It is probably a grace of the overall pattern that the young don't have to understand at the beginning how hard it will be later. Just as we don't understand how hard it will be for us complete a particular work. We're protected and shielded from how hard it is to build a Brooklyn Bridge because if we really knew the difficulties it would be impossible to begin. We're always protecting ourselves from the enormity of what we have to do.

I was just thinking as you were speaking about the opening chapter of Andrei Tarkovsky's book about filmmaking, *Sculpting in Time*. It is one of the best and most literate books about the process of art that I've ever read. The breadth of Tarkovsky's understanding about all art and its uses is beautifully articulated. He insists that art is for people, and that it has to be good for them in some fundamental way, the way the books of Tolstoy, and the films of Dovzhenko and Eisenstein, Bergmann and Buñuel were good for him as a young artist. He begins the book by excerpting a number of letters from his film audience, both grateful and critical, including some bitter remarks sparked by viewer's incomprehension of his films' symbolism and unconventional structure. Other letters thanked him for making a profound connection to them, saying that "Your film changed my life, or, I understood my mother and my father for the first time. Thank you so much for your work."

In this book, Tarkovsky discusses the process of his work, the role of the artist in society, the impossibility of arguing the merits of a work of art to someone who is not constitutionally set up to understand it. This kind of honest report is the best form of advice any of us can give to a young artist or writer.

As working artists we will engender enormously varied responses. Regardless of this, we need to maintain a faith that our work will find its way to the right people.

This interview is excerpted from a longer conversation between Alan Magee and Barry Lopez, which took place at Alan's home in Cushing, Maine, October 12-13 2002.

REALIST PAINTING

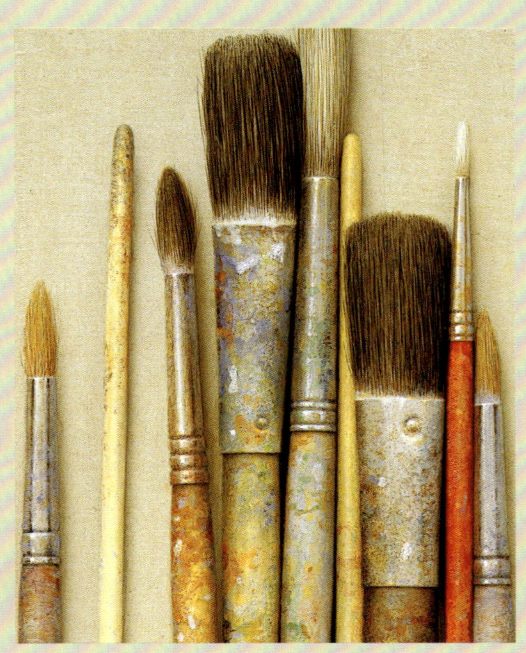

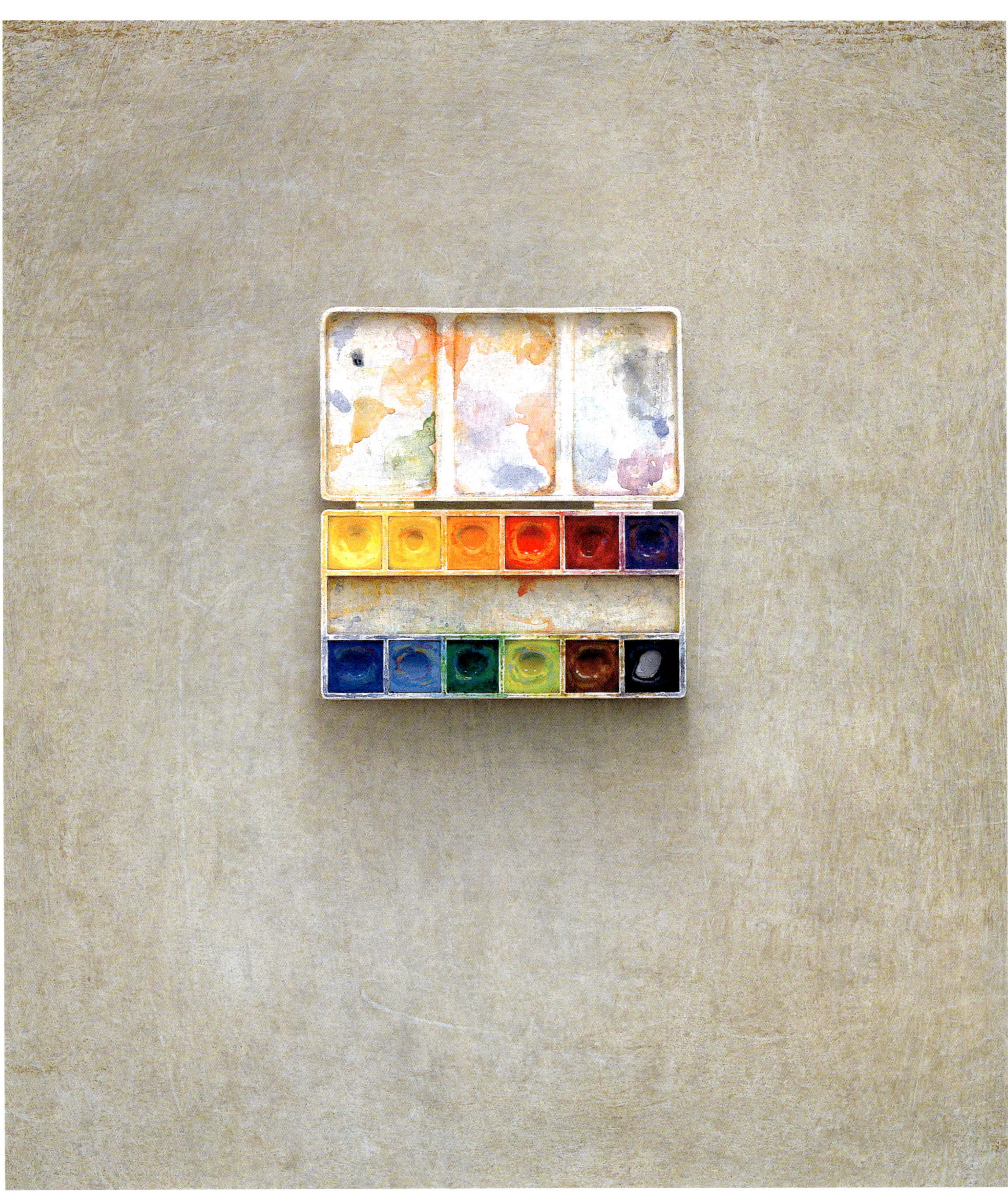

Primer, 2000, acrylic and oil on panel, 16 ¼ x 14"

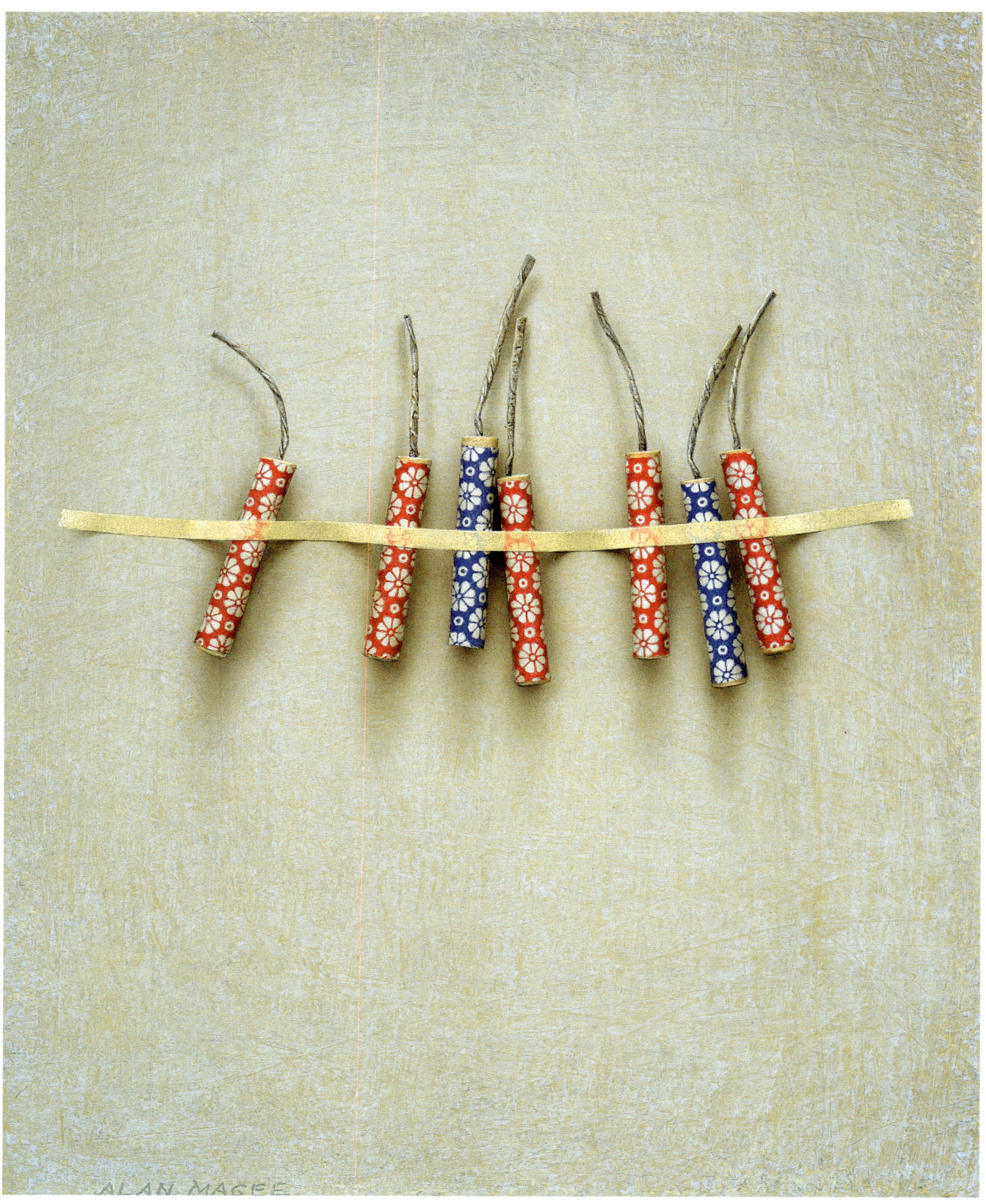

Garland, 2001, acrylic on panel, 10 ¼ x 8"

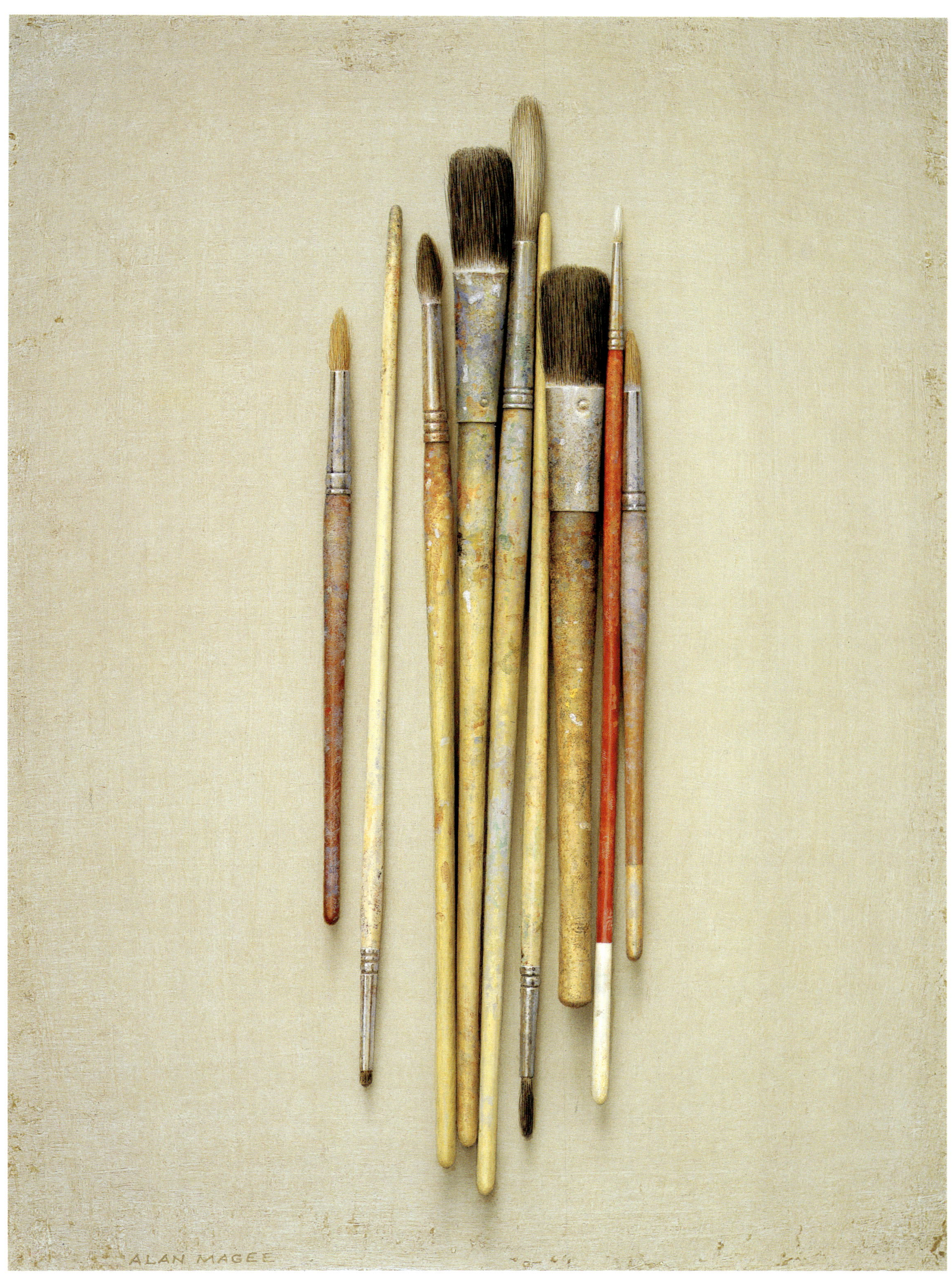

Résumé, 2001, acrylic and oil on panel, 15 ¾ x 11 ¾"

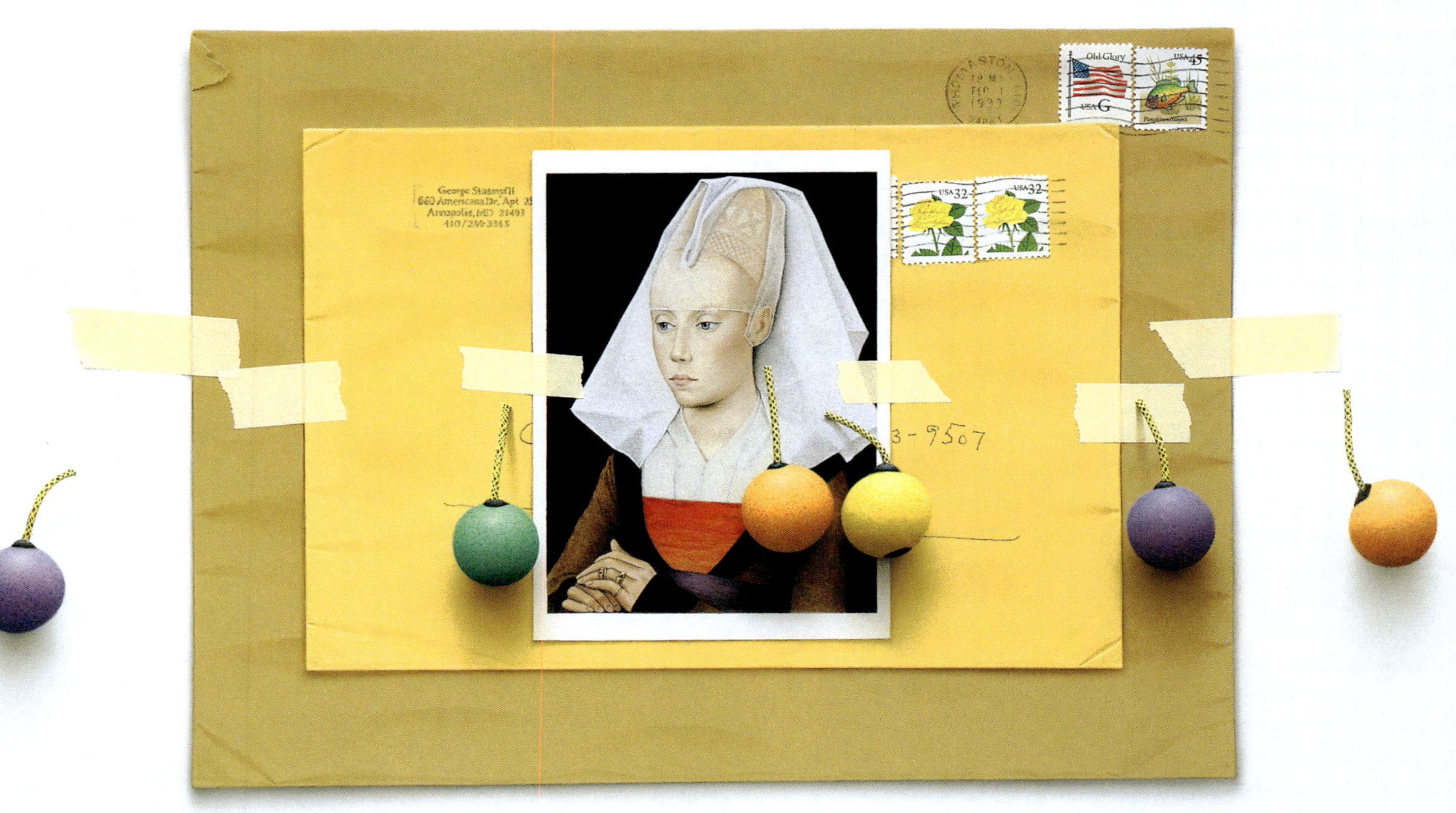

Old Glory
USA G
USA 45
USA 32
USA 32
3-9507

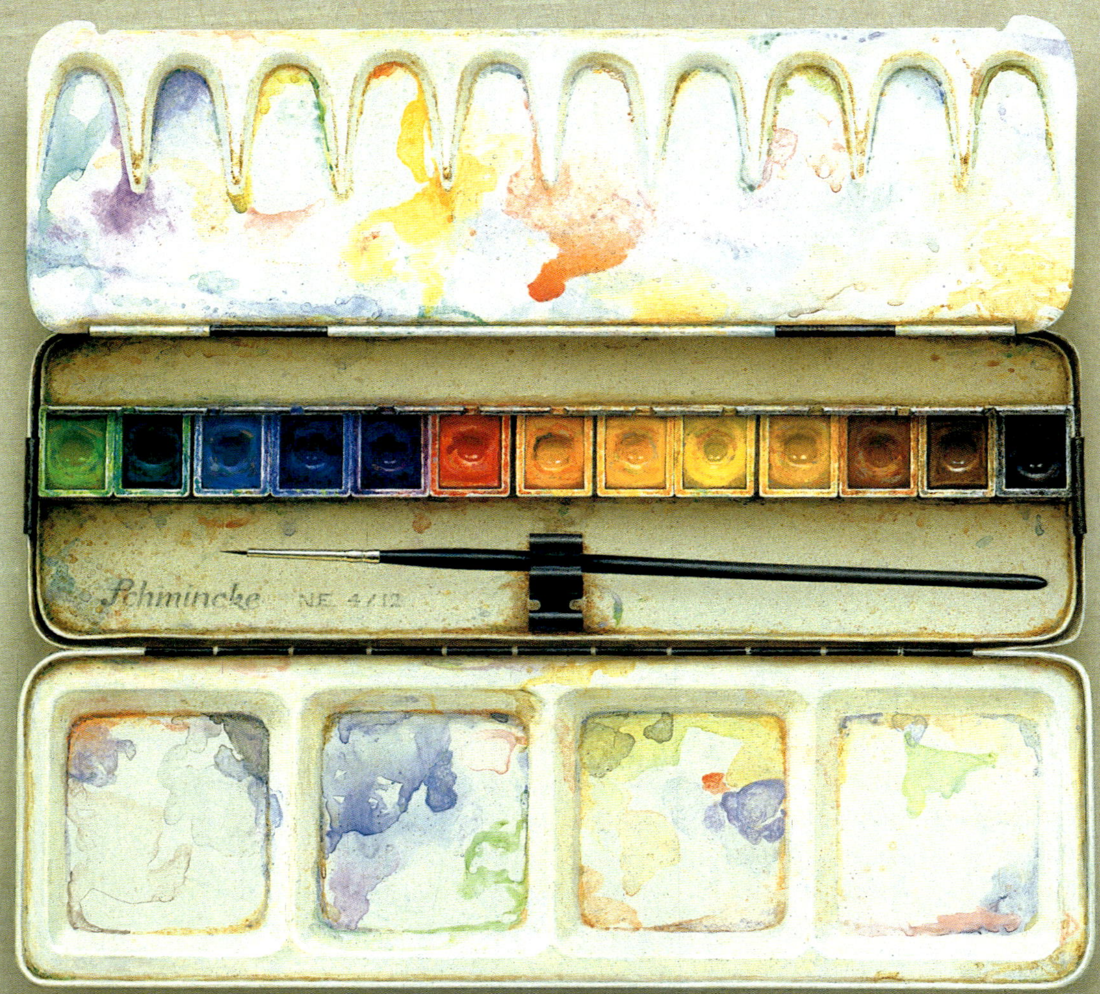
Schmincke NE 4/12

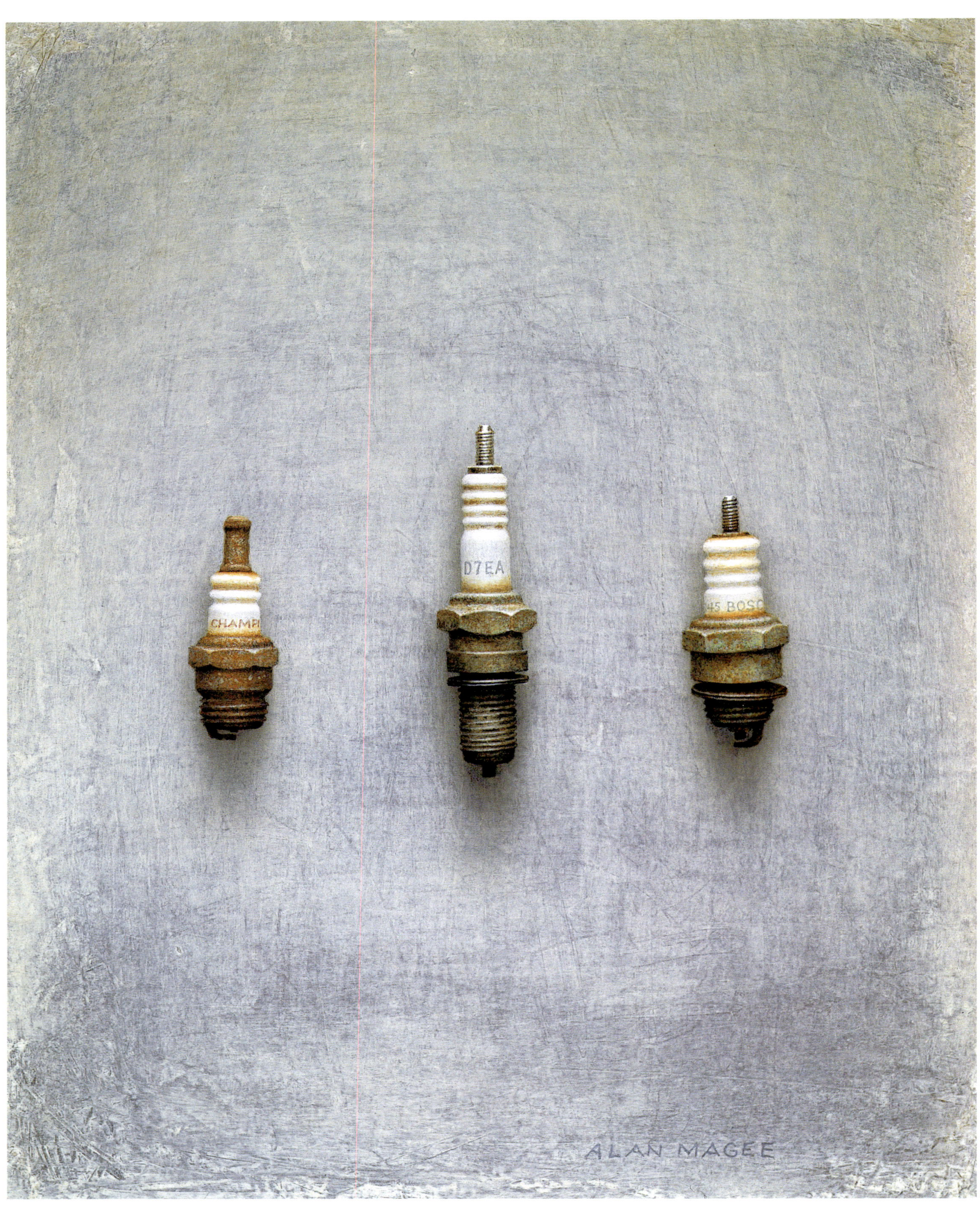

Pact, 2000, acrylic and oil on panel, 10 x 8"

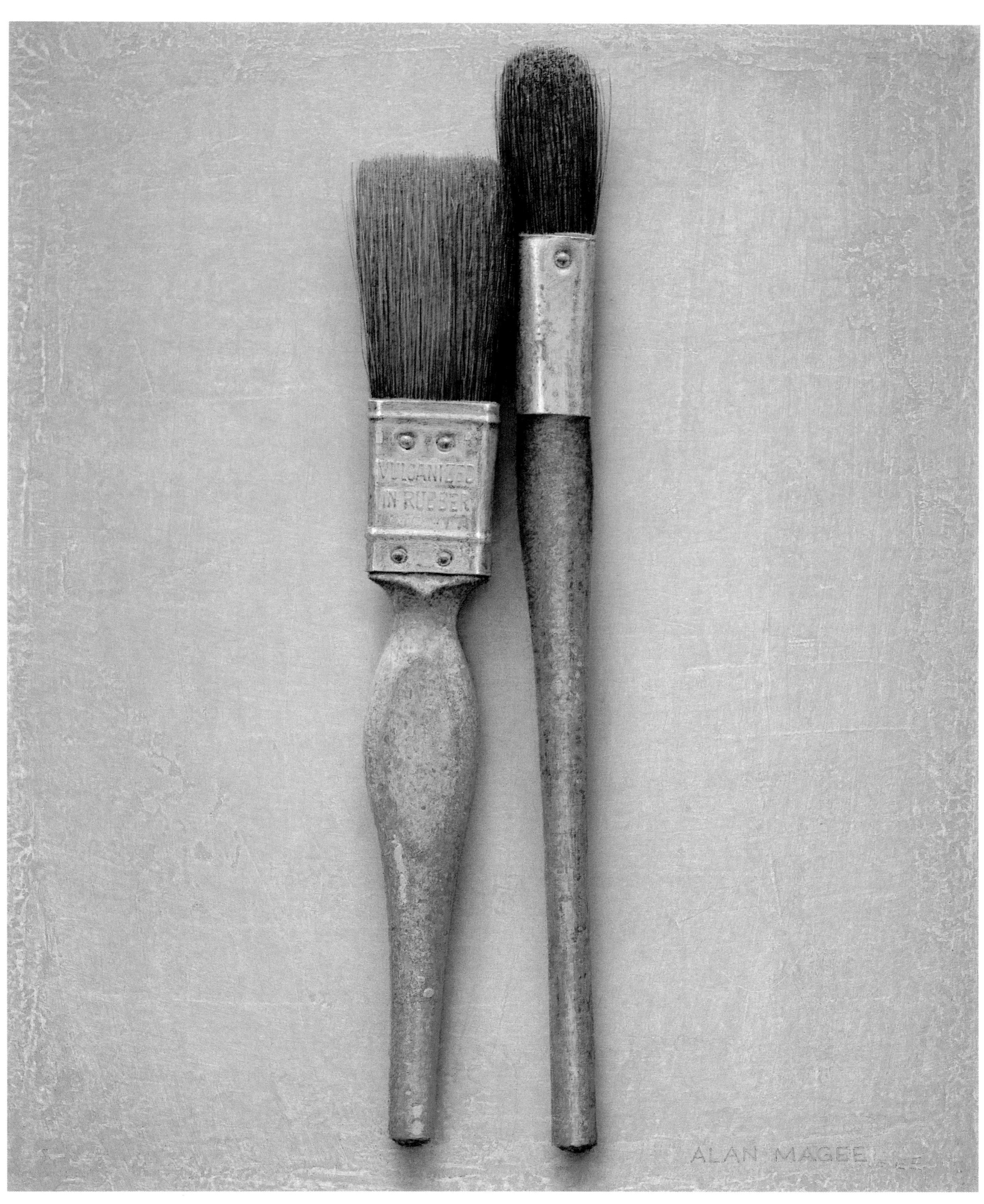

Rhyme, 2000, acrylic and oil on panel, 10 x 8"

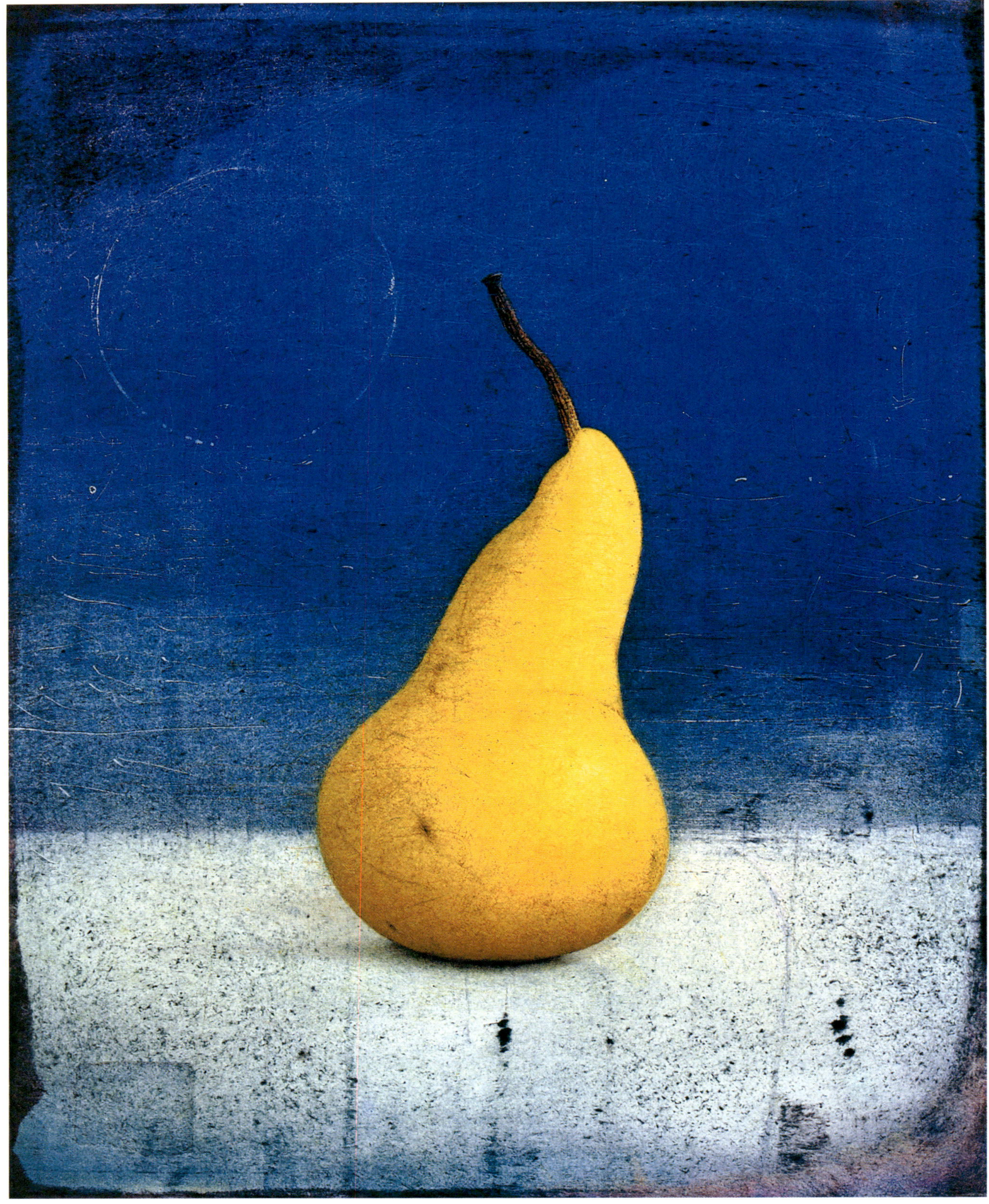

Pear and Moon, 1993, watercolor over monotype, 14 x 11"

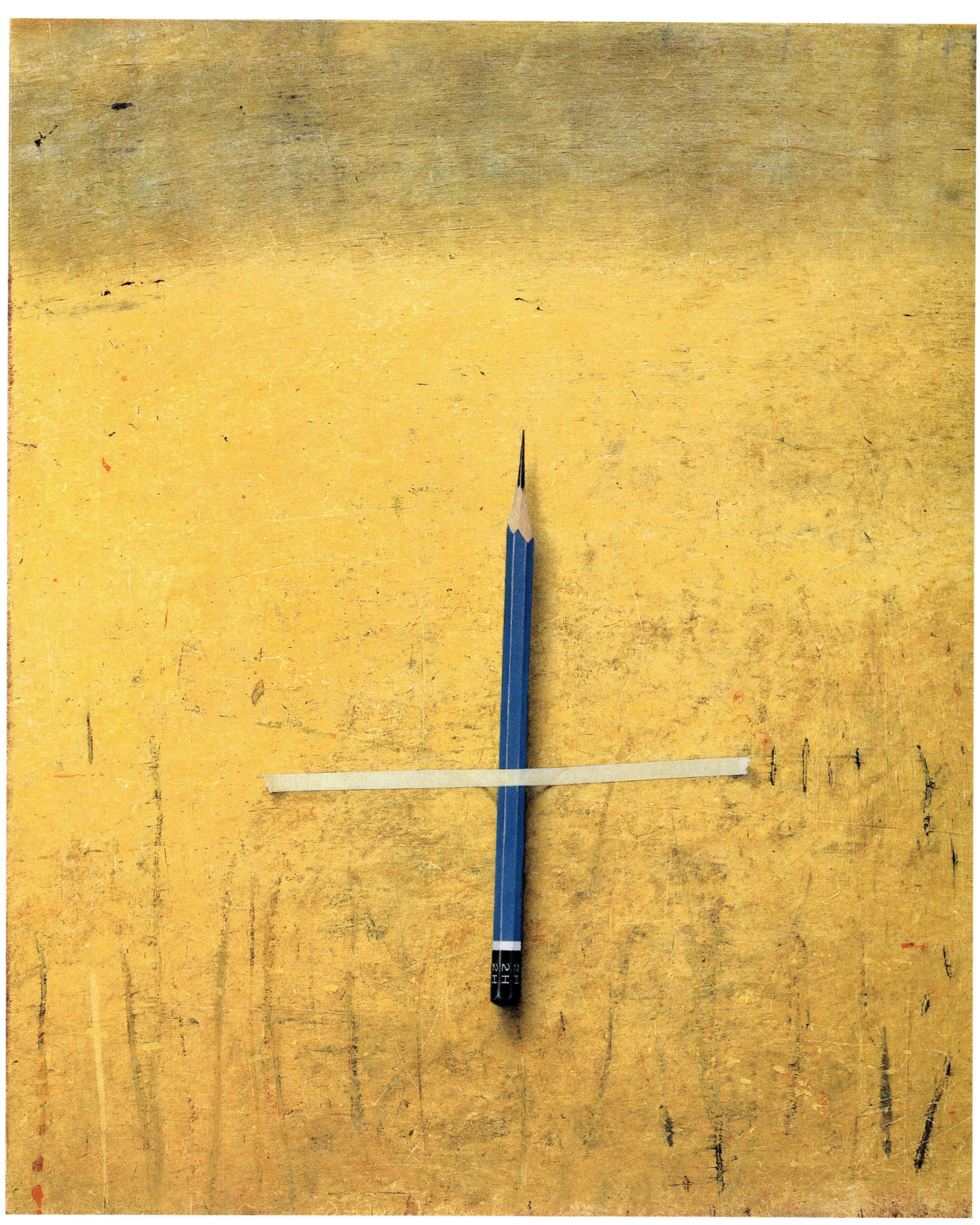

November Meadow, 1995, acrylic and watercolor over monotype, 14 x 11"

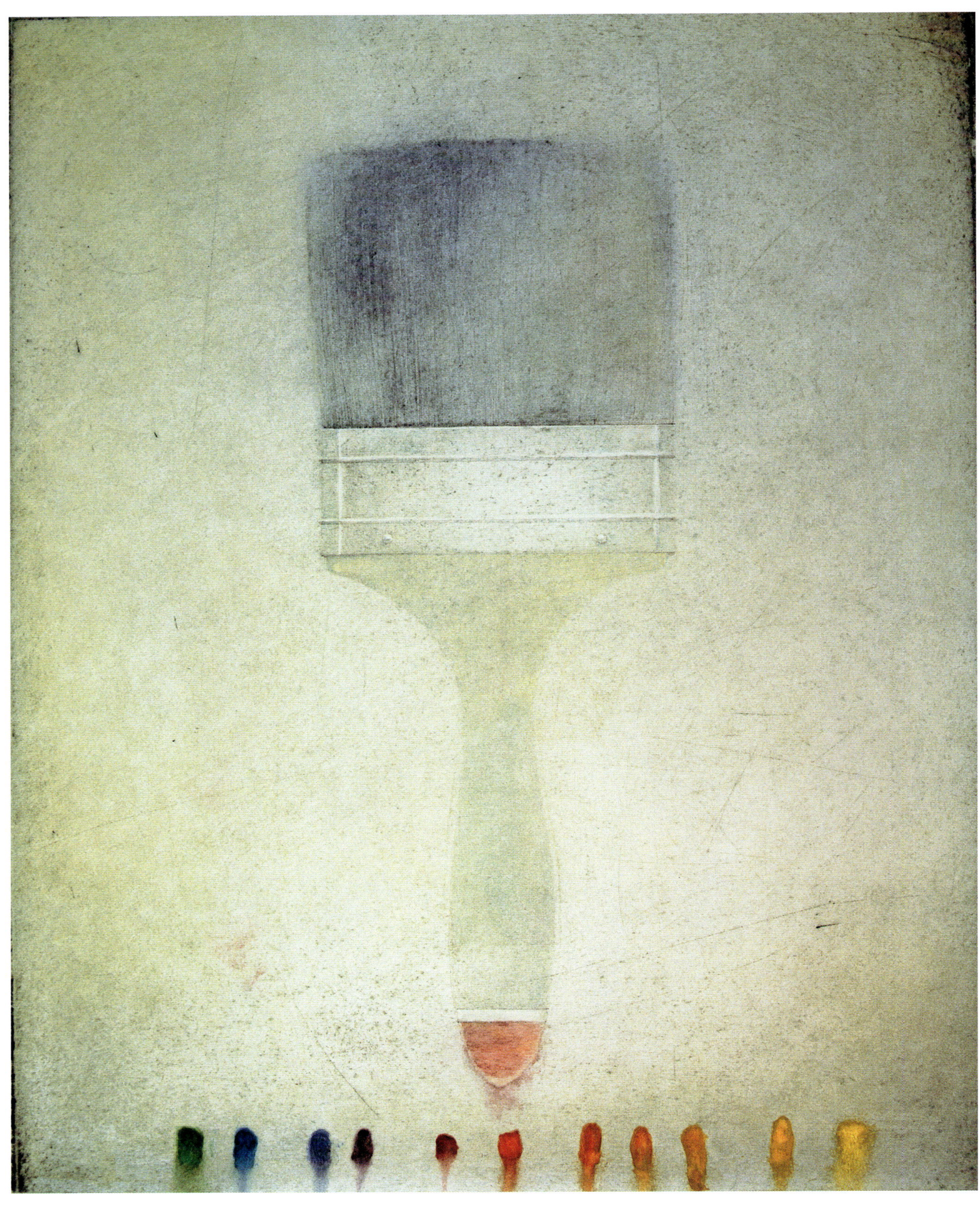

Colors, 1993, monotype, 14 x 11"

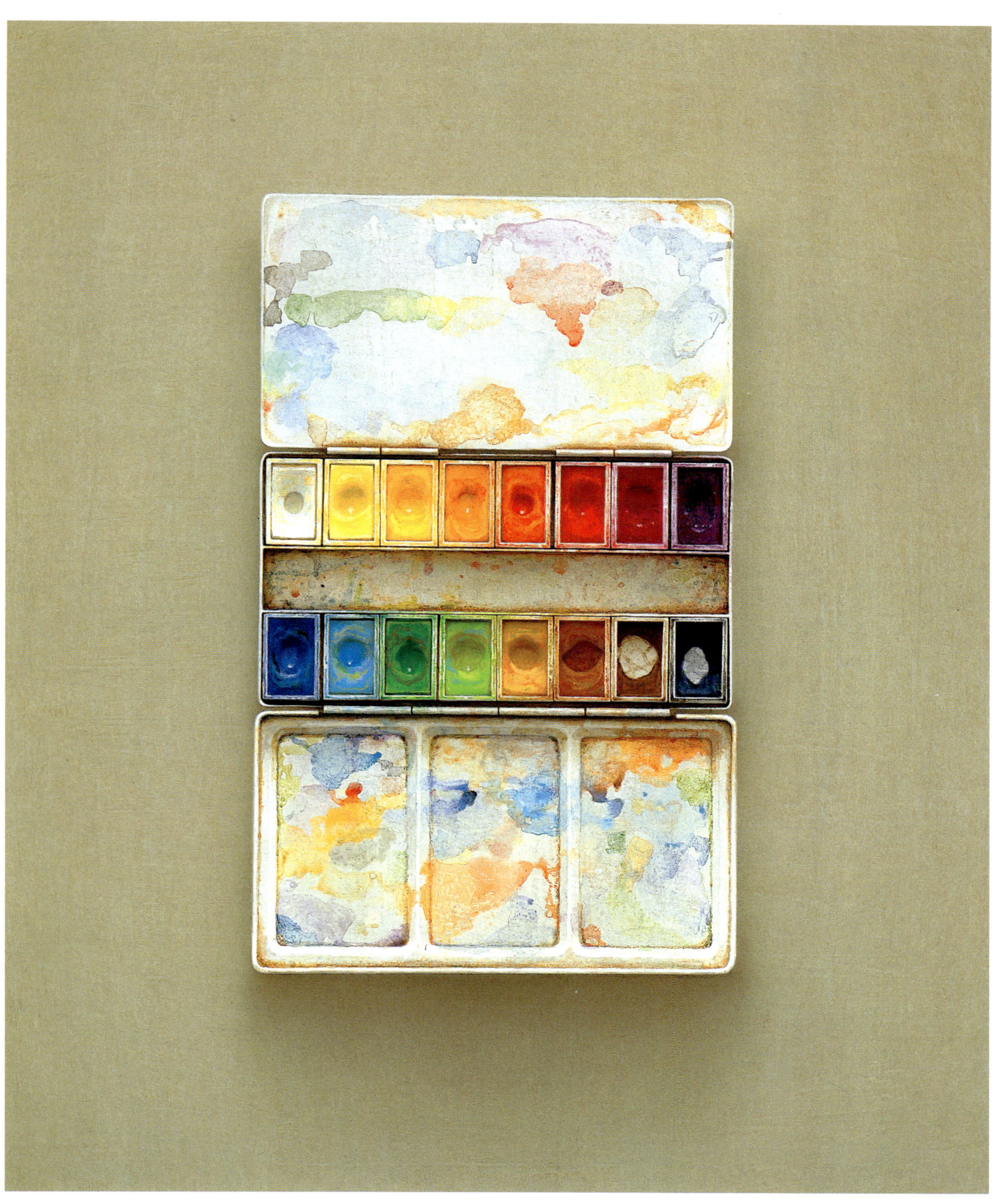

Array (detail), 2001, acrylic on panel, 20 x 16"

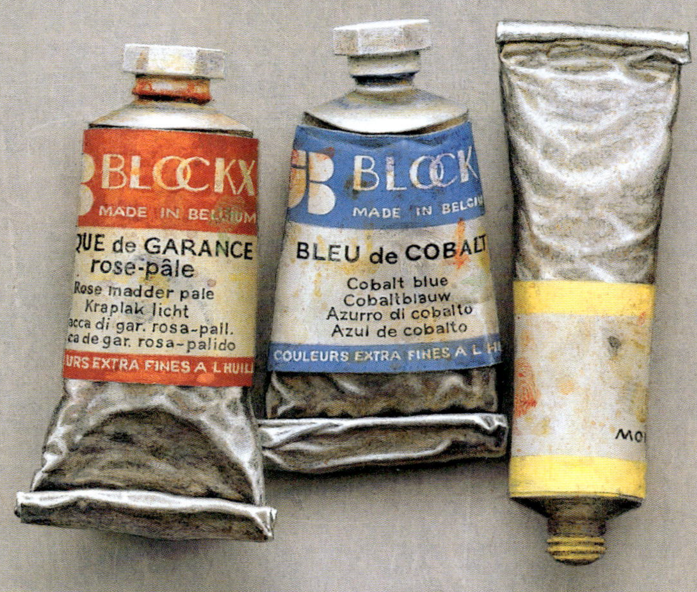

Guild, 2000, acrylic and oil on panel, 10 x 8"

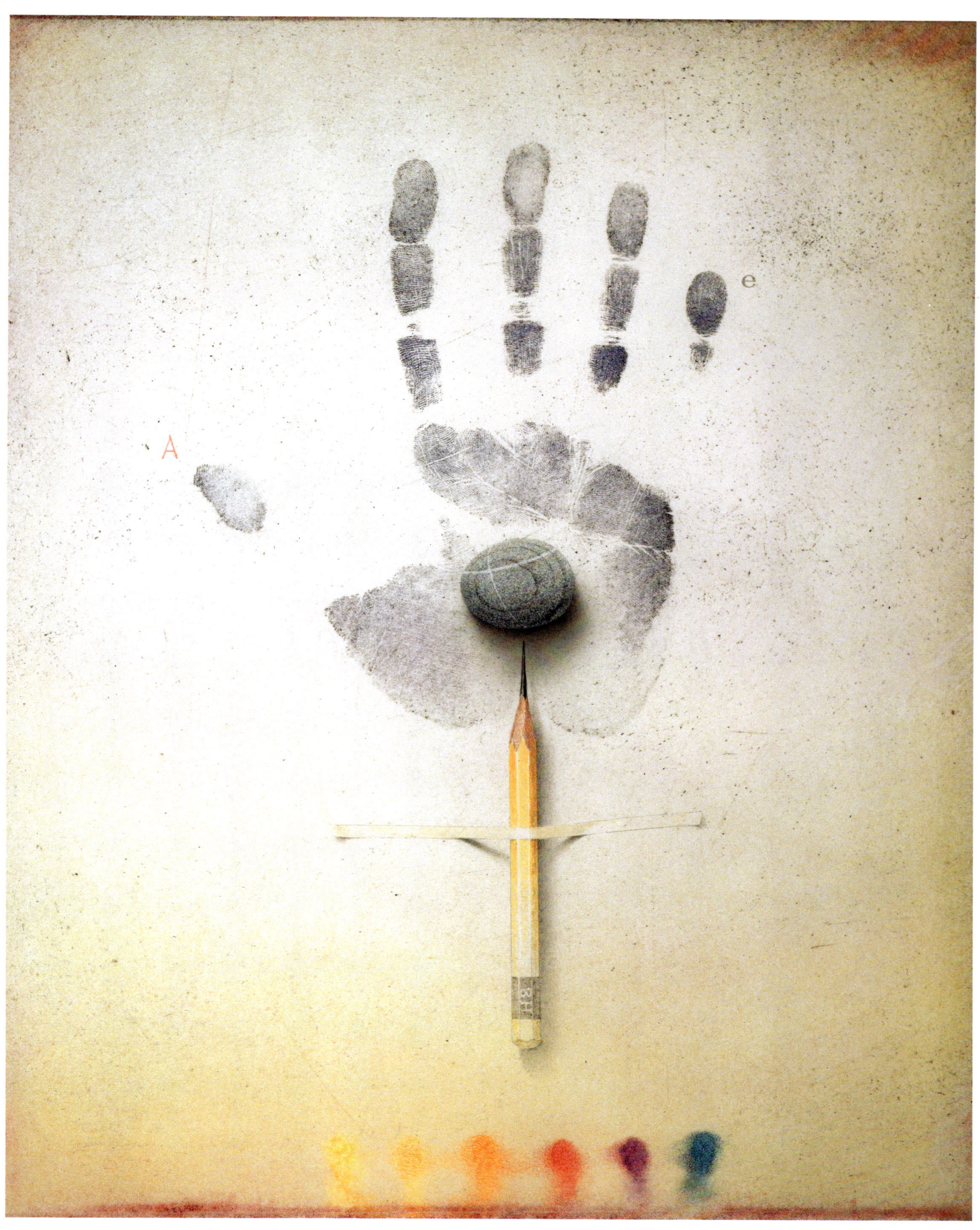

Selbstbildnis II, 1995, watercolor over monotype, 14 x 11"

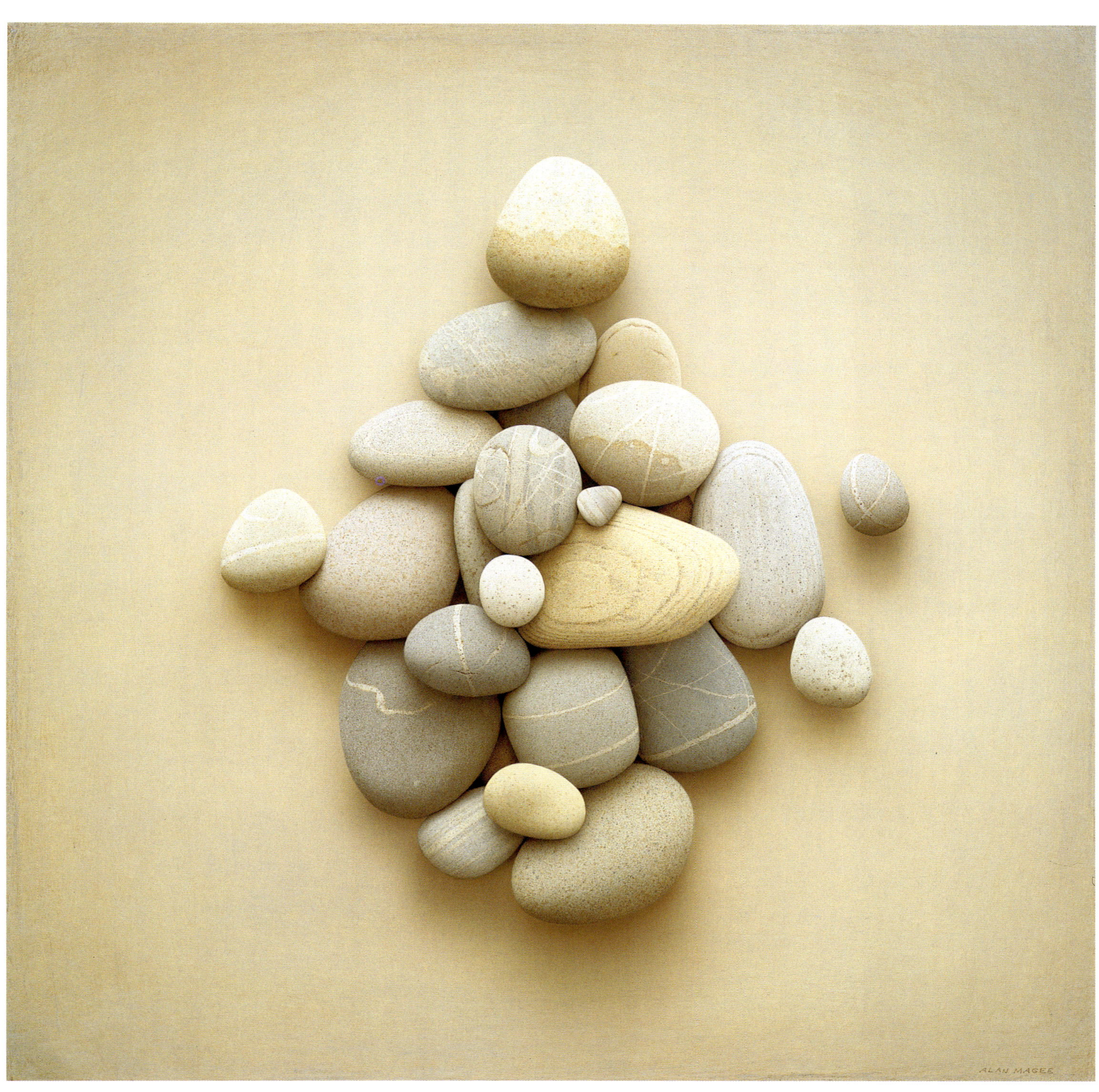

Zazen, 2001, acrylic and oil on panel, 30 x 30"

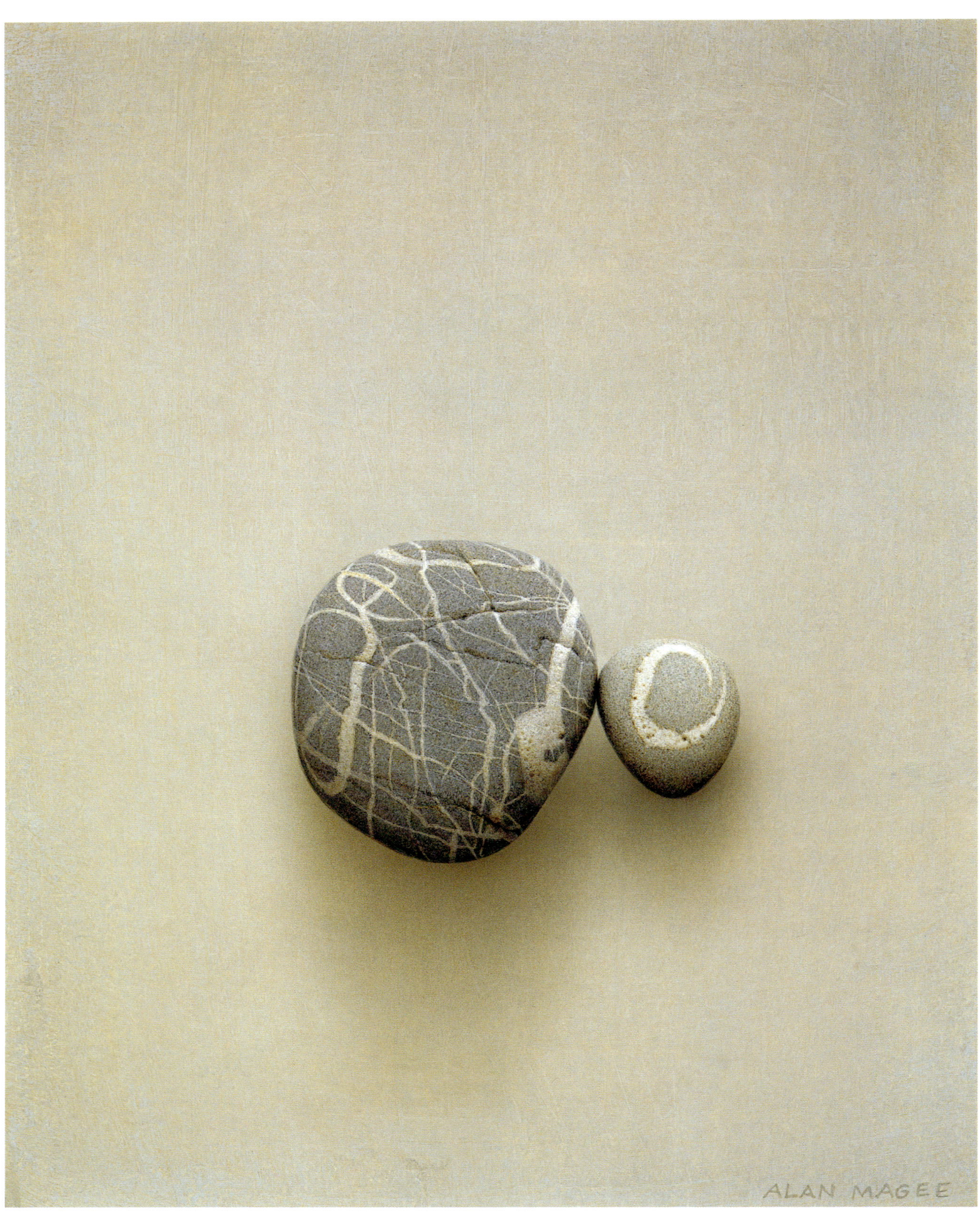

Paleographia, 2001, acrylic on panel, 10 ¼ x 8"

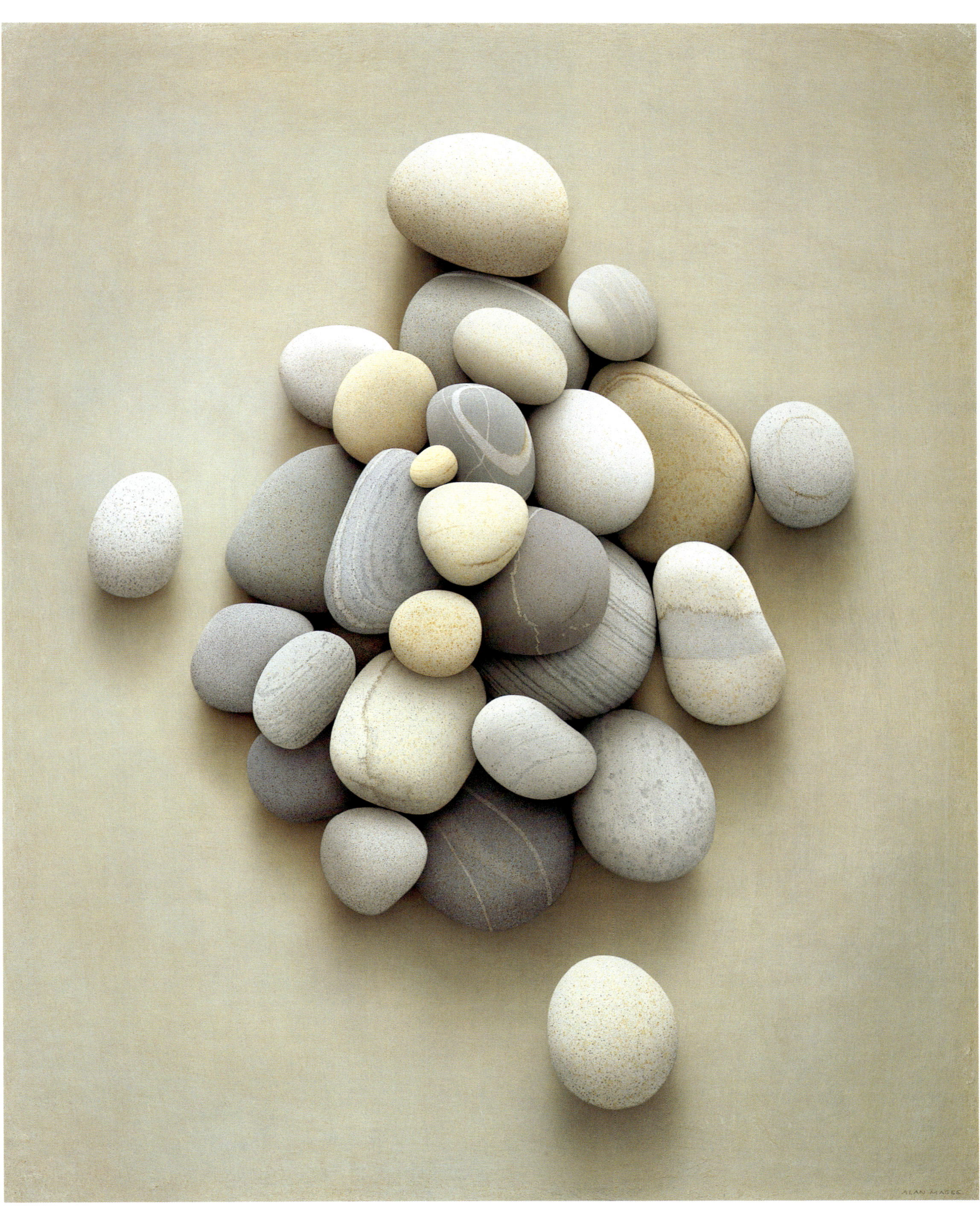

Convergence, 2002, acrylic and oil on panel, 50 x 40"

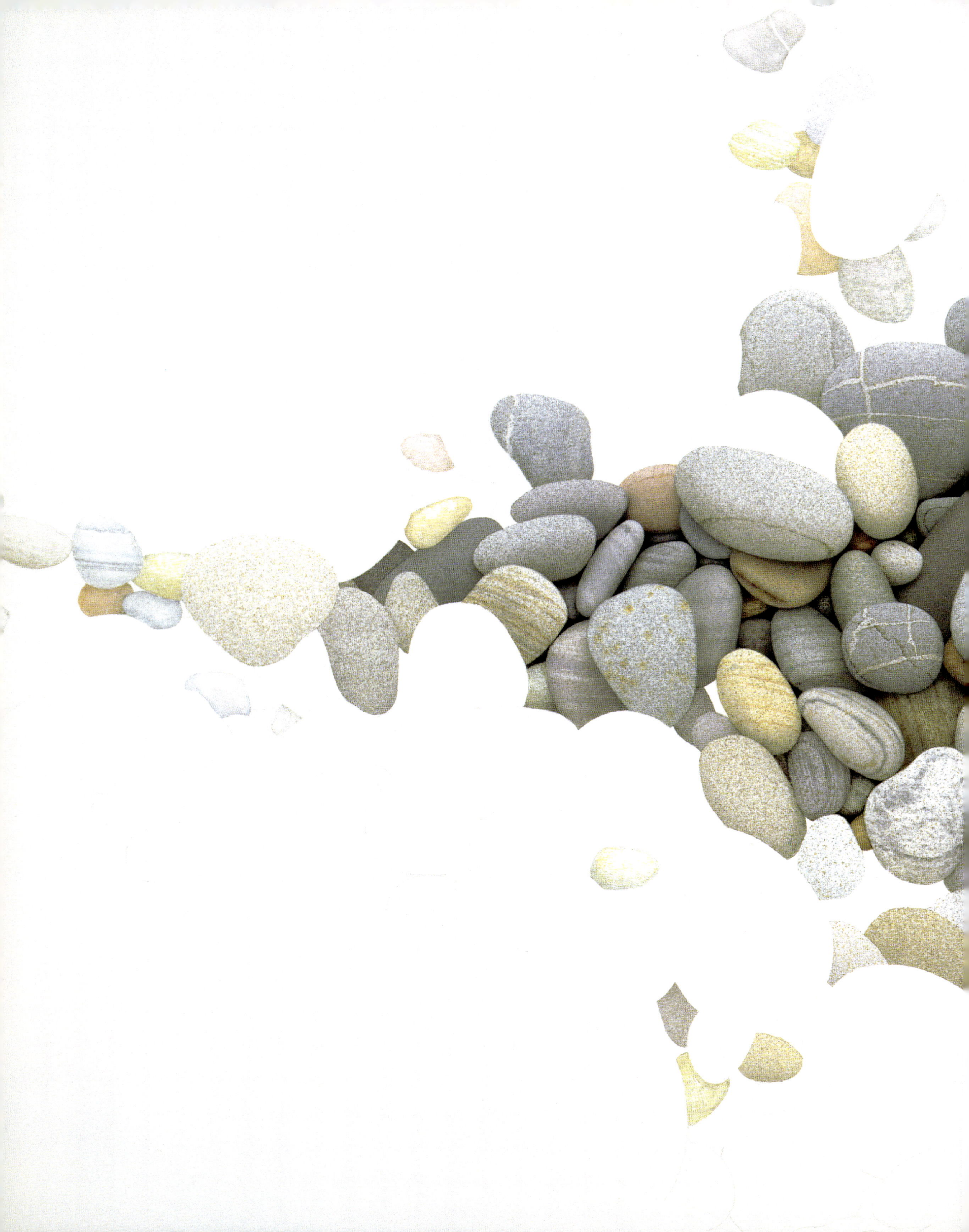

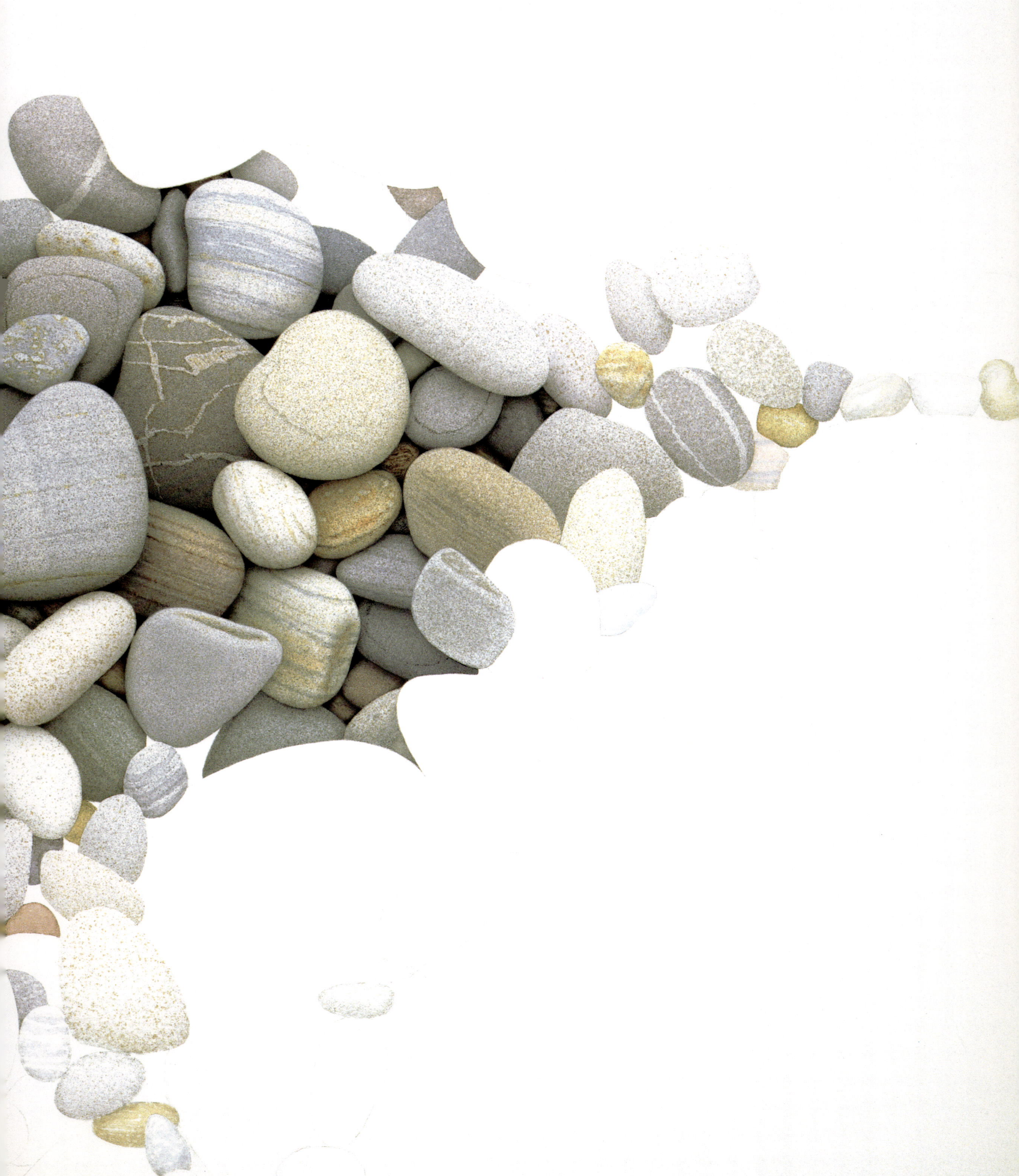

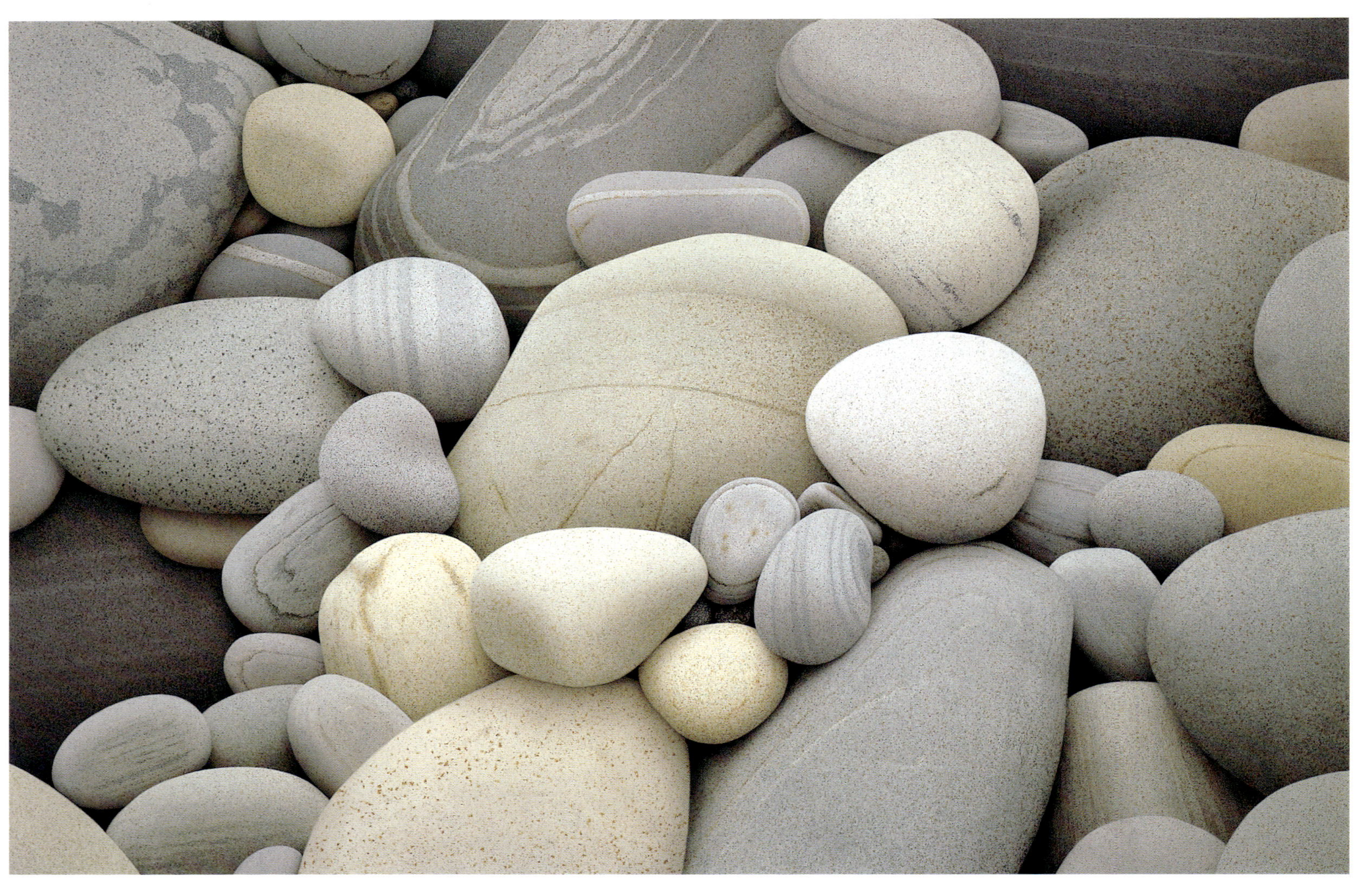

◁ *Excerpt (detail)*, 1998, watercolor and graphite on paper, 22 x 30"
Solaris, 2000, acrylic on canvas, 50 x 75"

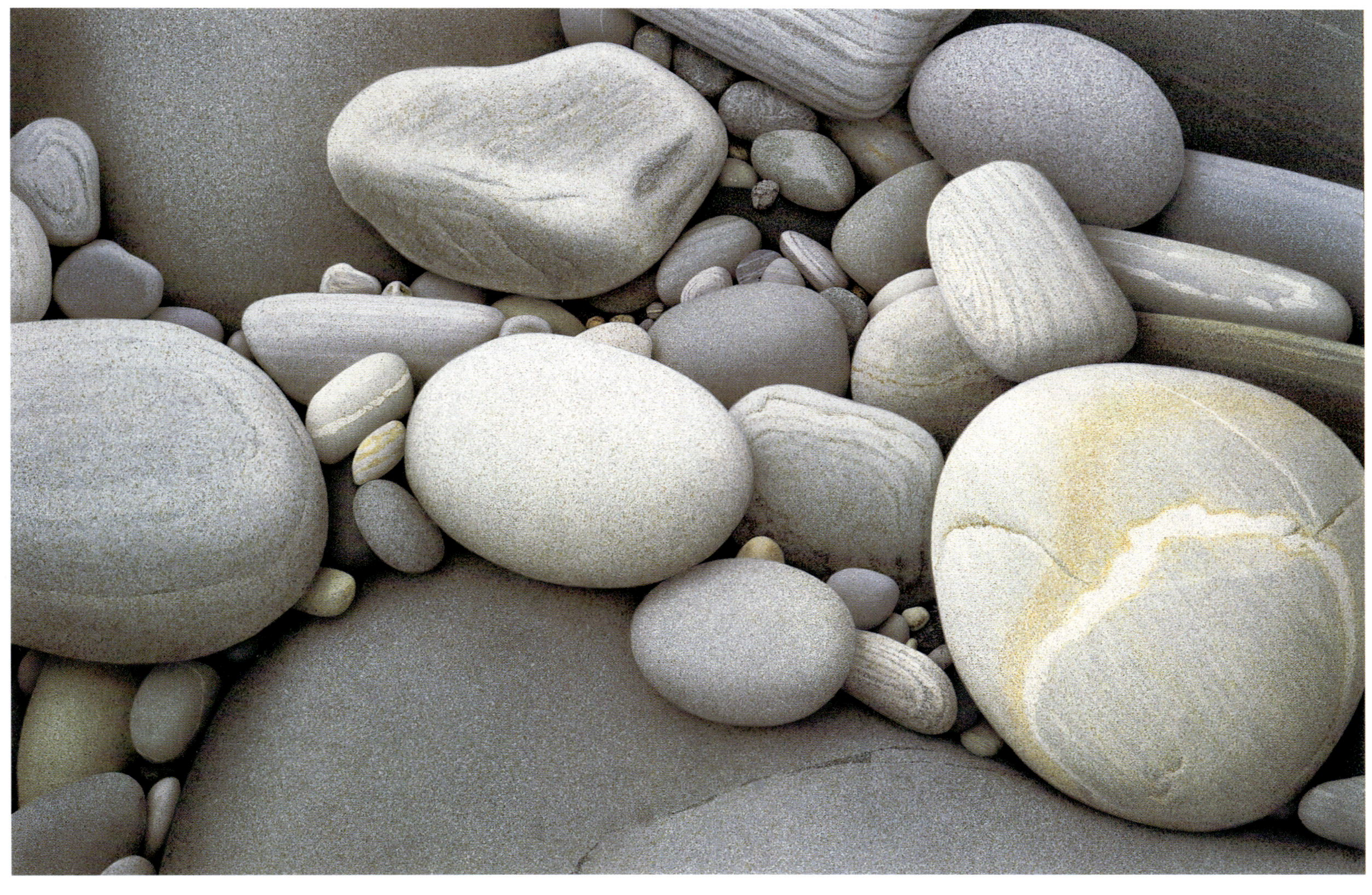

Stones, 1991, acrylic on canvas, 40 x 60"

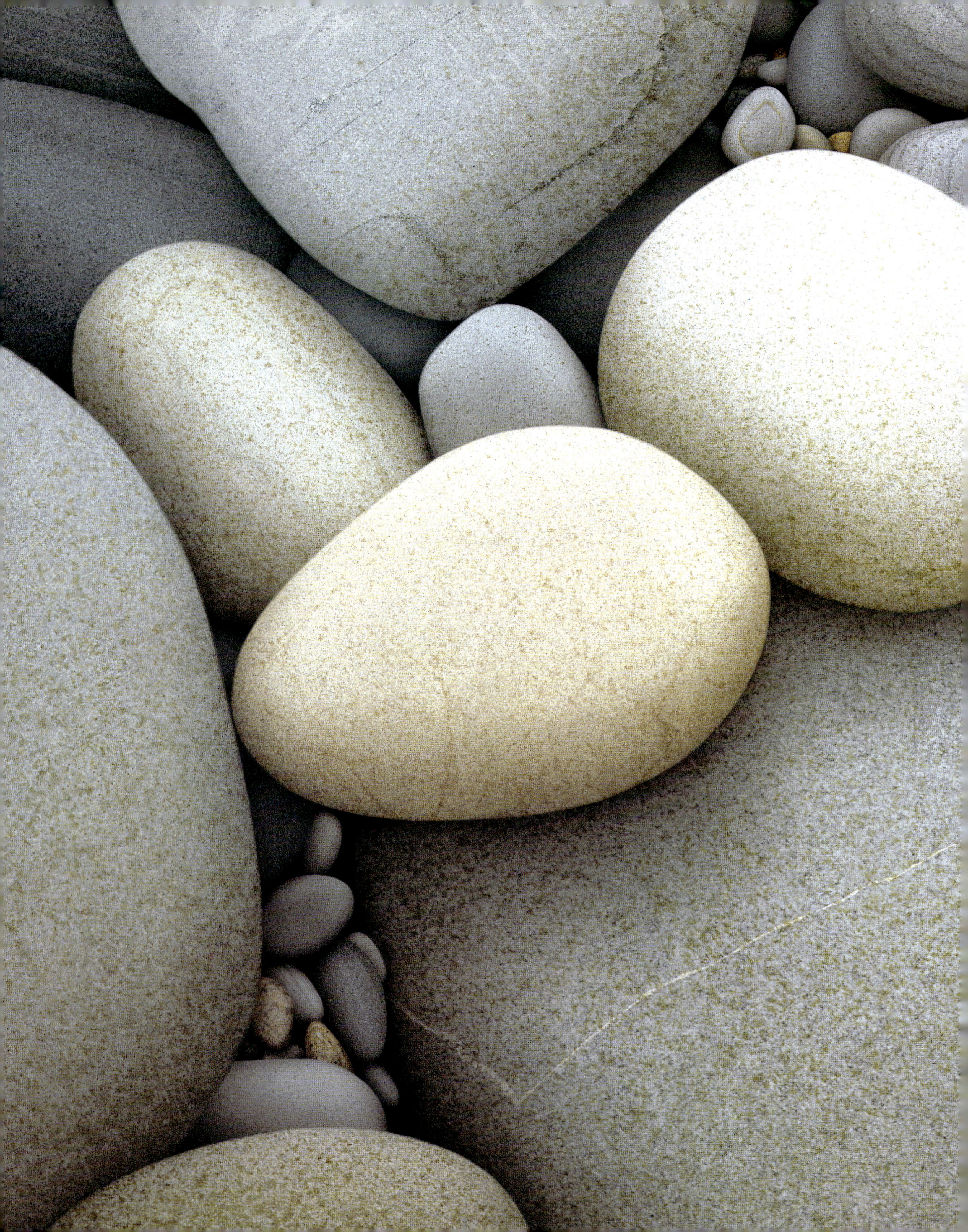

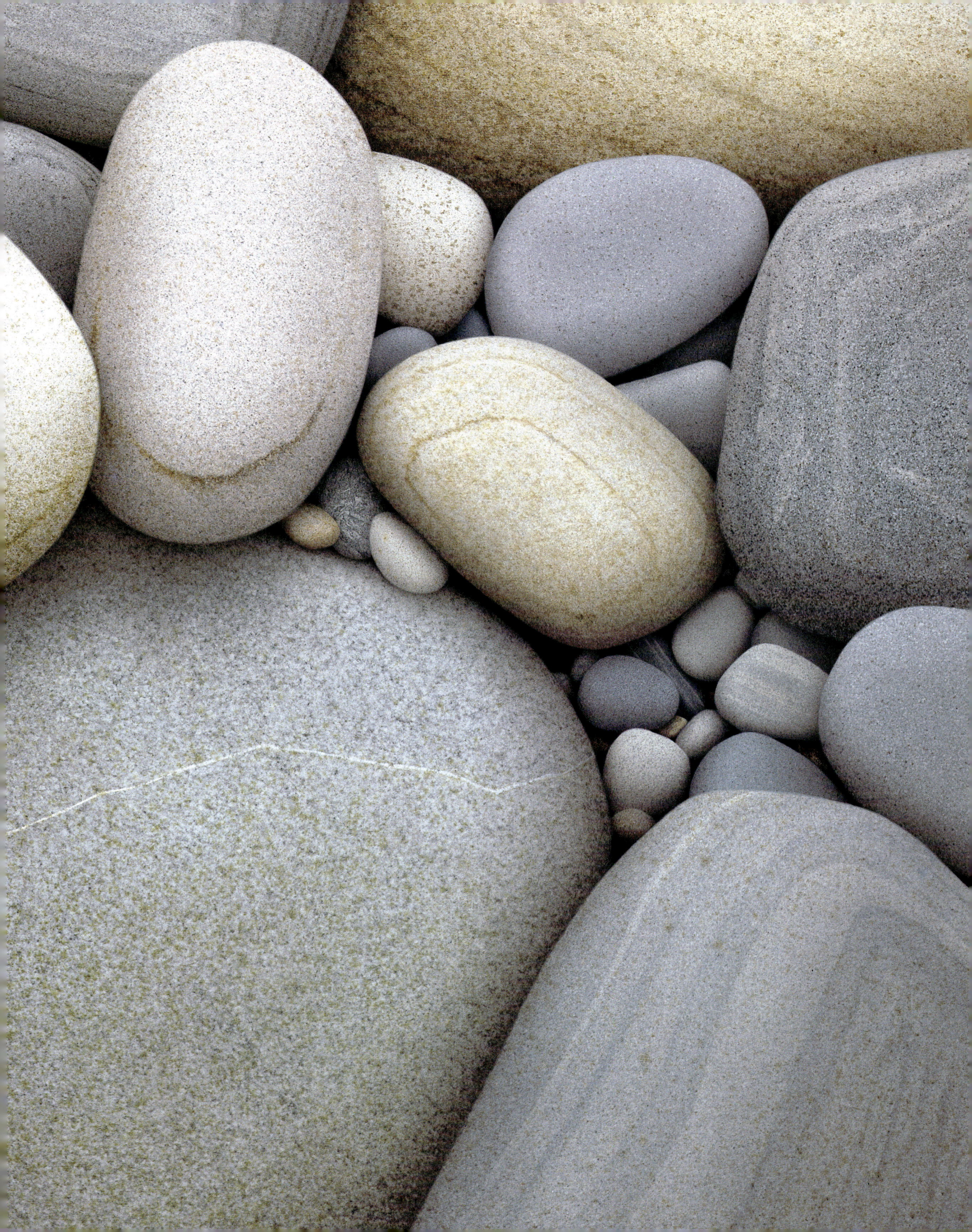

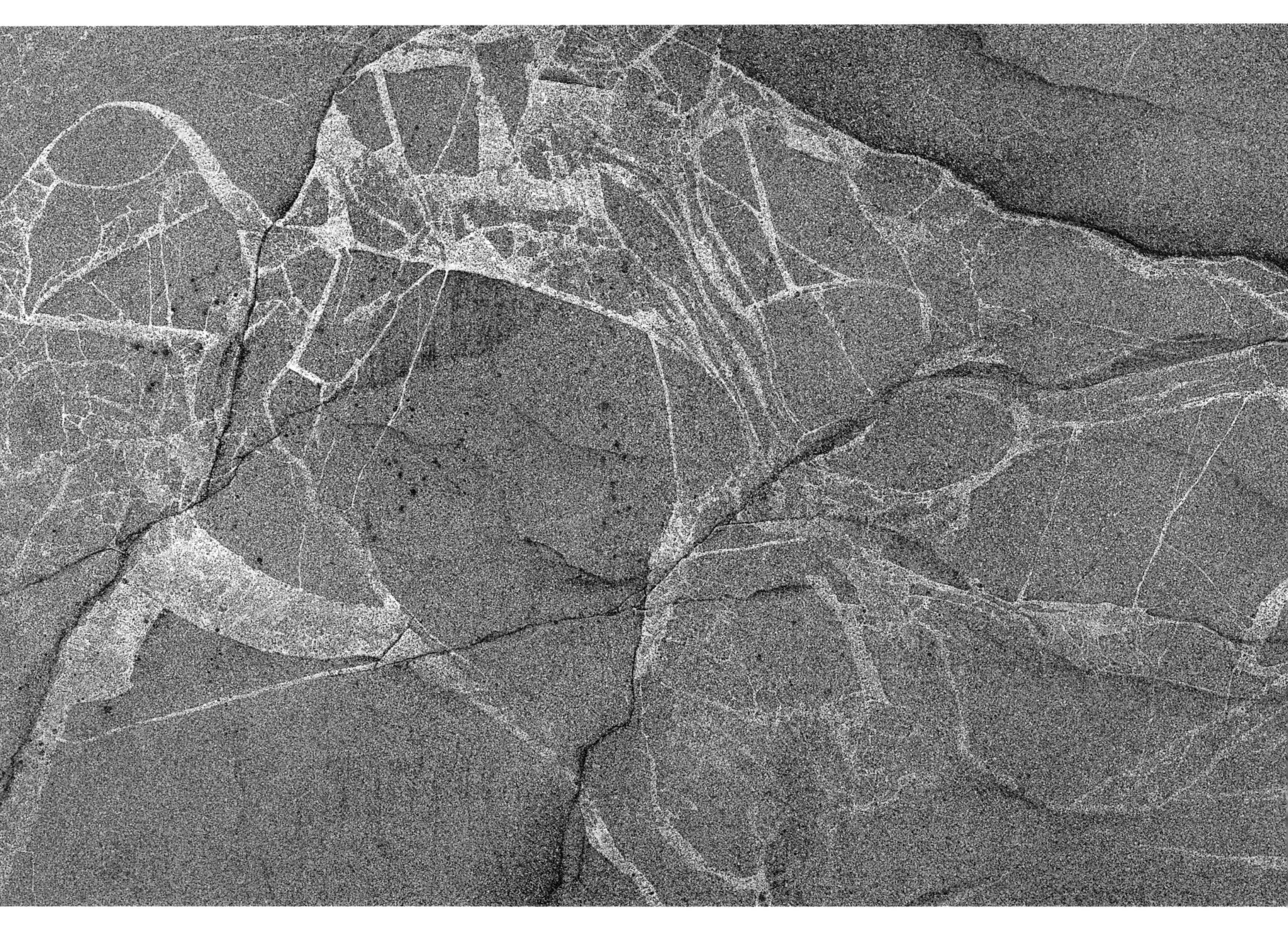

◁ *Quartet II*, 1996, acrylic on canvas 50 x 75"
Quartz Drawing II (detail), 1982, acrylic on canvas, 48 x 68"

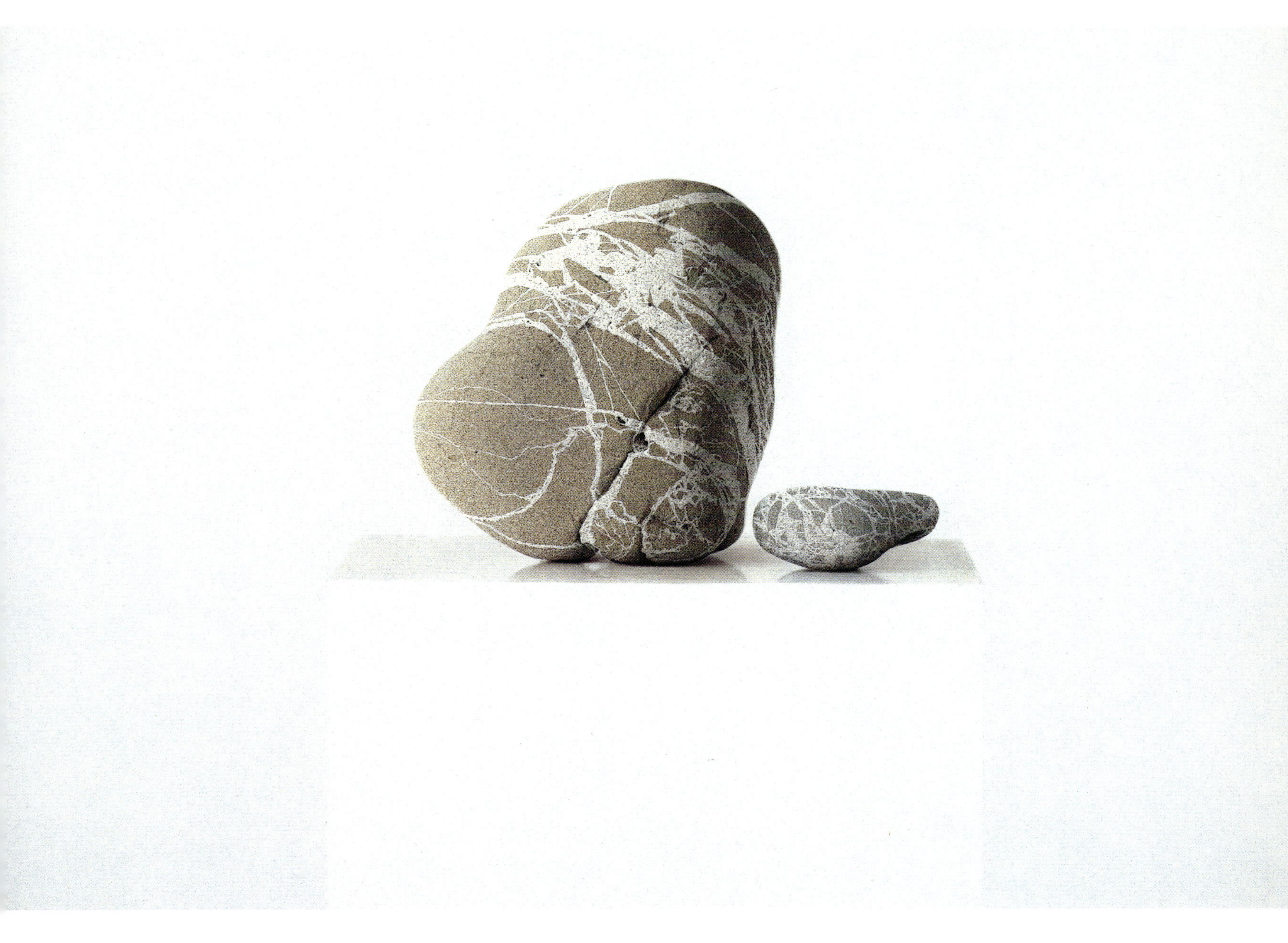

Two Stones (detail), 1982, watercolor on paper, 15 ½ x 19"

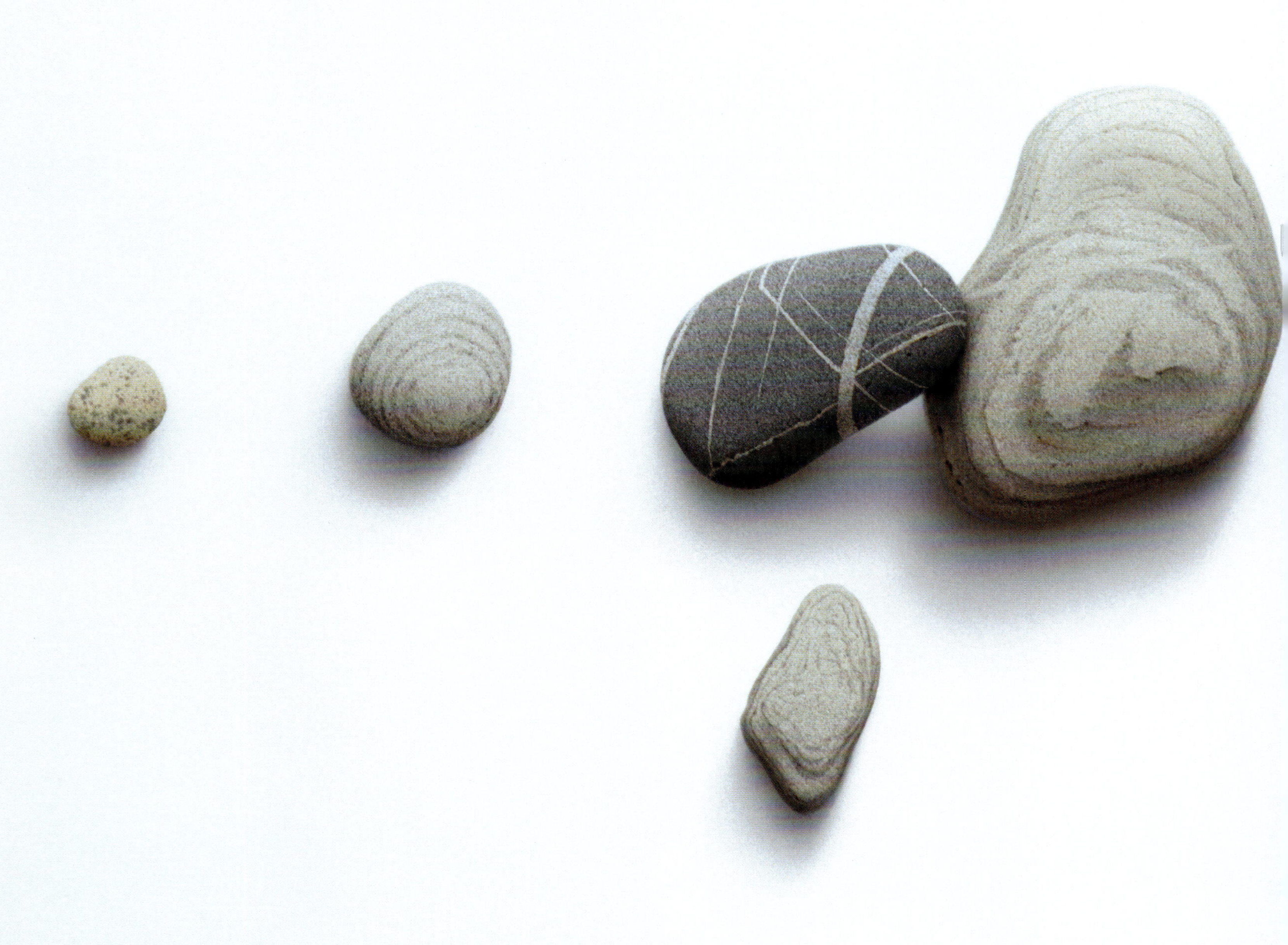

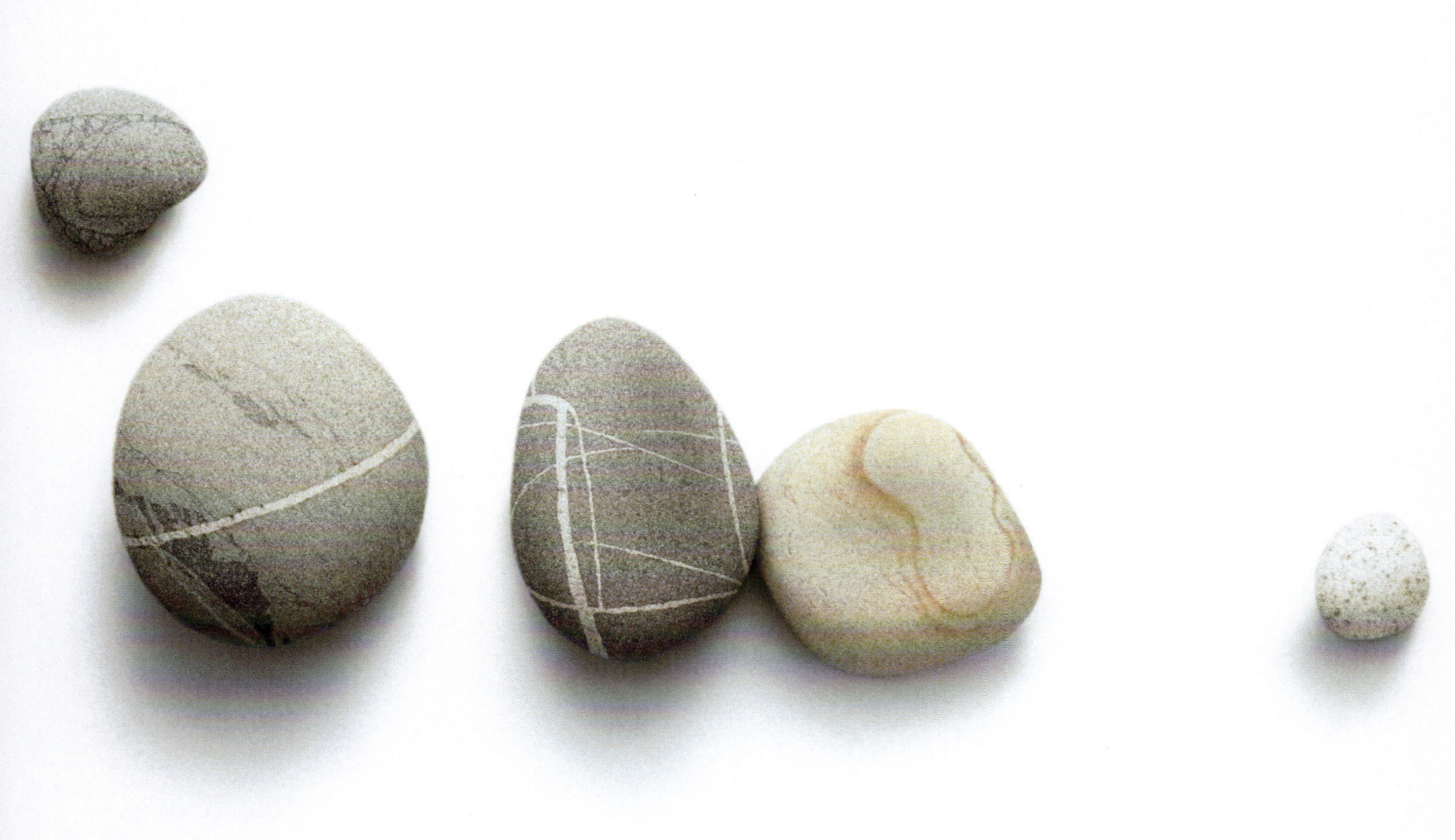

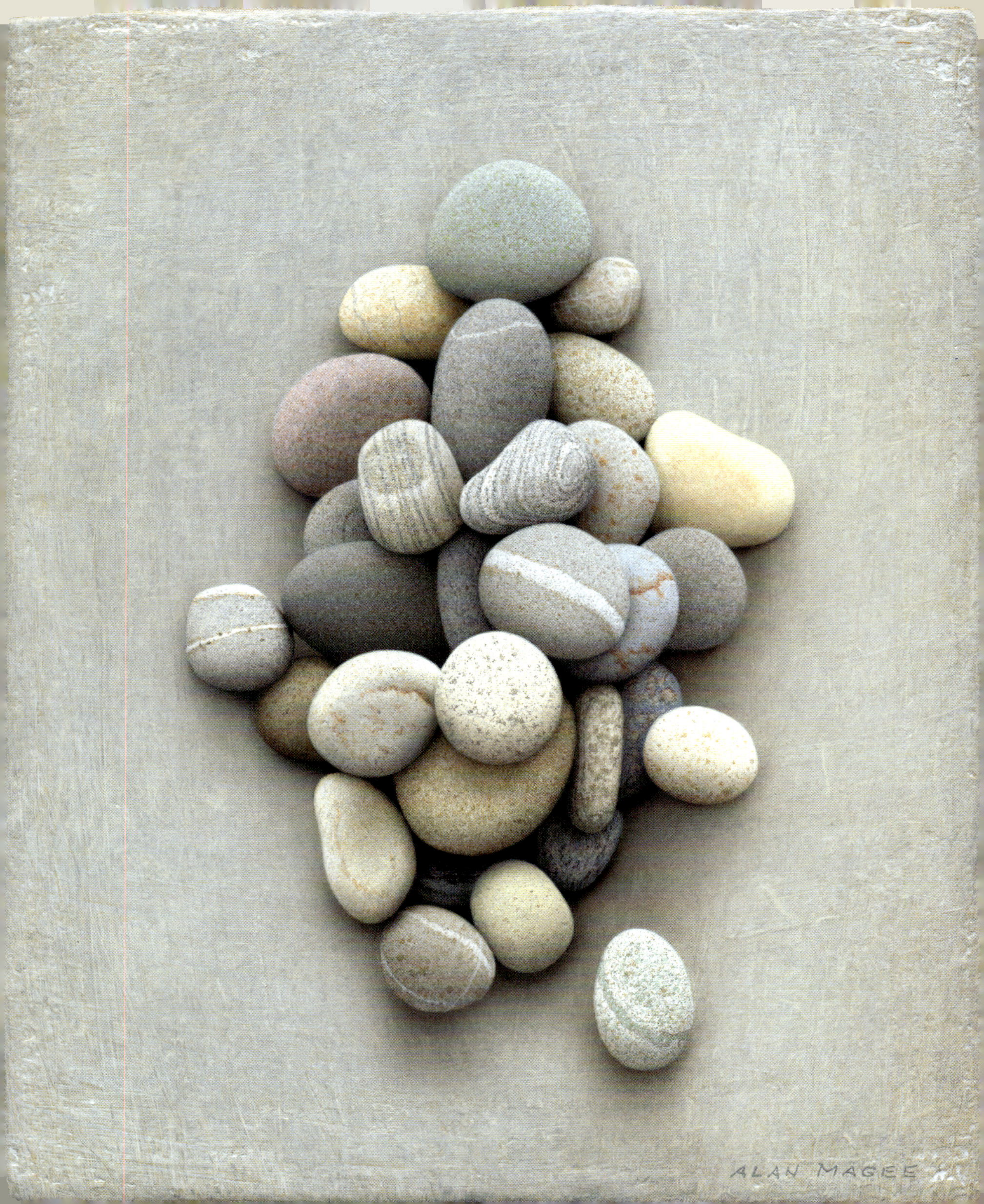
ALAN MAGEE

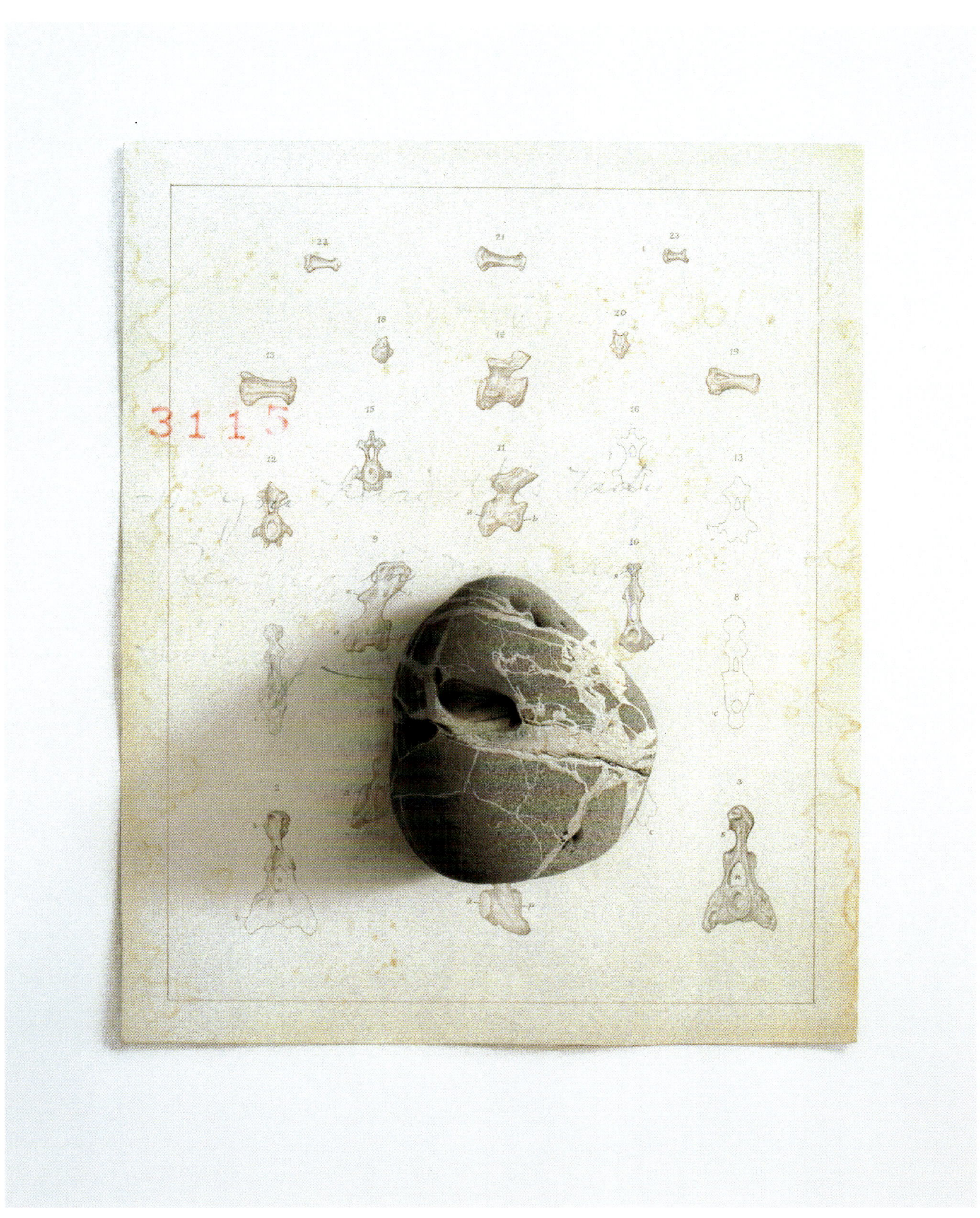

Strange Bones, 1982, watercolor, graphite and colored pencil on paper, 15 ½ x 19"

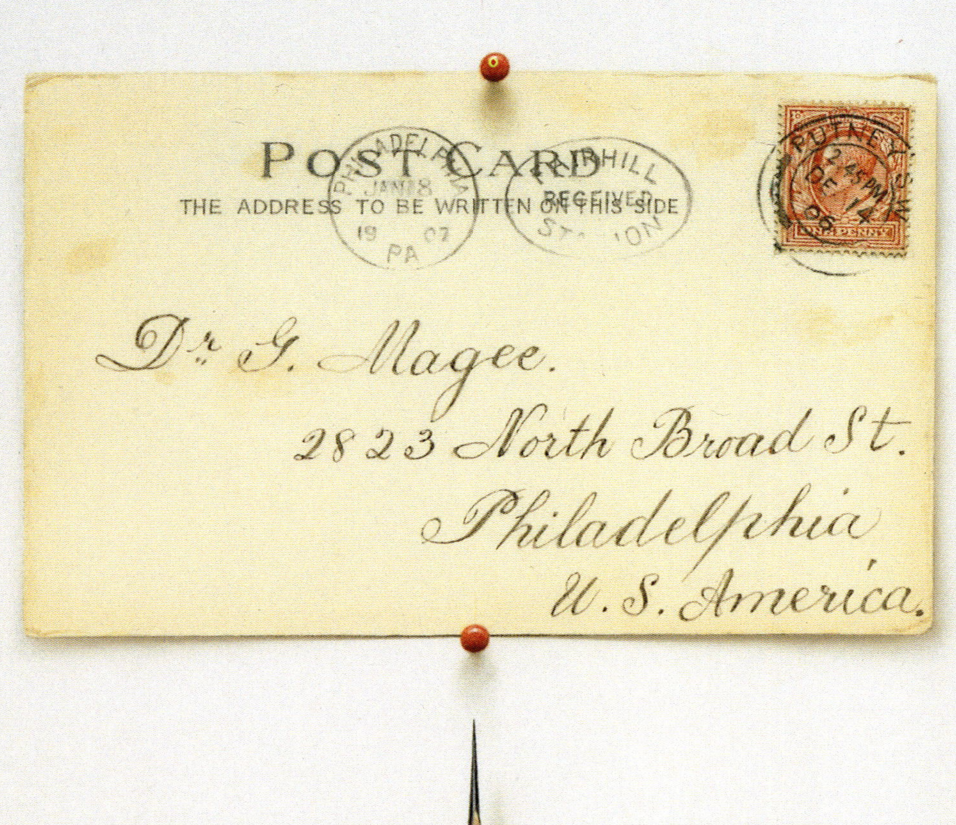
POST CARD
THE ADDRESS TO BE WRITTEN ON THIS SIDE
Dr. G. Magee.
2823 North Broad St.
Philadelphia
U. S. America.

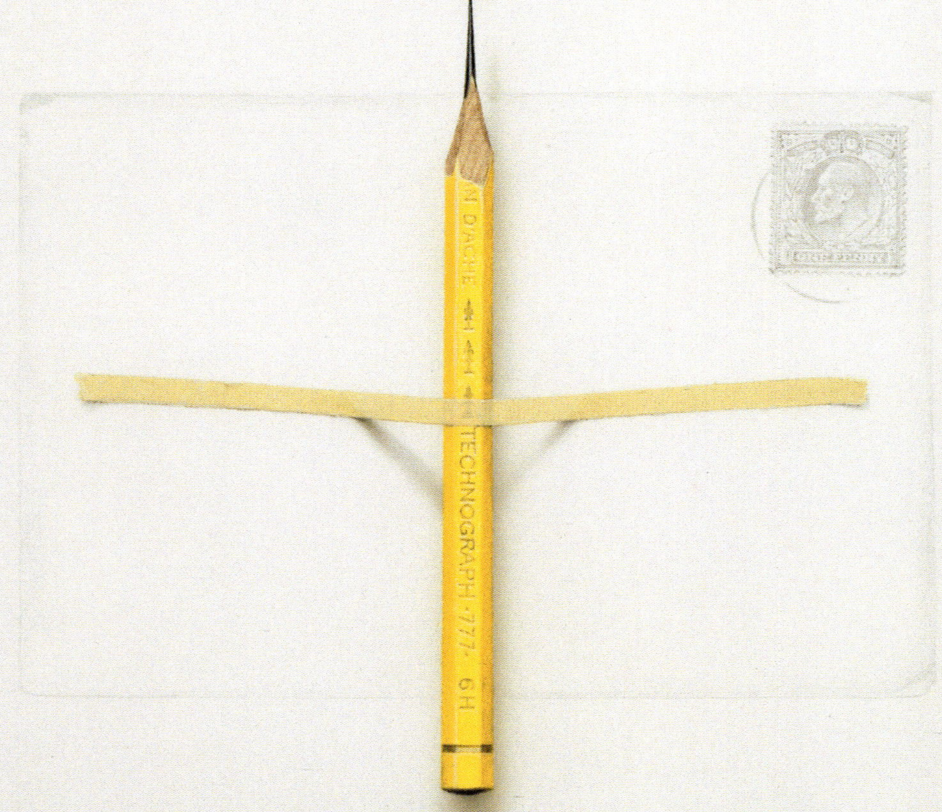
TECHNOGRAPH · 777 · 6H

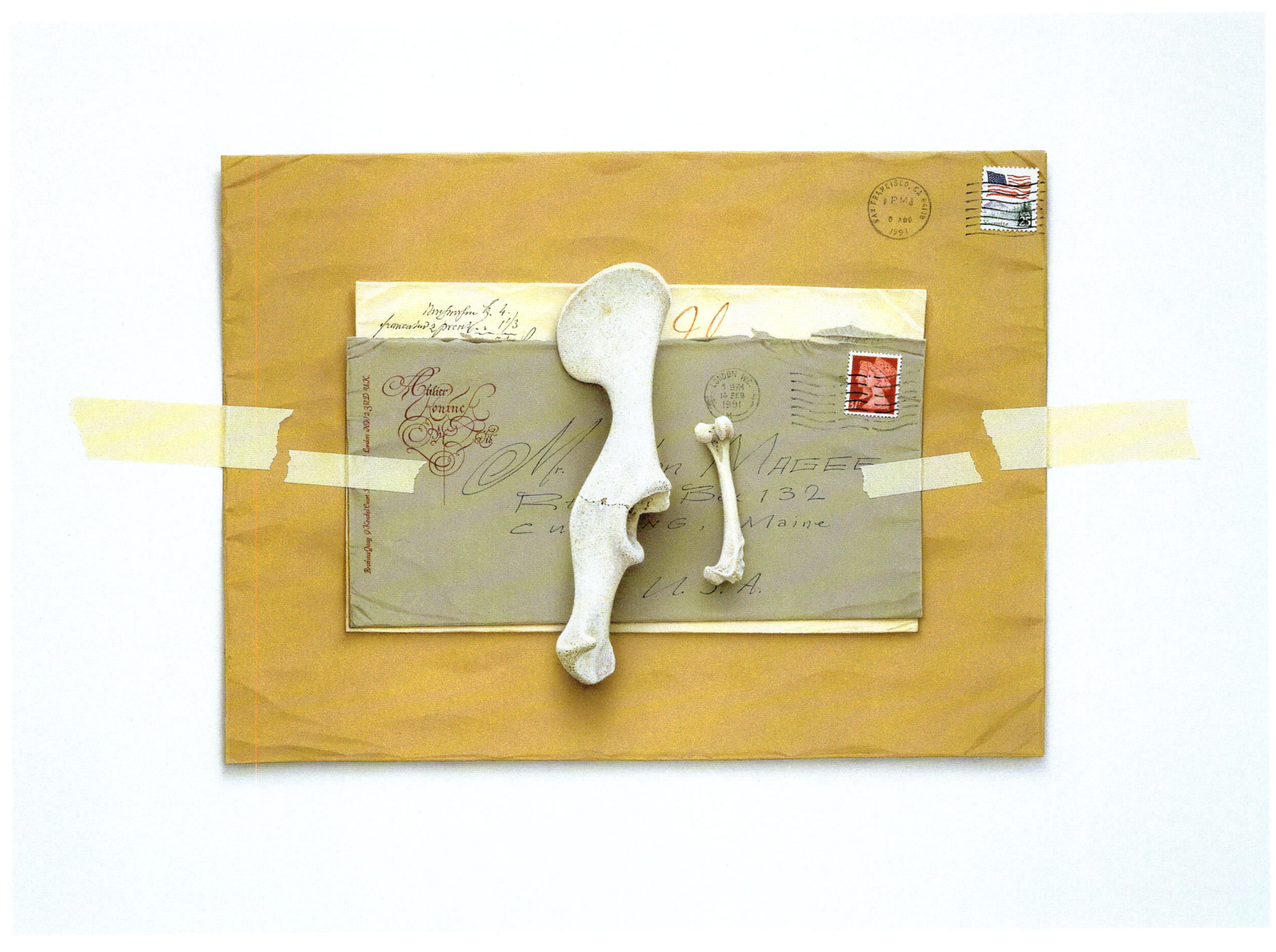

⊲ *Mimesis (detail)*, 1999, acrylic and graphite on paper, 15 ½ x 19"
A Letter from London, 1998, acrylic, graphite and colored pencil on paper, 19 x 24"

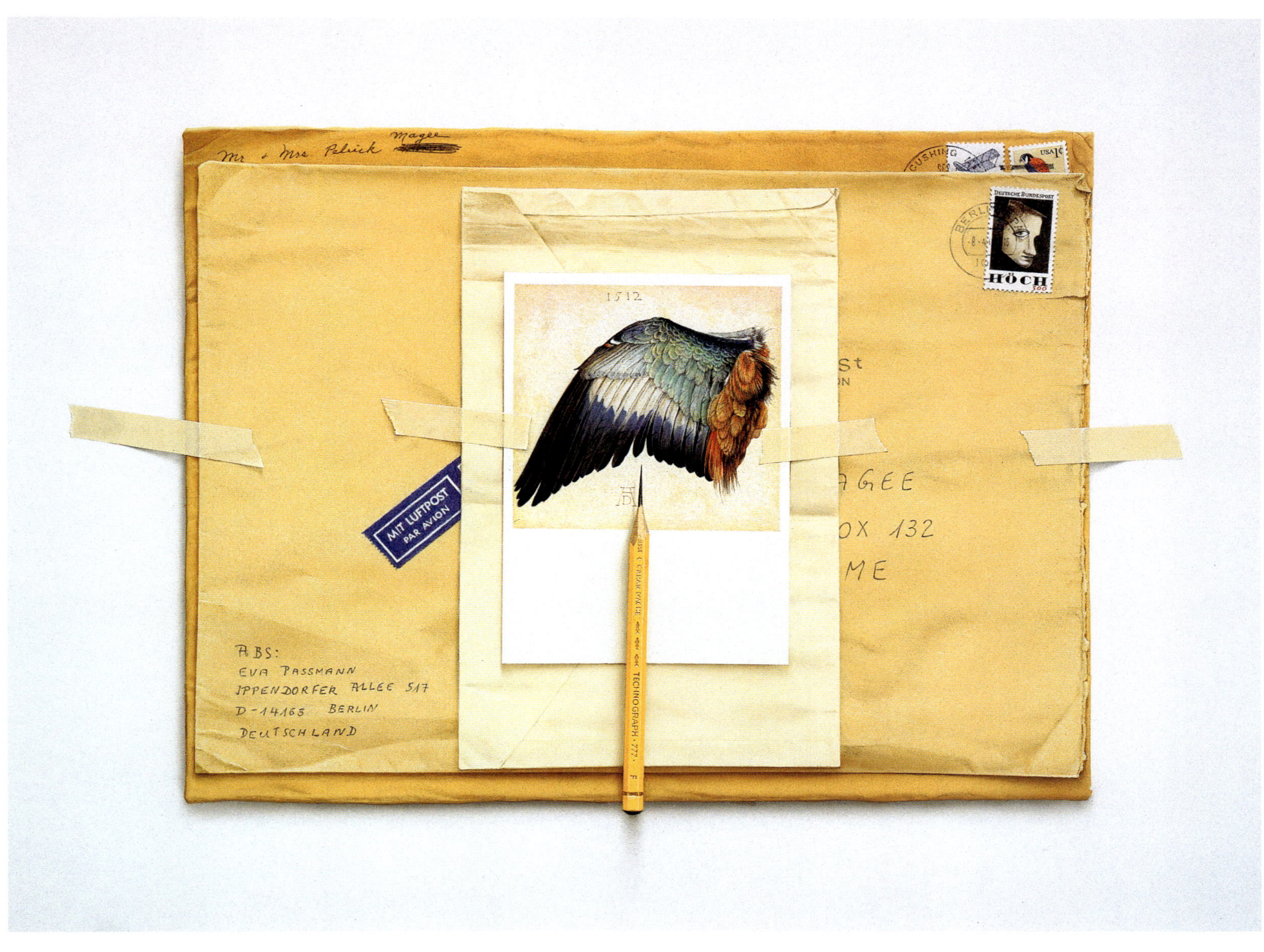

Luftpost, 1998, acrylic, graphite and colored pencil on paper, 19 x 23"

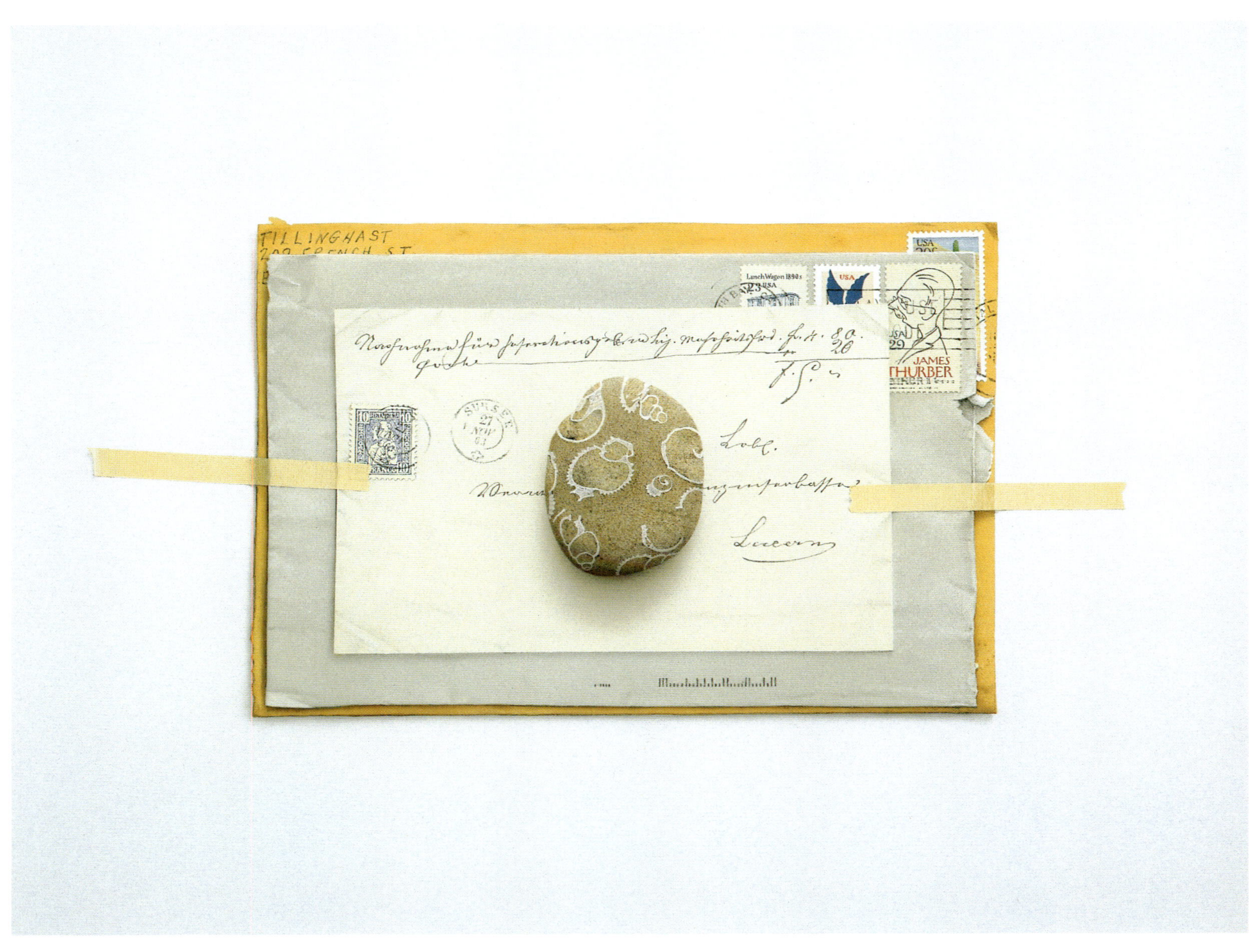

An Extended Correspondence, 1997, watercolor on paper, 15 ¼ x 19"

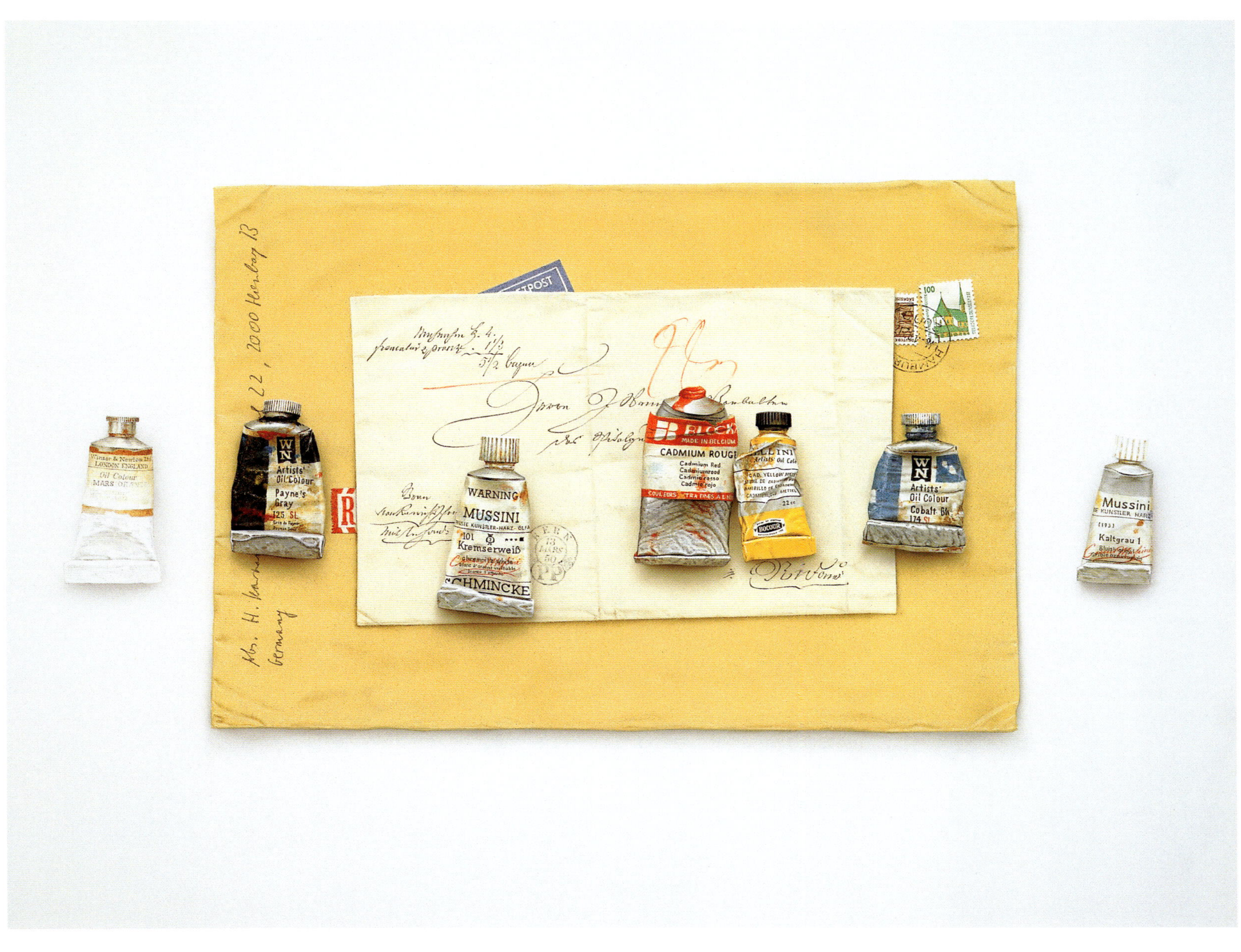

Paper and Paint, 1997, watercolor, graphite, and colored pencil on paper, 19 x 24"

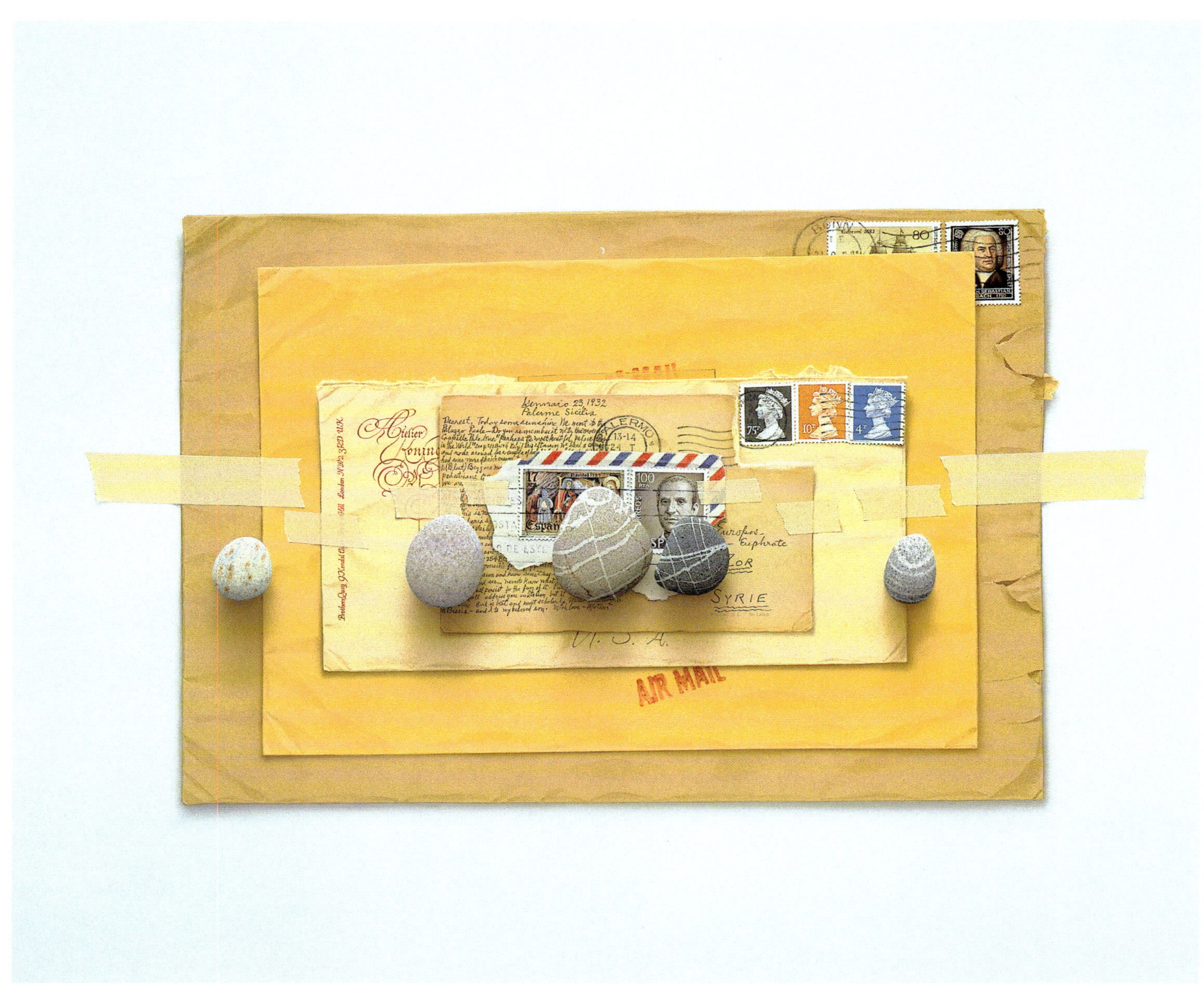

An Archaeology of the Fugue, 1998, acrylic and colored pencil on paper, 19 ½ x 24"
Paper Garden (detail), 1998, acrylic and graphite on paper, 19 ½ x 24" ▹

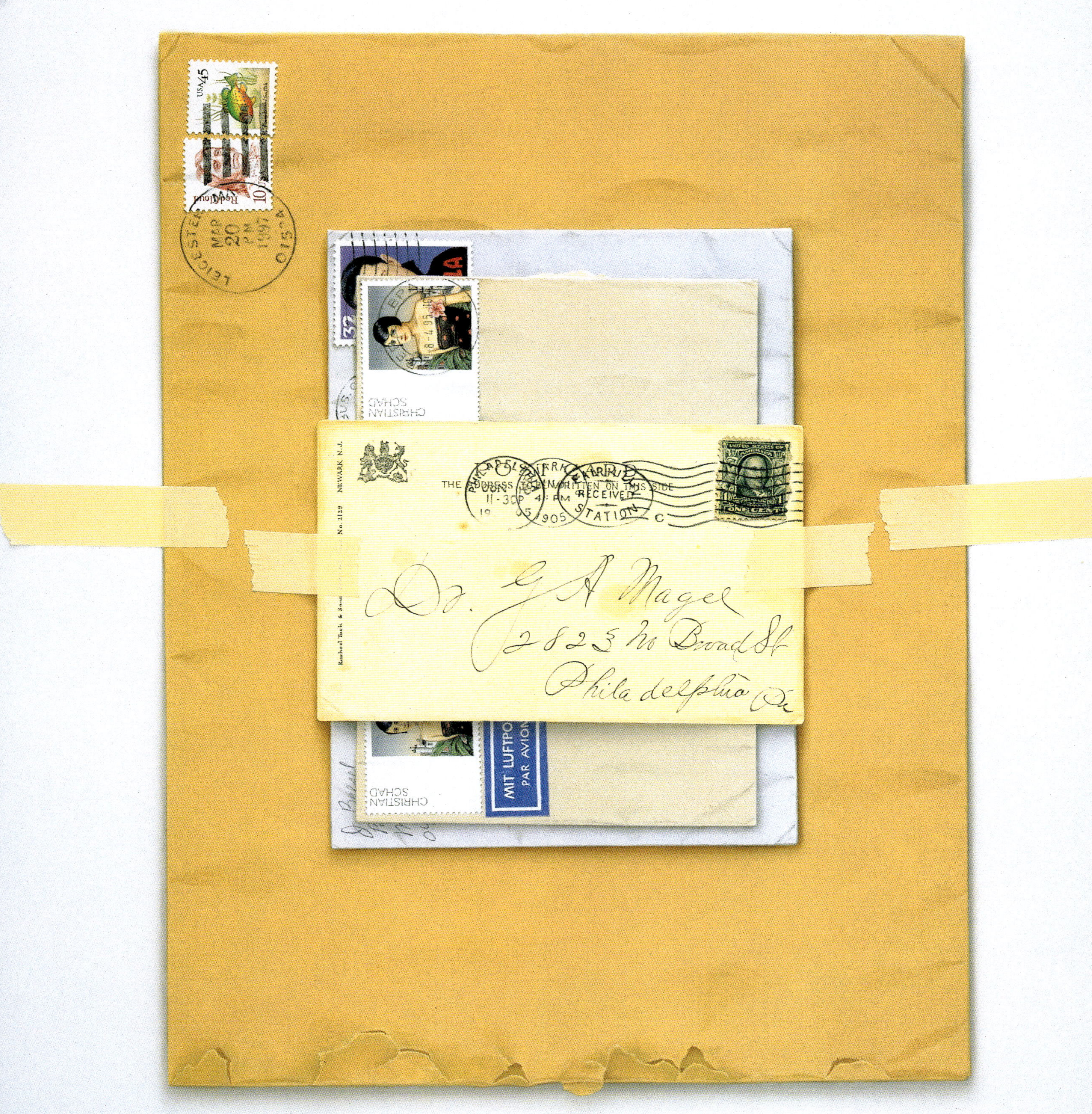

NEWARK N.J.
RECEIVED
STATION
ONE CENT
CHRISTIAN SCHAD
CHRISTIAN SCHAD
PAR AVION

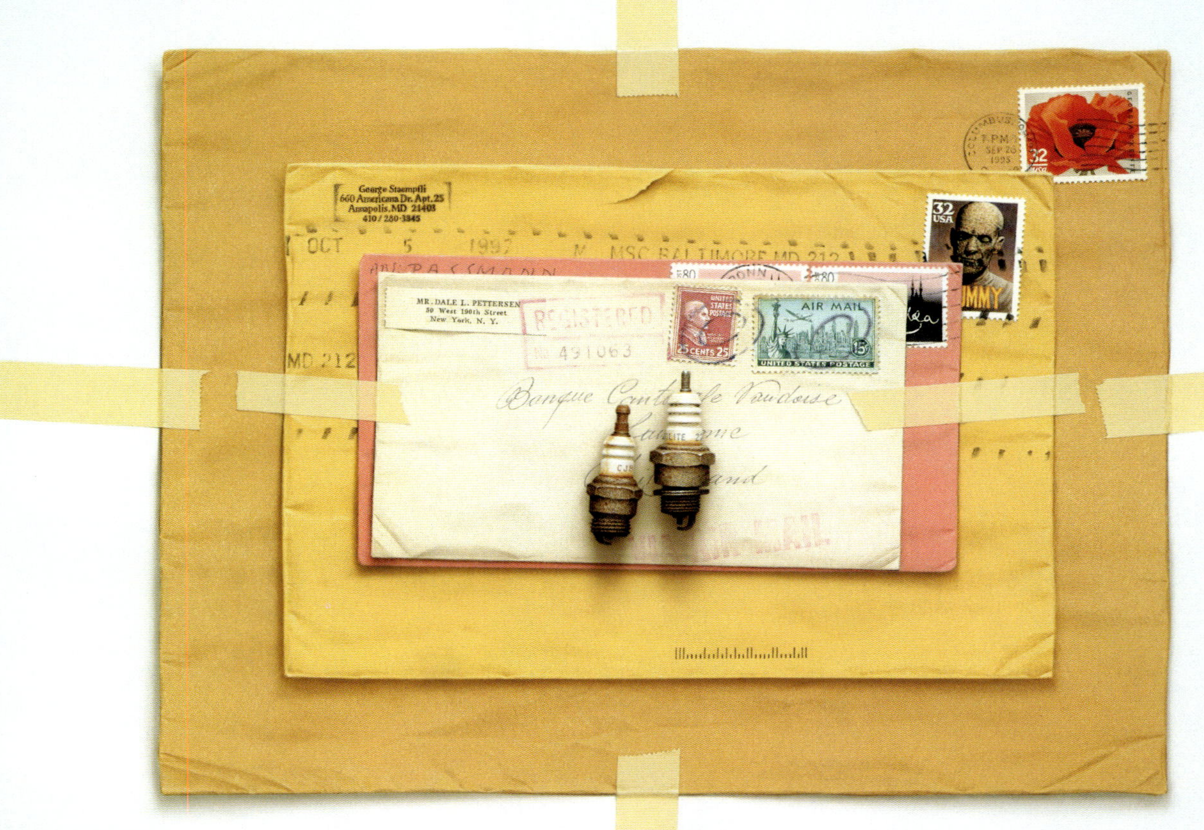
George Staempfli
660 Americana Dr. Apt. 25
Annapolis, MD 21403
410 / 280-3845
OCT 5 1997
MR. DALE L. PETTERSEN
50 West 190th Street
New York, N. Y.
REGISTERED
491063
AIR MAIL
UNITED STATES POSTAGE
25 CENTS 25
32 USA
MUMMY

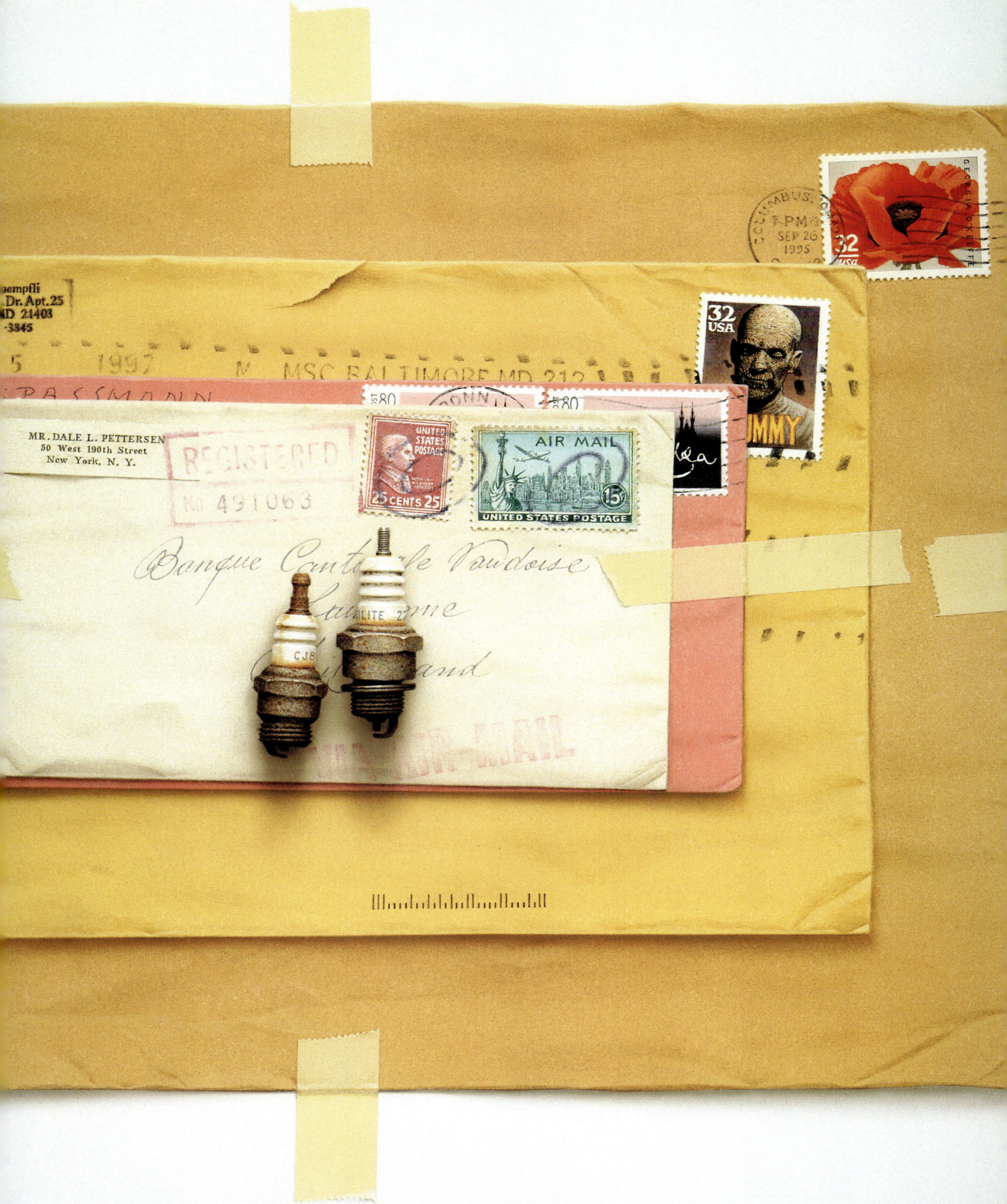

MR. DALE L. PETTERSEN
50 West 190th Street
New York, N. Y.

REGISTERED
No 491063

UNITED STATES POSTAGE
25 CENTS 25

AIR MAIL
UNITED STATES POSTAGE
15¢

32
USA
MUMMY

COLUMBUS
SEP 26
1995

GEORGIA O'KEEFFE
32
USA

MSC BALTIMORE MD 212

Dr. Apt. 25
MD 21403
-3345

Banque Cantonale Vaudoise
Lausanne
Switzerland

CJ8
LITE

AIR MAIL

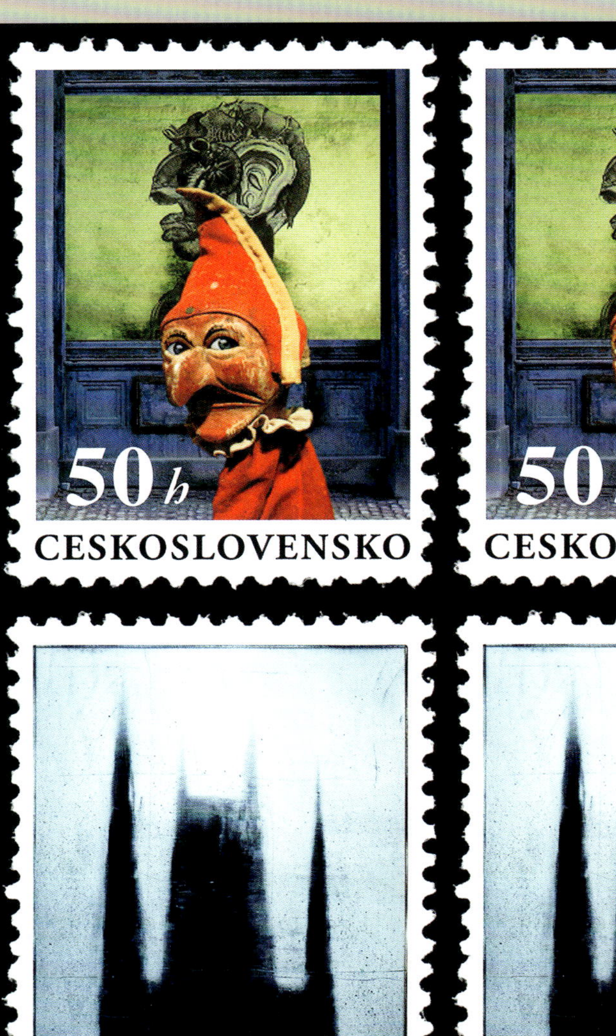

Stamp Designs, 1999, digital montages, sizes variable

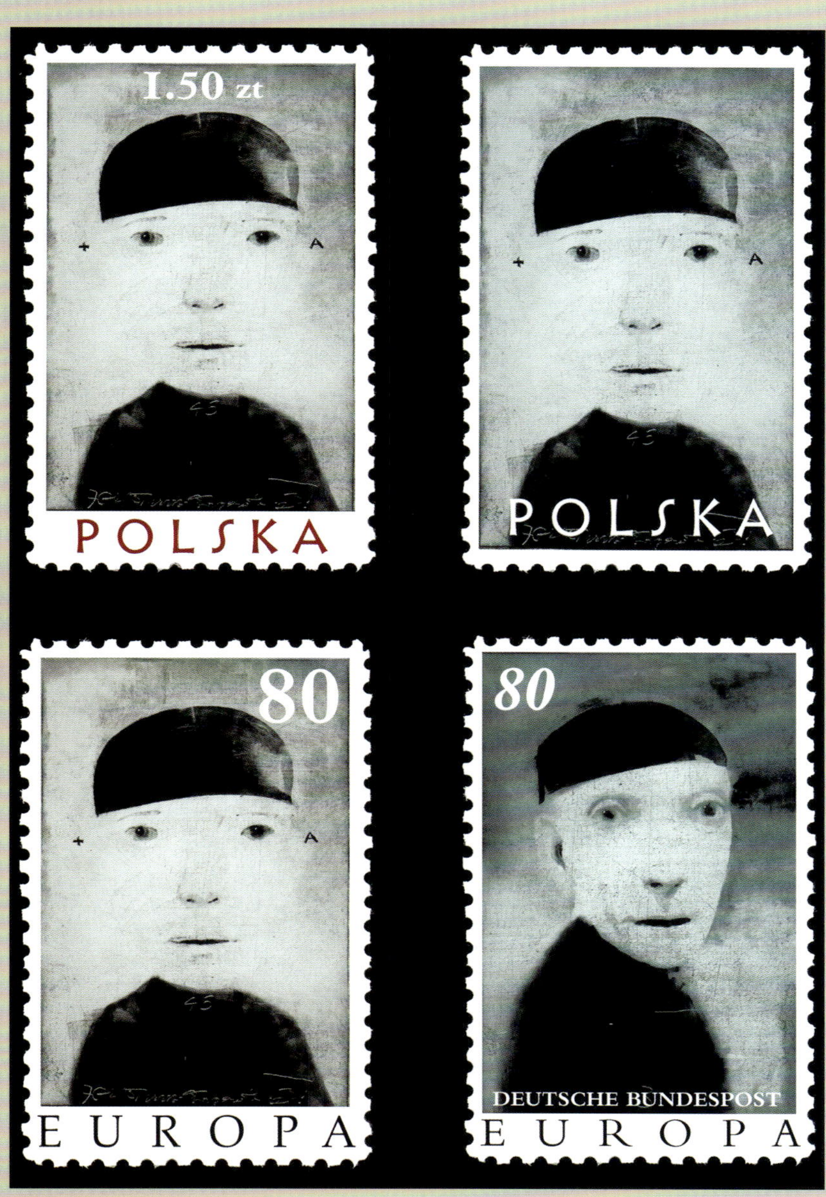
1.50 zt
POLSKA
POLSKA
80
EUROPA
80
DEUTSCHE BUNDESPOST
EUROPA

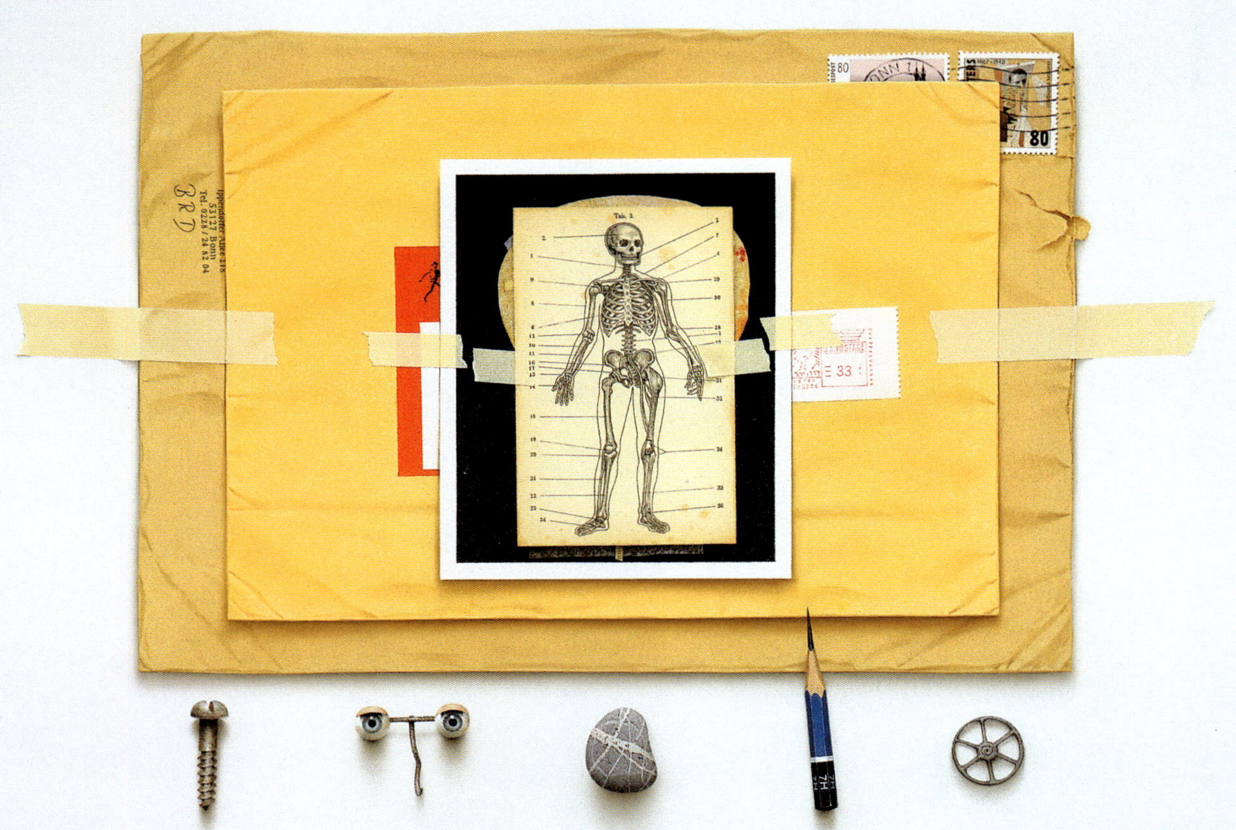

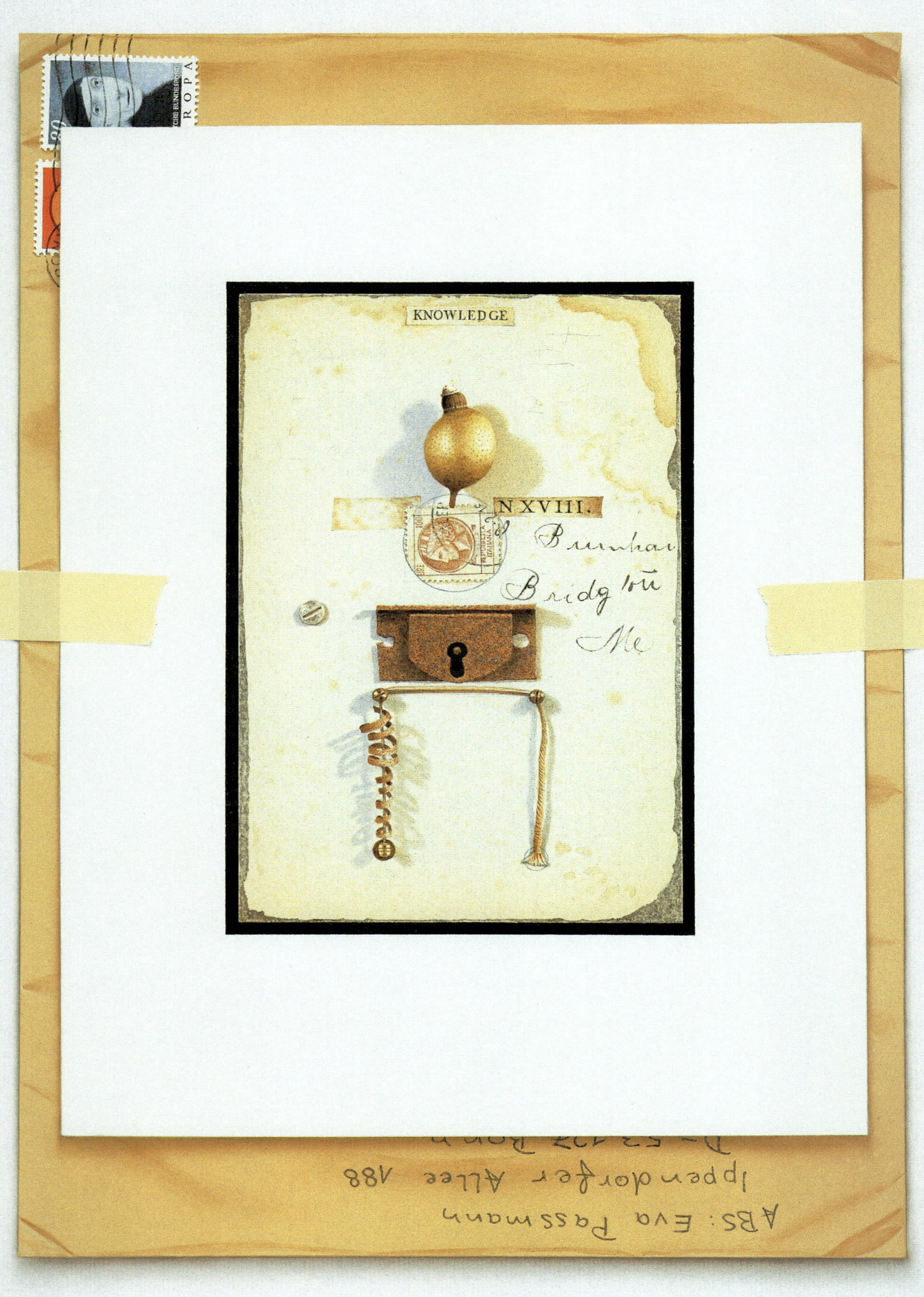
KNOWLEDGE
N XVIII.
ABS: Eva Passmann
Ippendorfer Allee 188

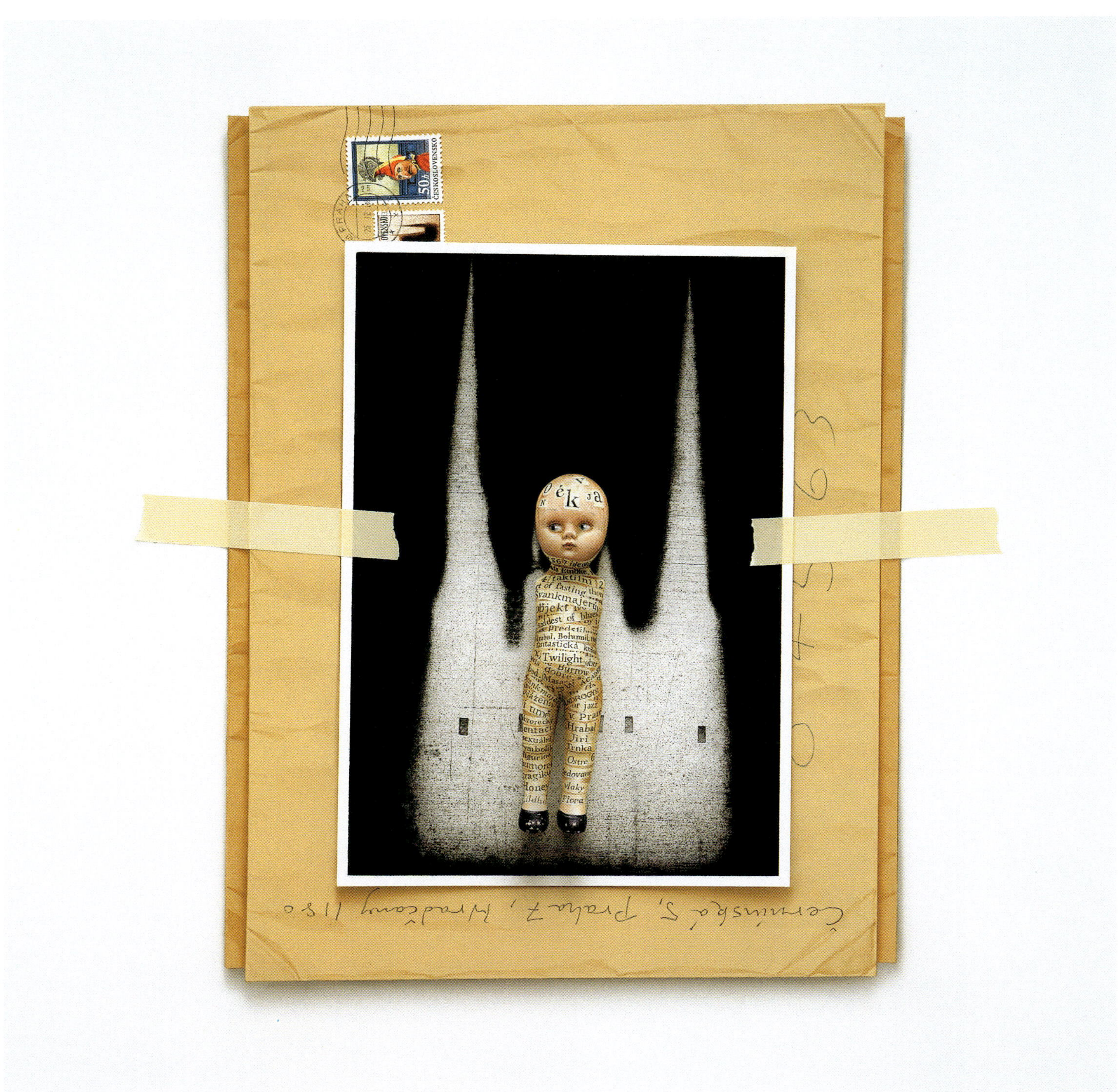

Samizdat (and detail), 1999, acrylic, graphite and colored pencil on paper, 19 ½ x 24"

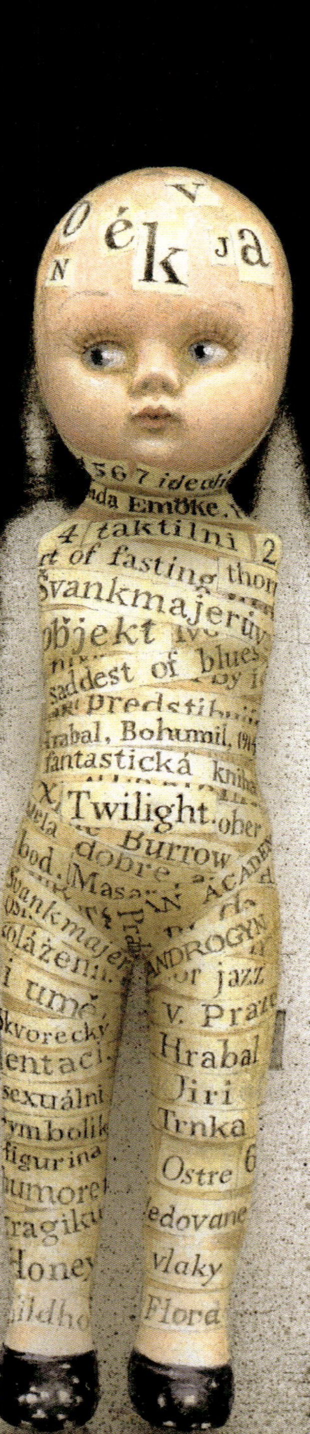

Emöke
taktilni
of fasting
Švankmajerův
objekt
saddest of blues
Hrabal, Bohumil
fantastická
Twilight
Burrow
dobre
ANDROGYN
jazz
v. Praze
Skvorecky
Hrabal
sexuální
Jiri
Trnka
figurina
Ostre
Honey
vlaky
Flora

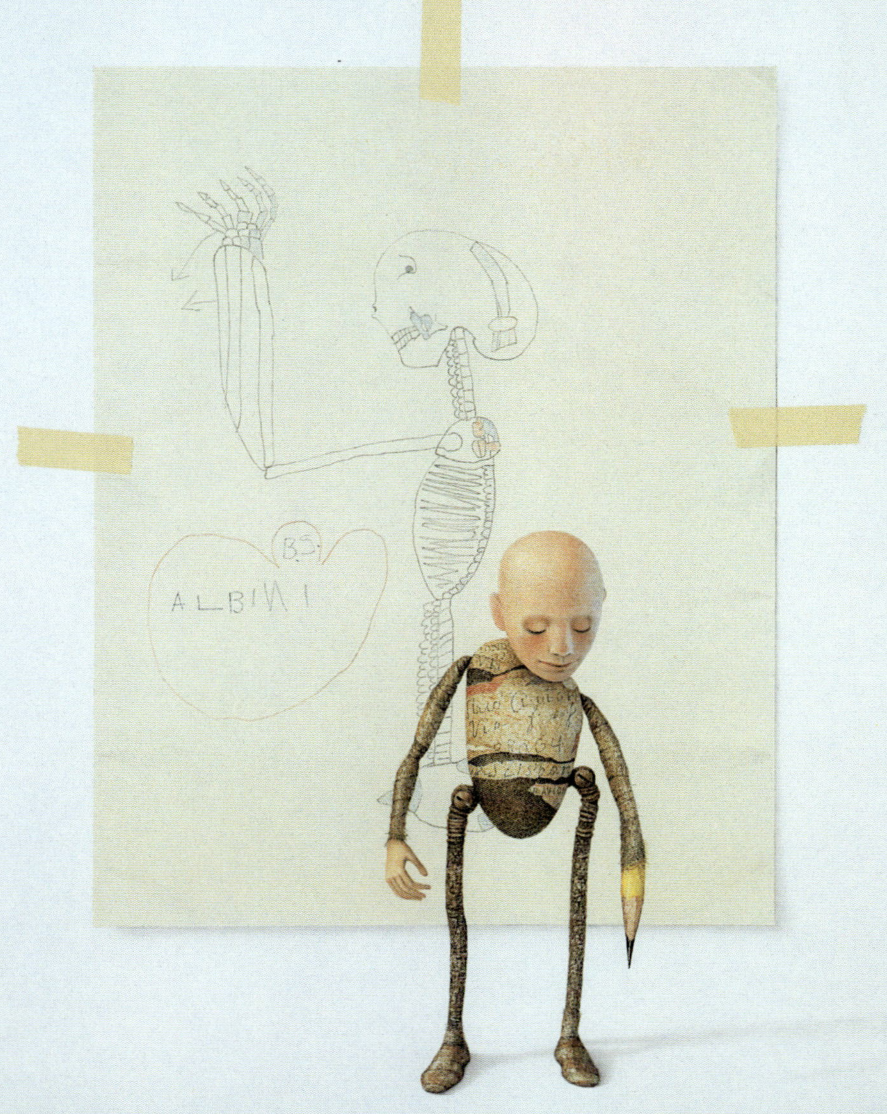
B.S.
ALBINI

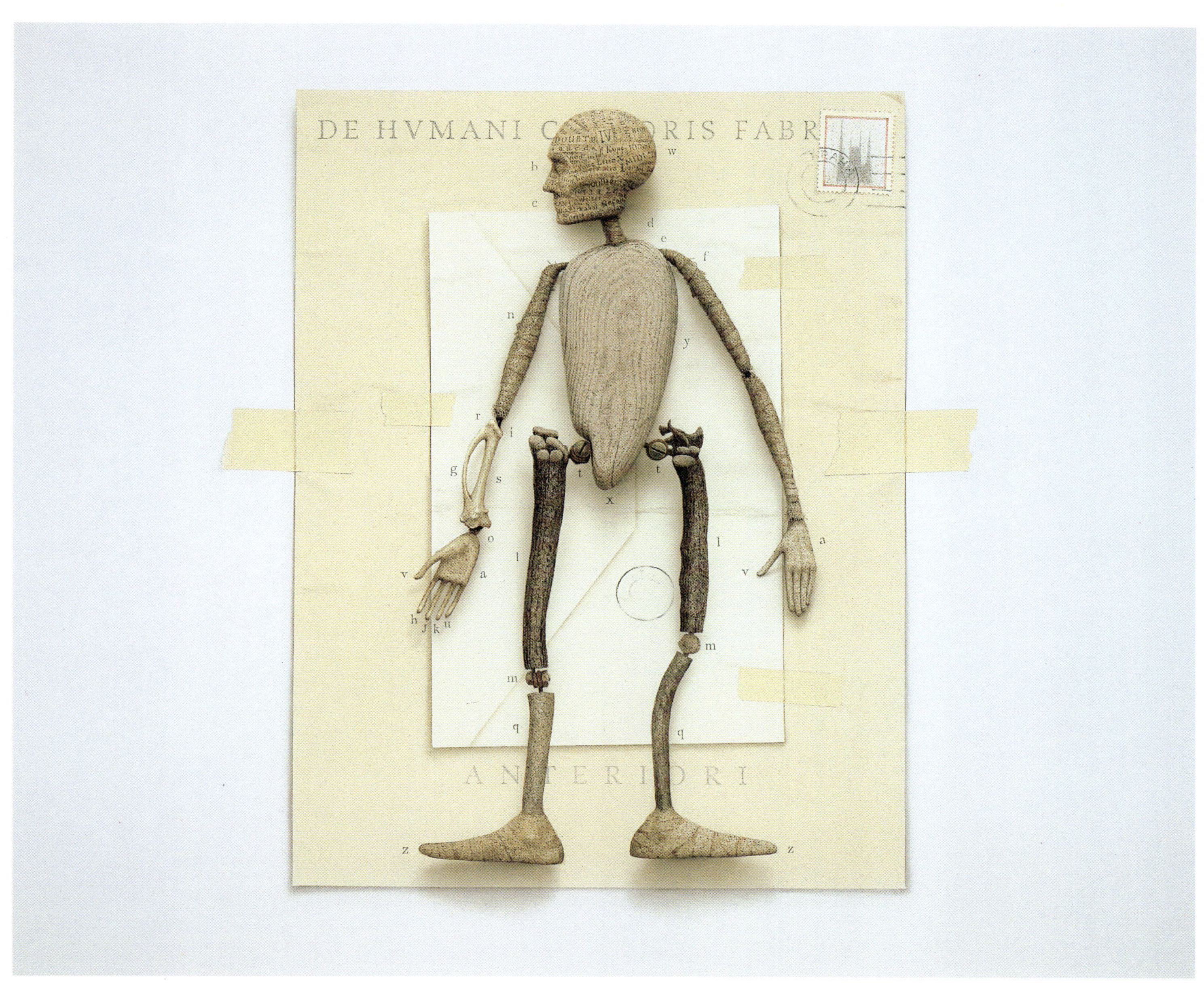

An Exact Anatomy of Man, 1997, watercolor and graphite on paper, 18 x 22"

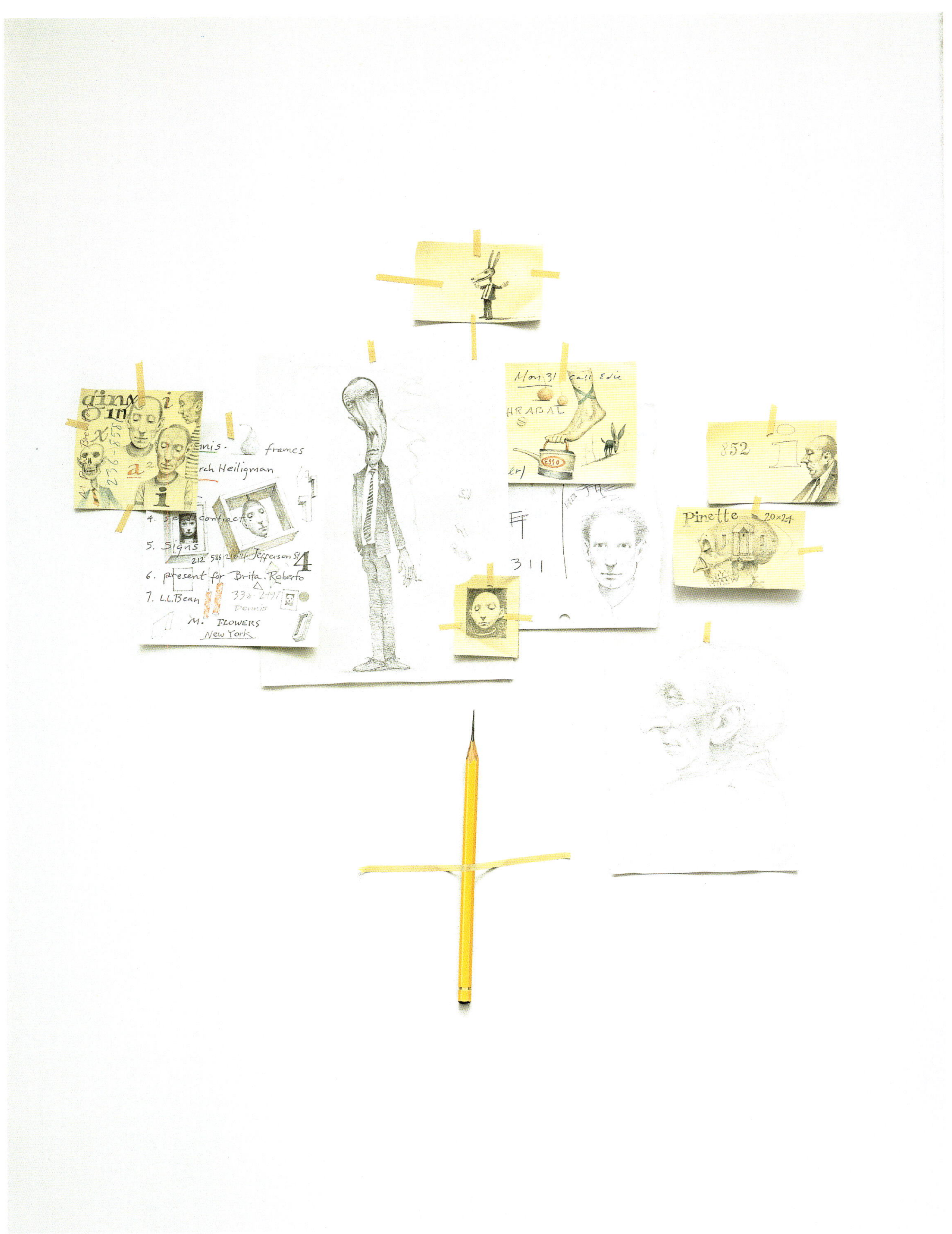

Works on Paper, 1996, watercolor on paper, 30 x 22"

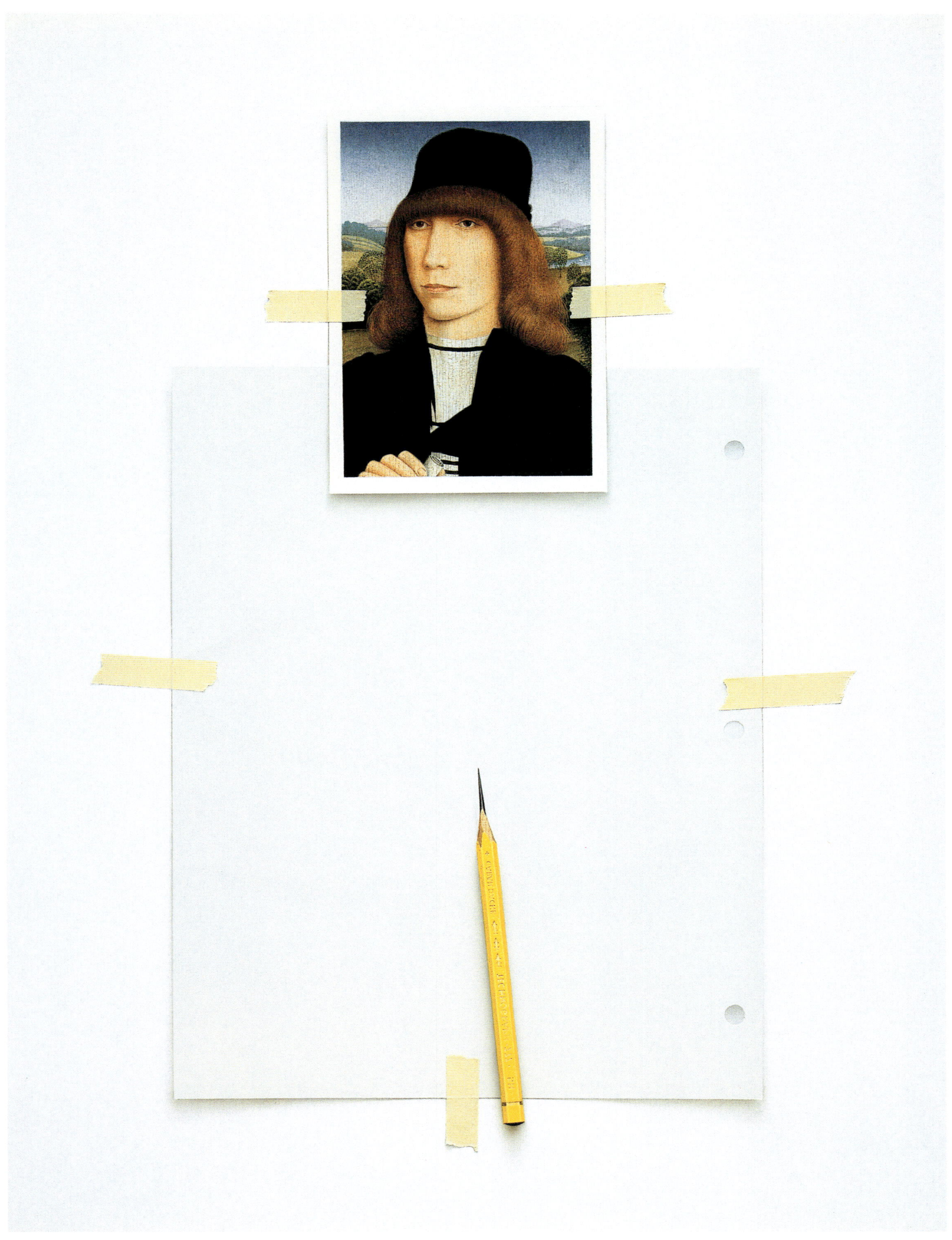

After Memling, 1999, acrylic, graphite and colored pencil on paper, 19 x 15"

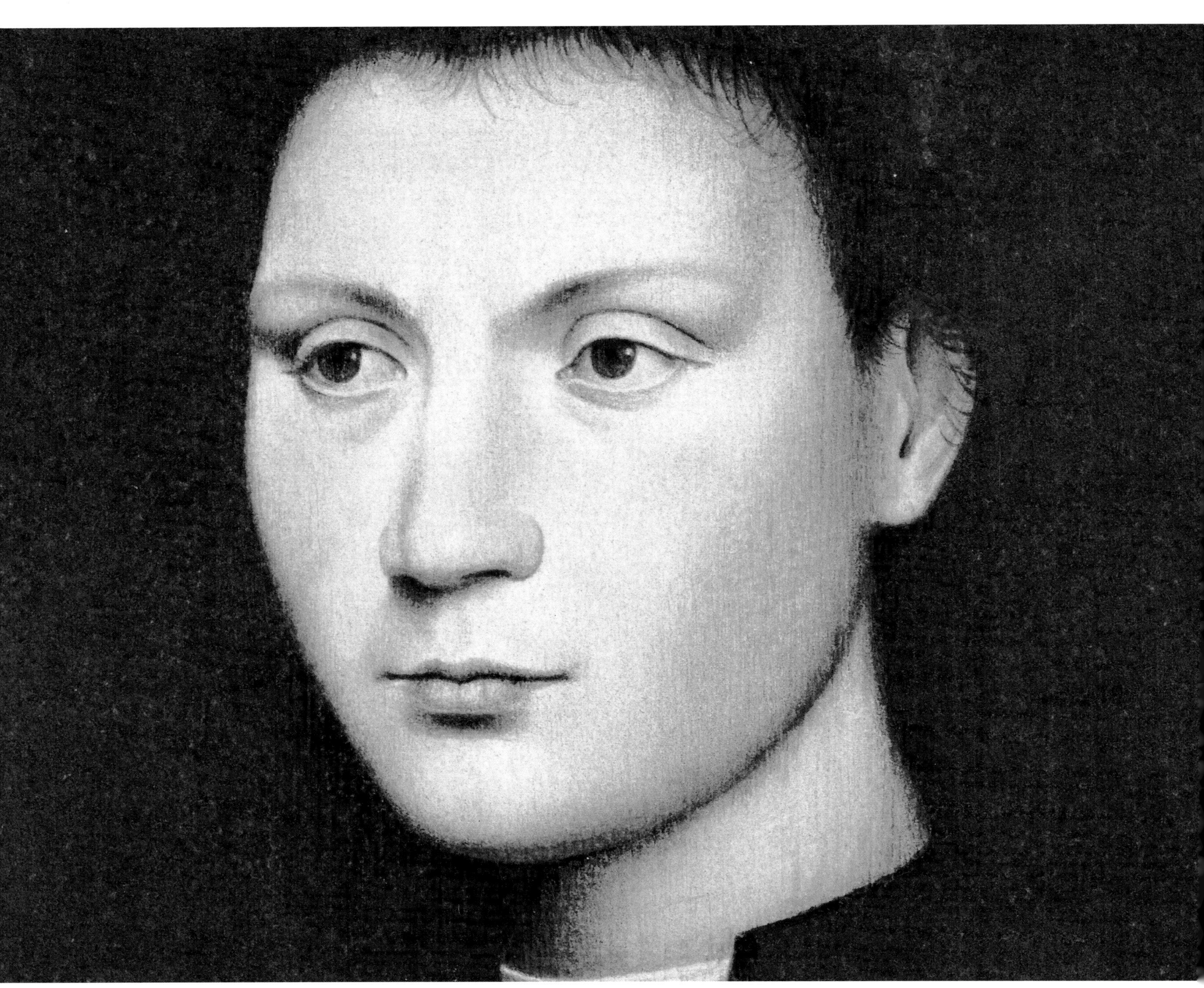

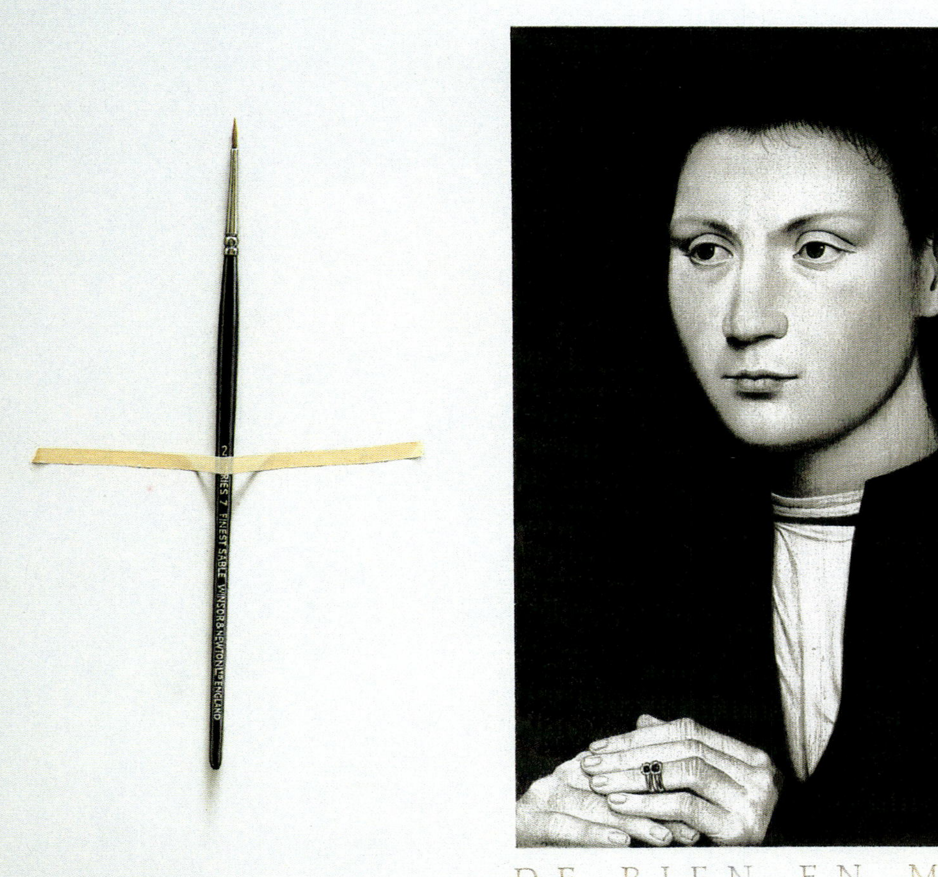

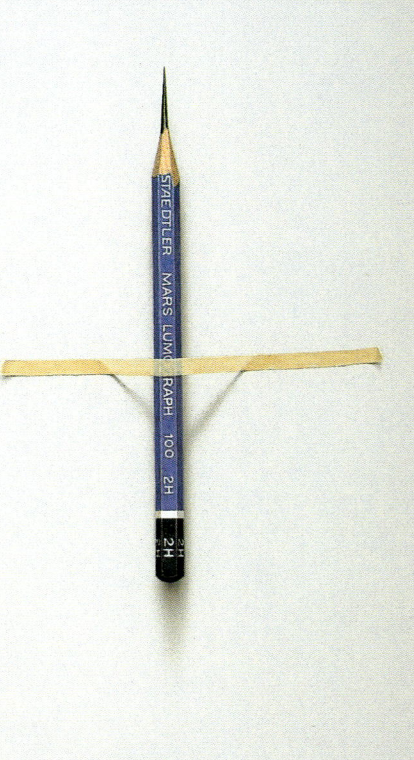

The Lost Memling (and detail), 2000, acrylic and graphite on paper, 15 x 19"

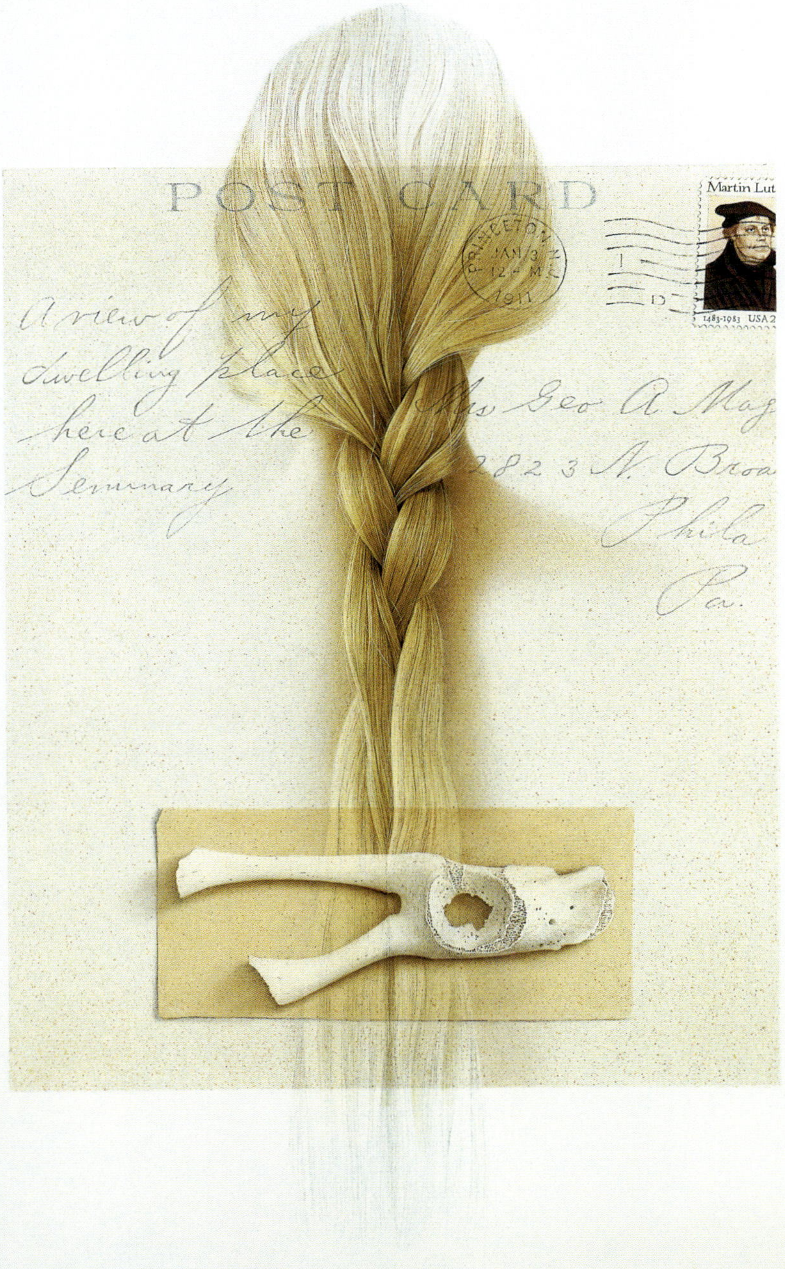

POST CARD
PRINCETON
JAN 3
1911
Martin Lut
1483-1983 USA 2
A view of my
dwelling place
here at the
Seminary
Mrs Geo A Mag
2823 N. Broa
Phila
Pa.

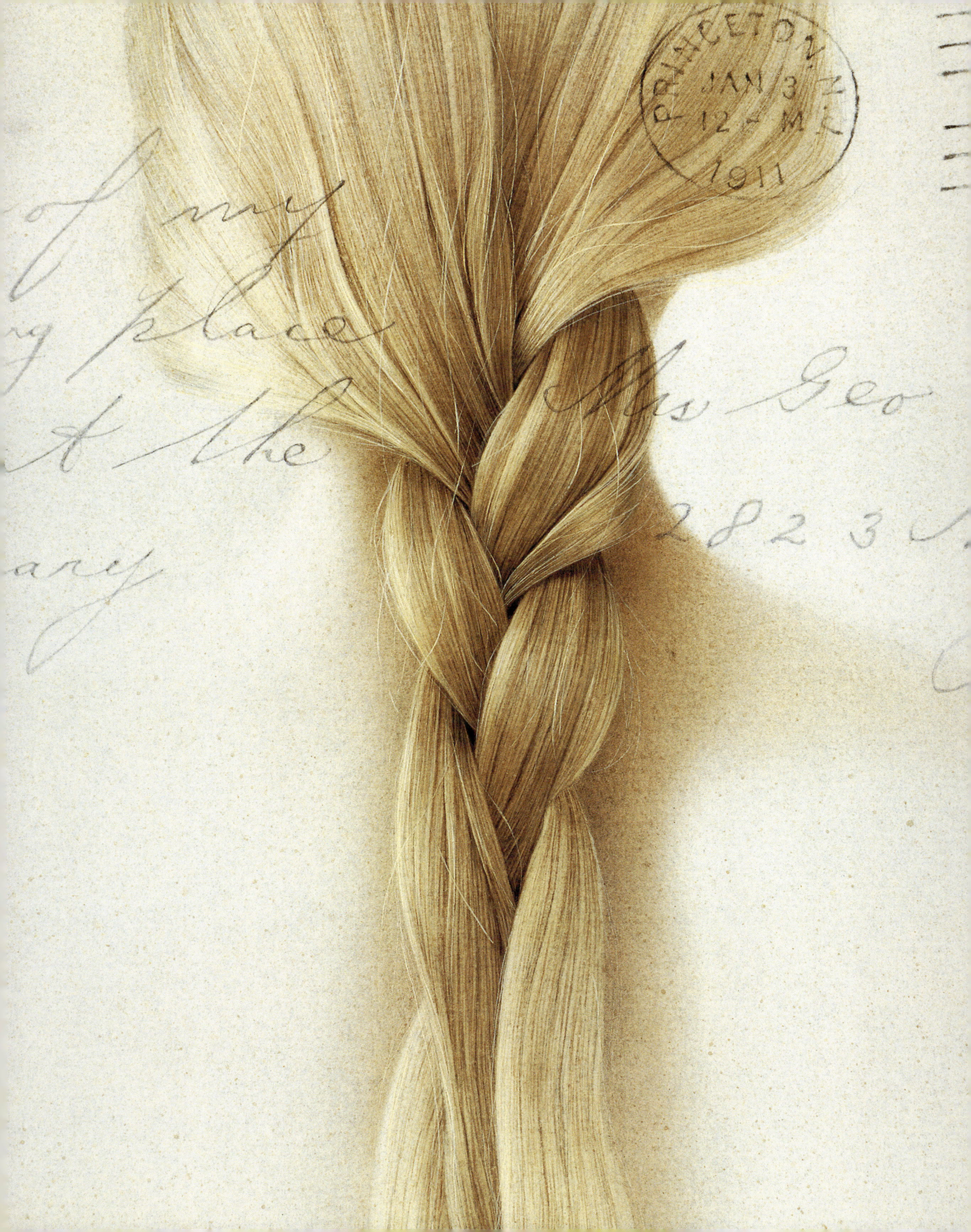
PRINCETON
JAN 3
12 M
1911
Mrs Geo
2823

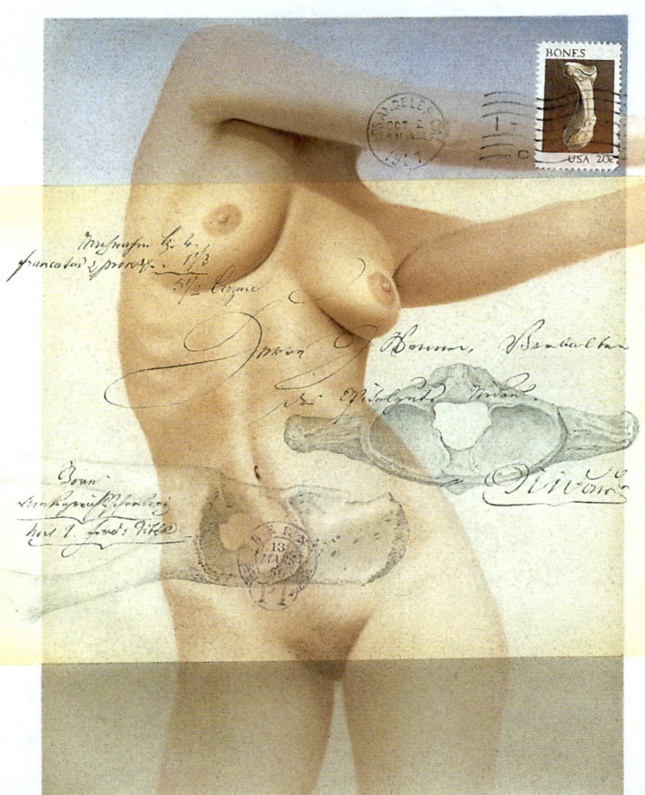
BONES
USA 20c

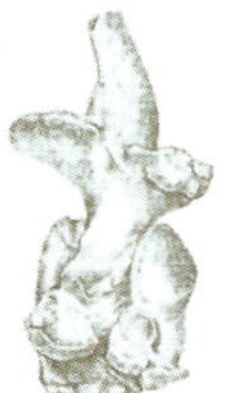

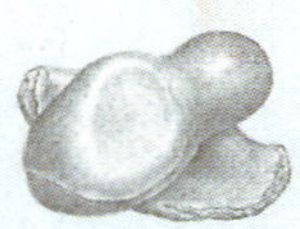

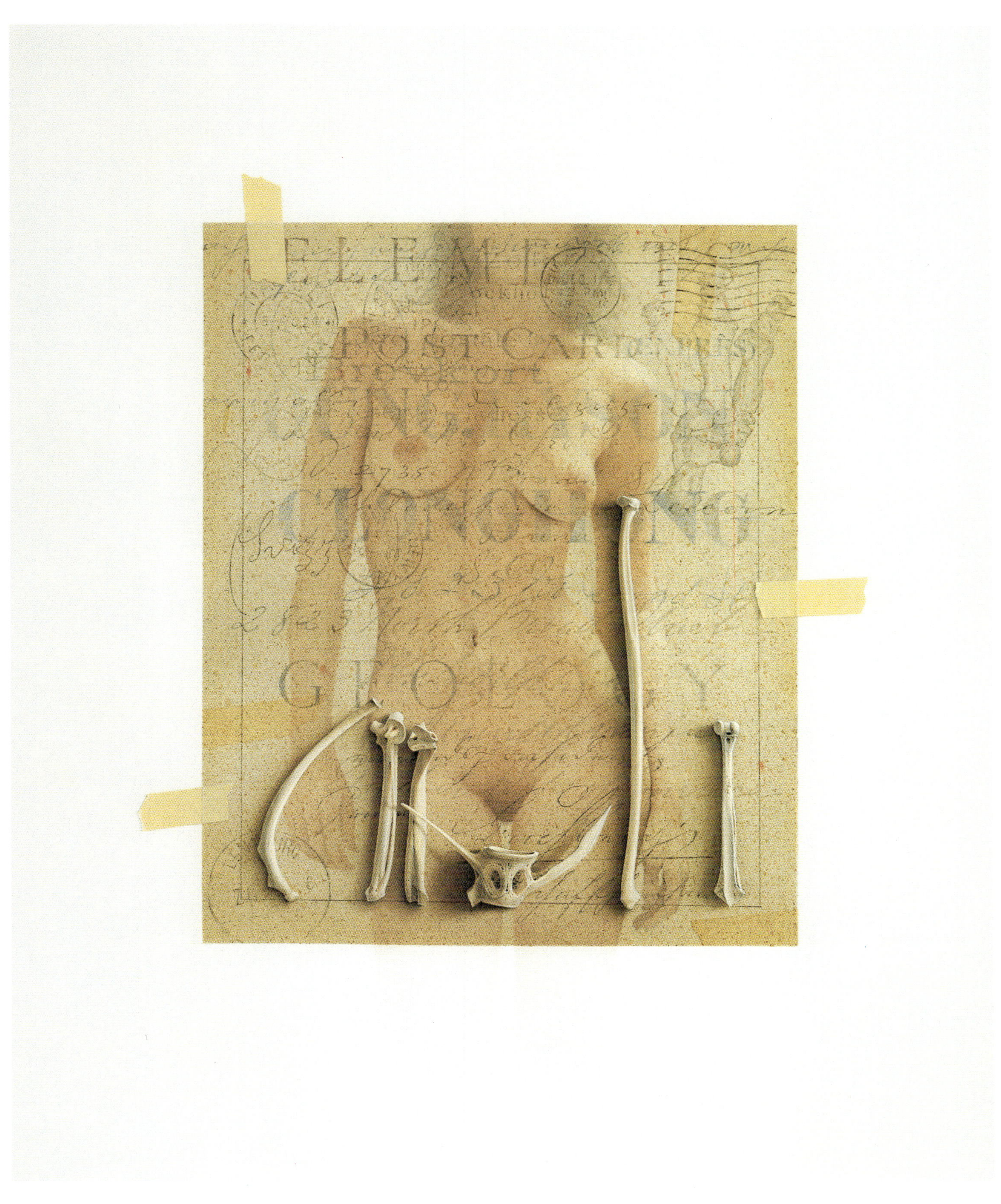

Palimpsestos (detail), 1984, watercolor and colored pencil on paper, 18 ½ x 22"

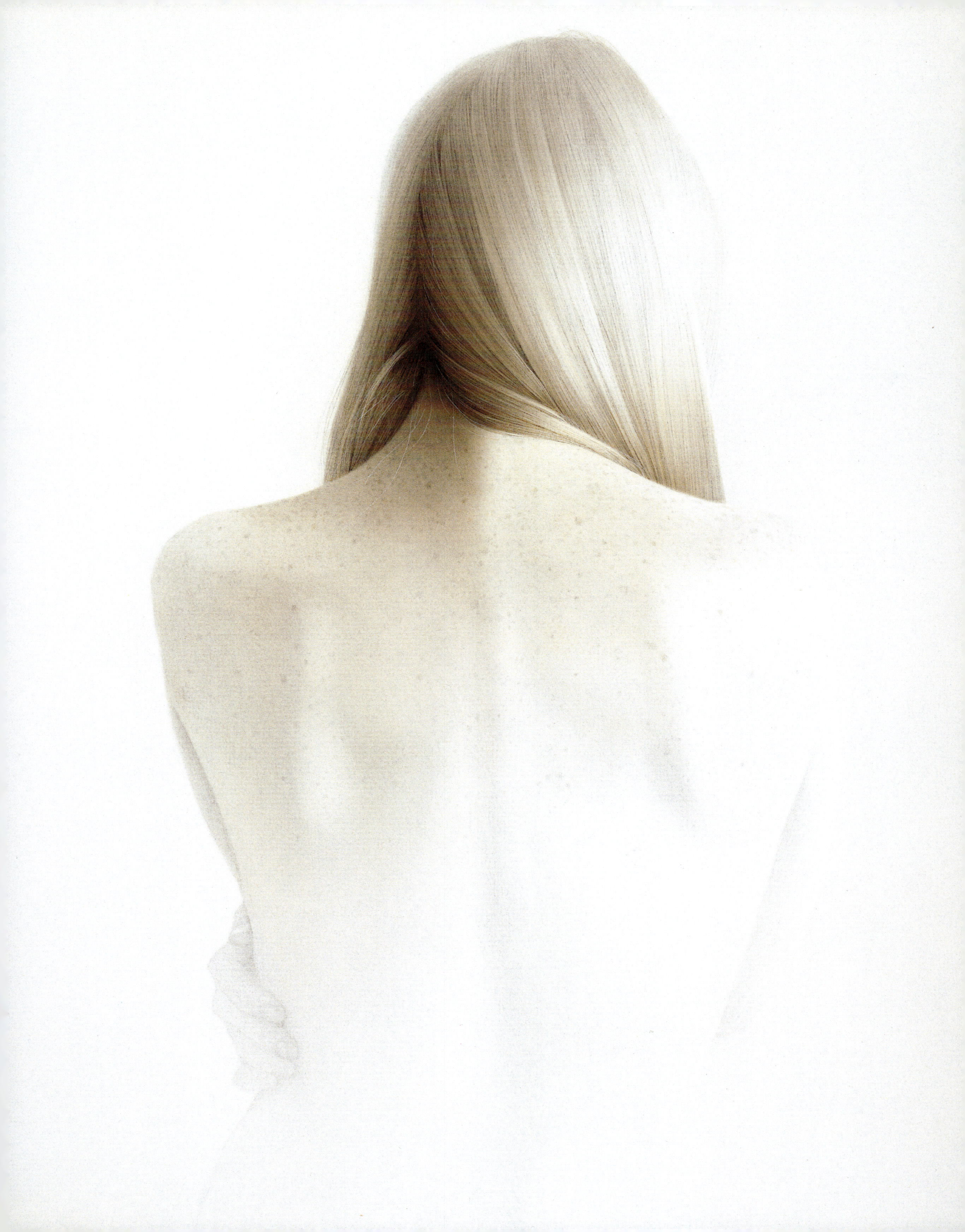

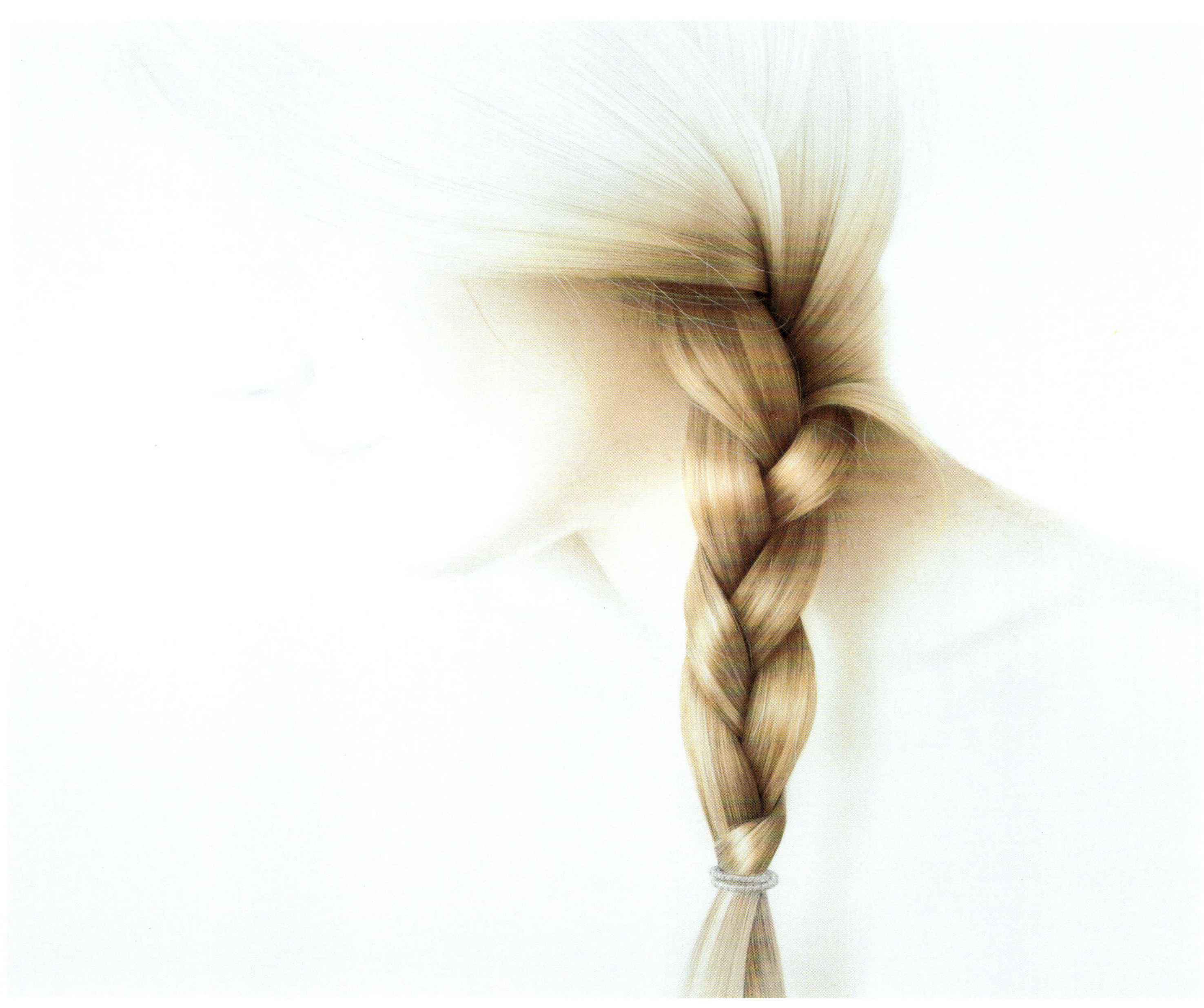

◁ *Monika (detail)*, 1983, watercolor on paper, 18 x 22"
Braid (detail), 1980, watercolor on paper, 22 x 30"

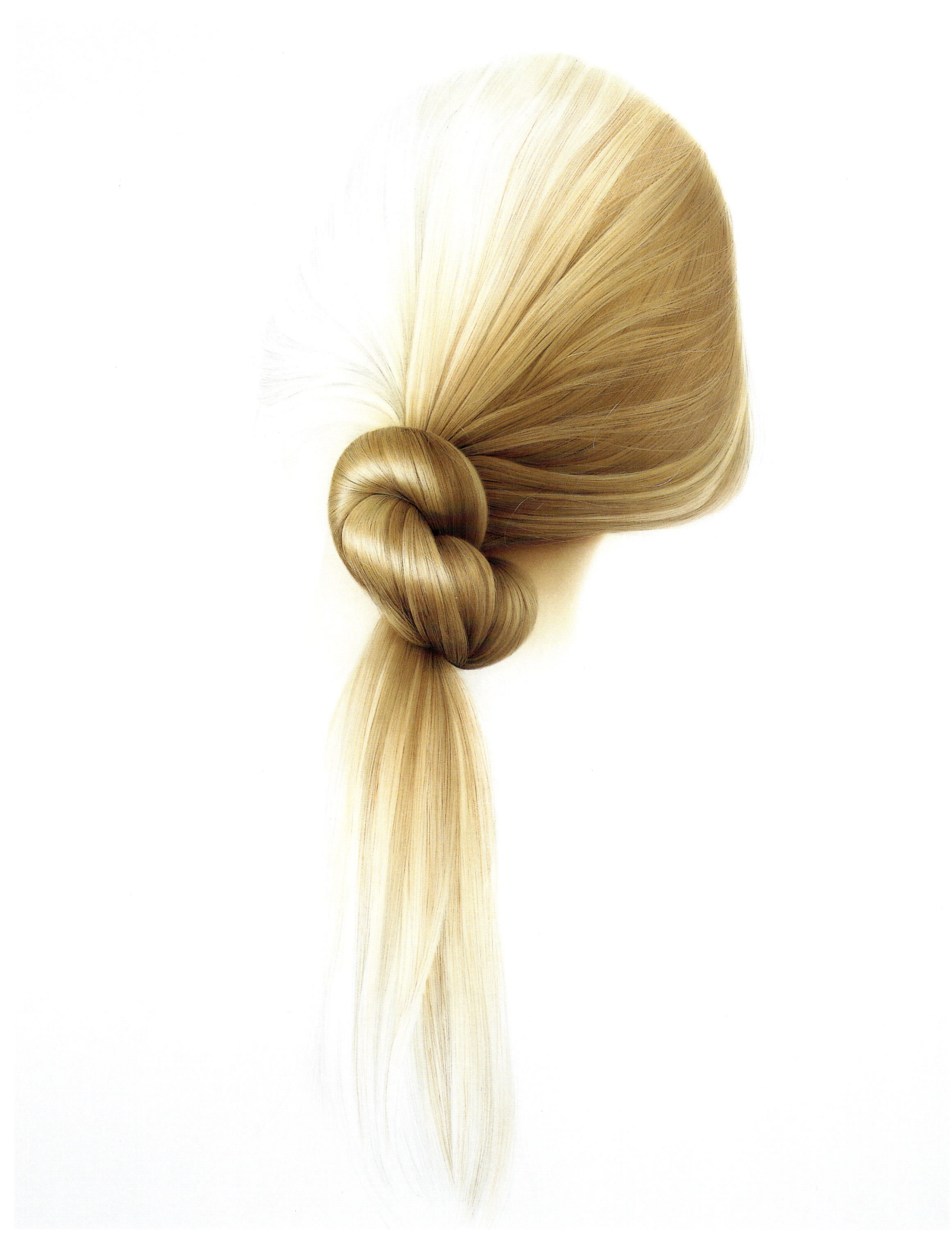

Knot (detail), 1984, watercolor and graphite on paper, 18 1/4 x 25"

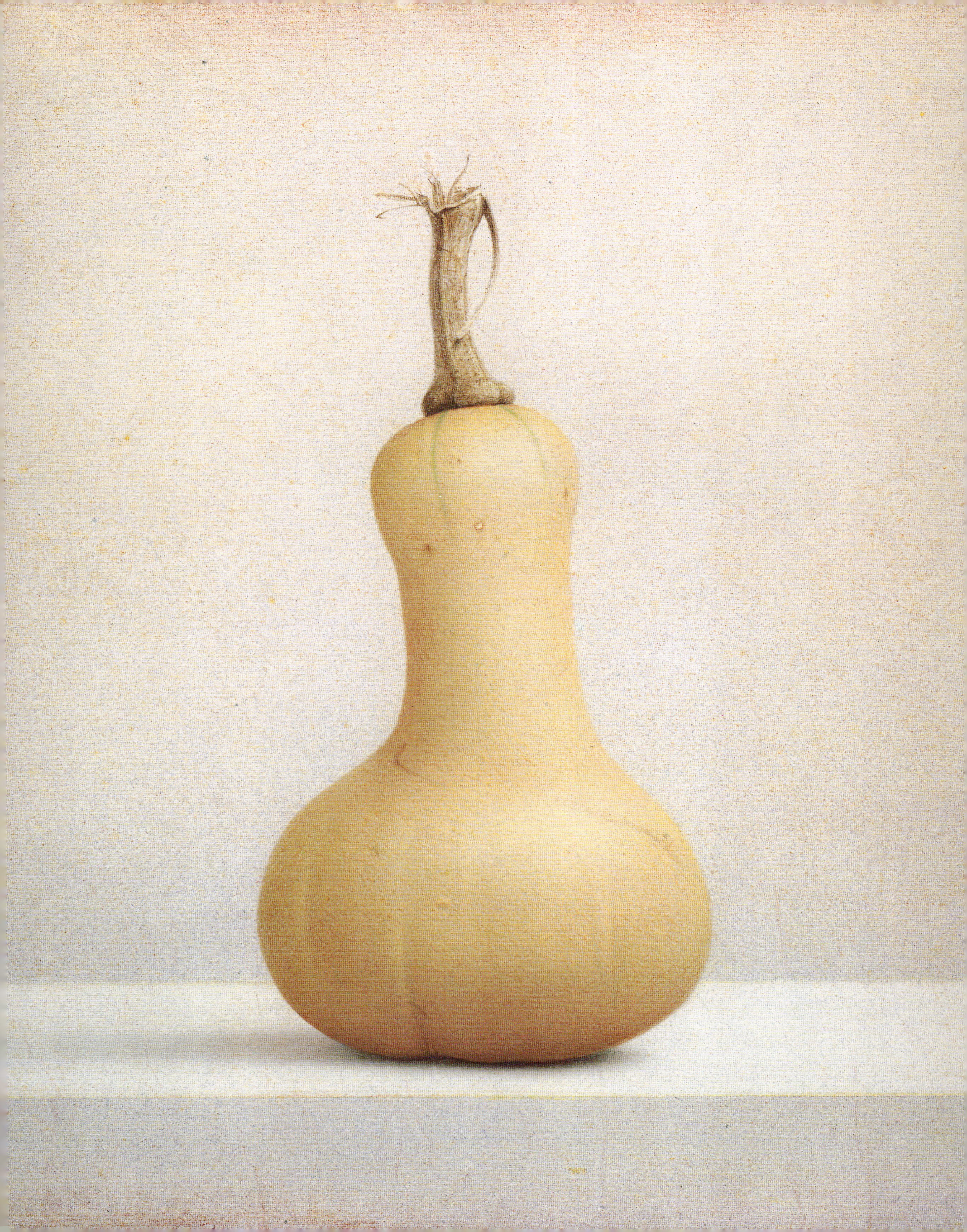

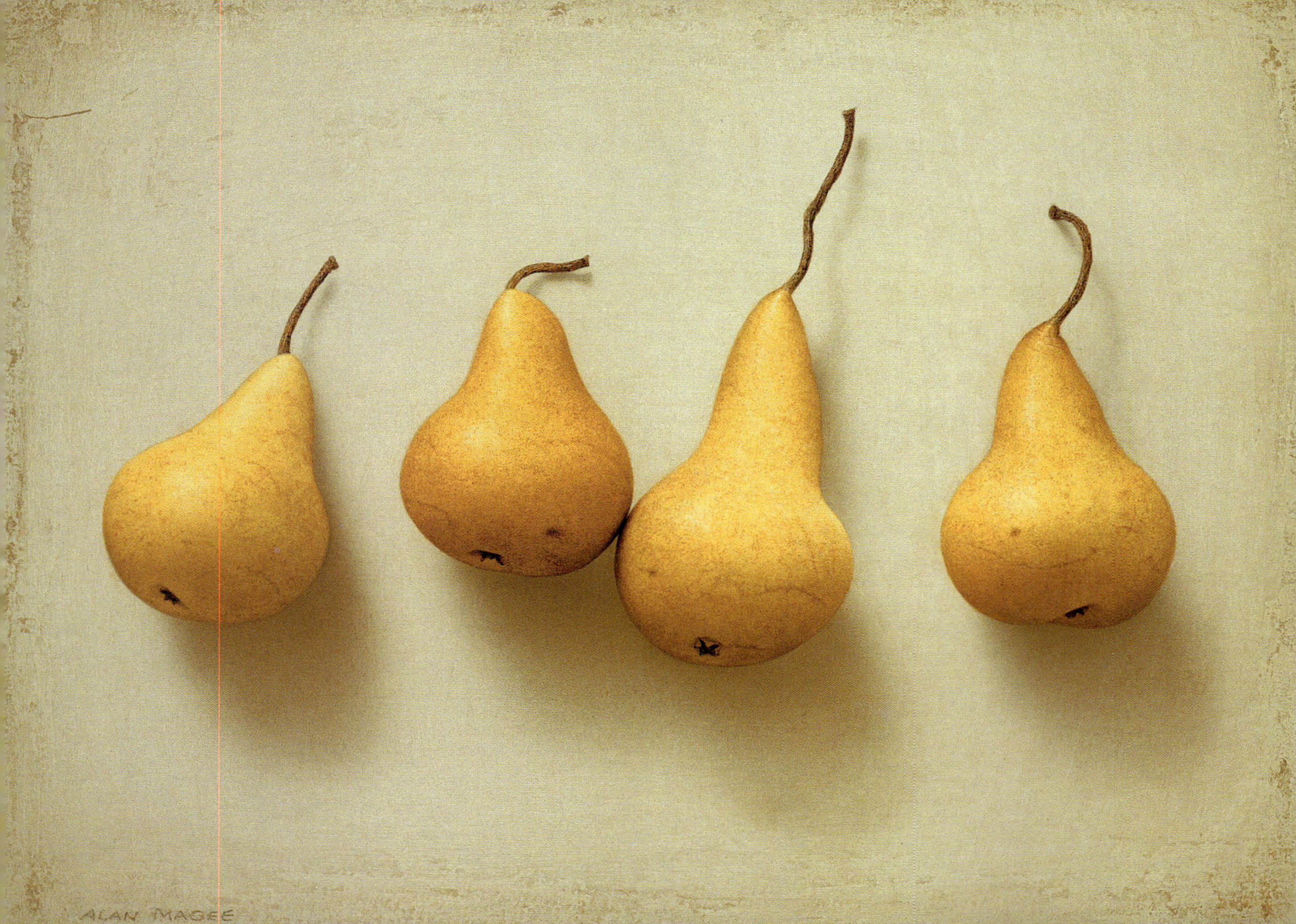
ALAN MAGEE

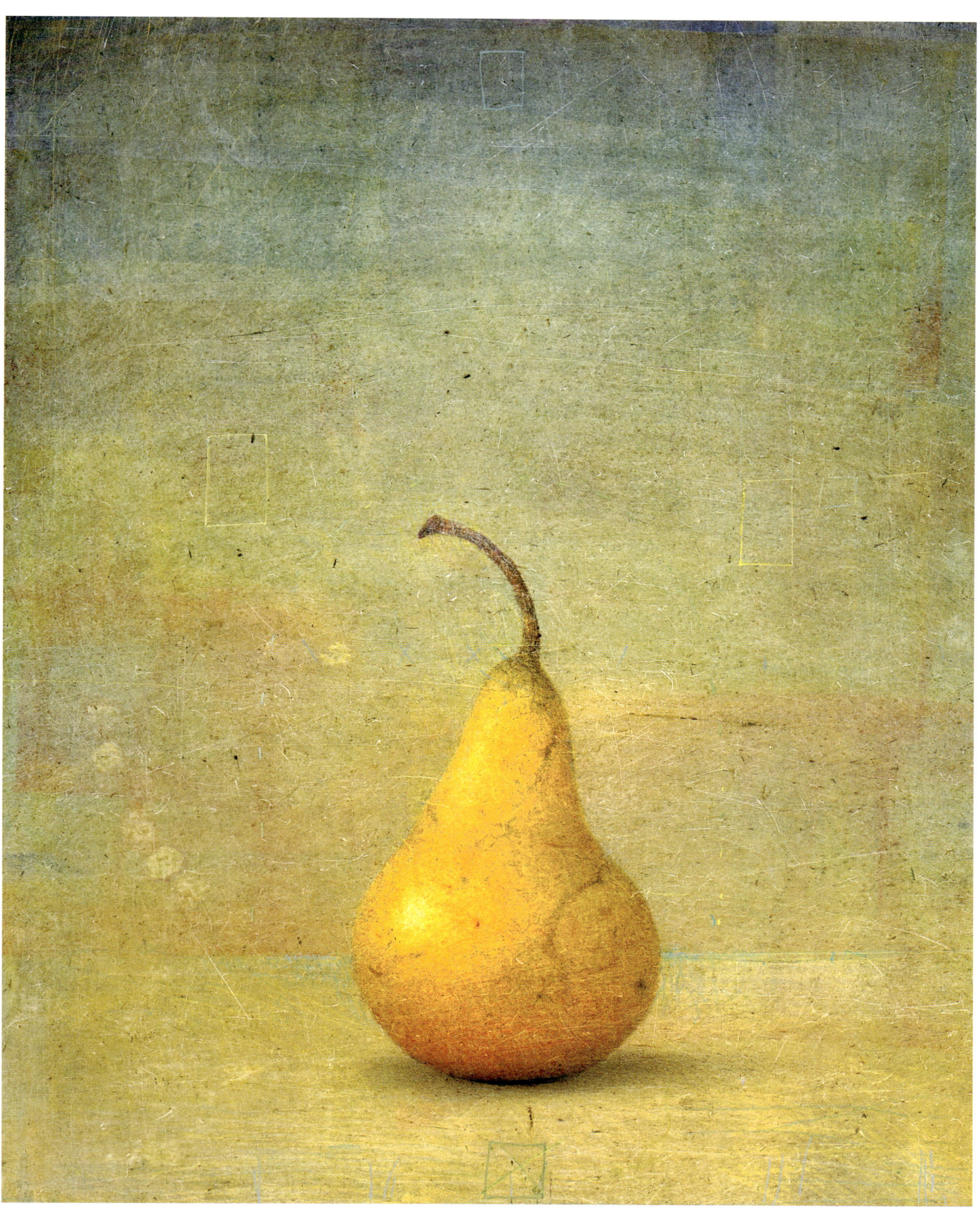

Pear, 1992, monotype, 14 x 11"

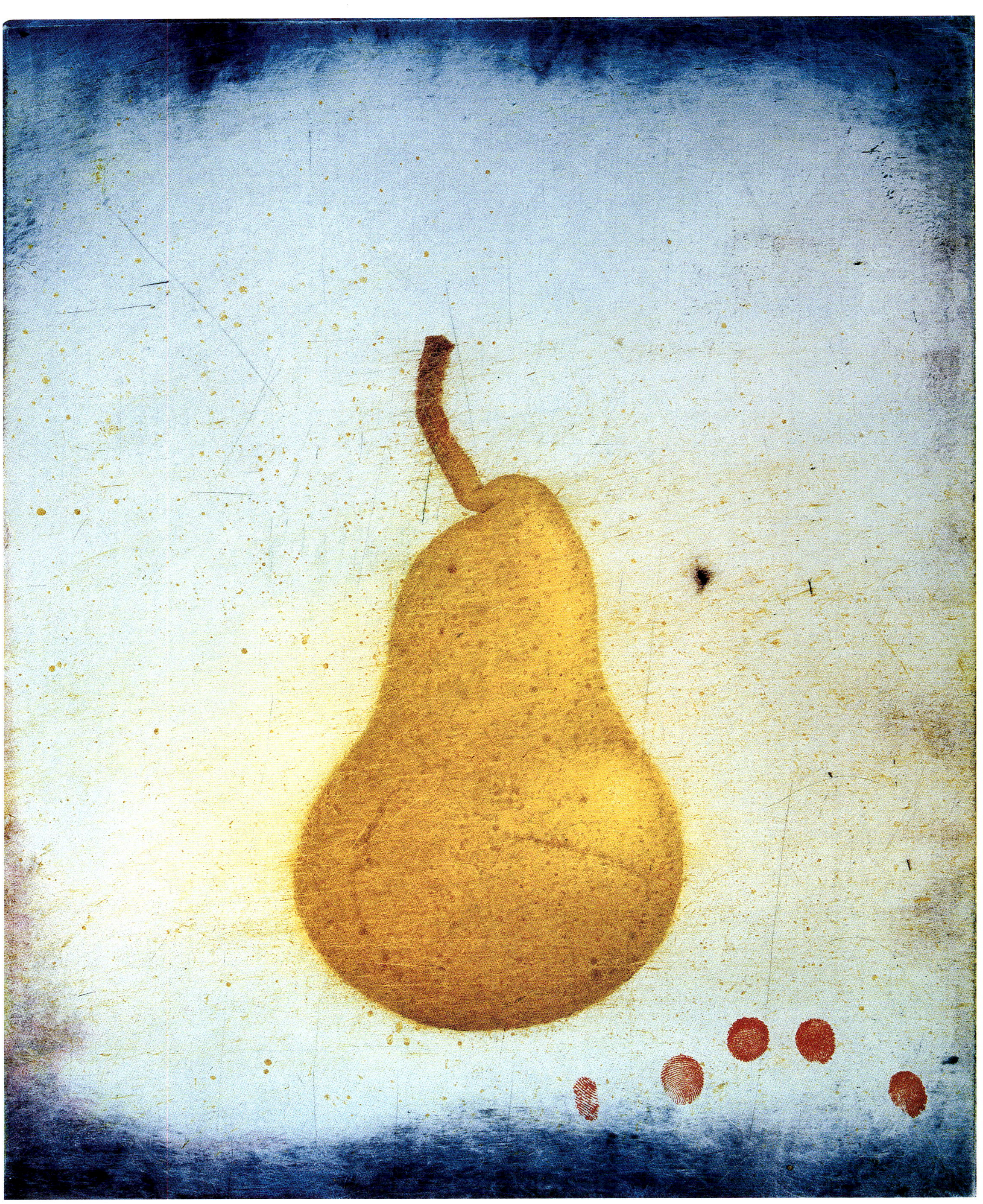

Pear with Fingerprints, 1993, monotype with watercolor, 14 x 11"

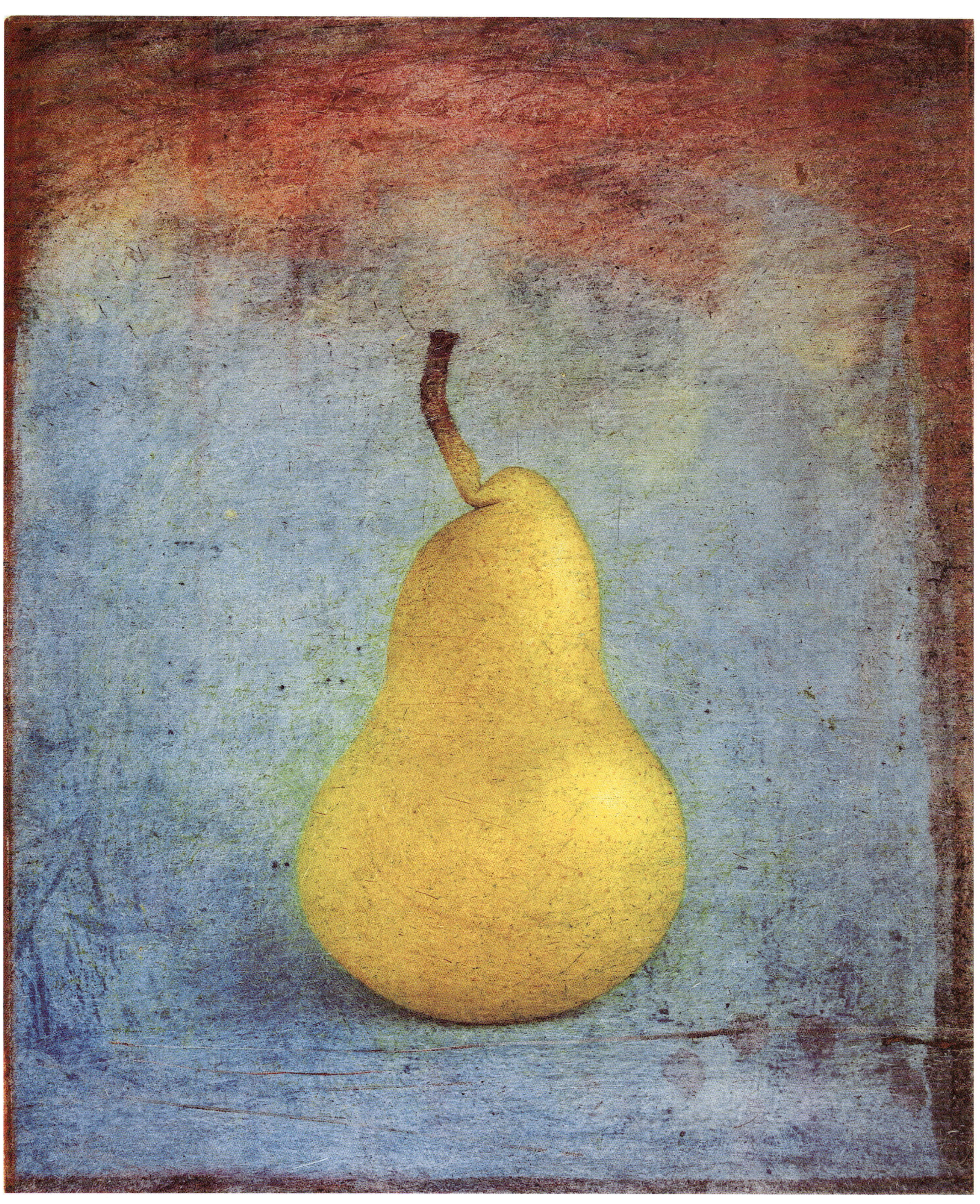

Pear in Blue Weather, 1993, monotype with watercolor, 14 x 11"

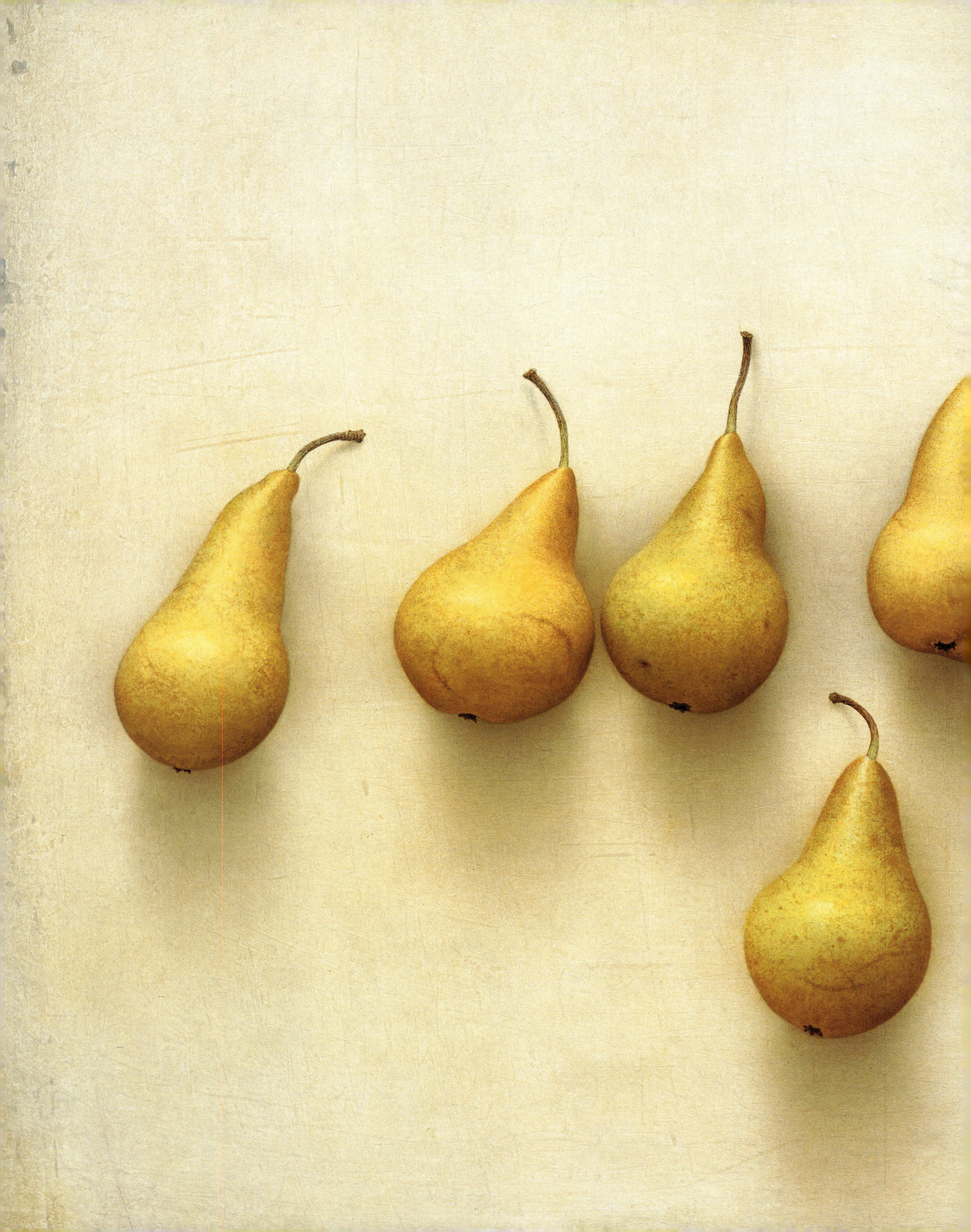

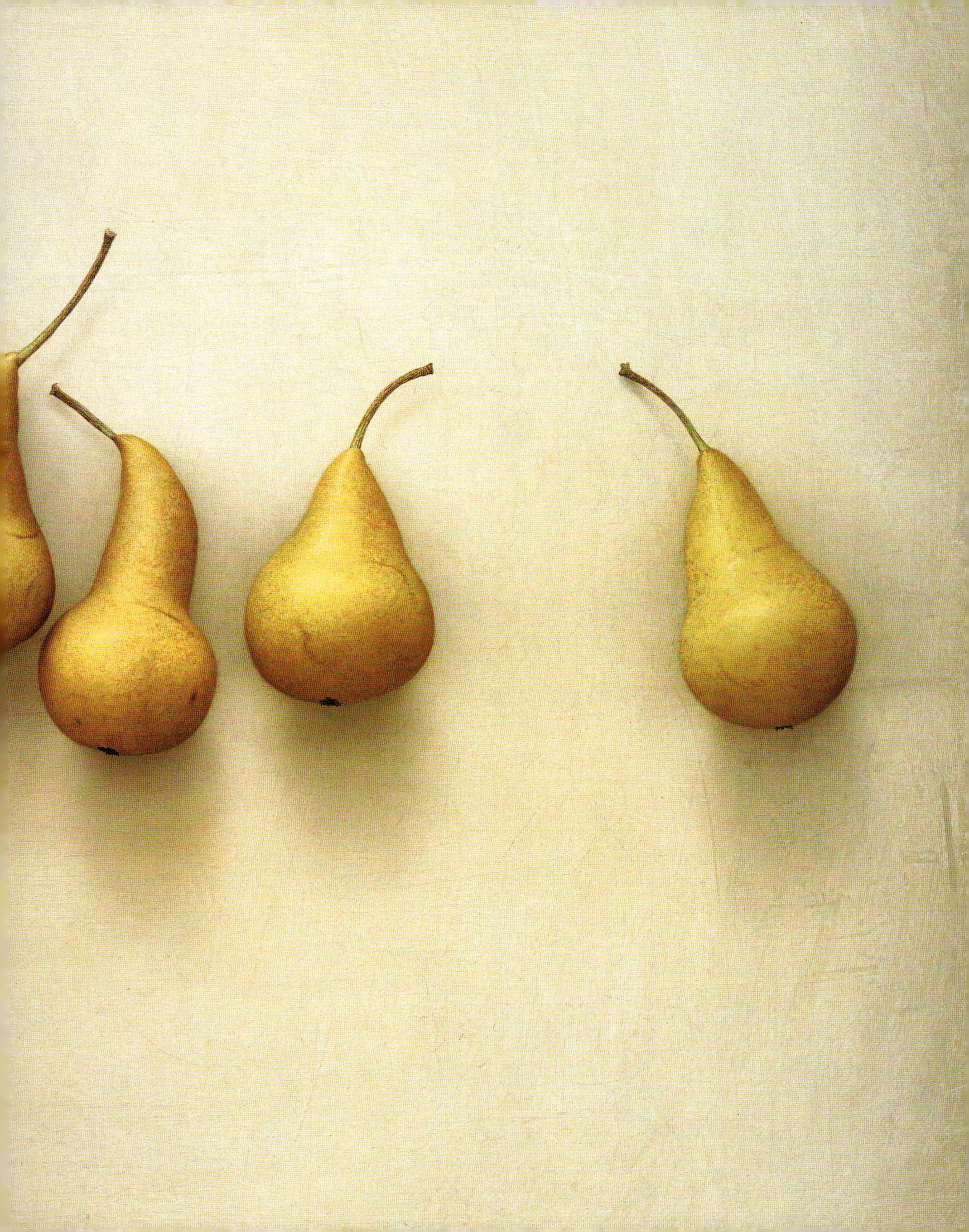

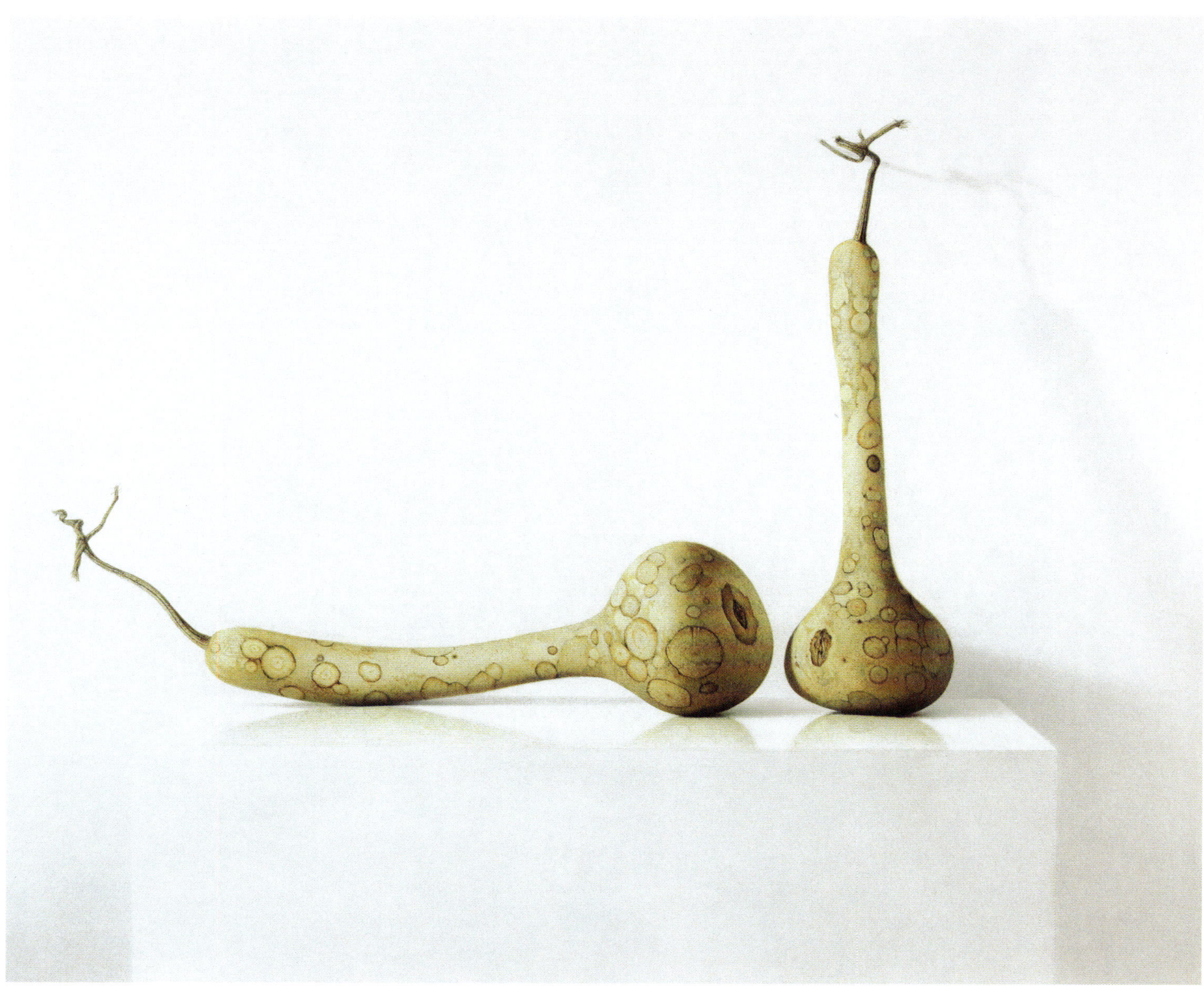

◁ *Harmonic (detail)*, 2000, acrylic on panel, 24 x 30"
Gourds, 1983, watercolor and colored pencil on paper, 15 x 19"

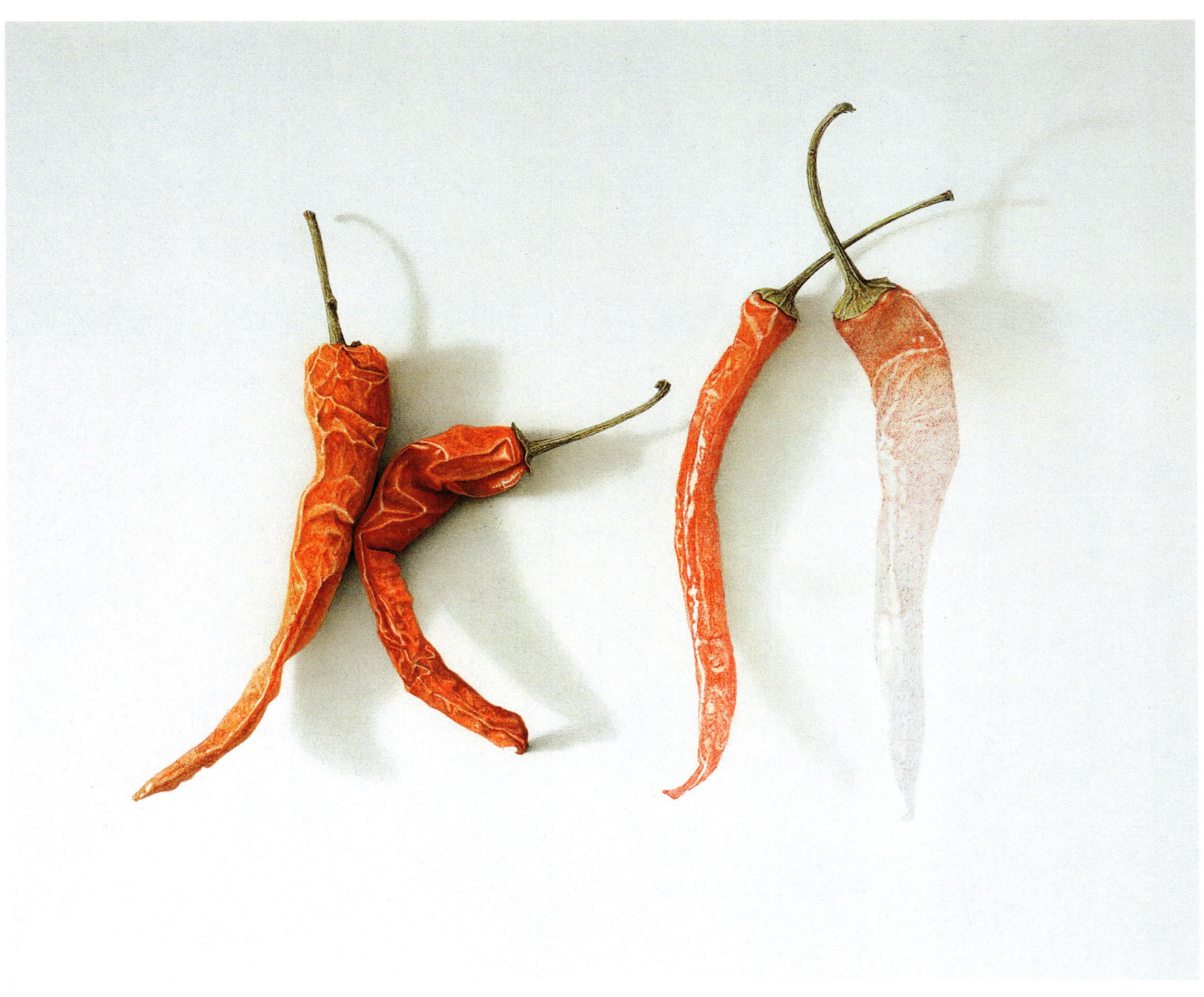

Peppers (detail), 1989, watercolor, graphite and colored pencil on paper, 15 x 19"

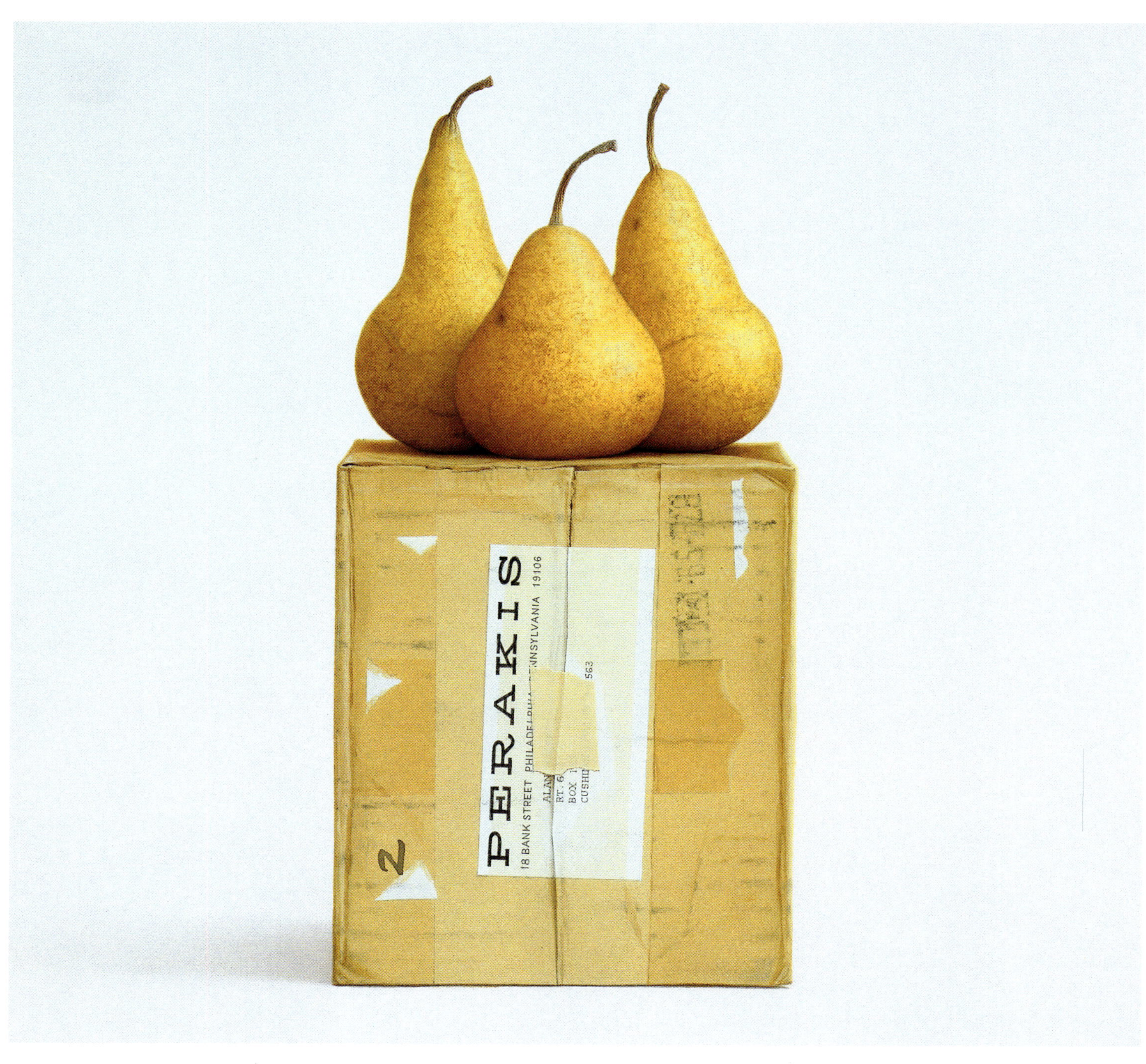

Monument, 2000, acrylic on paper, 15 ½ x 19 ¾"

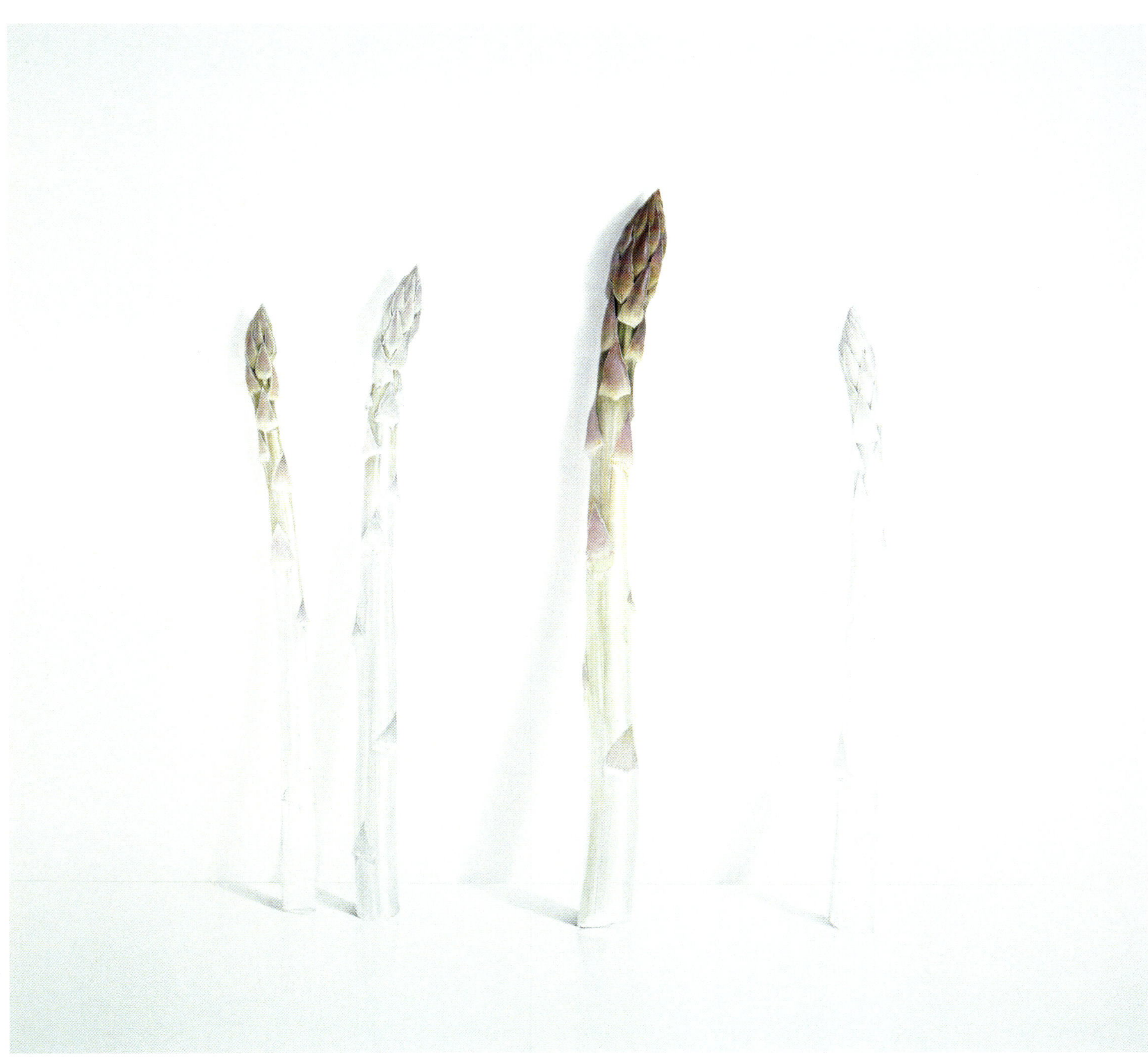

Asparagus, 1980, watercolor and graphite on paper, 17 x 22"

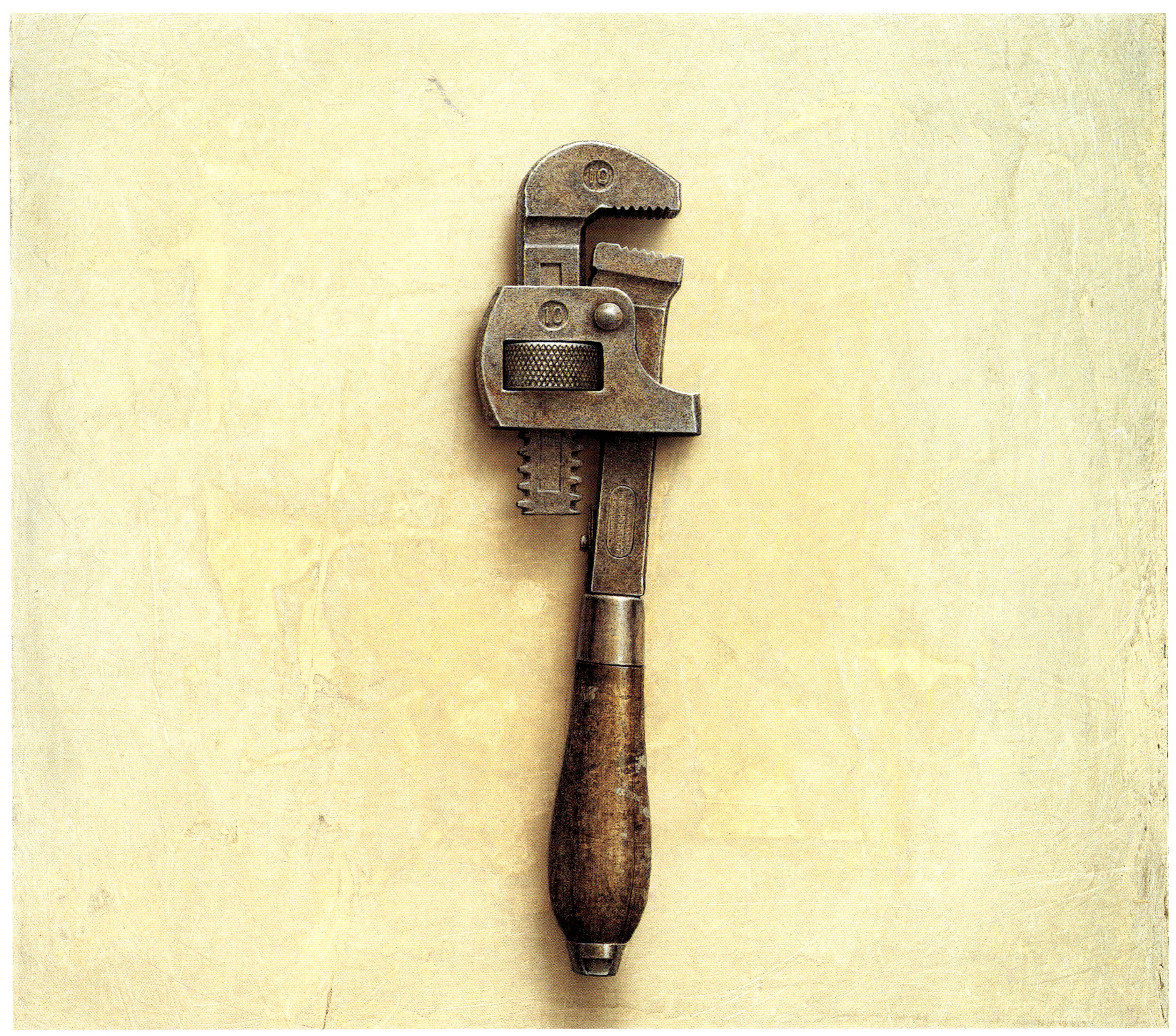

Wrench, 1997, acrylic and oil on panel, 14 x 14"

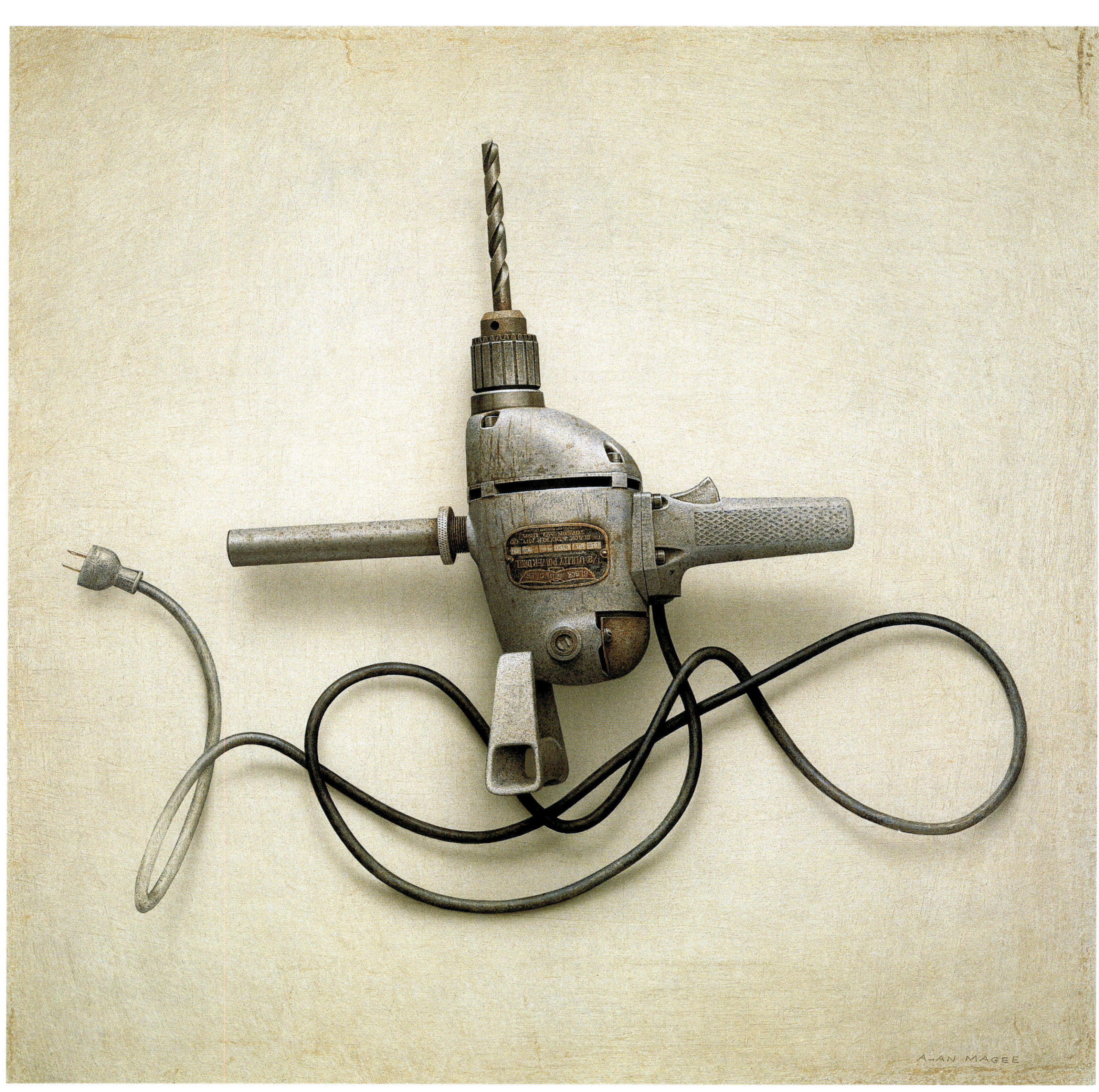

Emblem, 2000, acrylic on panel, 30 x 30"

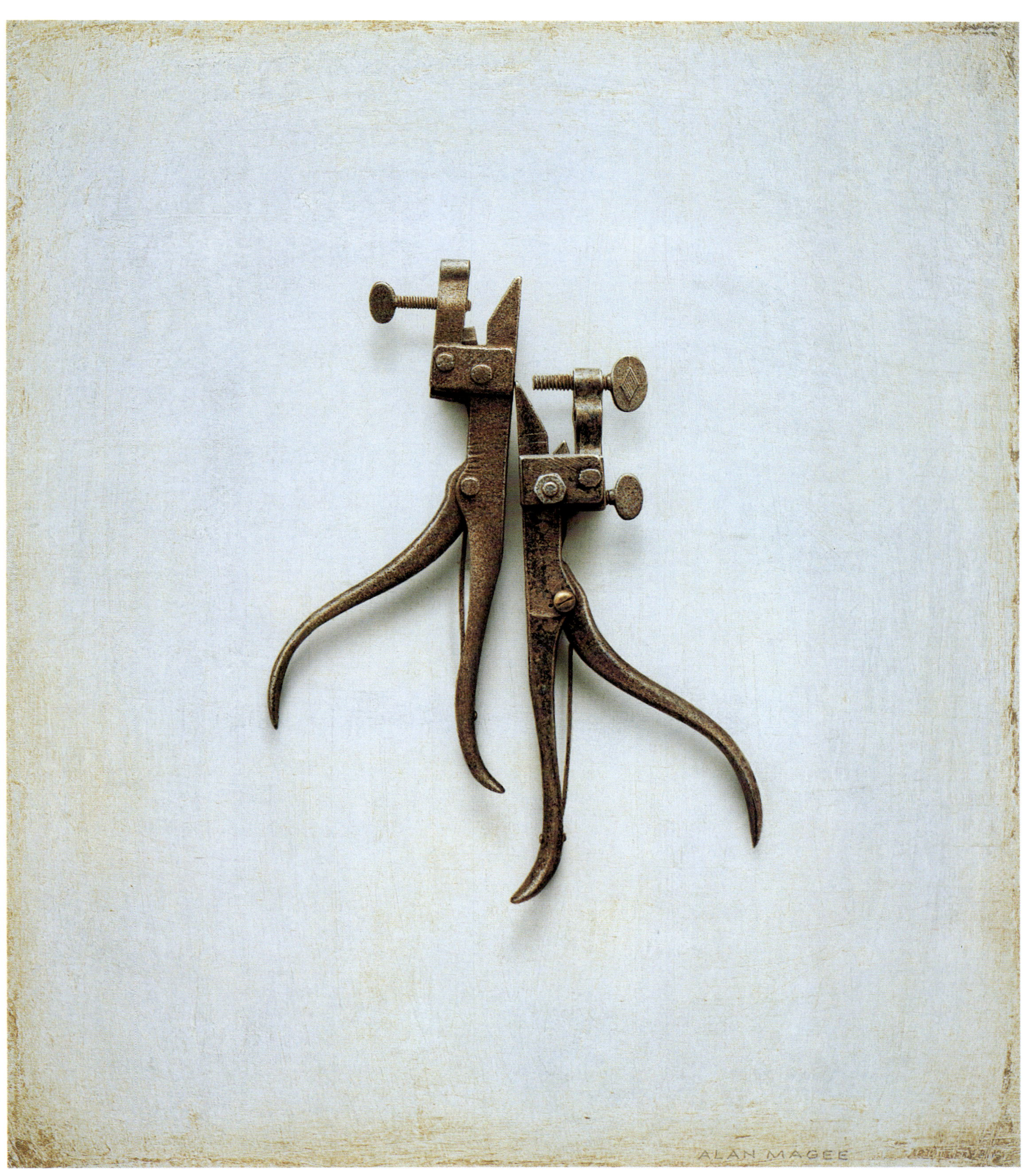

Couplet (Second Version), 2001, acrylic and oil on panel, 16 ¼ x 14"

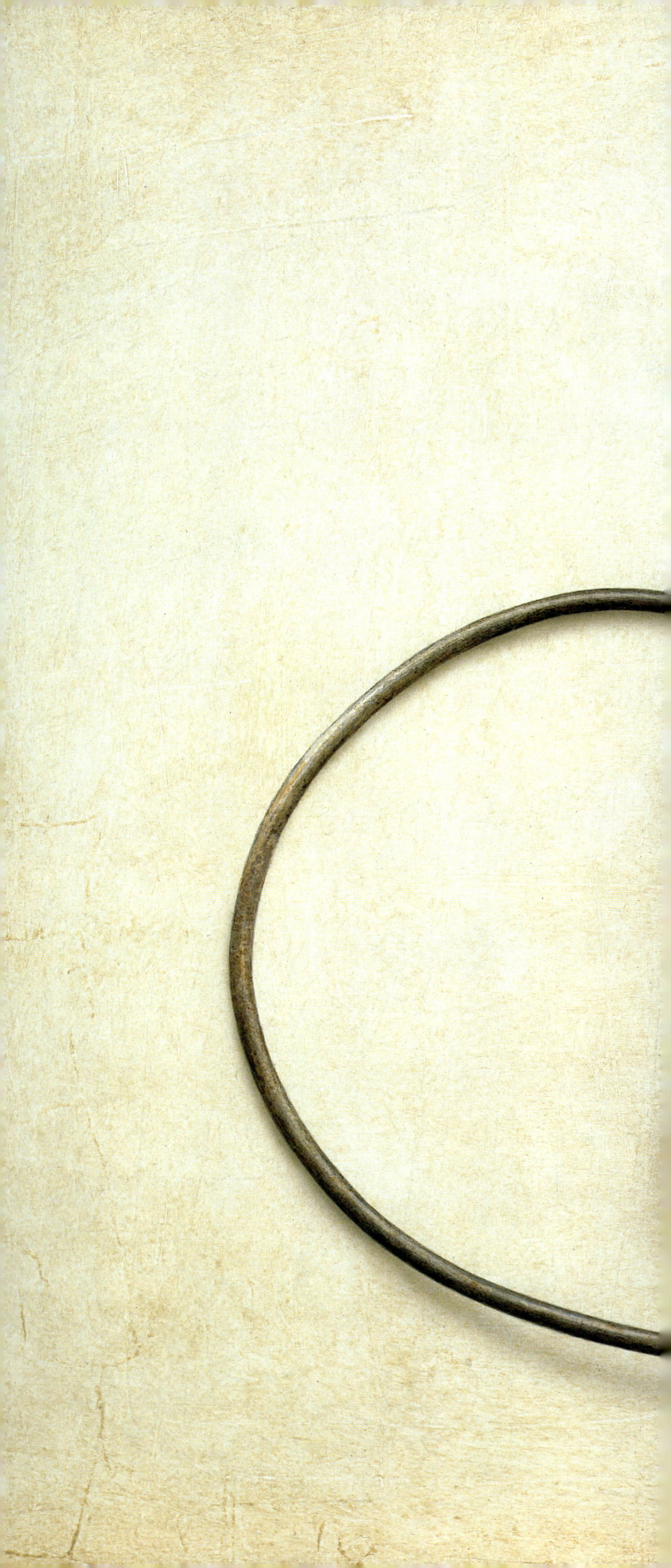

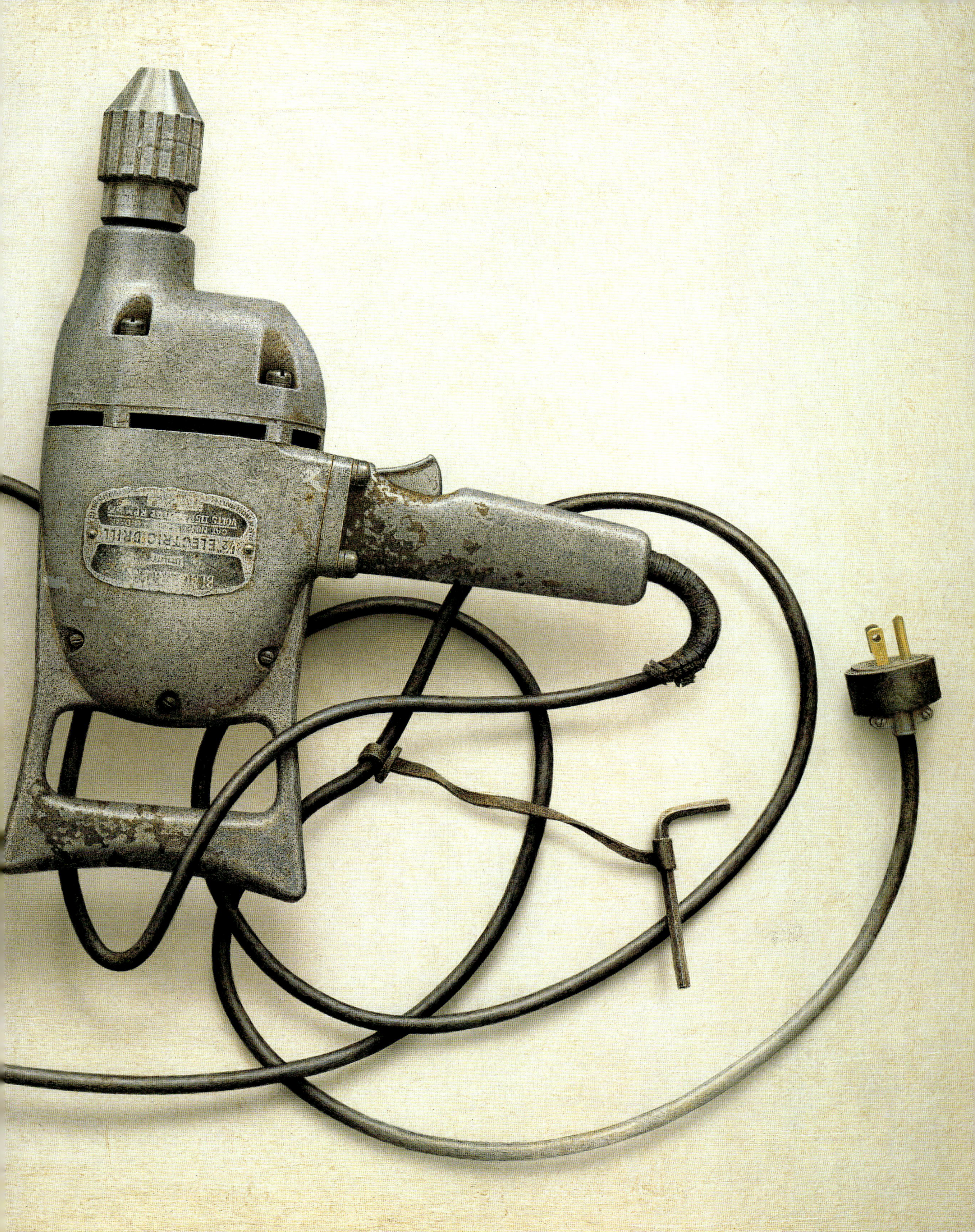
½" ELECTRIC DRILL
VOLTS 115

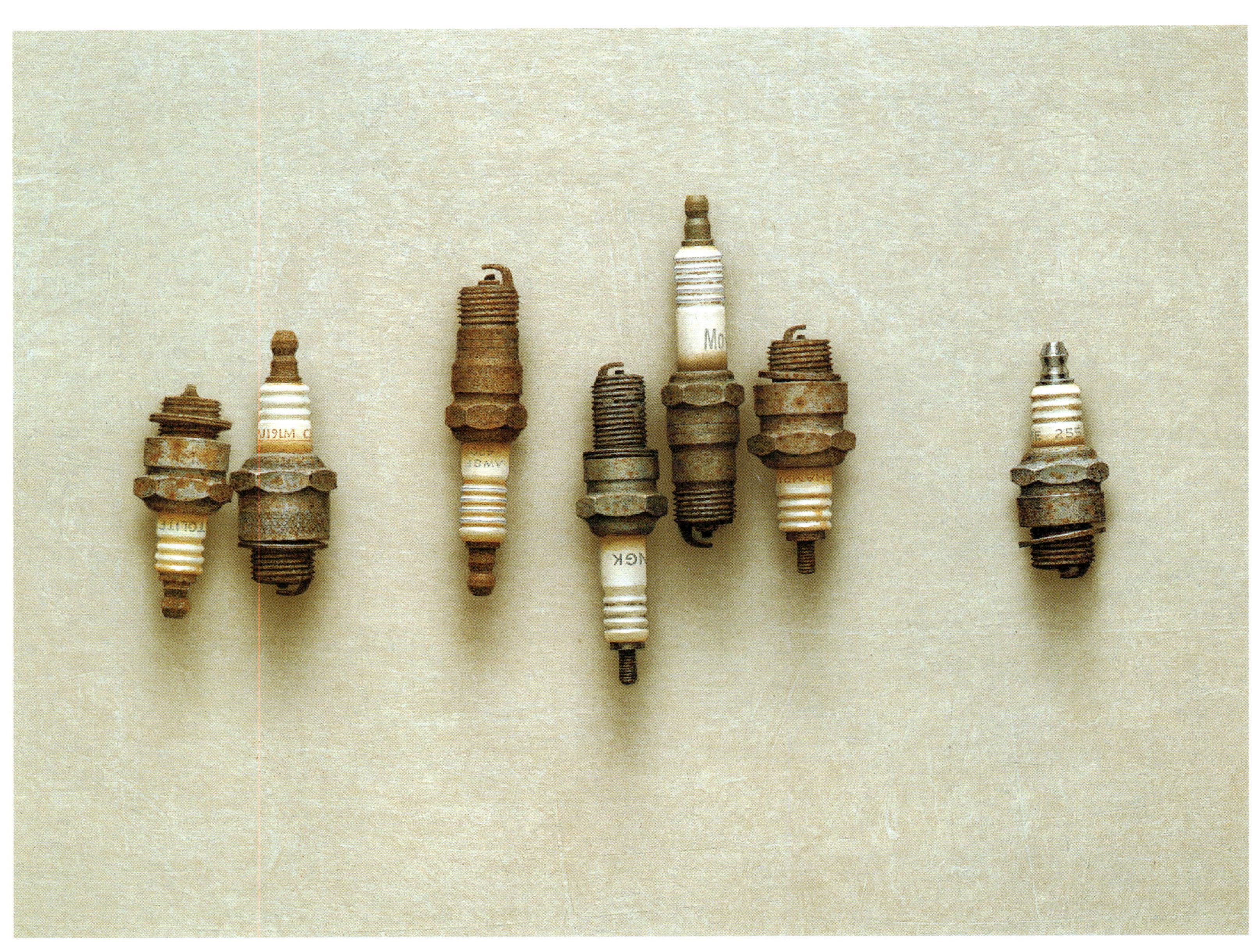

◁ *Artifact (detail)*, 1999, acrylic on panel, 24 x 30"
List II (detail), 1999, acrylic and oil on panel, 16 x 22"

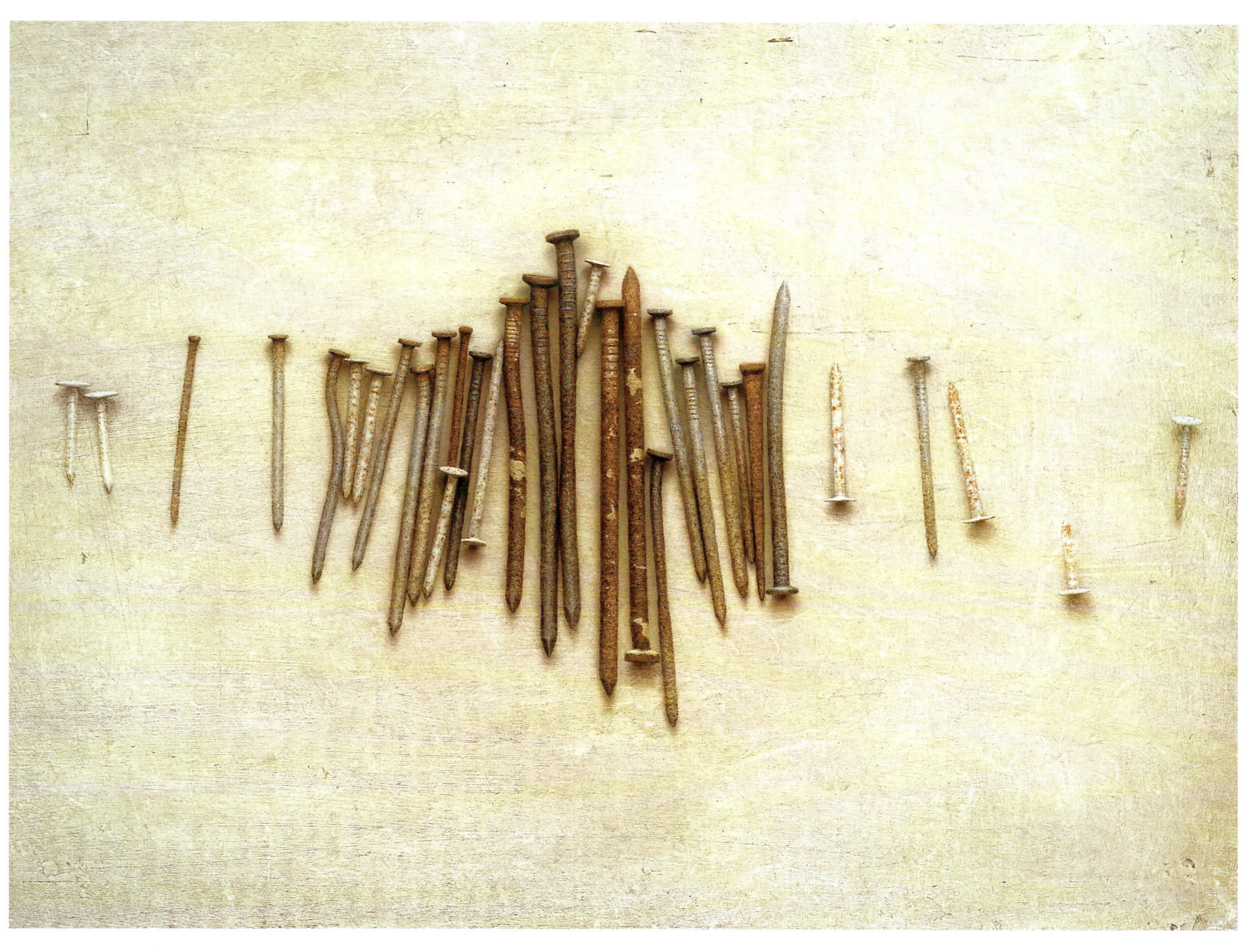

Nails (detail), 1997, oil on panel, 16 x 22"

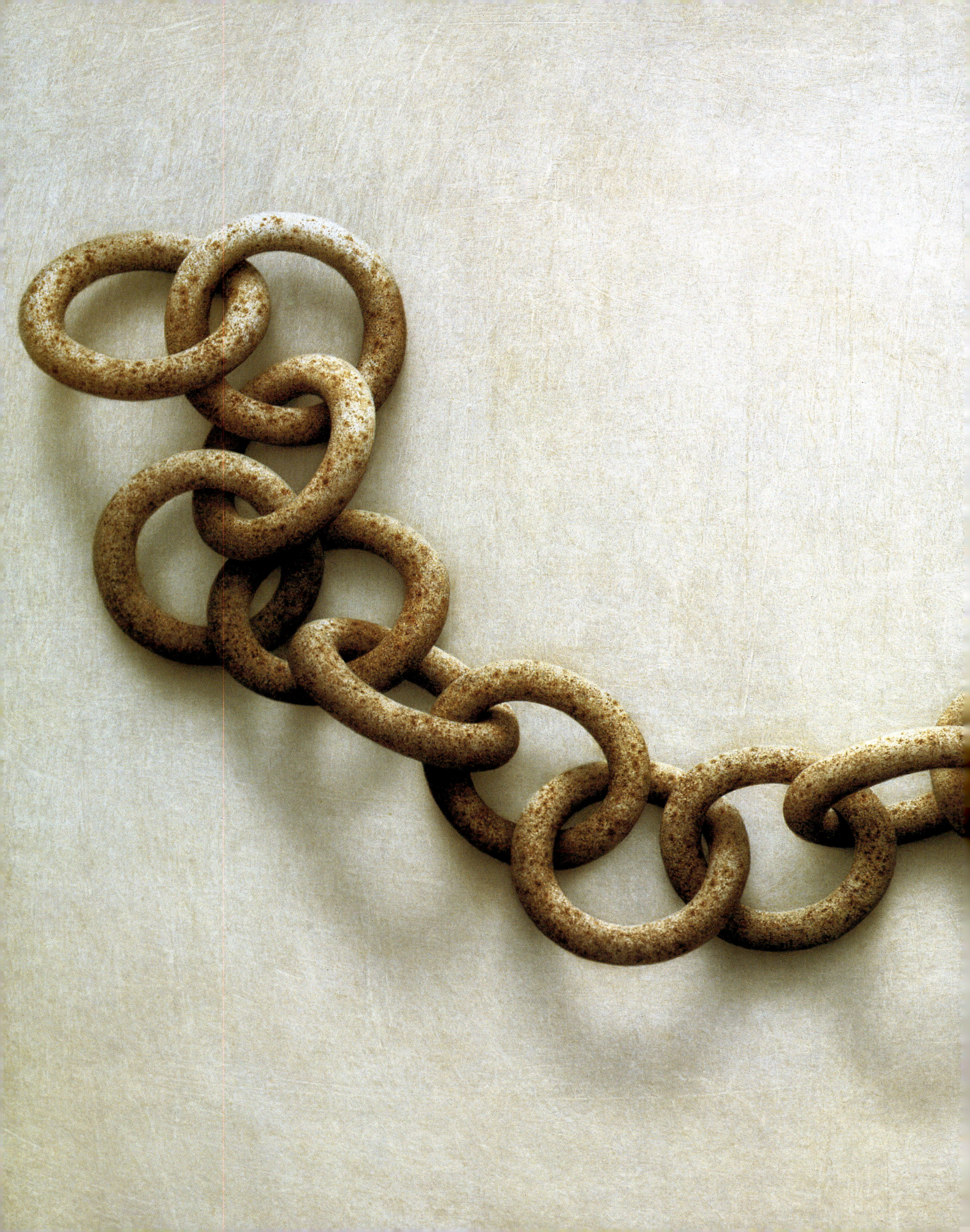

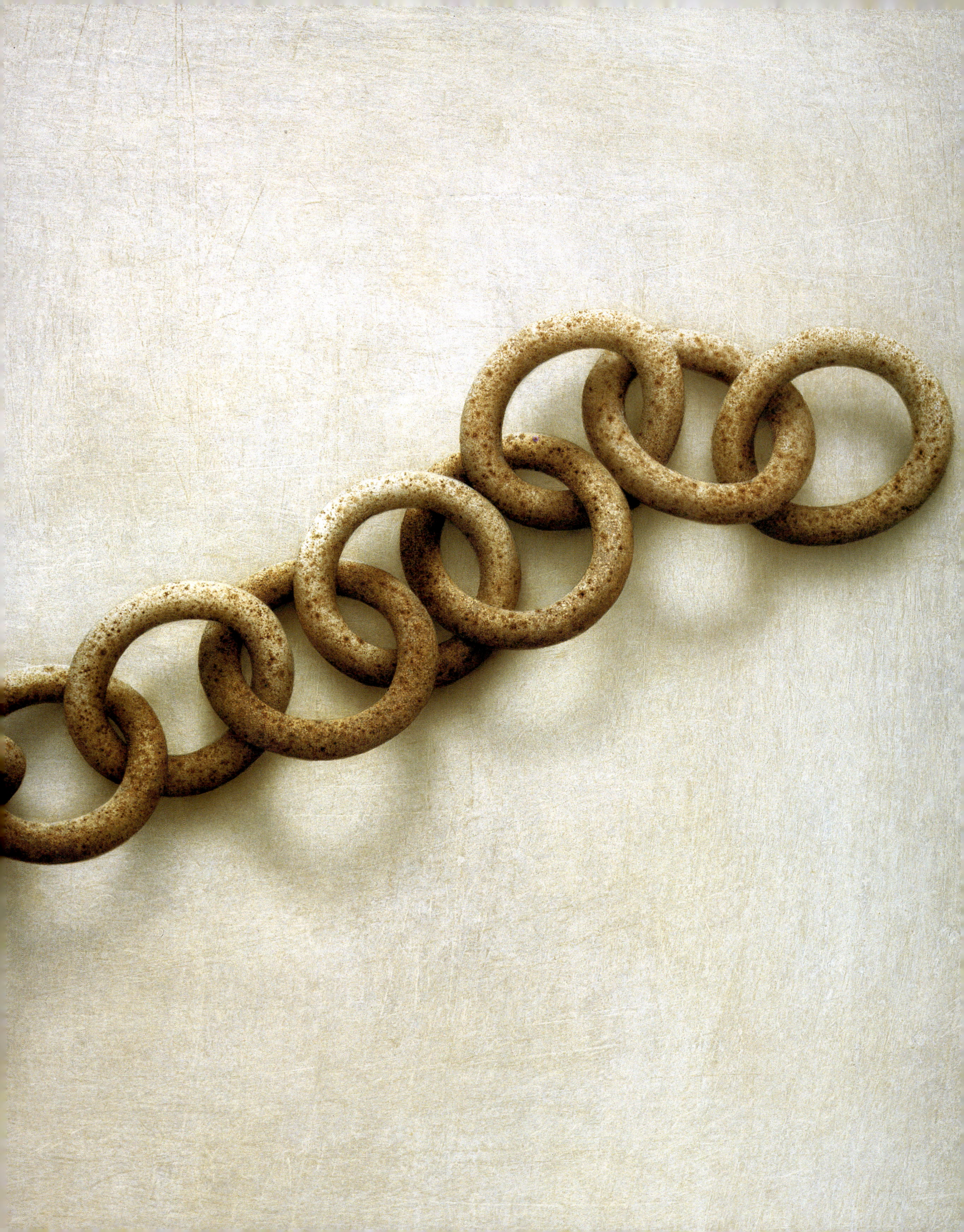

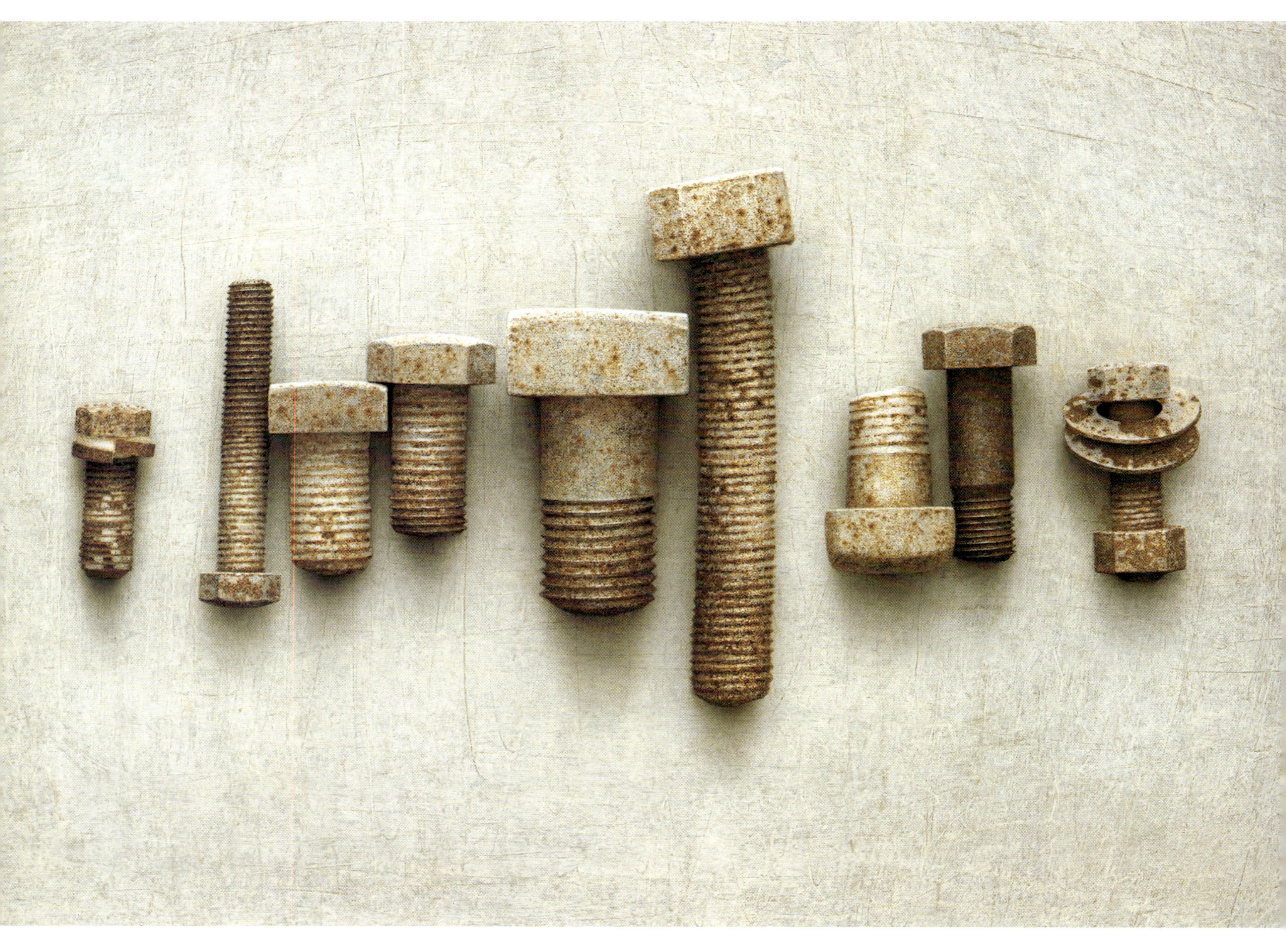

◁ *Catena (detail)*, 2000, acrylic on panel, 32 x 40"
Earthwork (detail), 2001, acrylic and oil on panel, 16 x 22"

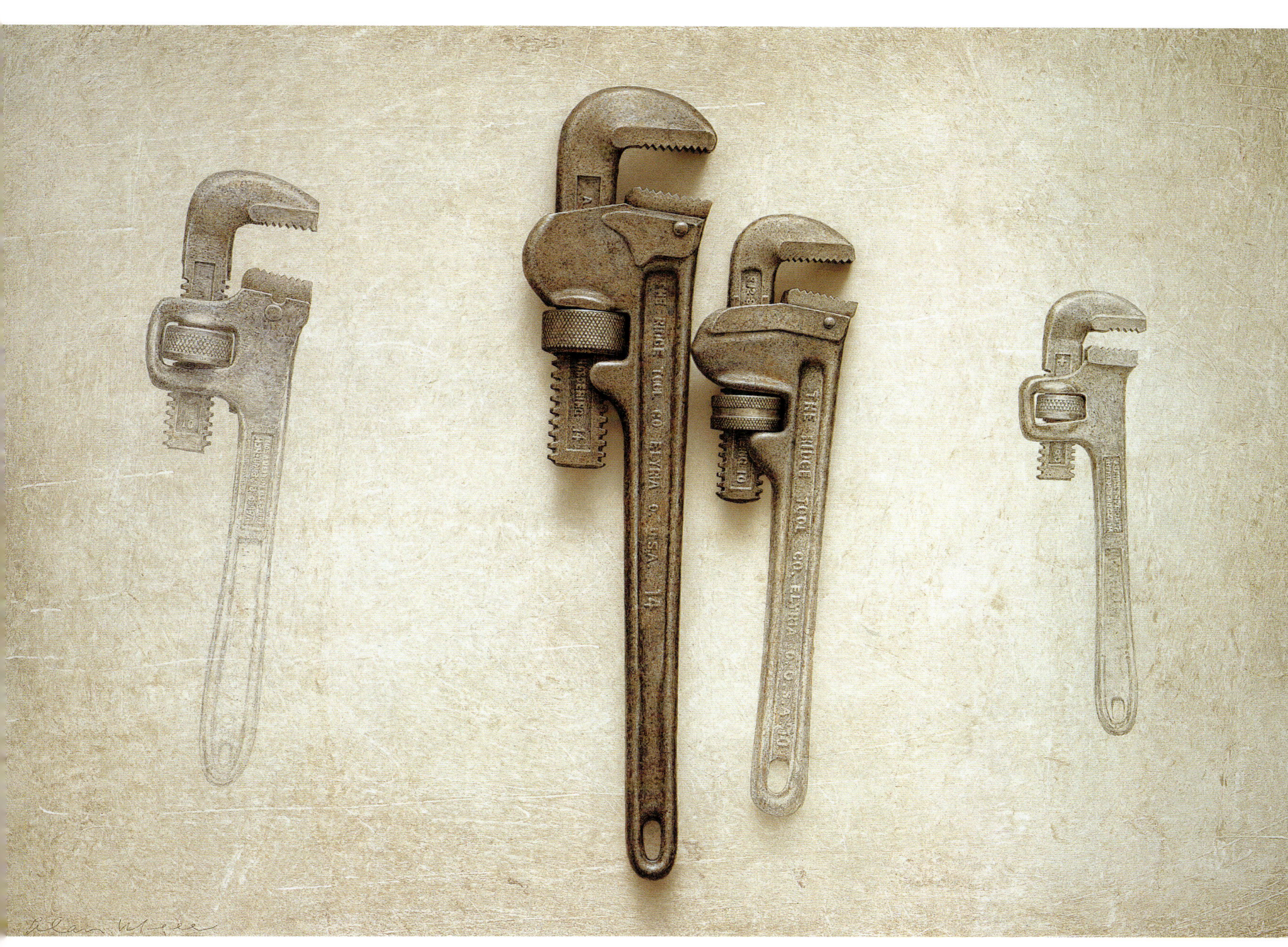

Natural History, 1997, acrylic and oil on panel, 16 x 22"

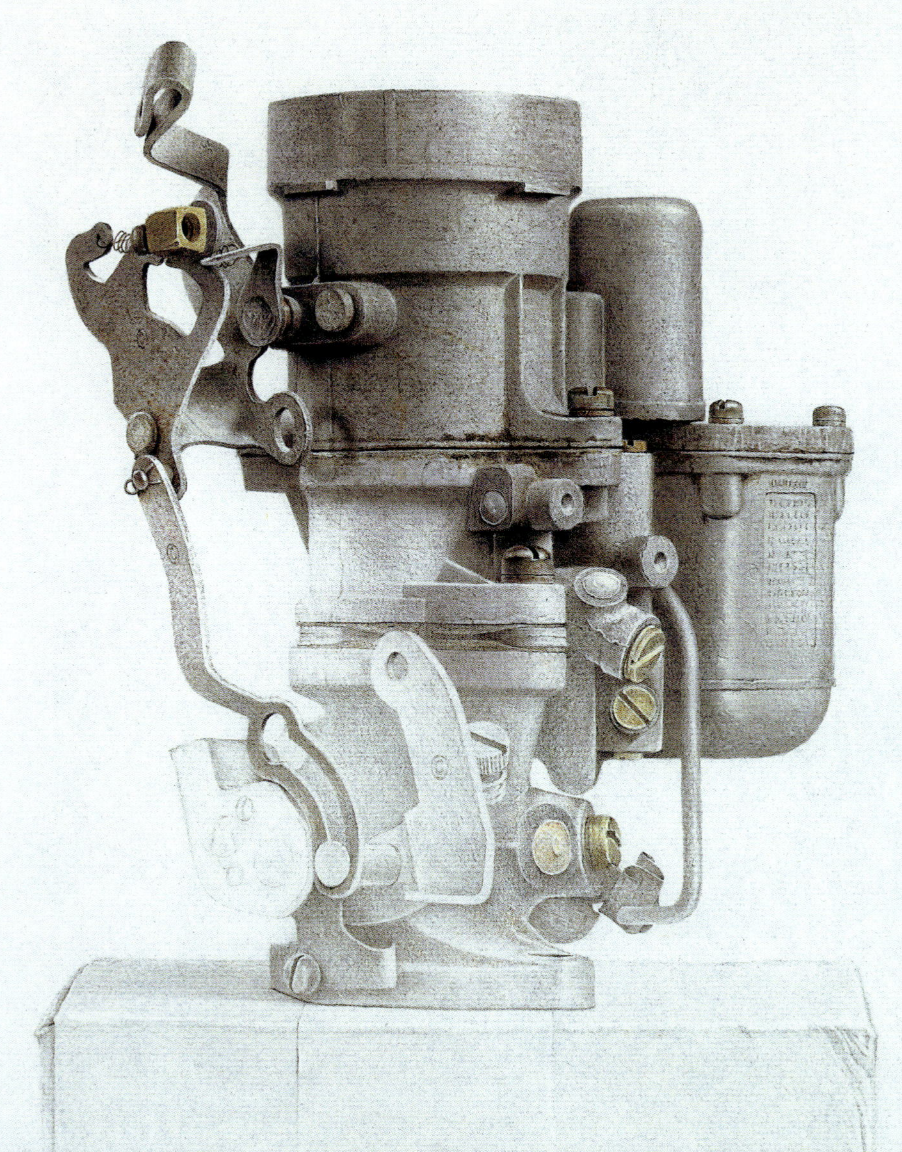

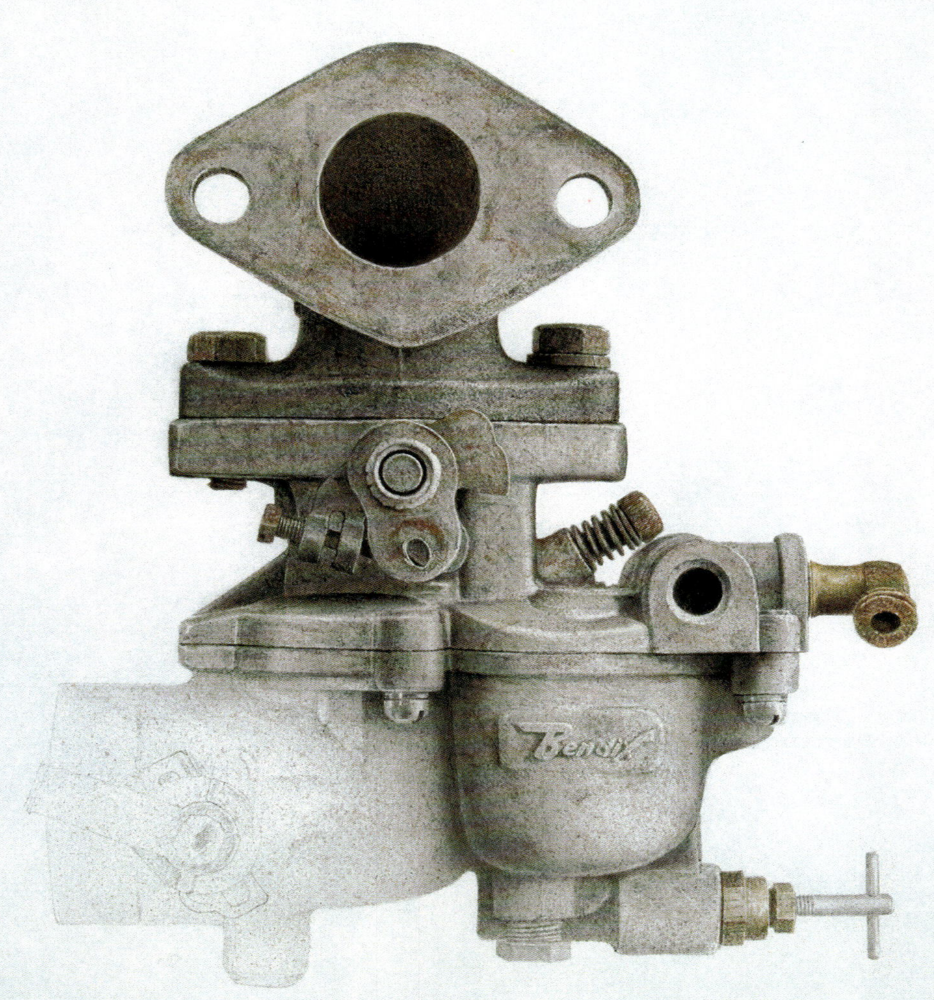
Bendix

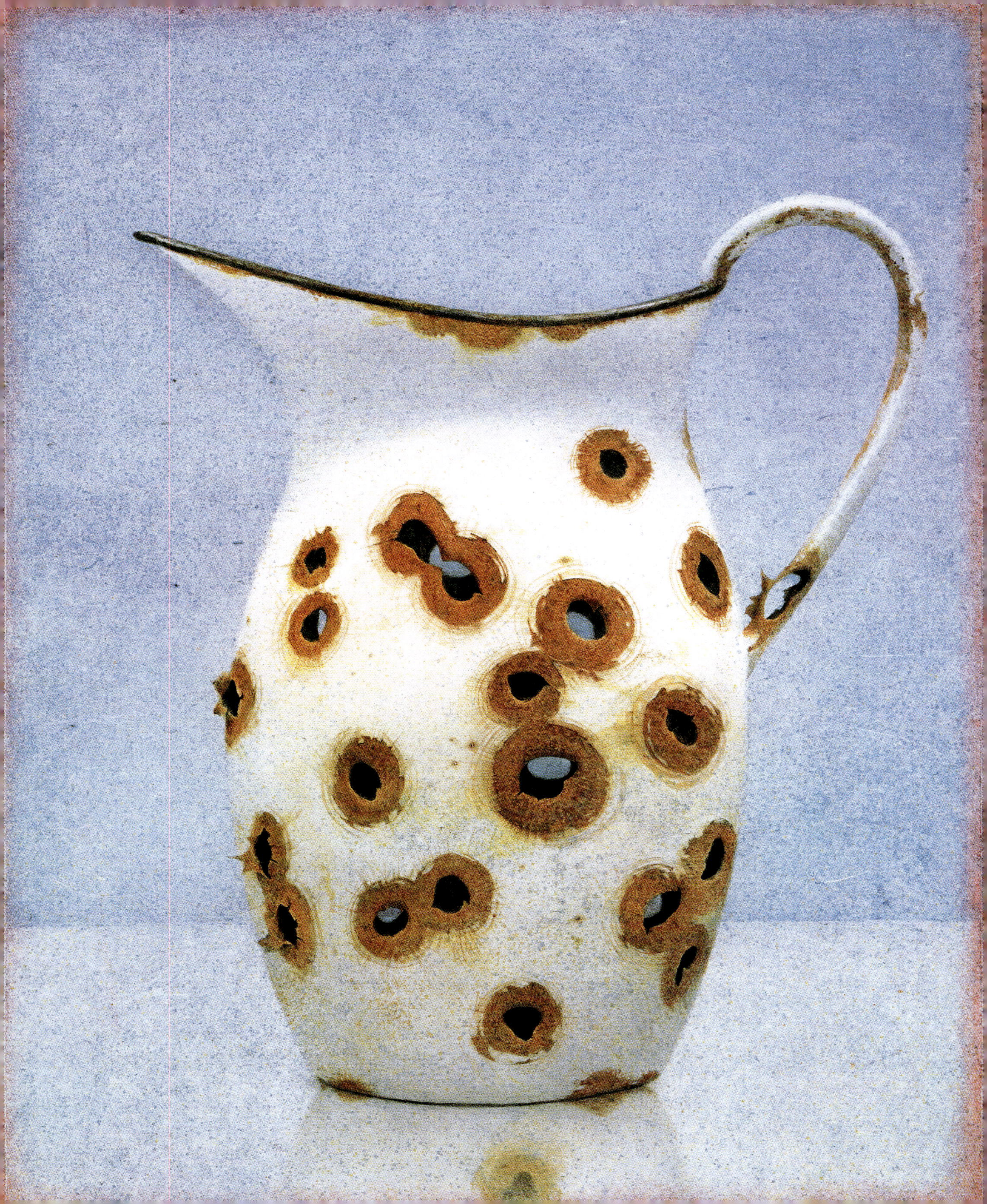

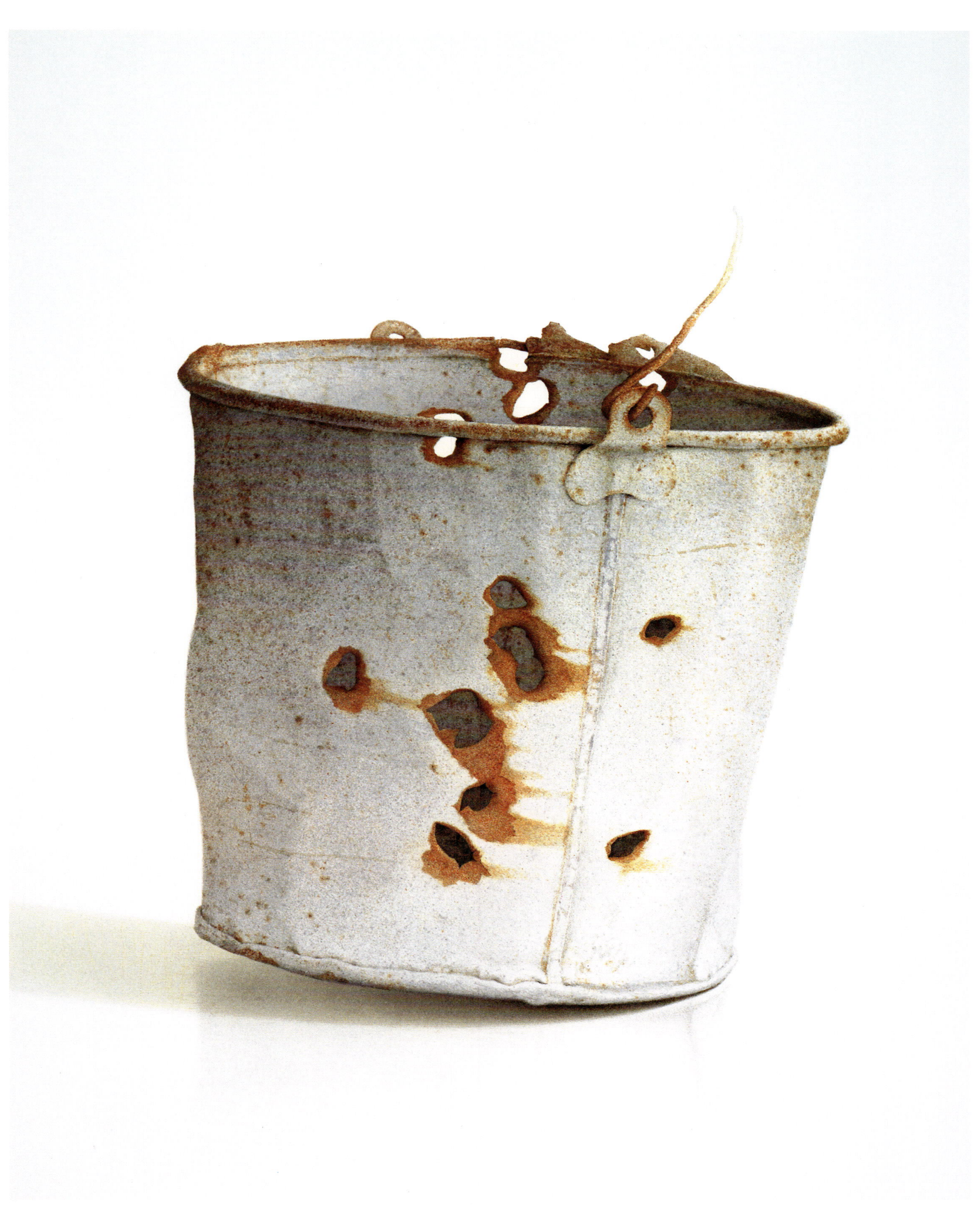

Gravitas (detail), 1995, watercolor on paper, 22 x 30"

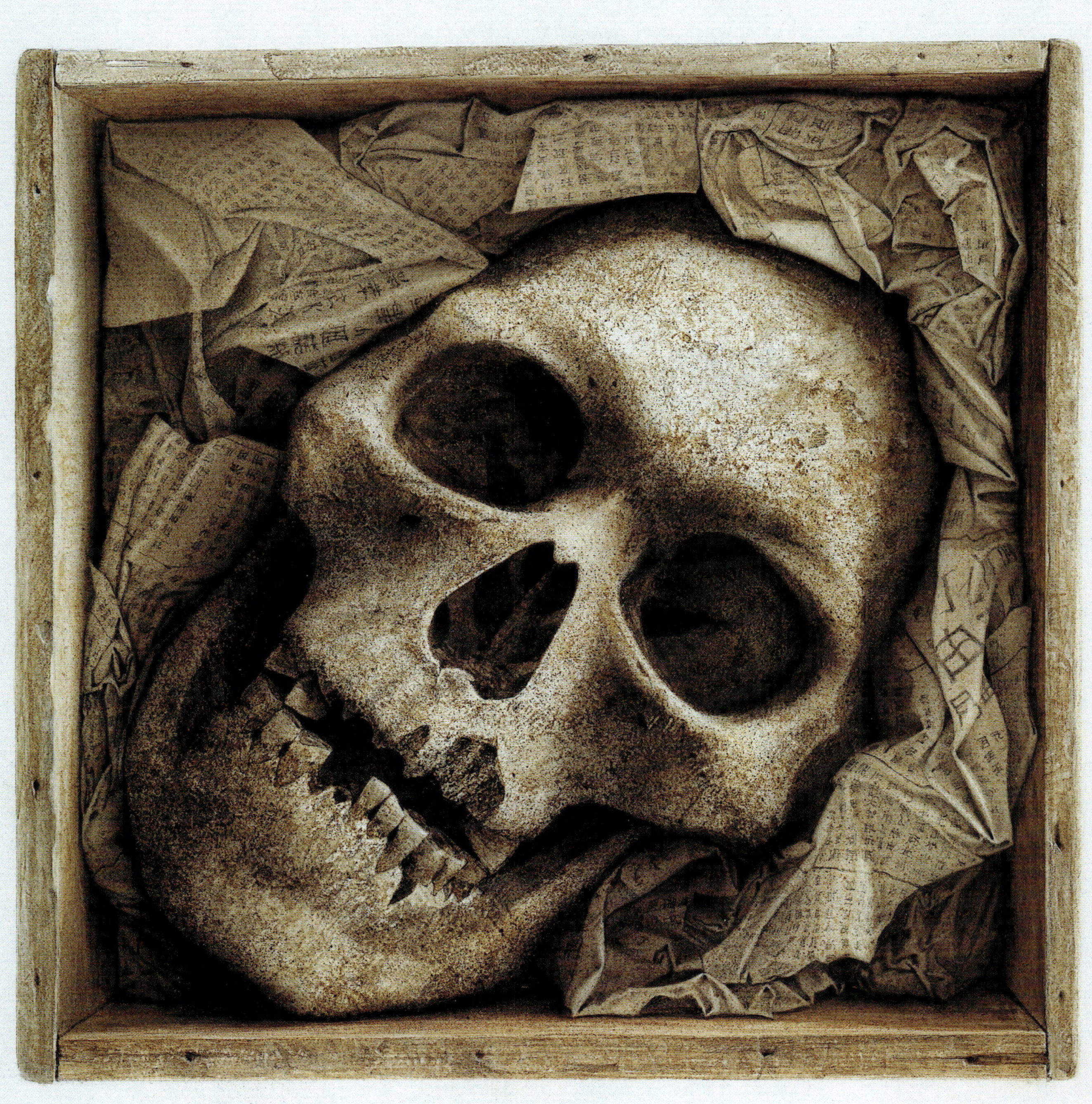

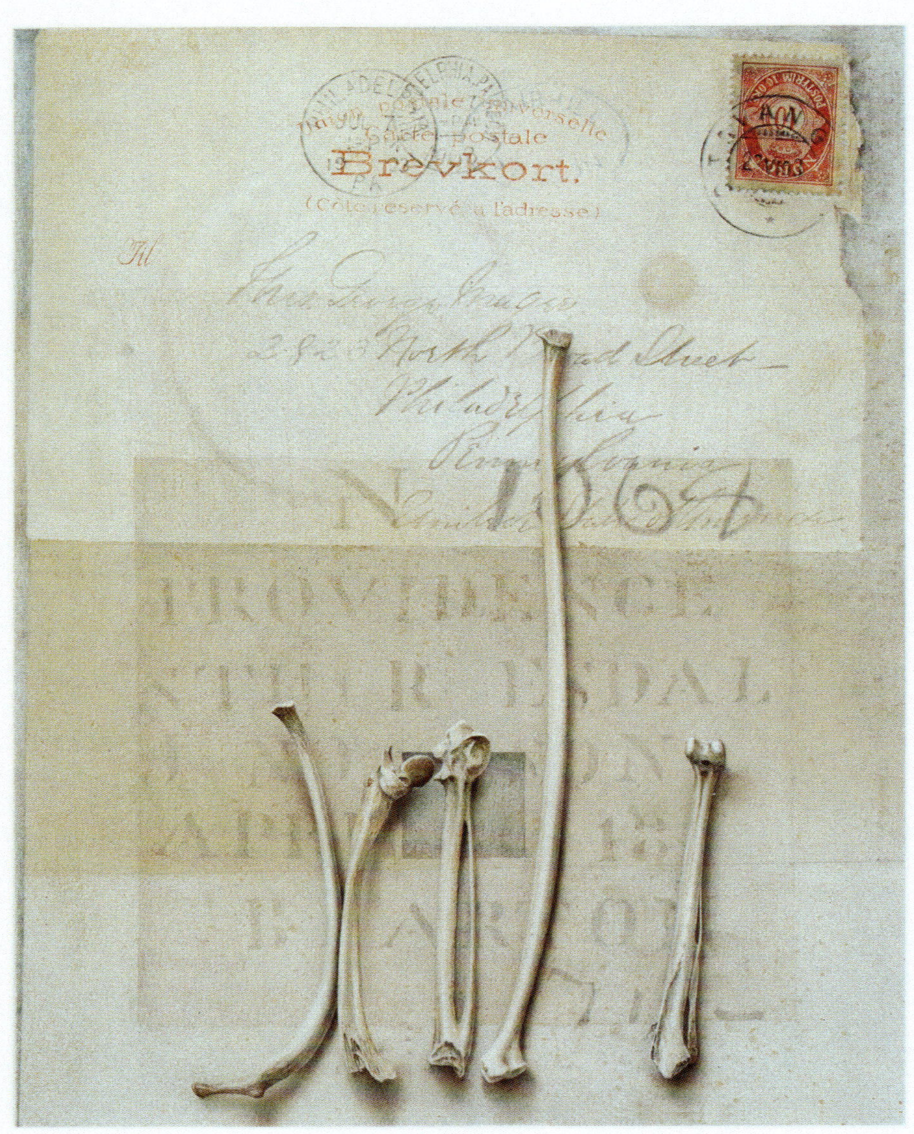

◁ *Gift (detail)*, 1983, watercolor on paper, 15 ¼ x 19"
Bones (detail), 1982, watercolor and colored pencil on paper, 15 ½ x 19"

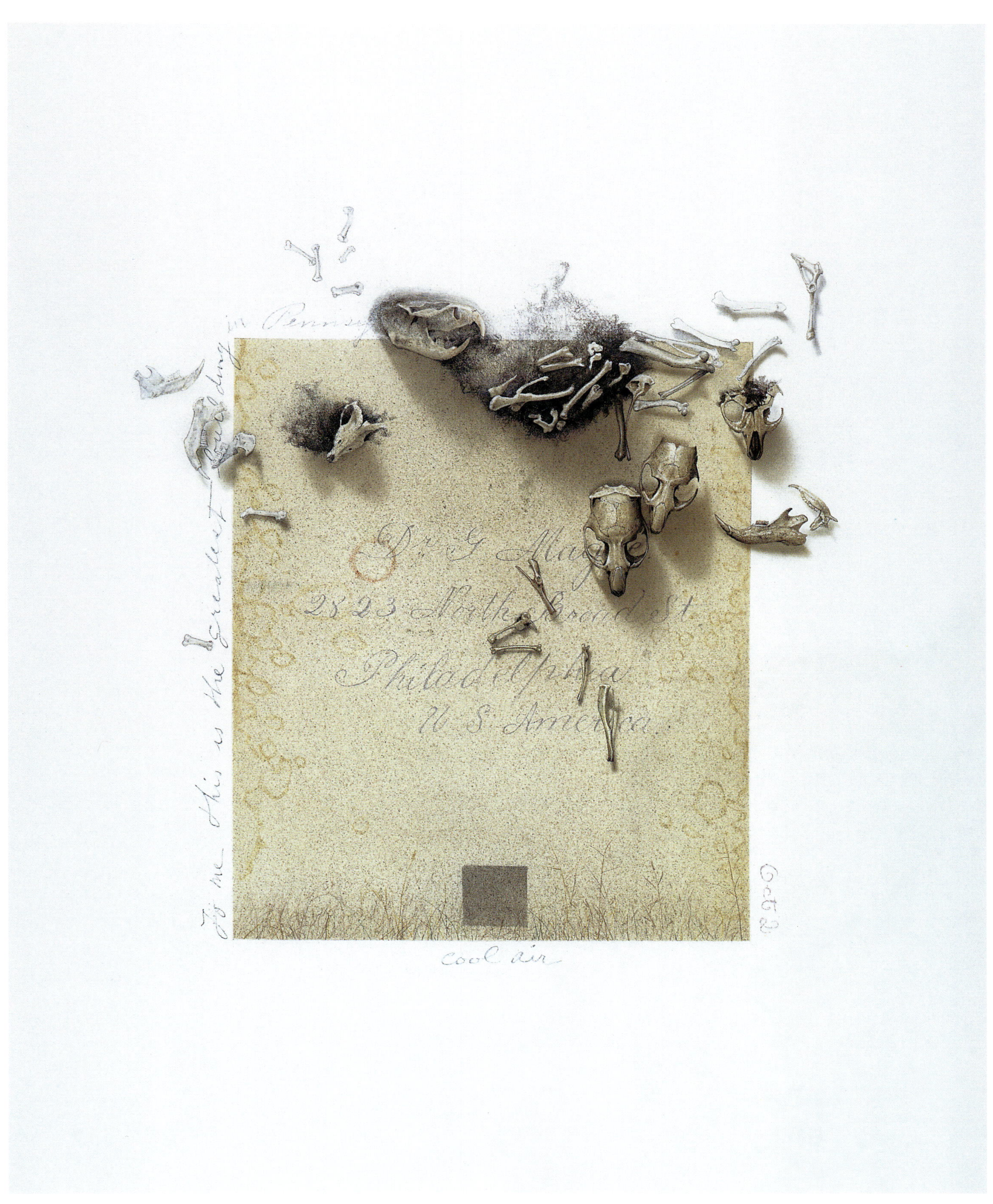

Cool Air, 1983, watercolor and colored pencil on paper, 18 ½ x 14"

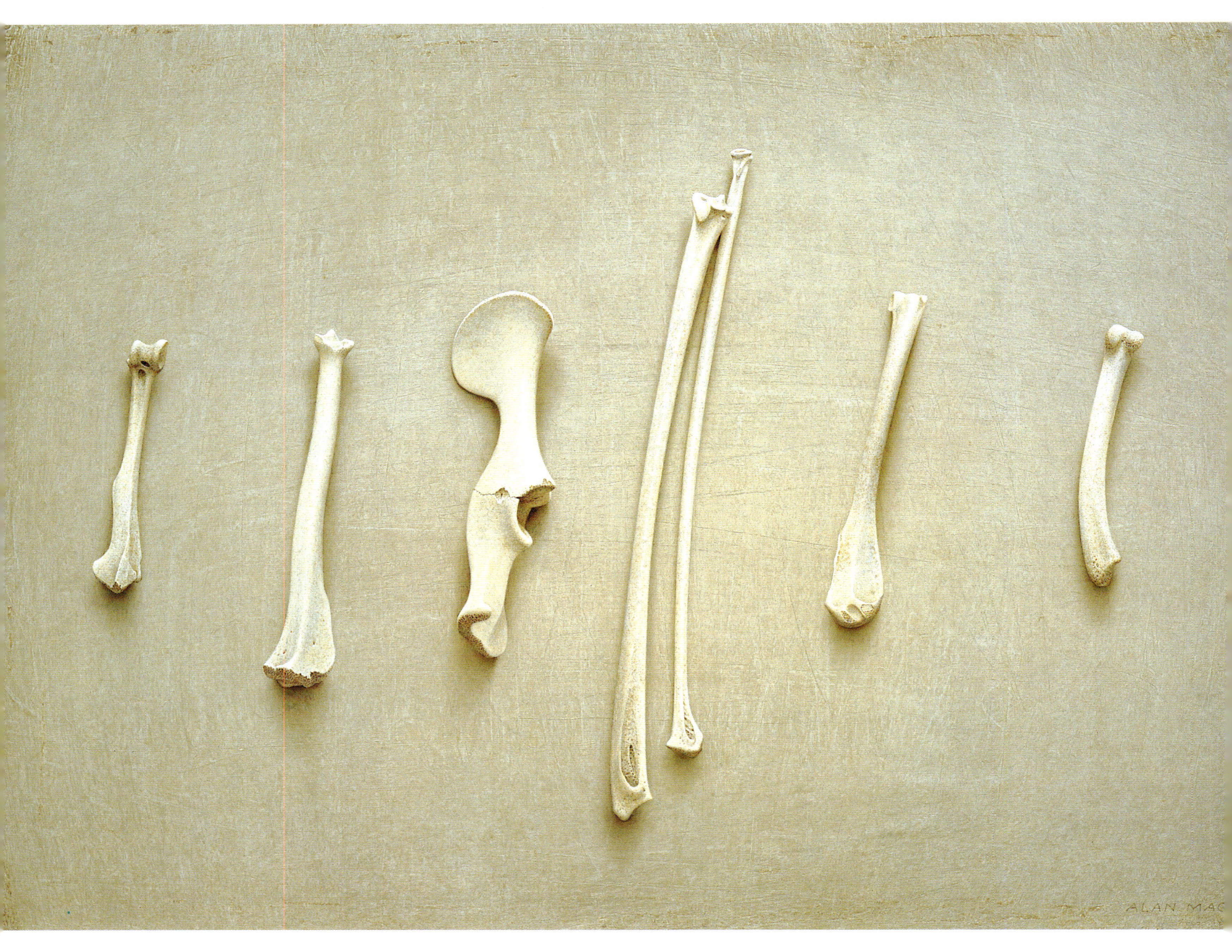

Still Life, 2001, acrylic and oil on panel, 16 x 22"

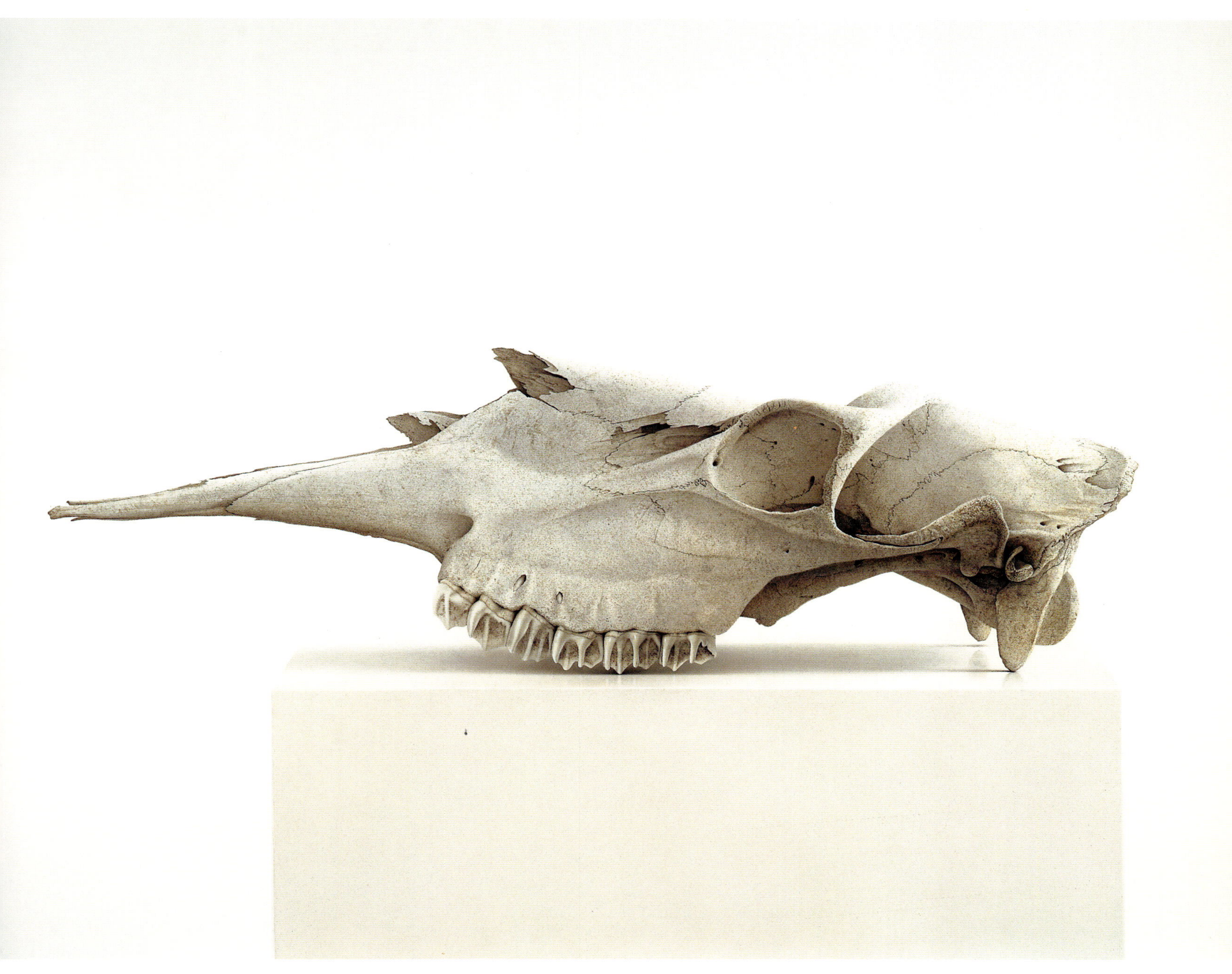

Mooseskull, 1986, watercolor on paper, 22 x 30"

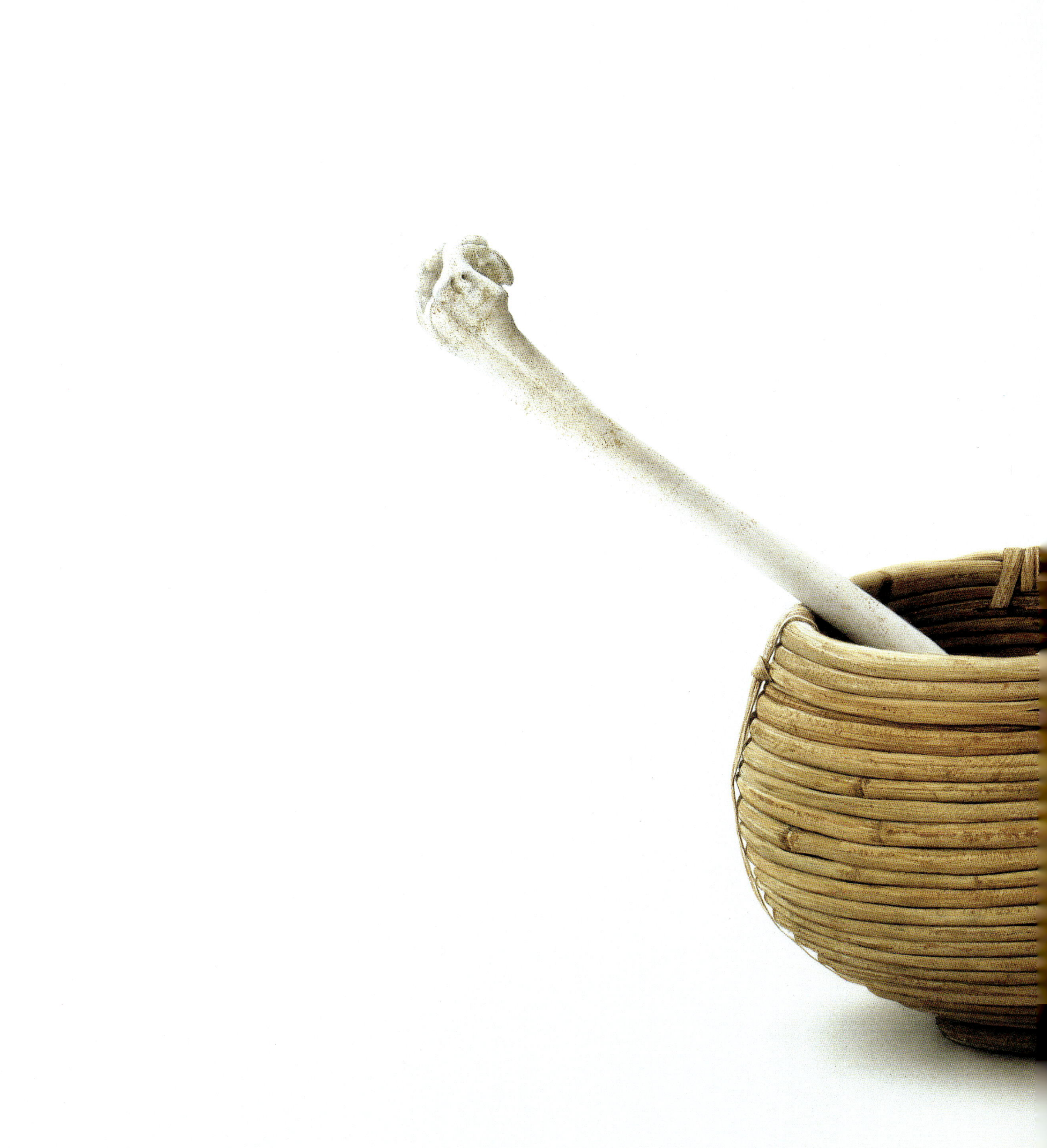

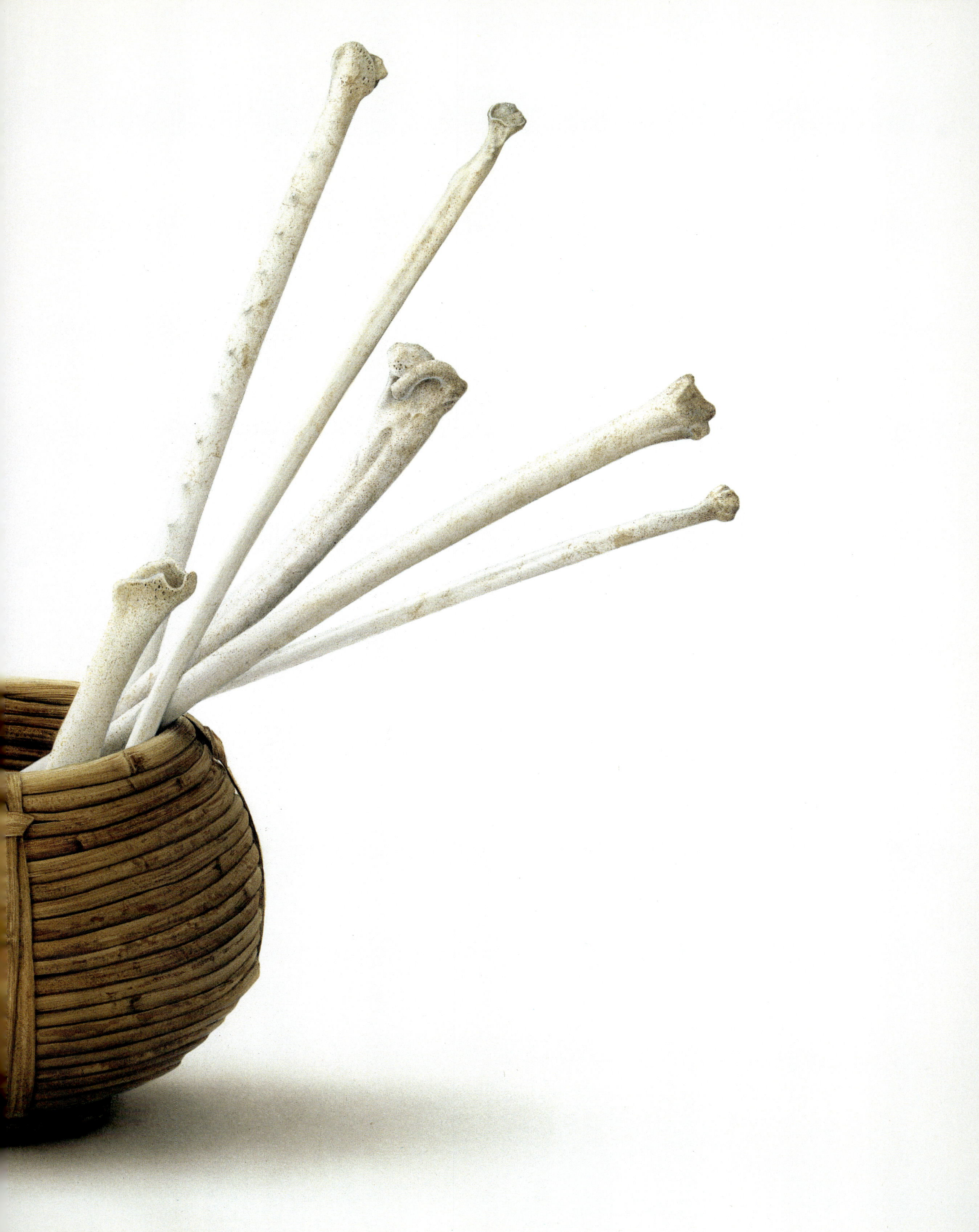

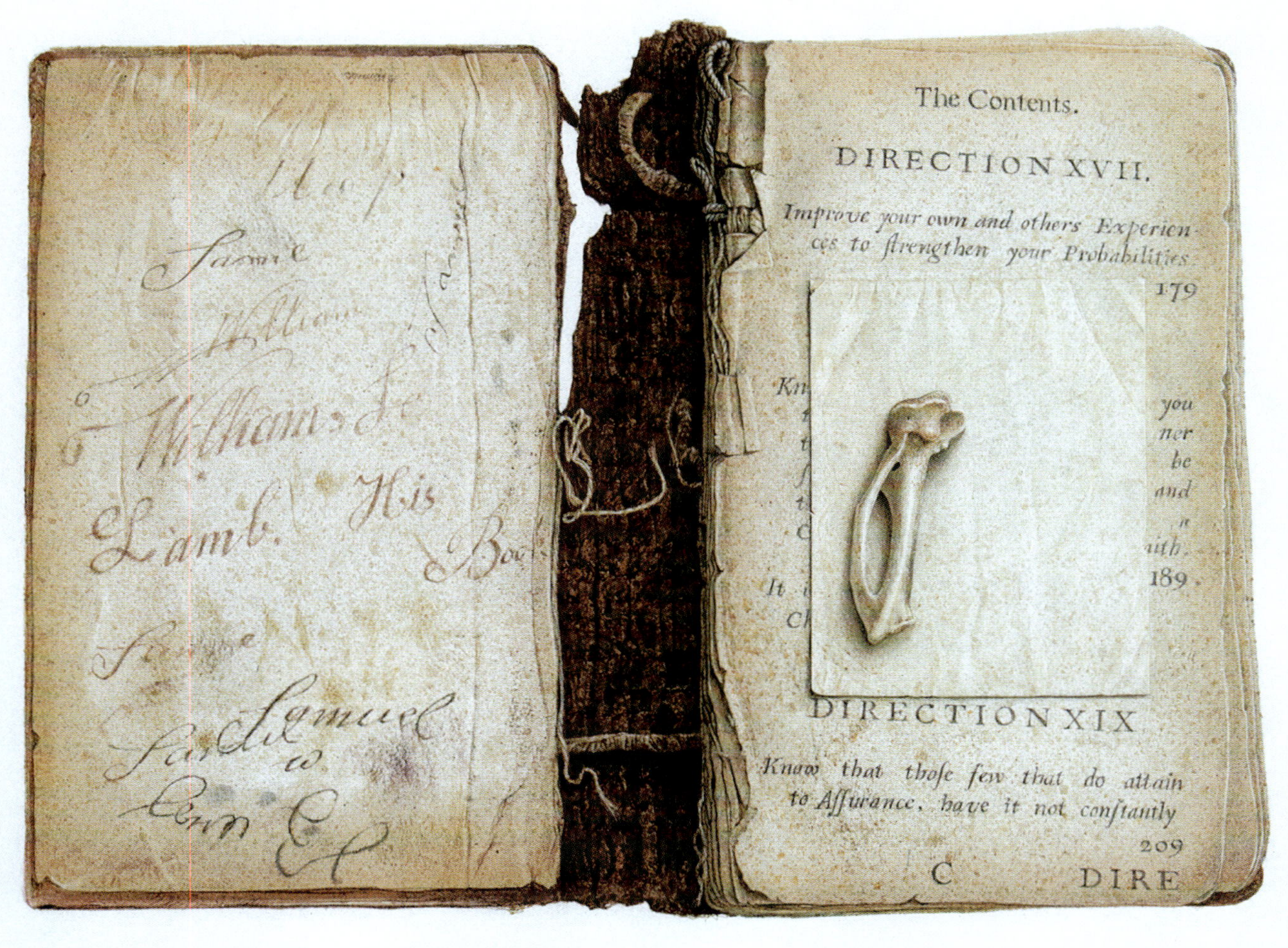

The Contents.
DIRECTION XVII.
Improve your own and others Experien-
ces to strengthen your Probabilities
179
189
DIRECTION XIX
Know that those few that do attain
to Assurance, have it not constantly
209
C
DIRE
William
Lamb. His
Samuel

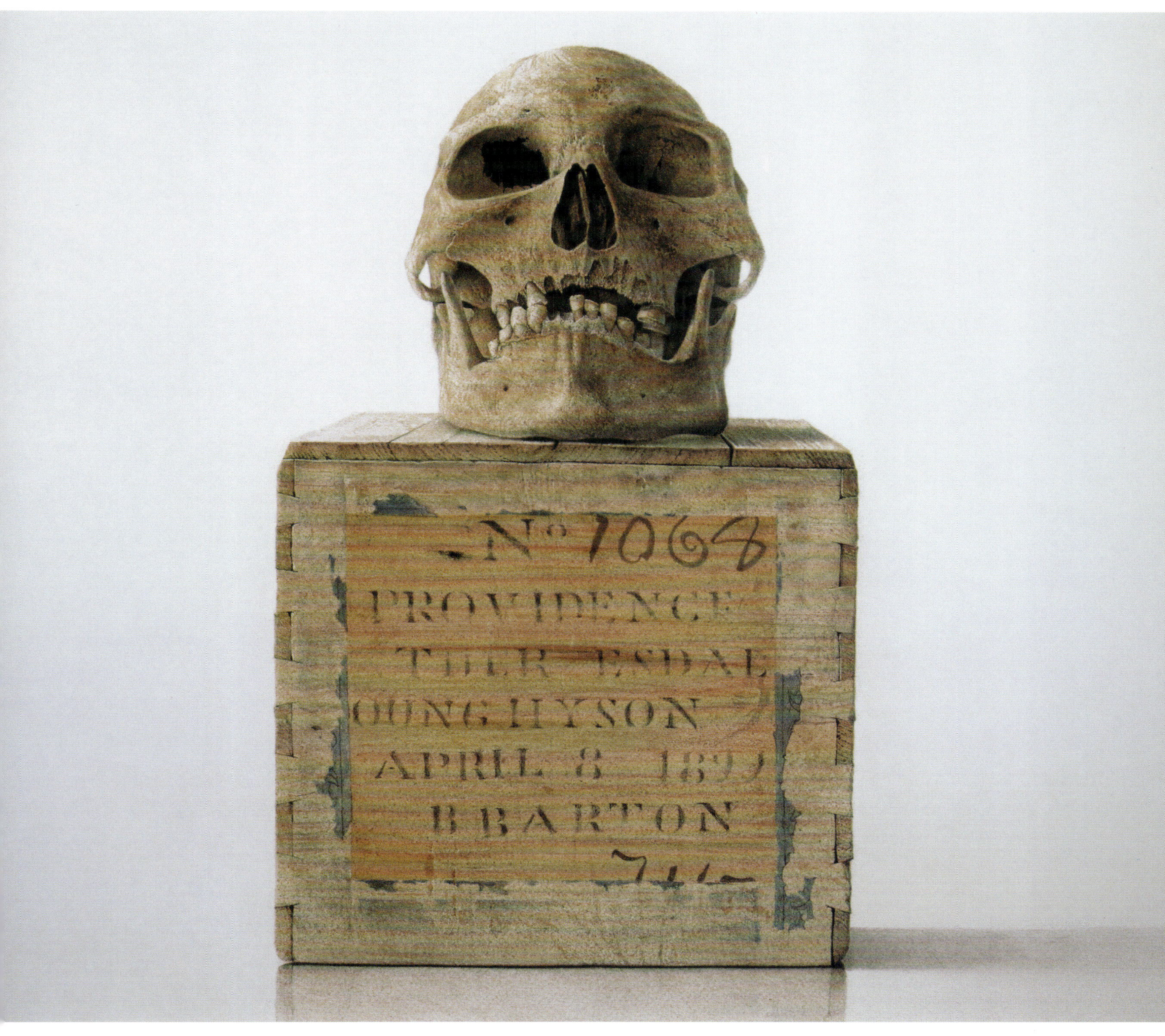

Skull, 1982, watercolor and colored pencil on paper, 18 x 22"

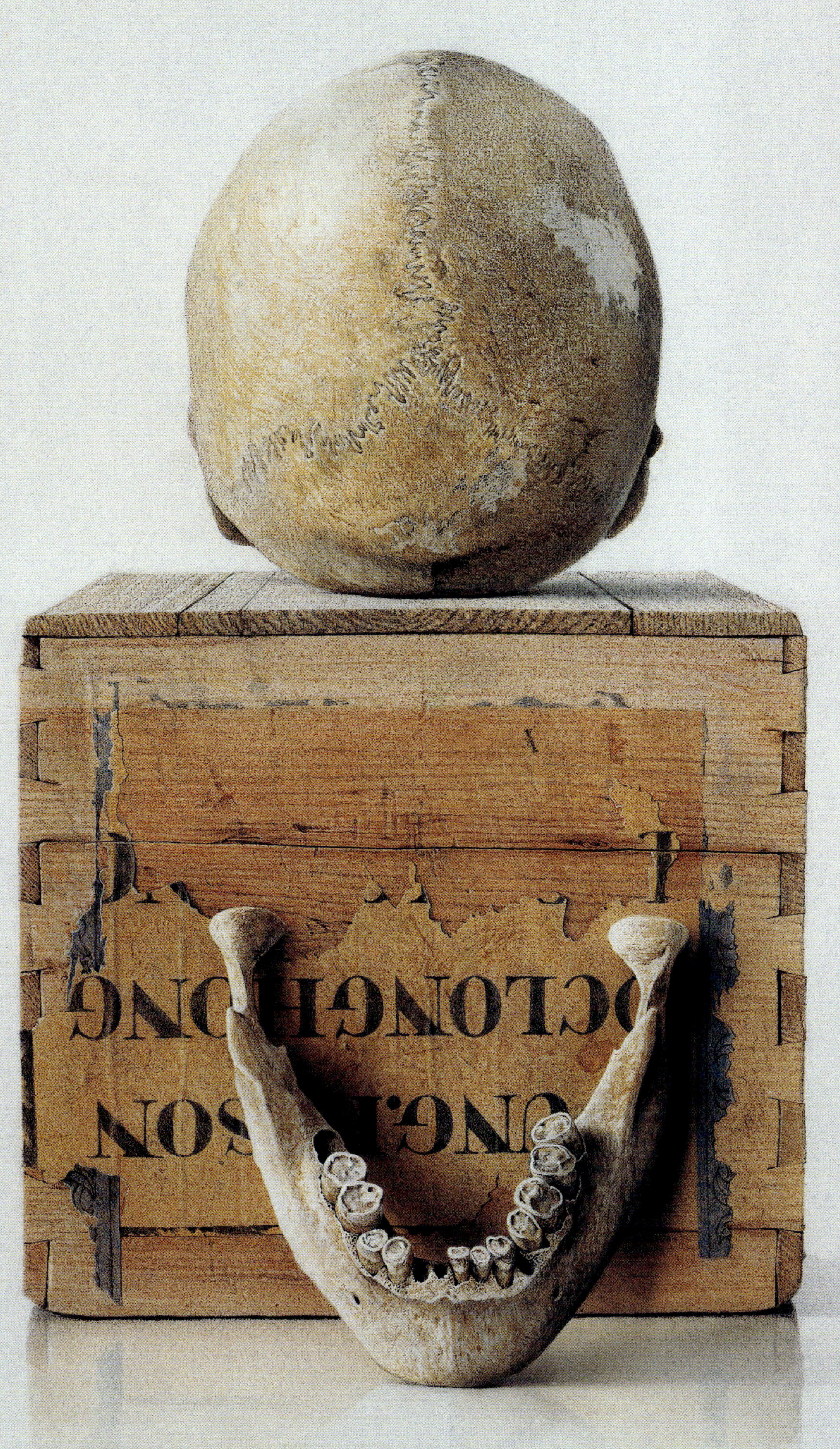

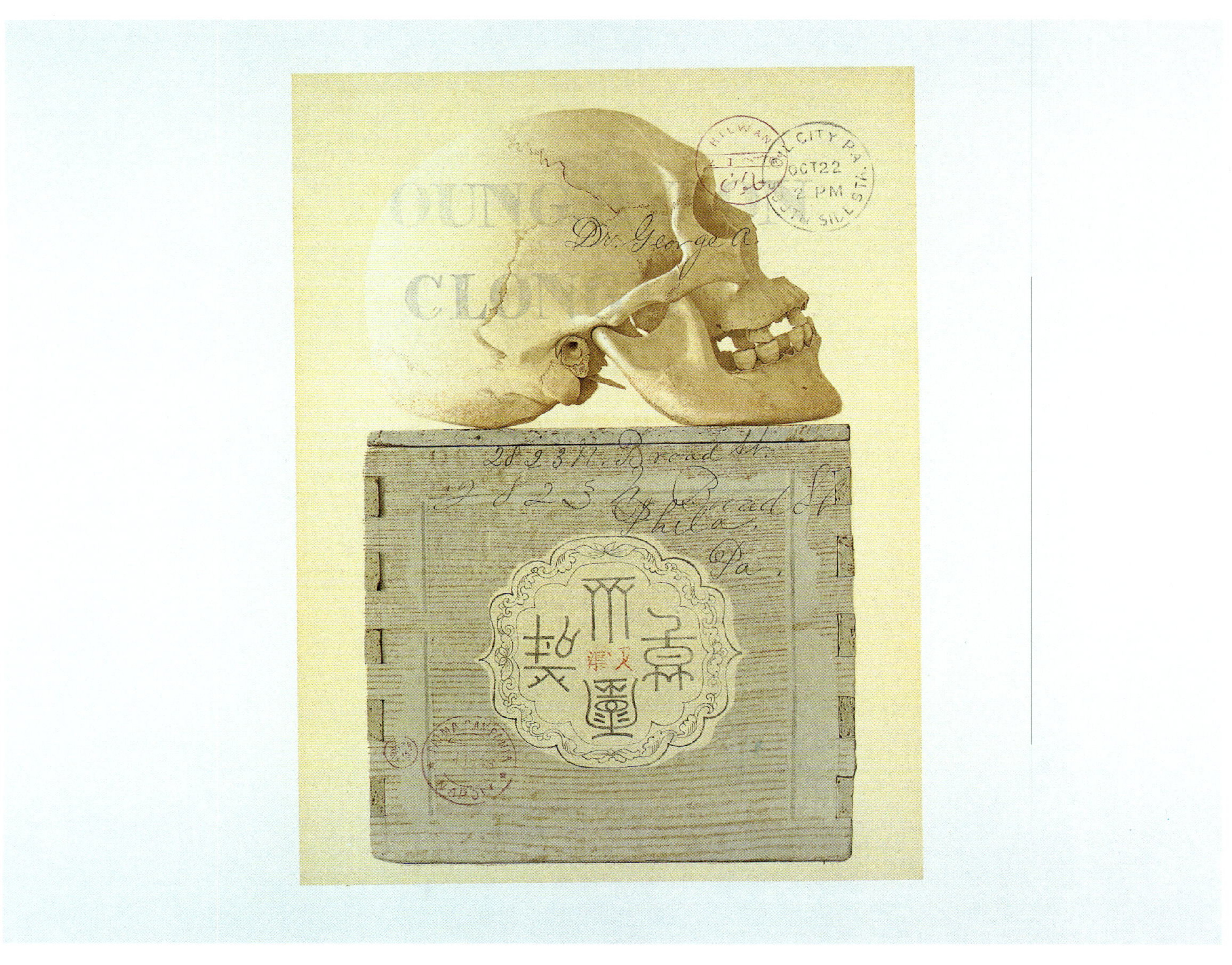

◁ *The Tea Box (detail)*, 1982, watercolor and colored pencil on paper, 18 x 22"
Collected Letters, 1984, ten-color lithograph, 18 x 22"

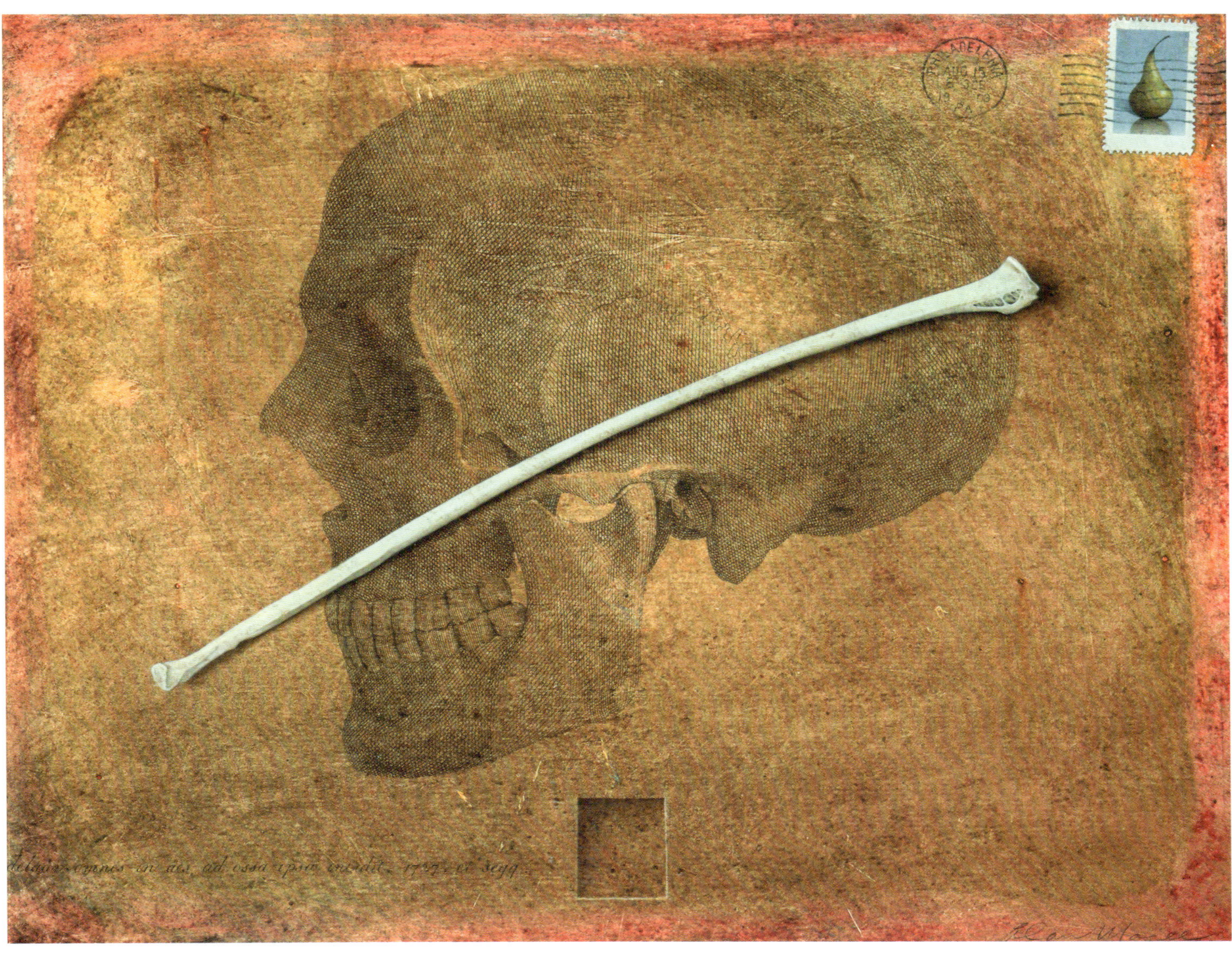

The Anatomist's Notebook, 1986, acrylic and watercolor over monotype, 11 x 14"

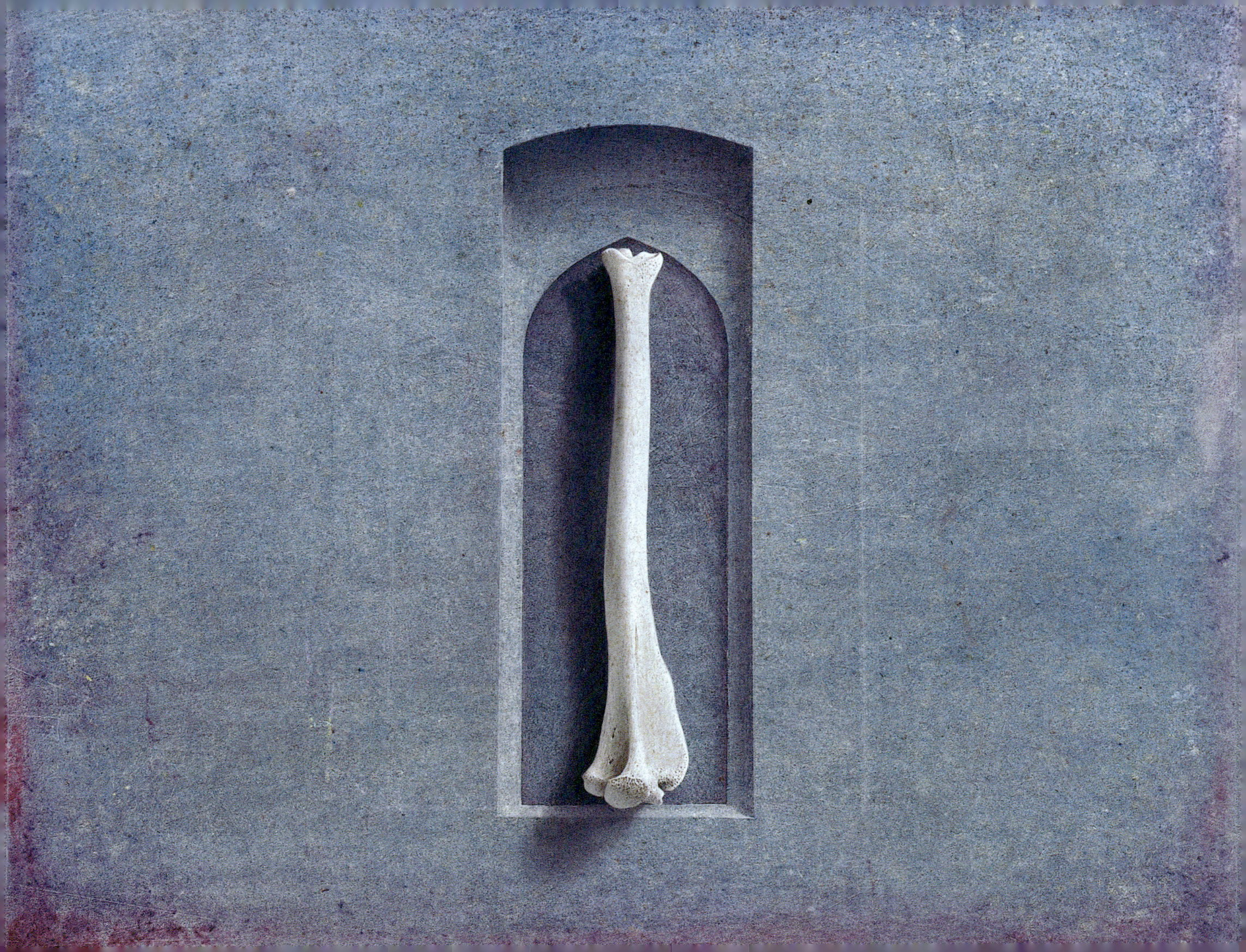

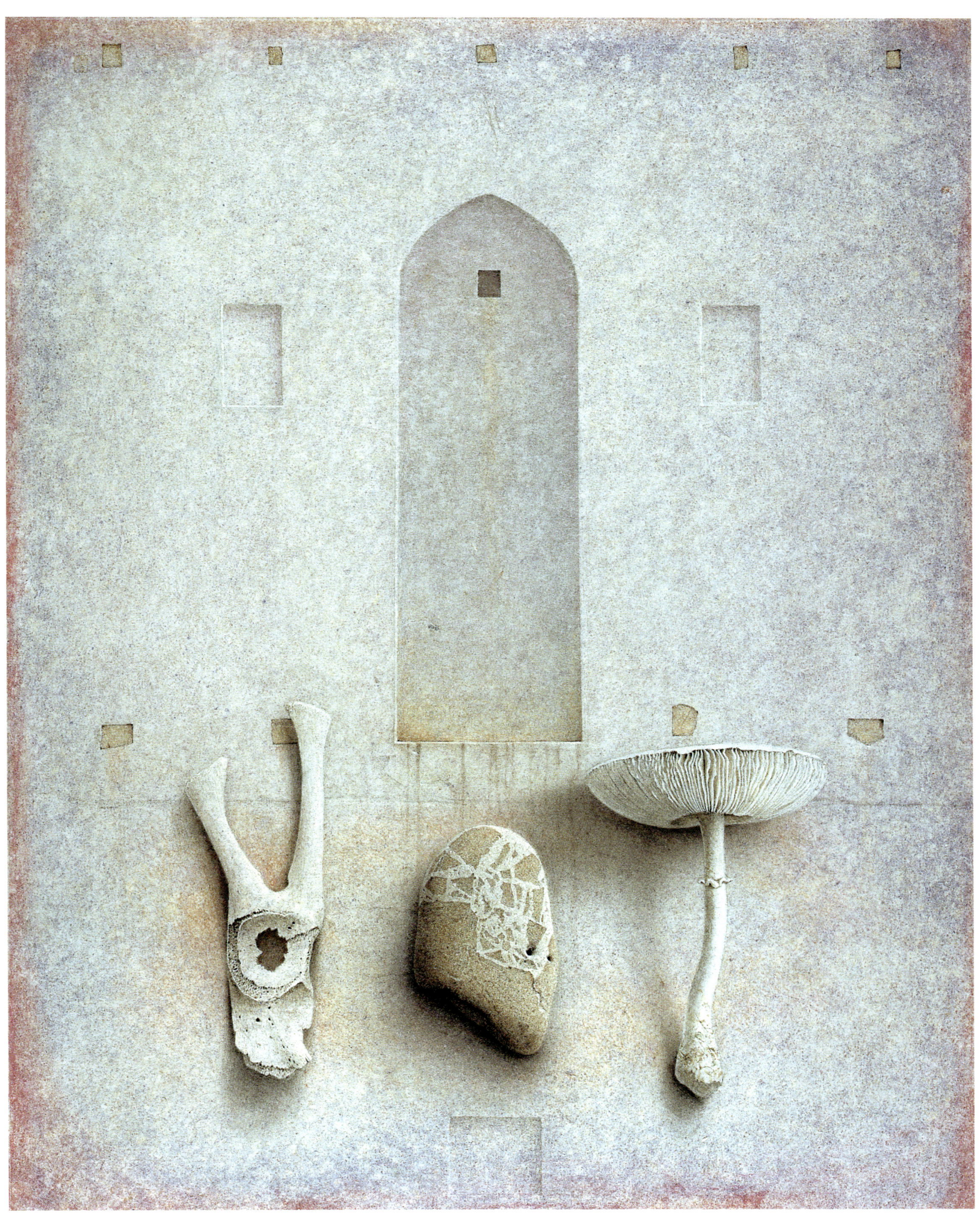

A First Seminary, 1986, acrylic and watercolor over monotype, 14 x 11"

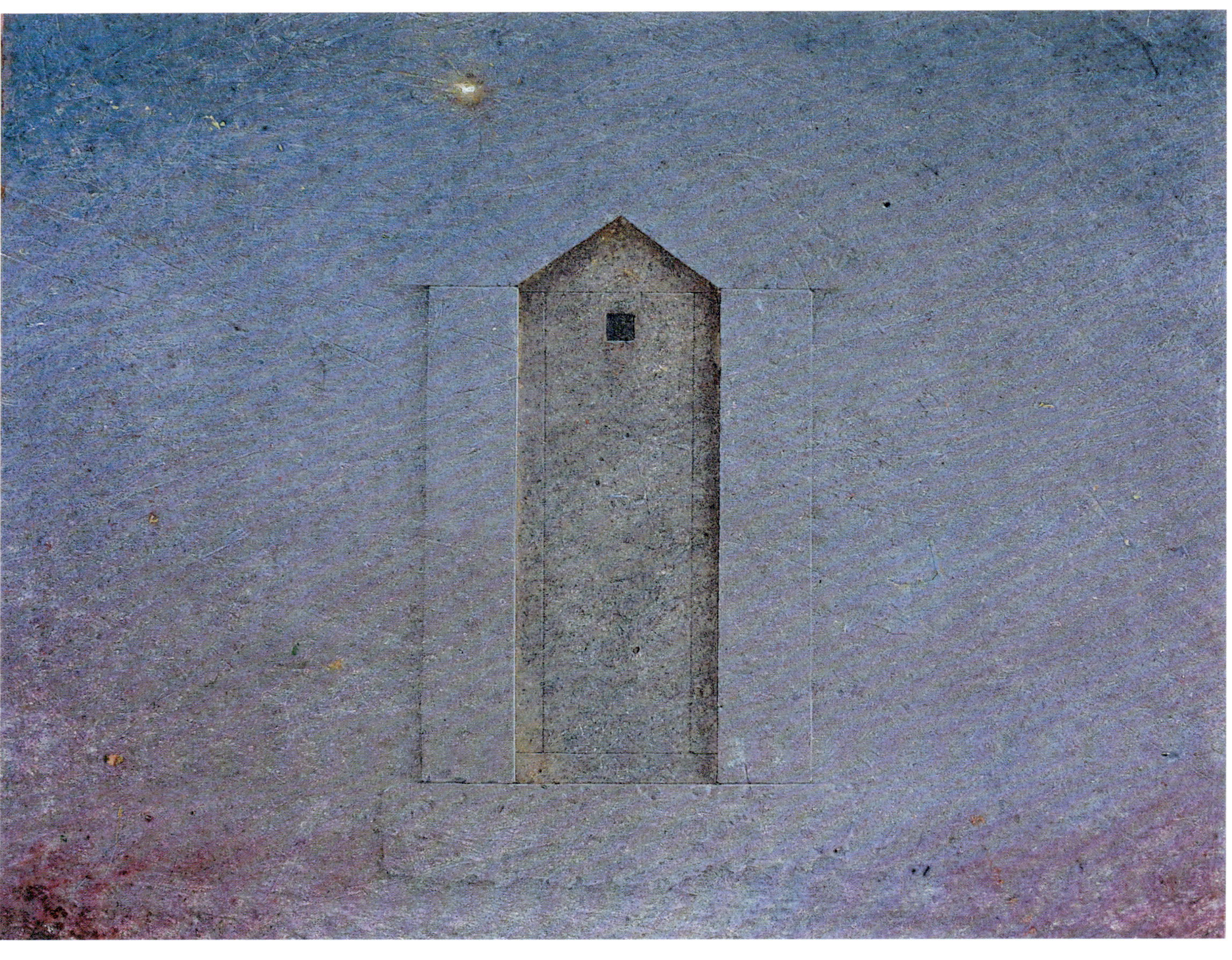

Inlet, 1985, monotype, 8 x 10"

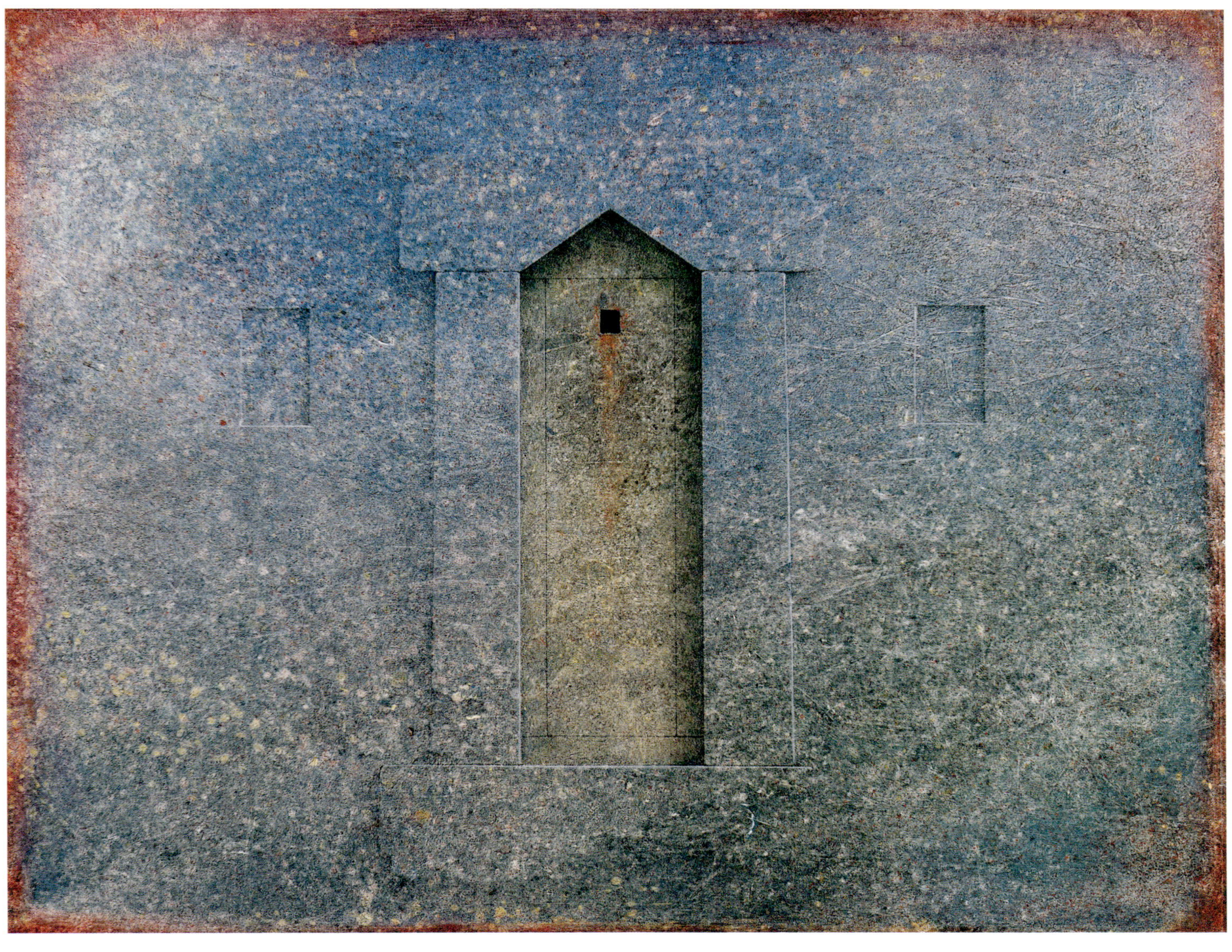

Inlet II, 1985, monotype, 14 x 11"

MONTAGE AND SCULPTURE

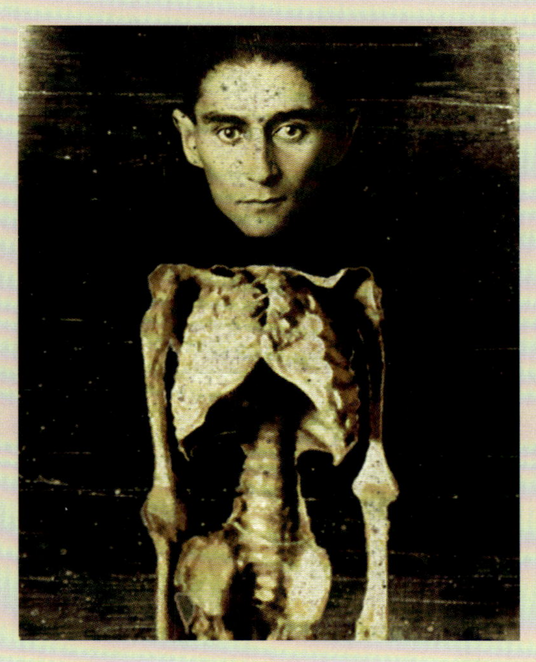

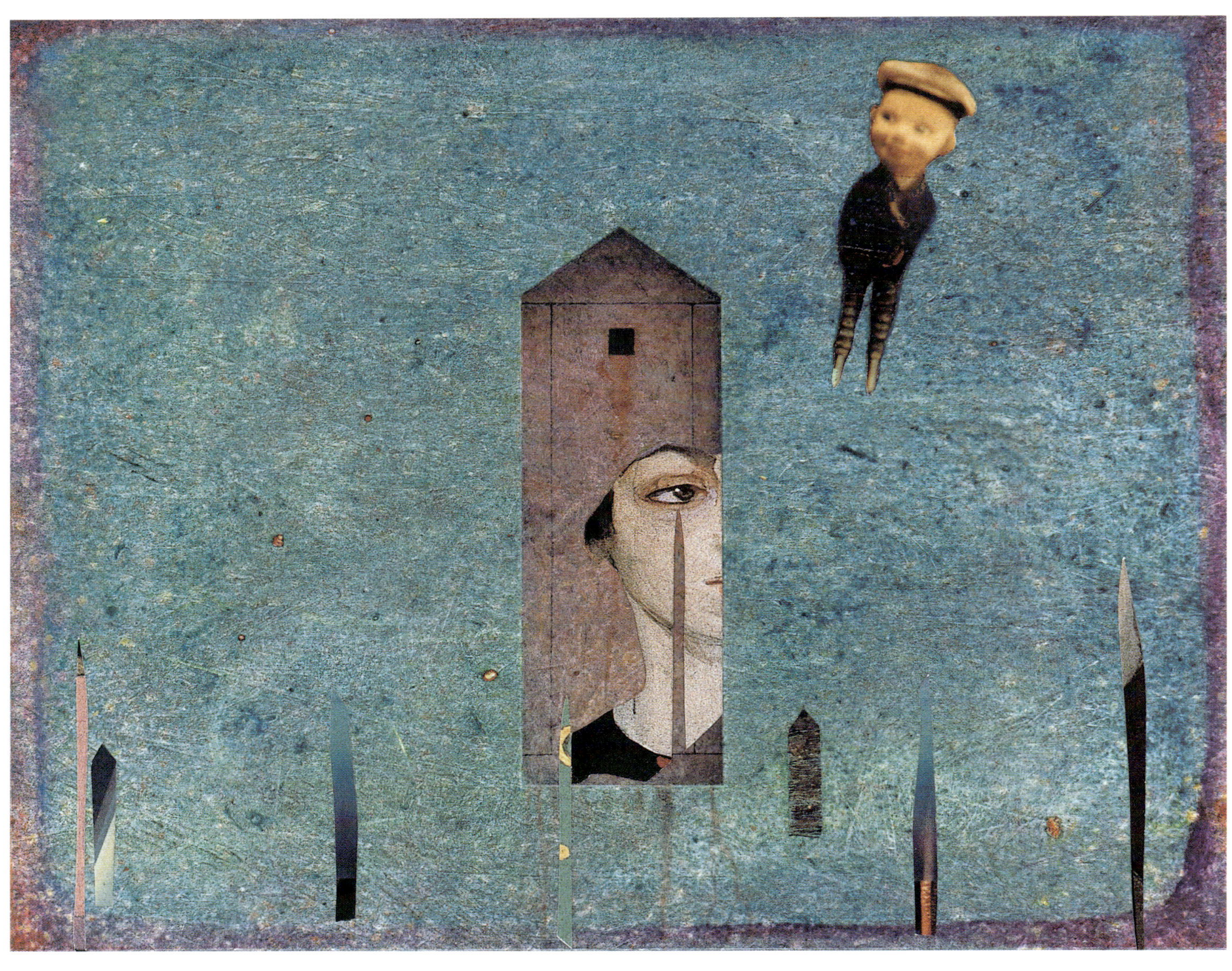

Going Over, 1988, monotype collage, 8 x 10"

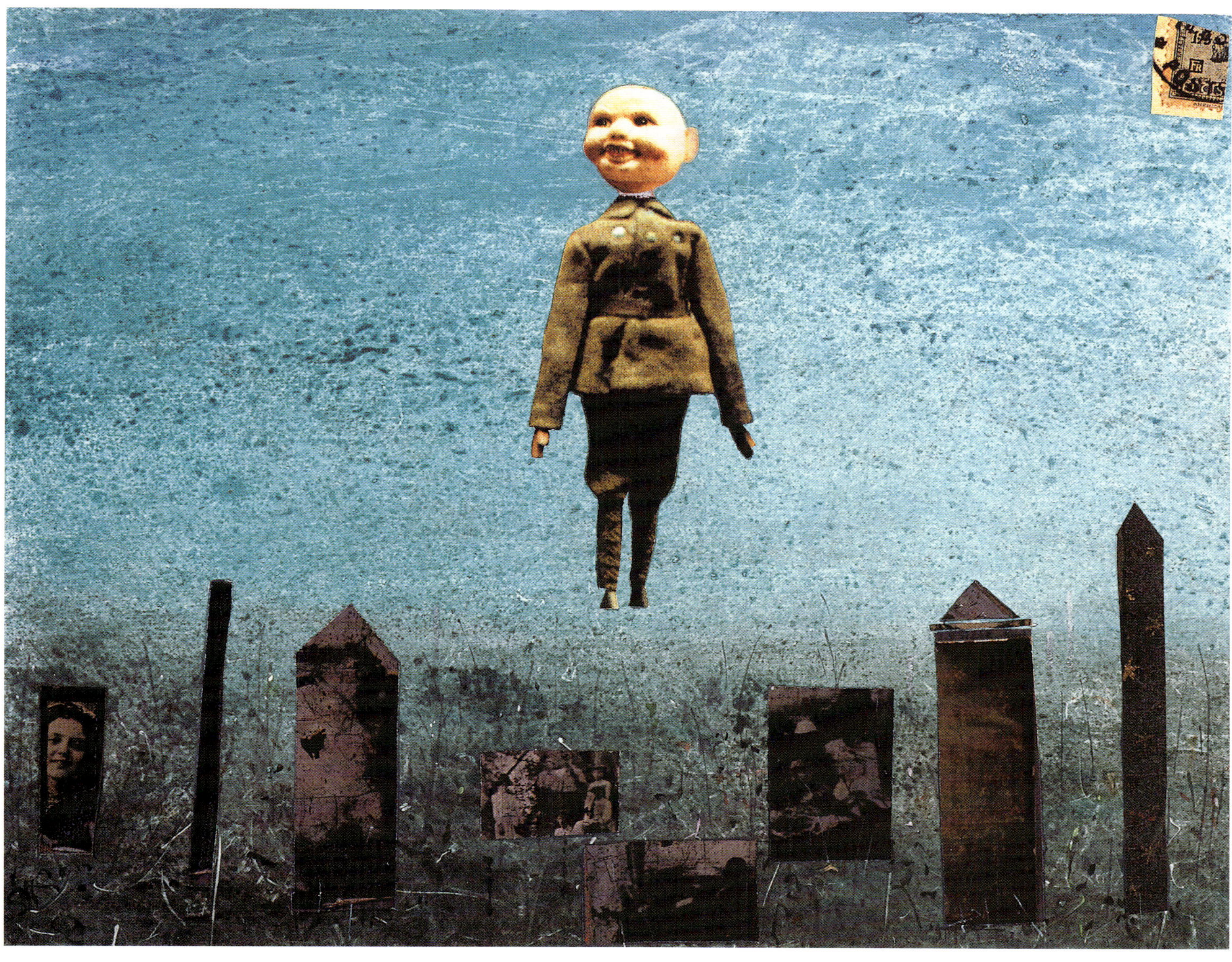

The Land of Ancestors, 1988, monotype collage, 8 x 10"

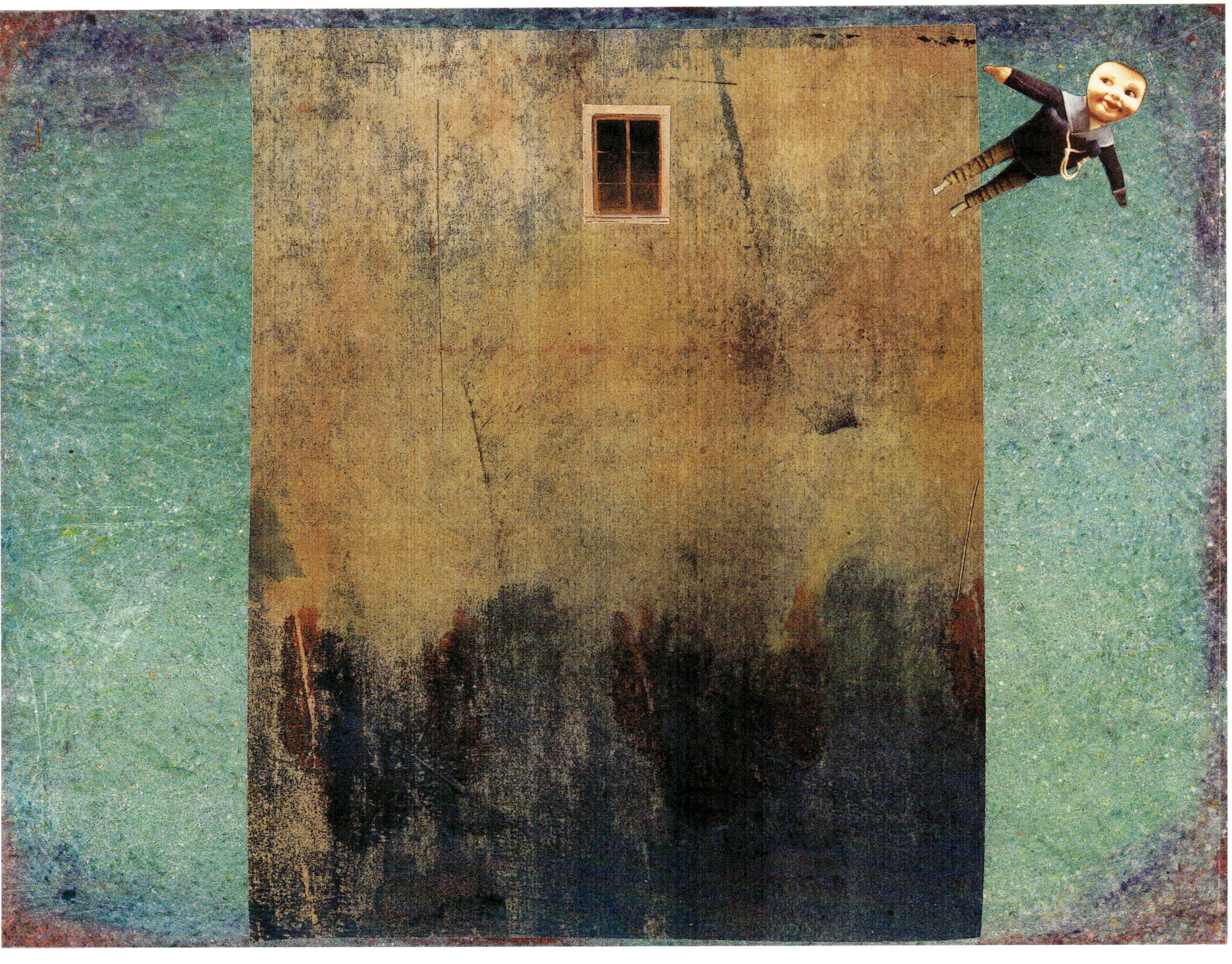

Flight, 1988, monotype collage, 11 x 14"

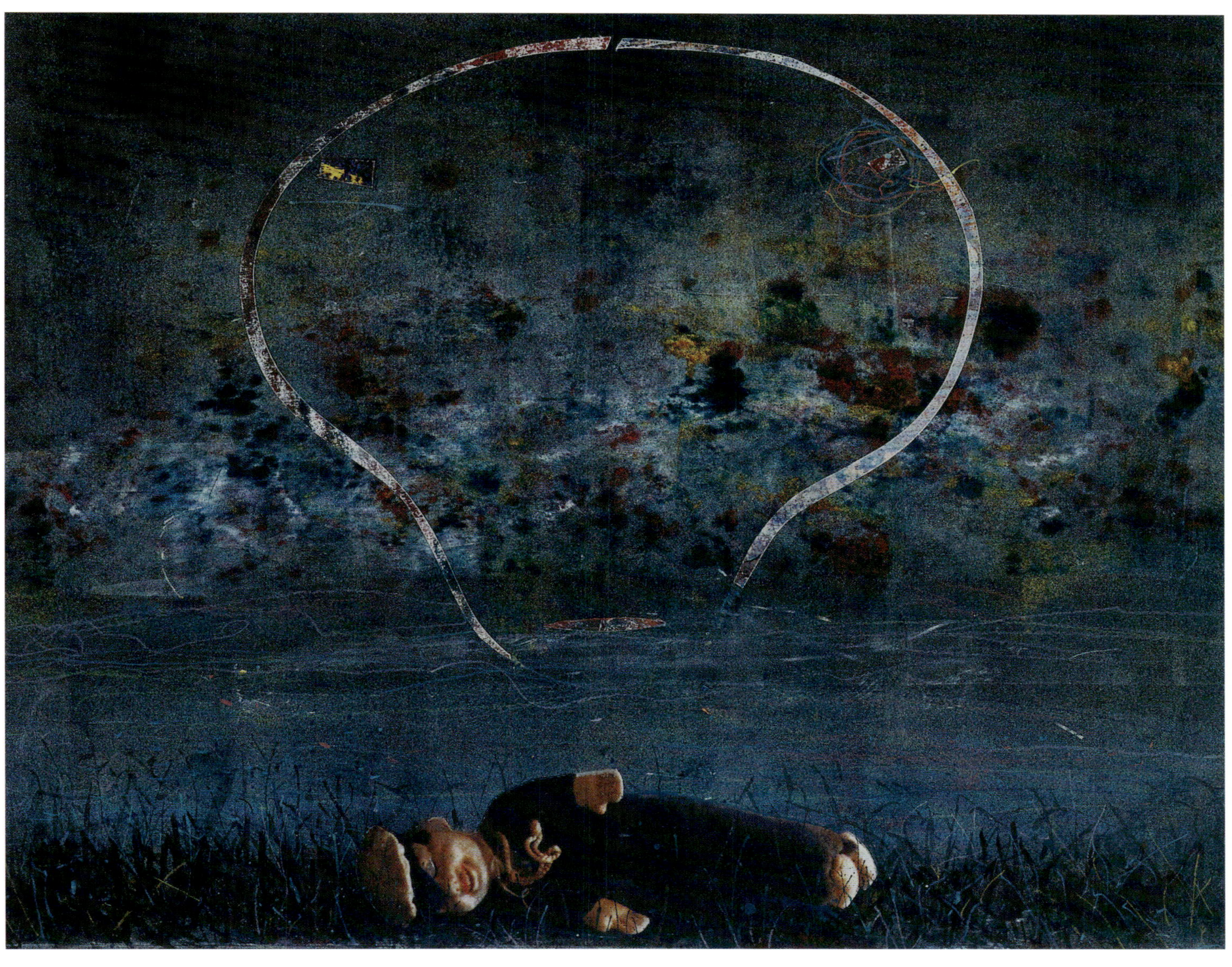

Noir, 1988, monotype collage, 8 x 10"

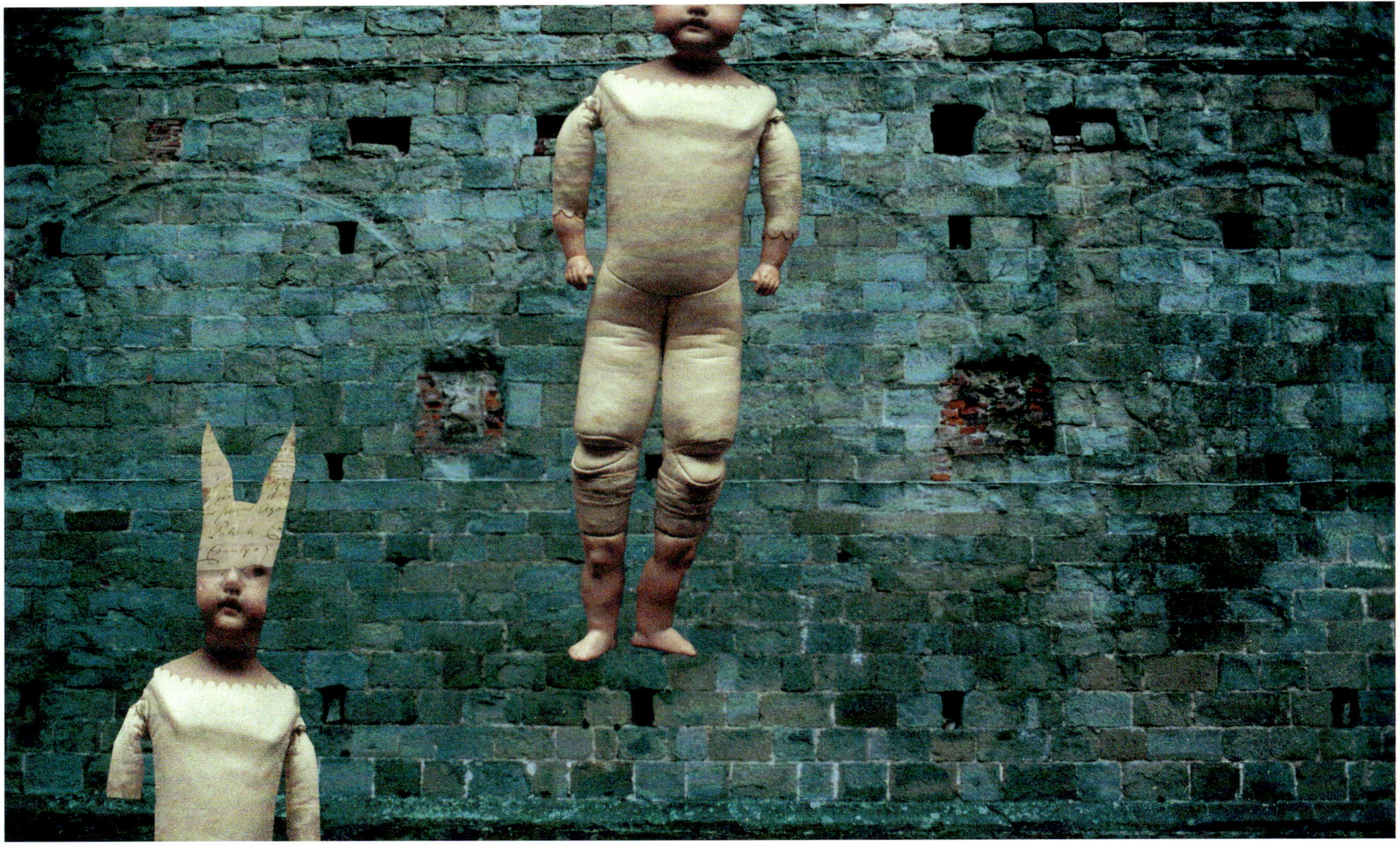

In Europa, 1992, digital photomontage, size variable

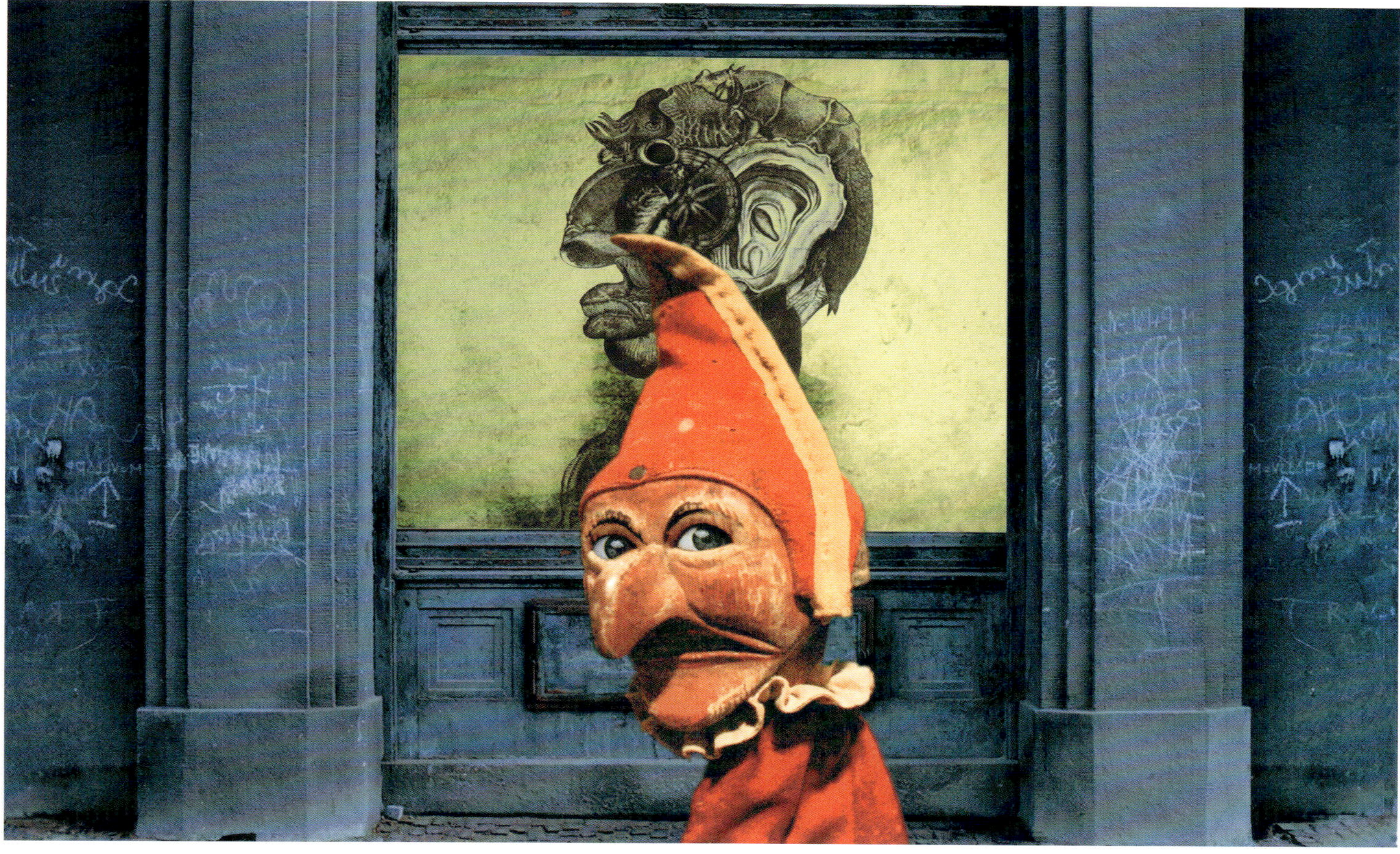

Portrait of Jan Švankmajer, 1992, digital photomontage, size variable

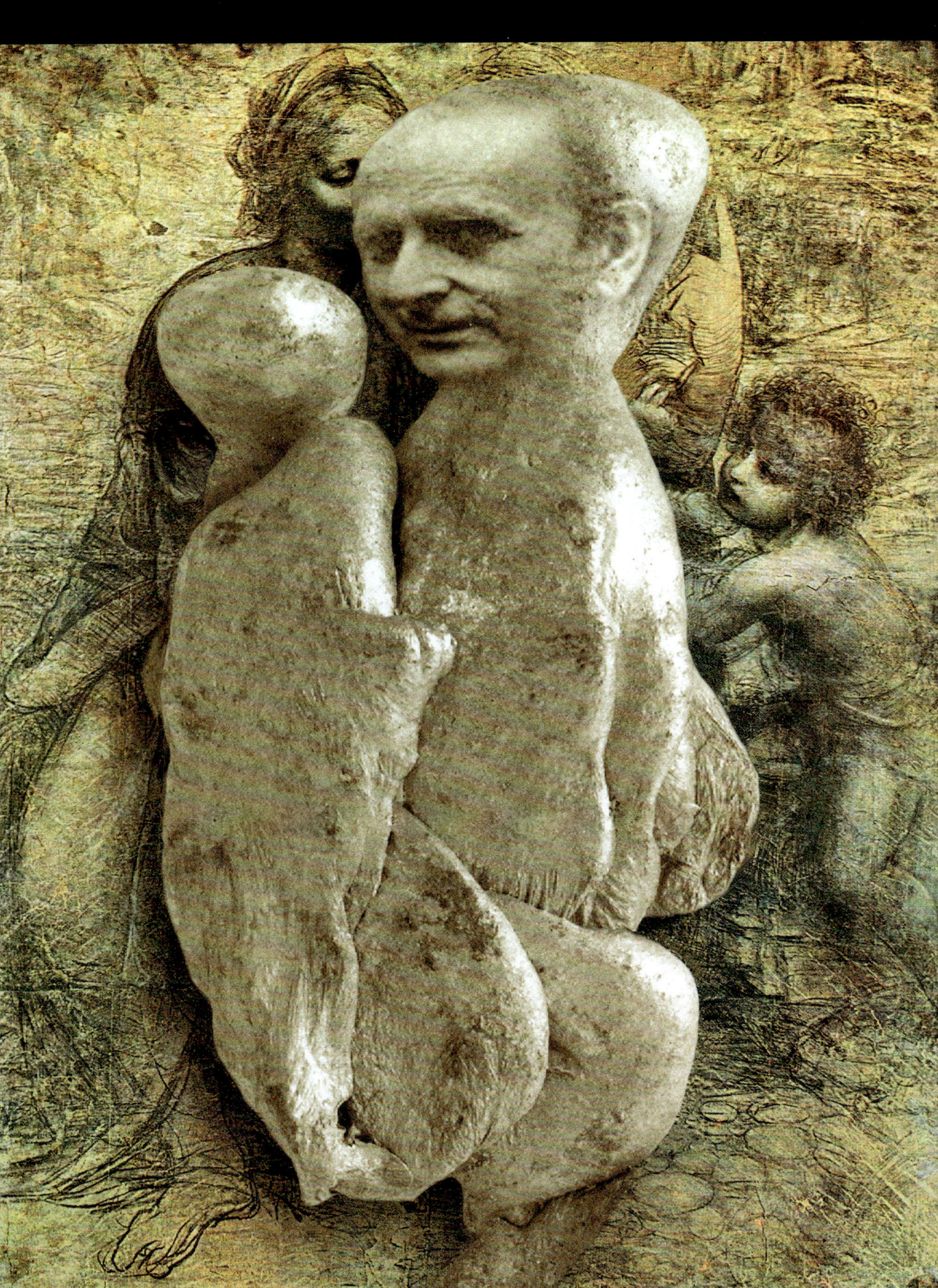

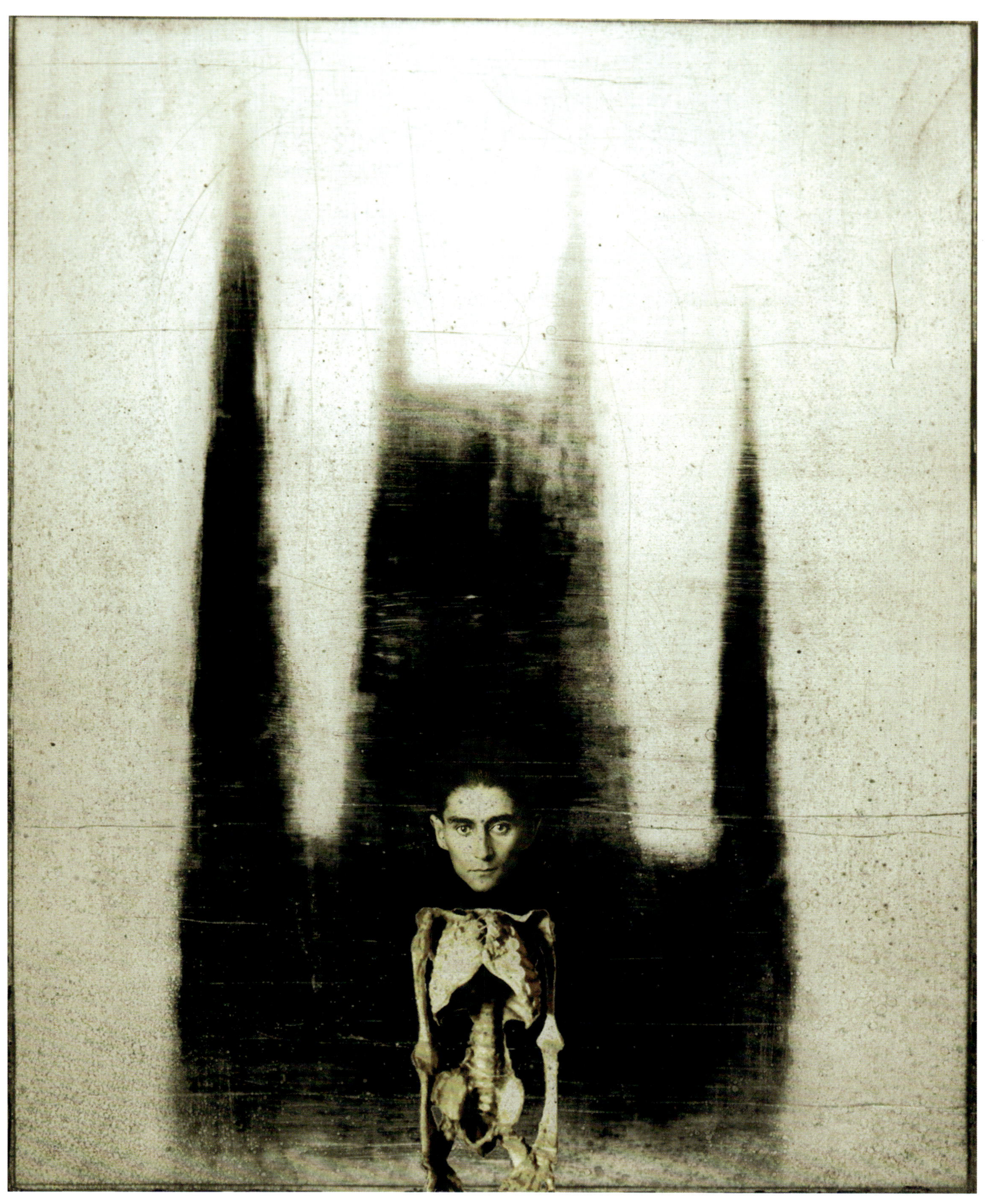

Portrait of Franz Kafka, 1992, digital photomontage, size variable

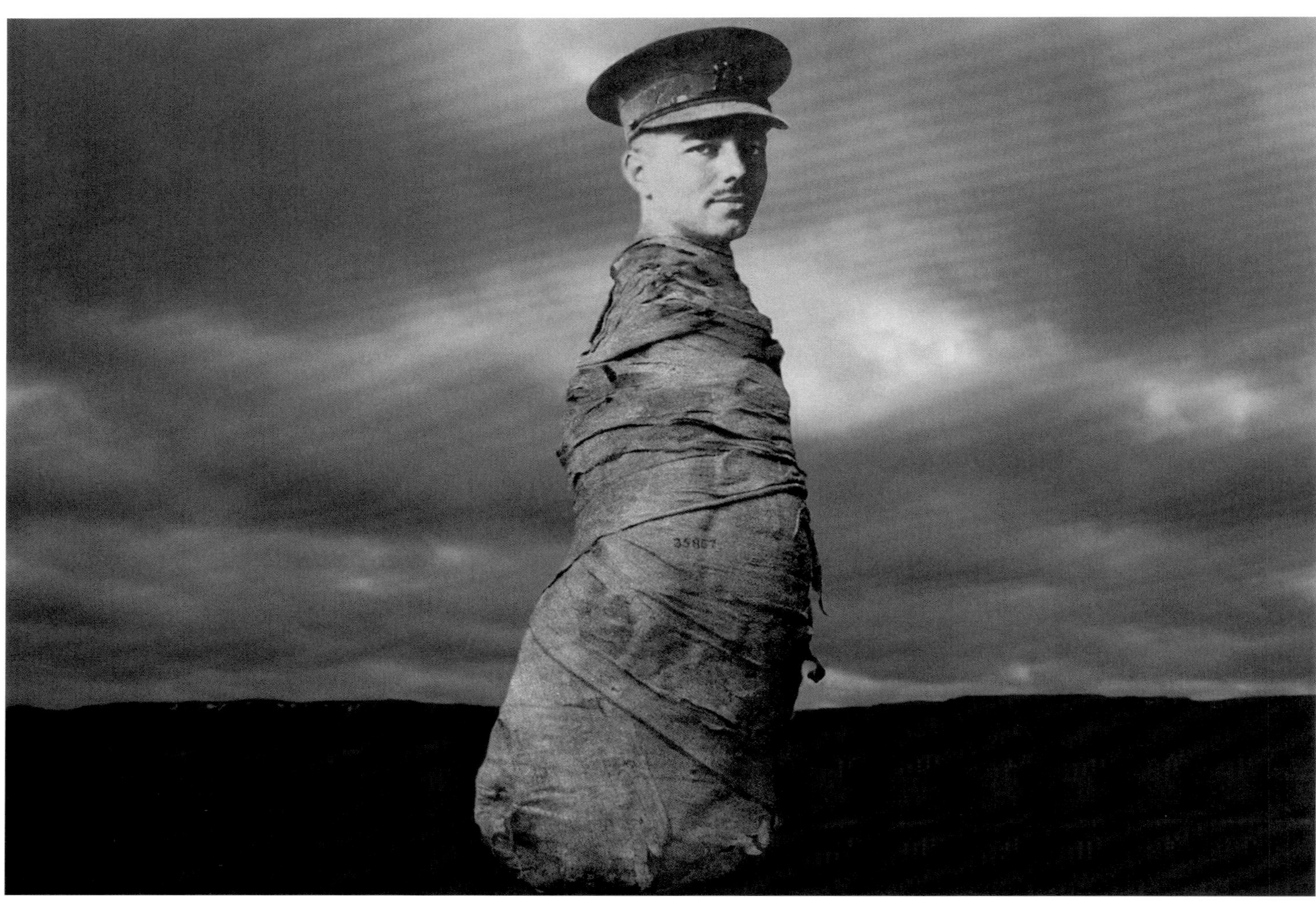

Portrait of Wilfred Owen, 1992, digital photomontage, size variable

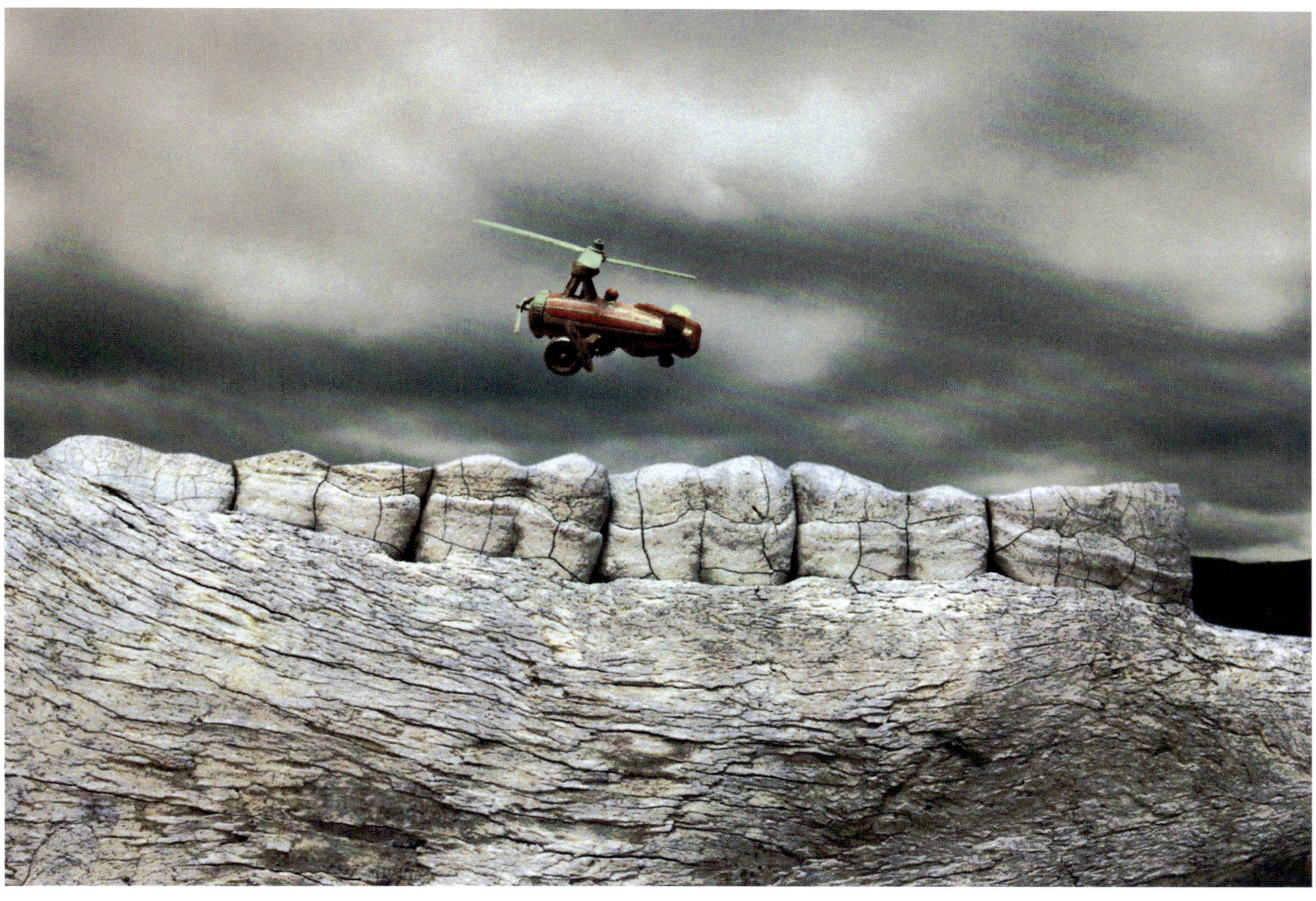

Mesa Blanca (for Emmet Gowin), 1992, digital photomontage, size variable

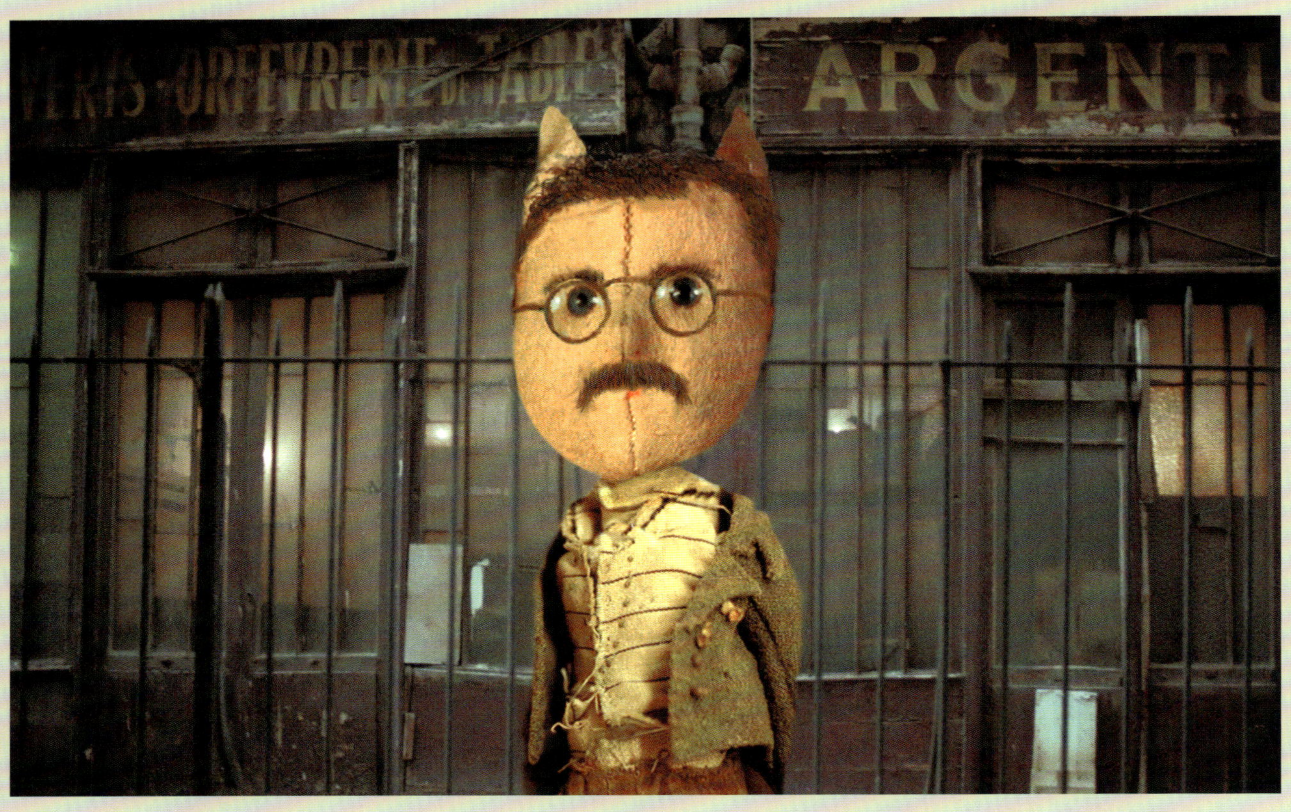

Walter Benjamin in Paris, 1992, digital photomontage, size variable

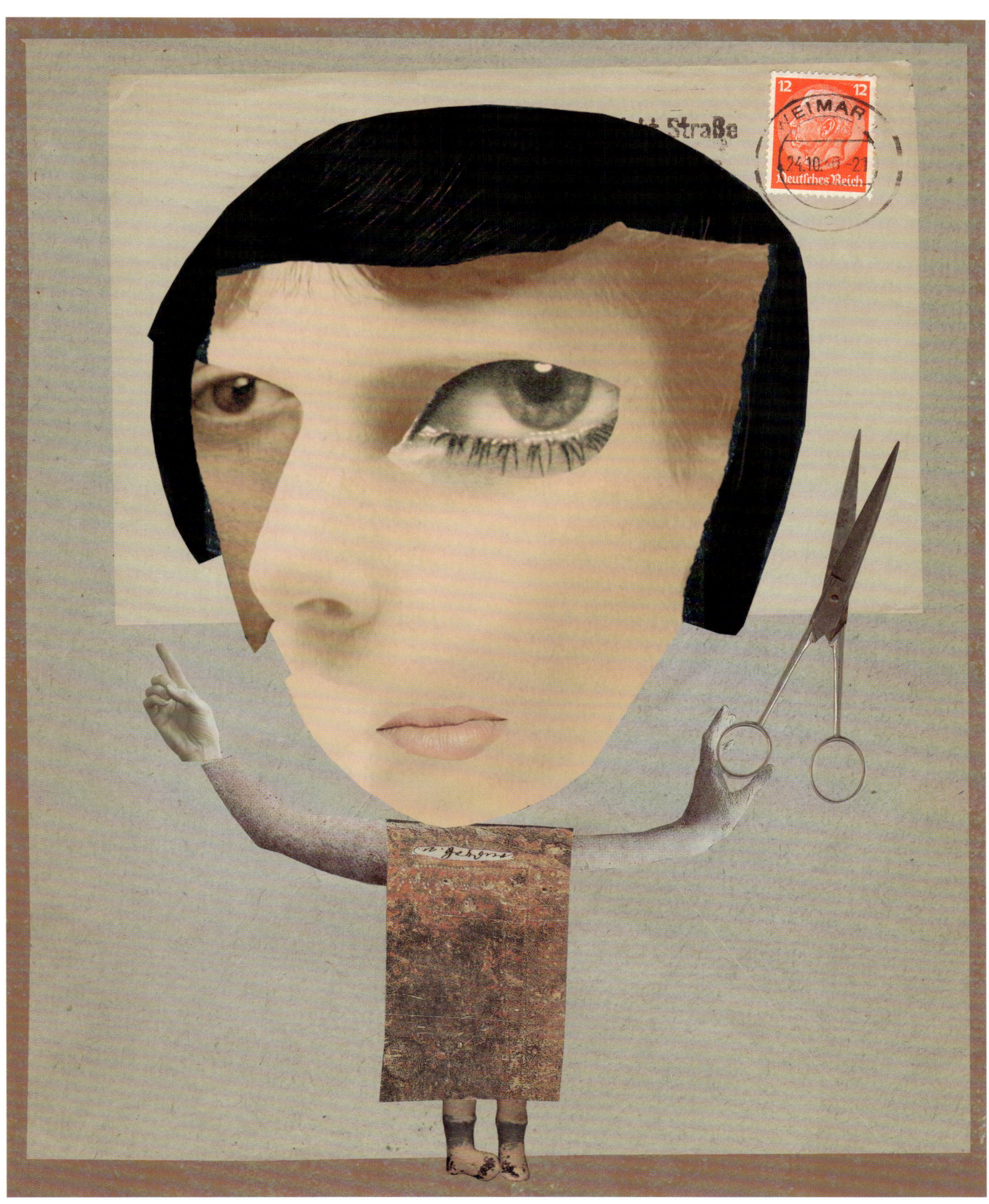

Portrait of Hannah Höch, 1992, digital photomontage, size variable

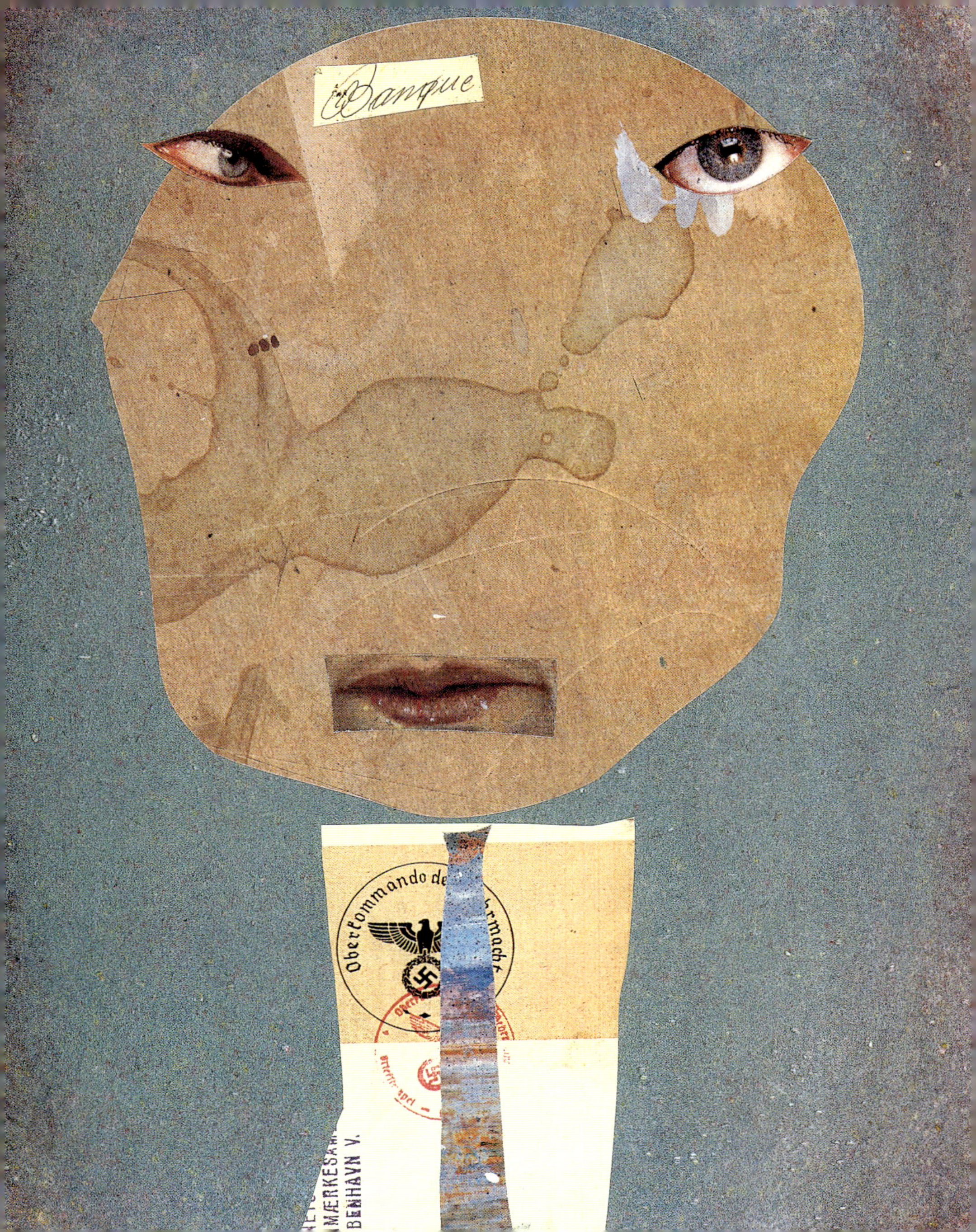
Banque
Oberkommando de
rmacht
MÆRKESA
BENHAVN V.

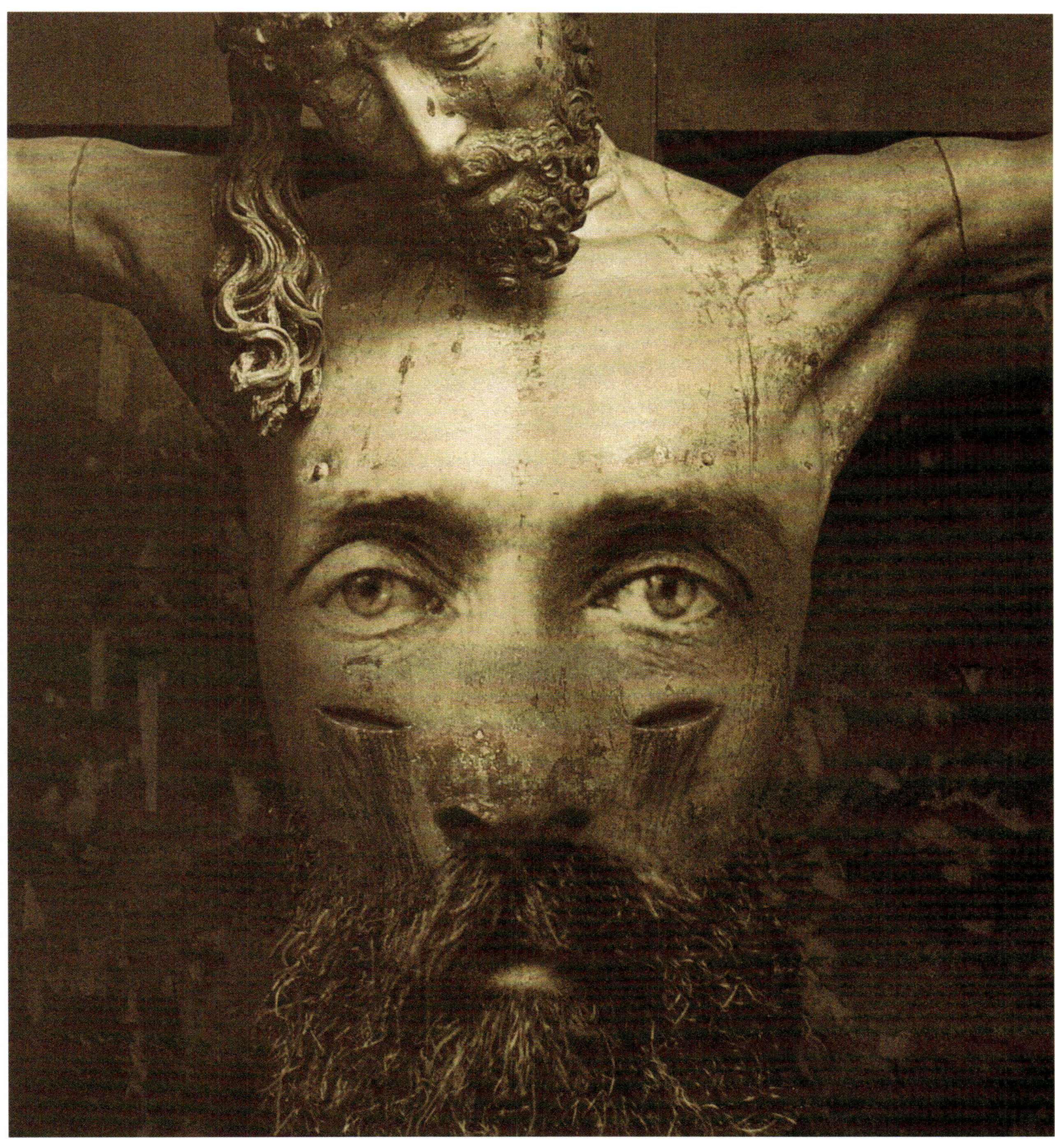

Portrait of Veit Stoss, 1992, digital photomontage, size variable

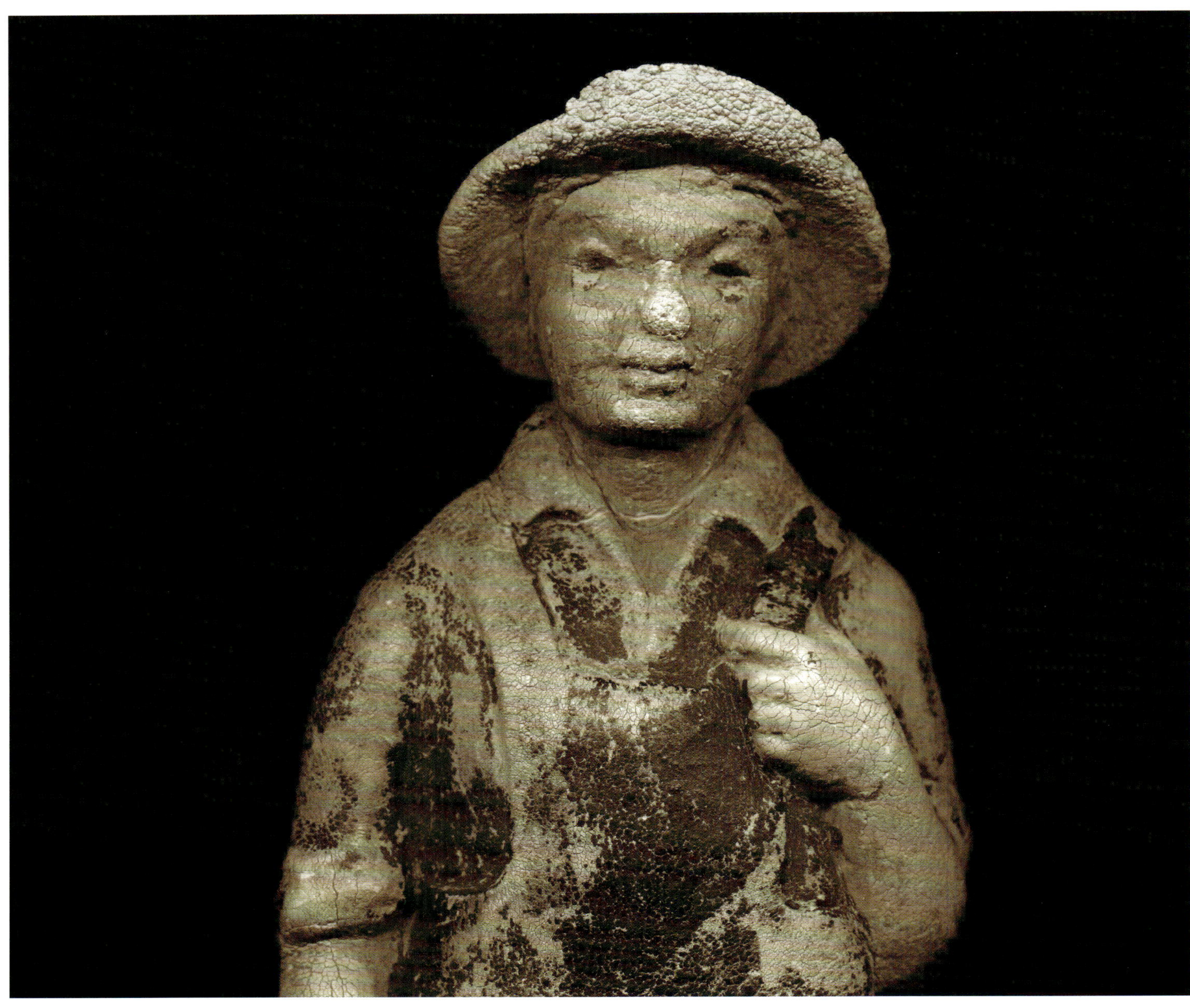

Heartland, 2001, photograph, 8 ½ x 11"

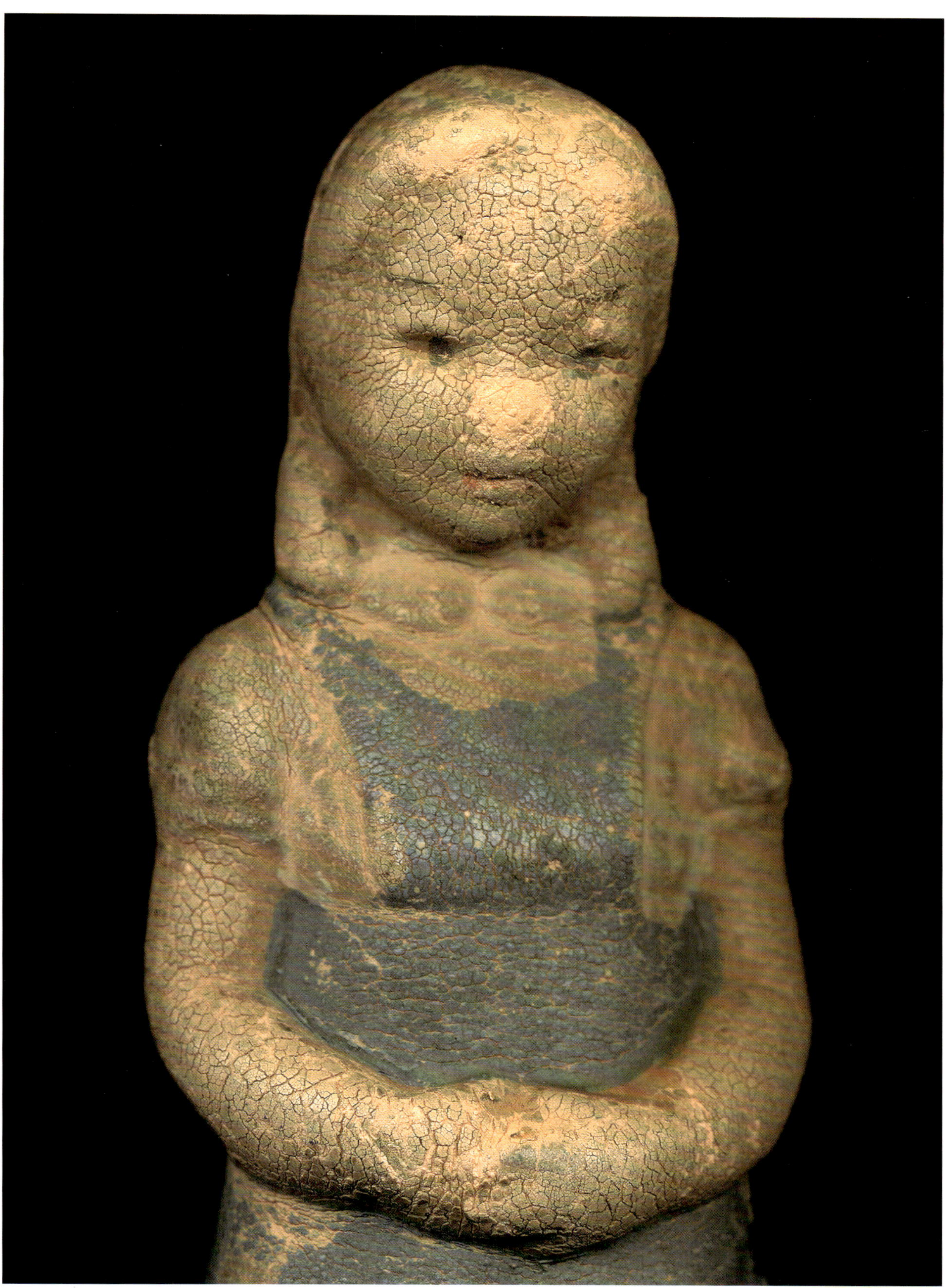

From an Anthology of Childhood, 2001, photograph, 11 x 8 ½"

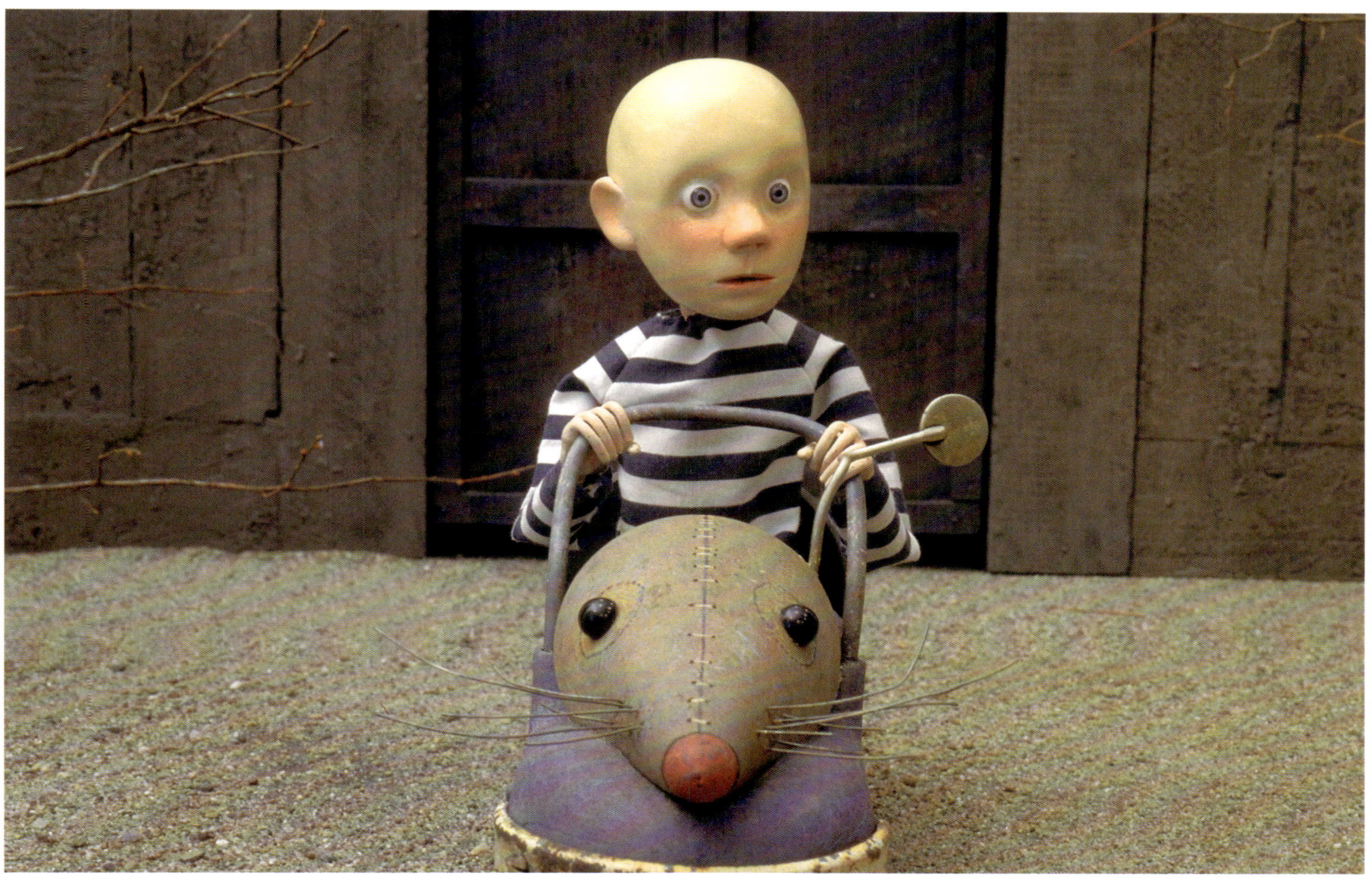

Wild Mouse, 1994, mixed materials, h. 10"

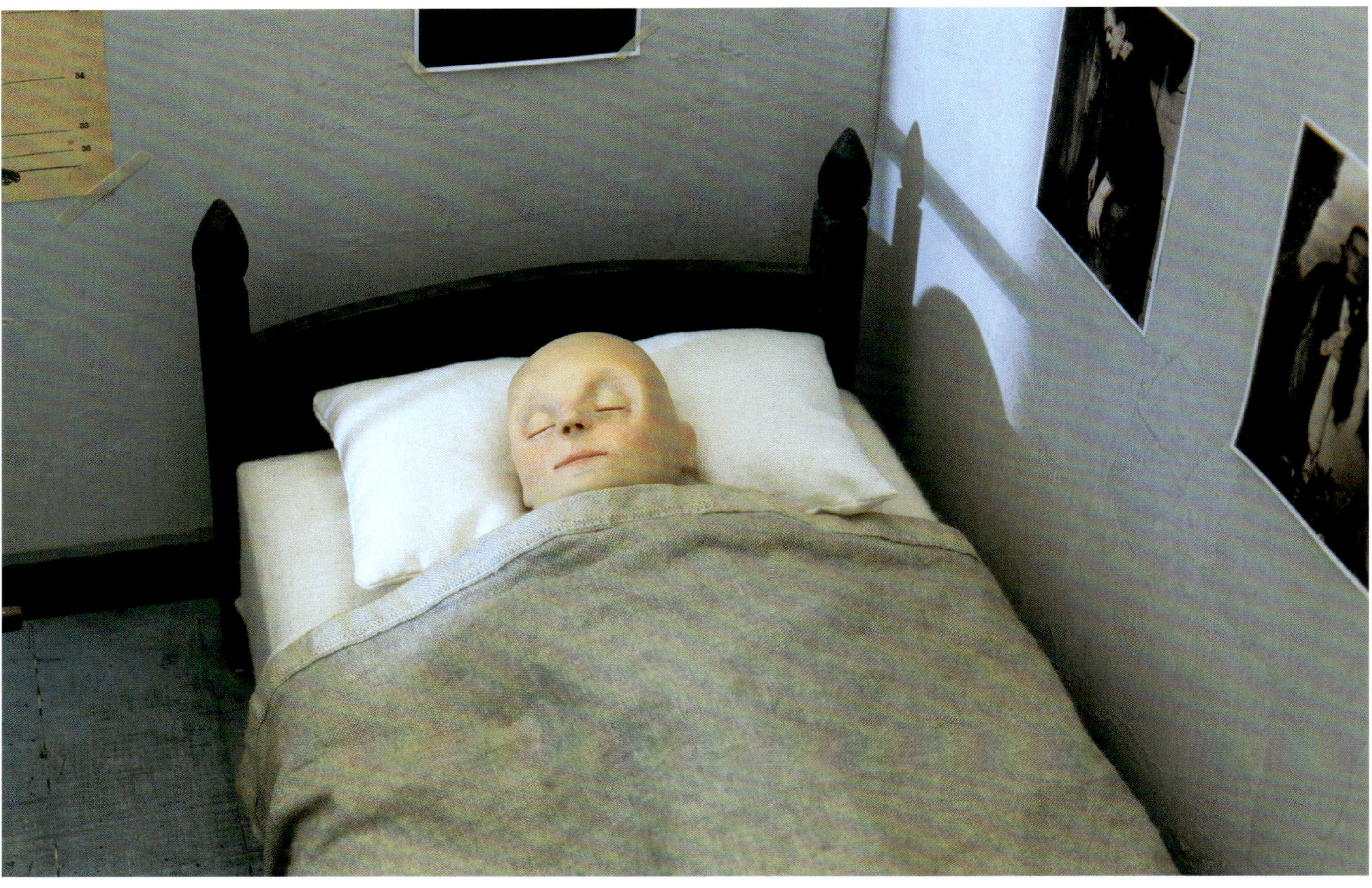

Moonlight (detail), 1994, mixed materials, 22 x 24 x 19"

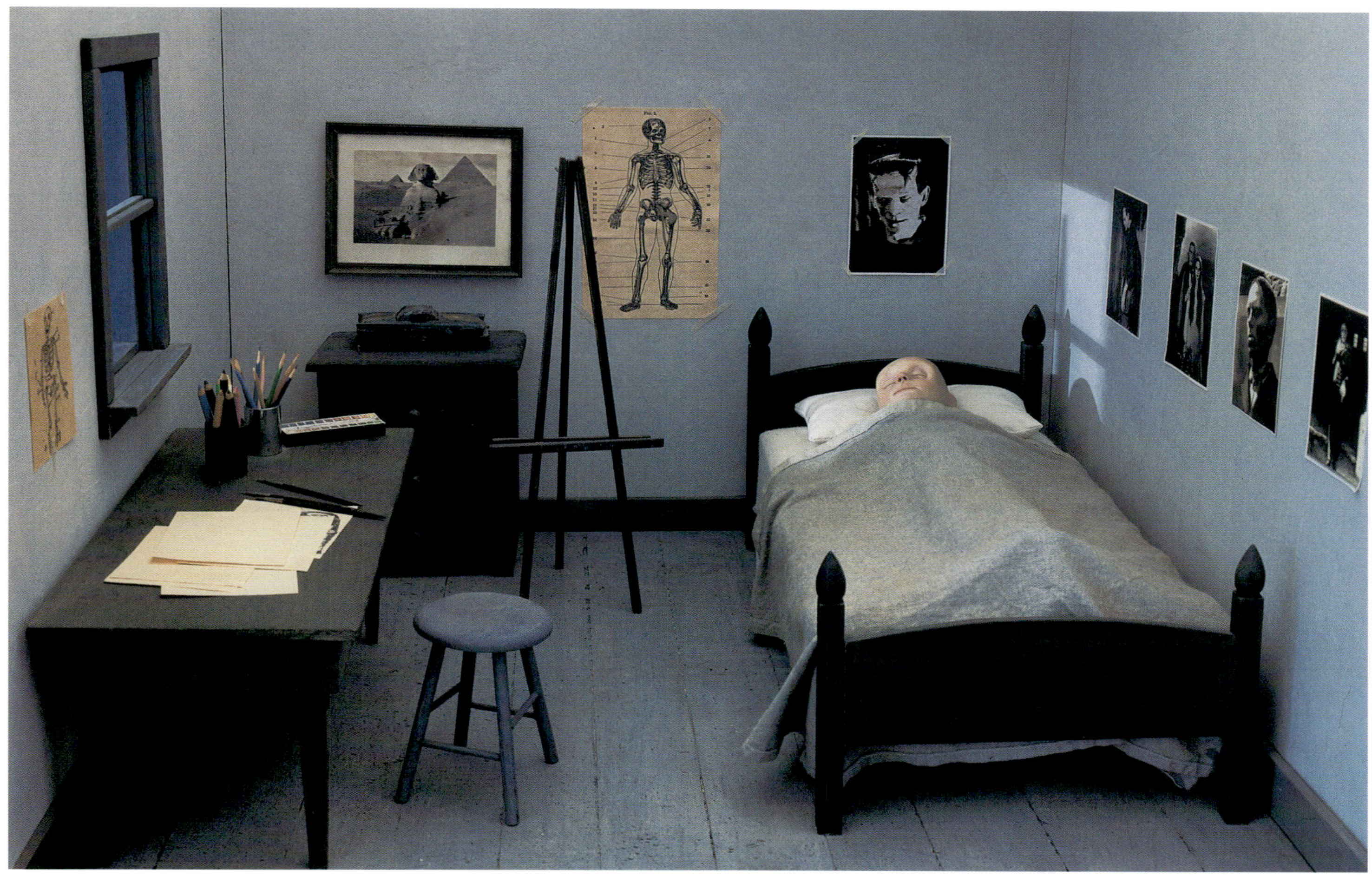

Moonlight, 1994, mixed materials, 22 x 24 x 19"

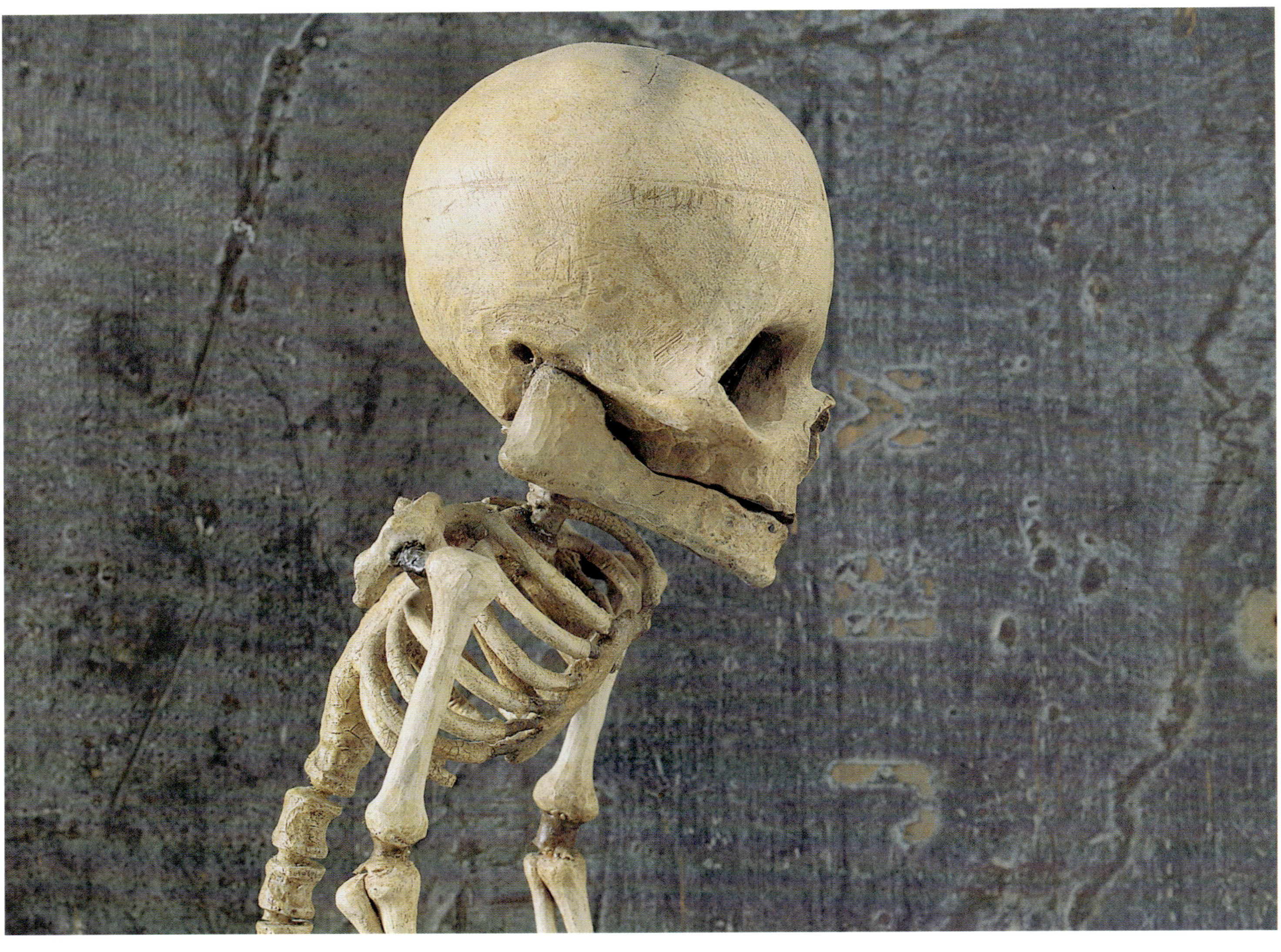

Anatomical Model (and detail), 1994, mixed materials, h. 14"

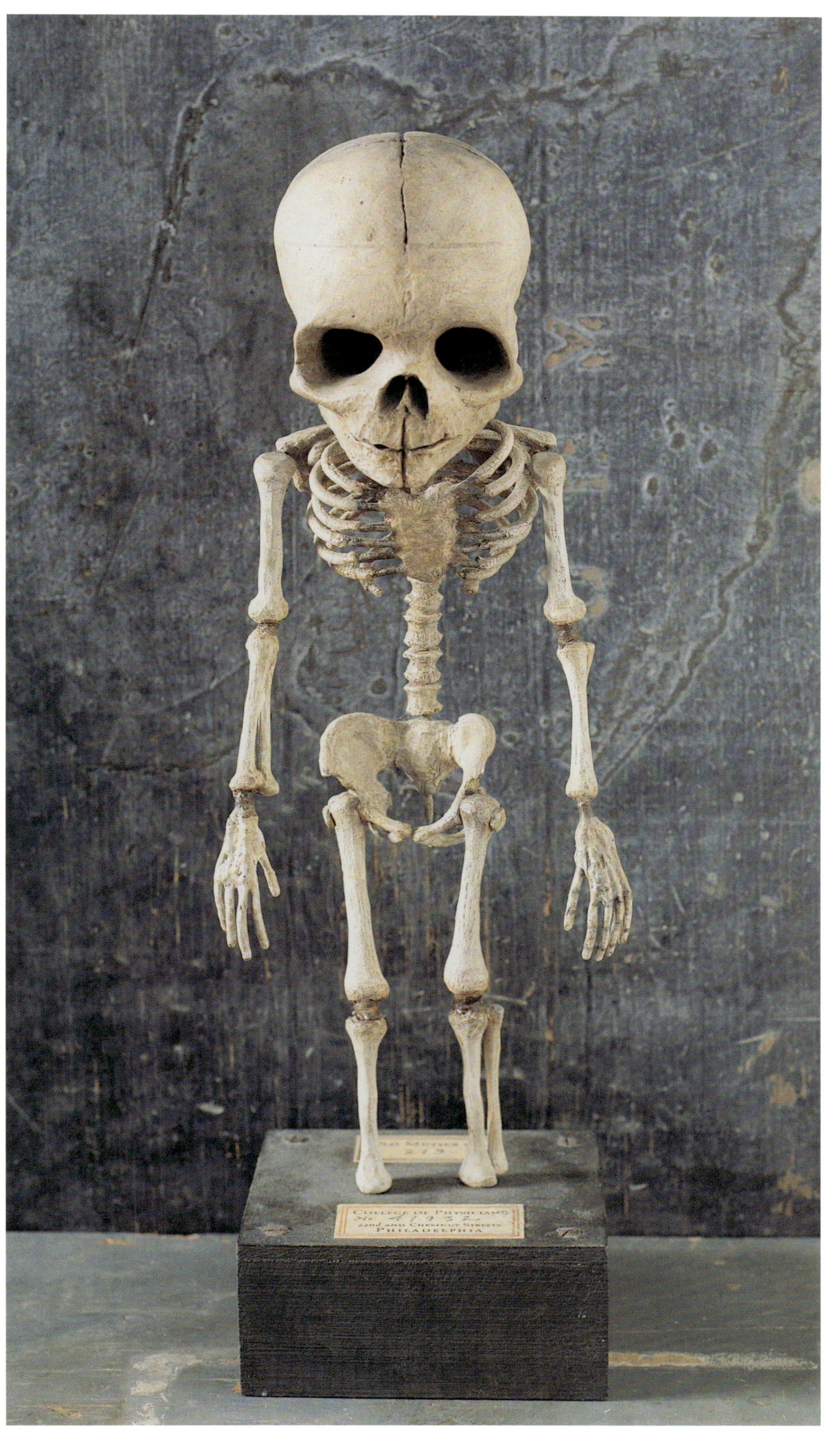
College of Physicians
22nd and Chestnut Streets
Philadelphia

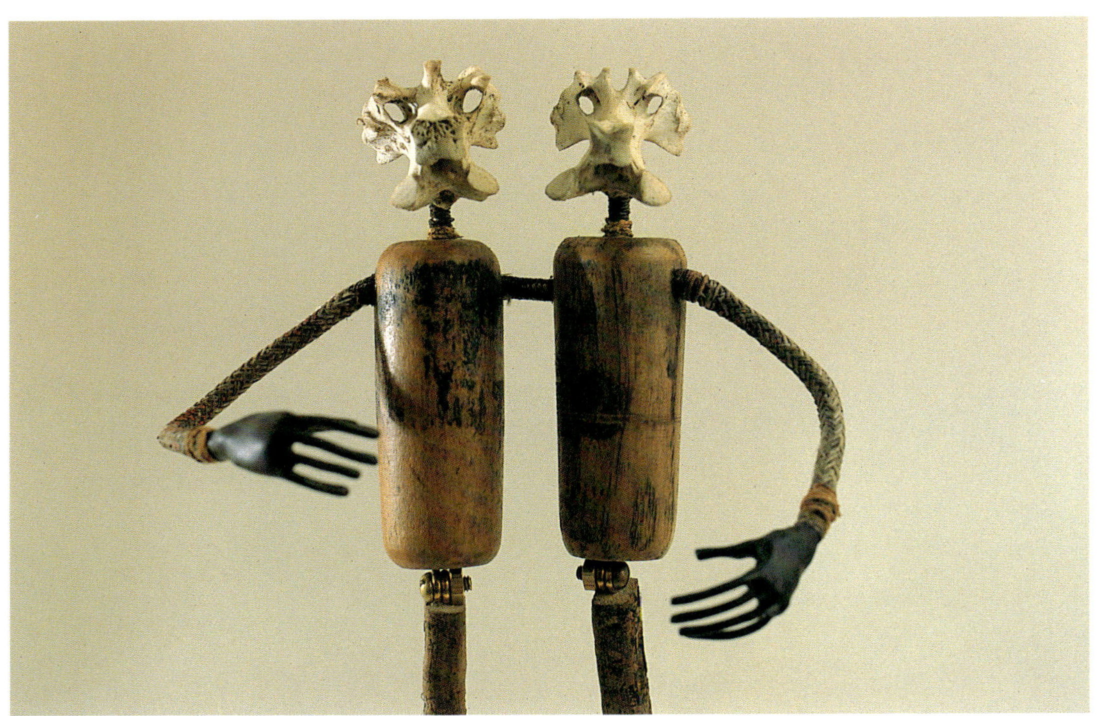

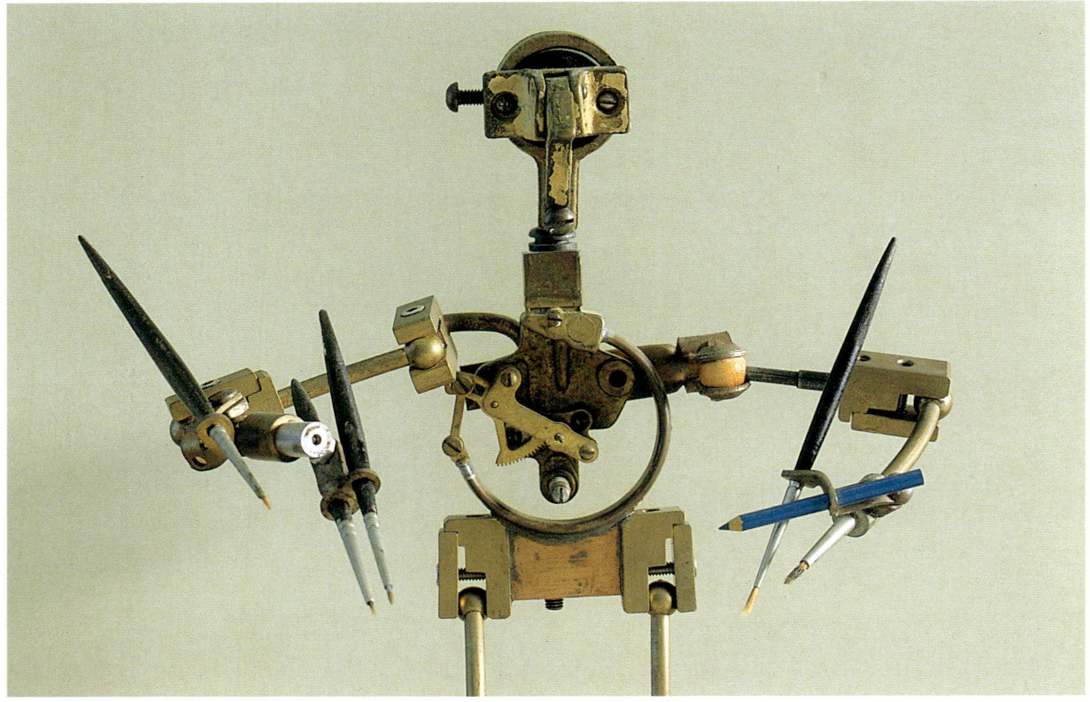

Twins (detail), 1994, mixed materials, h (approximate) 18"
Painter (detail), 1994, mixed materials, h. 11 ¾"

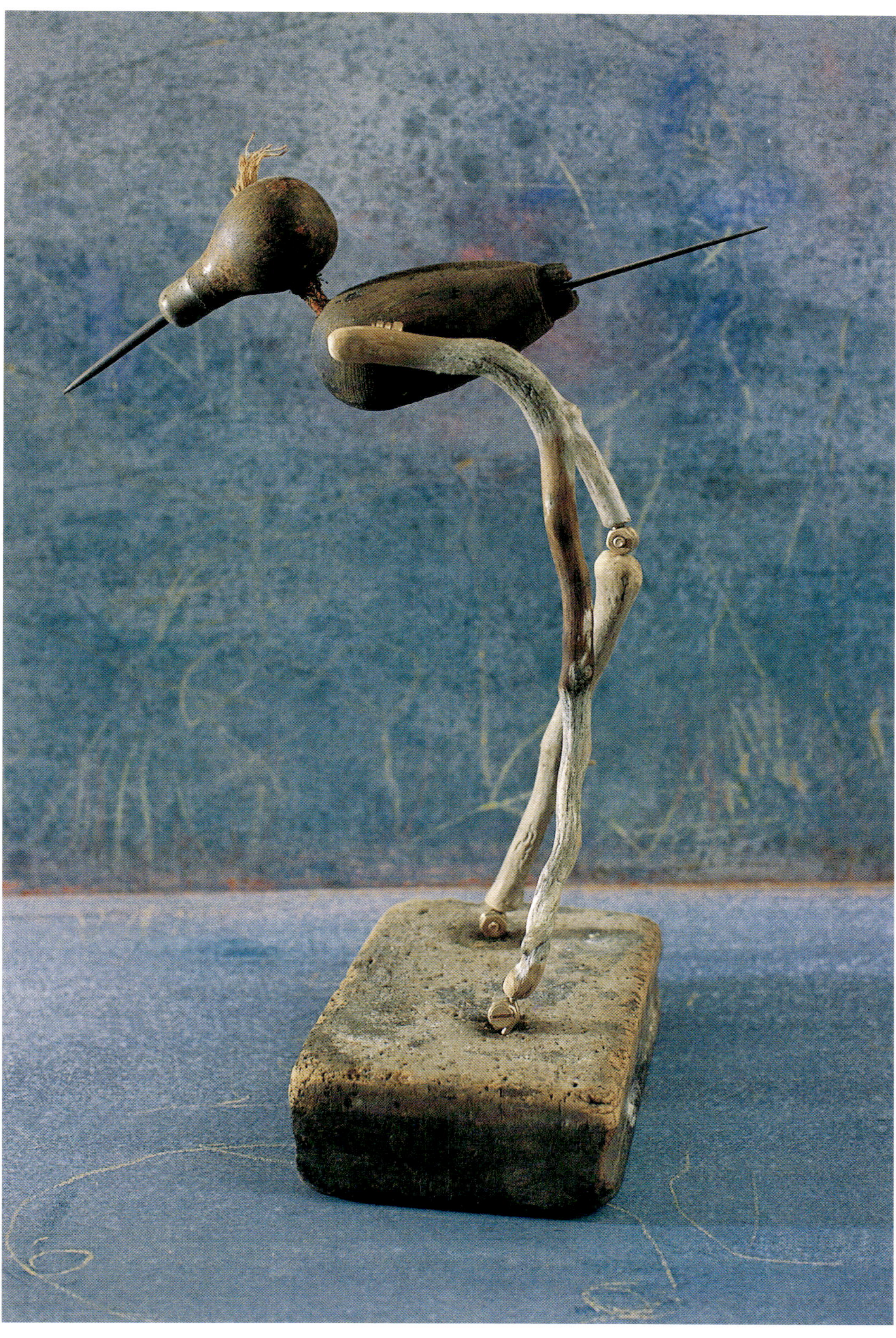

Bird, 1992, mixed materials, h. 9"

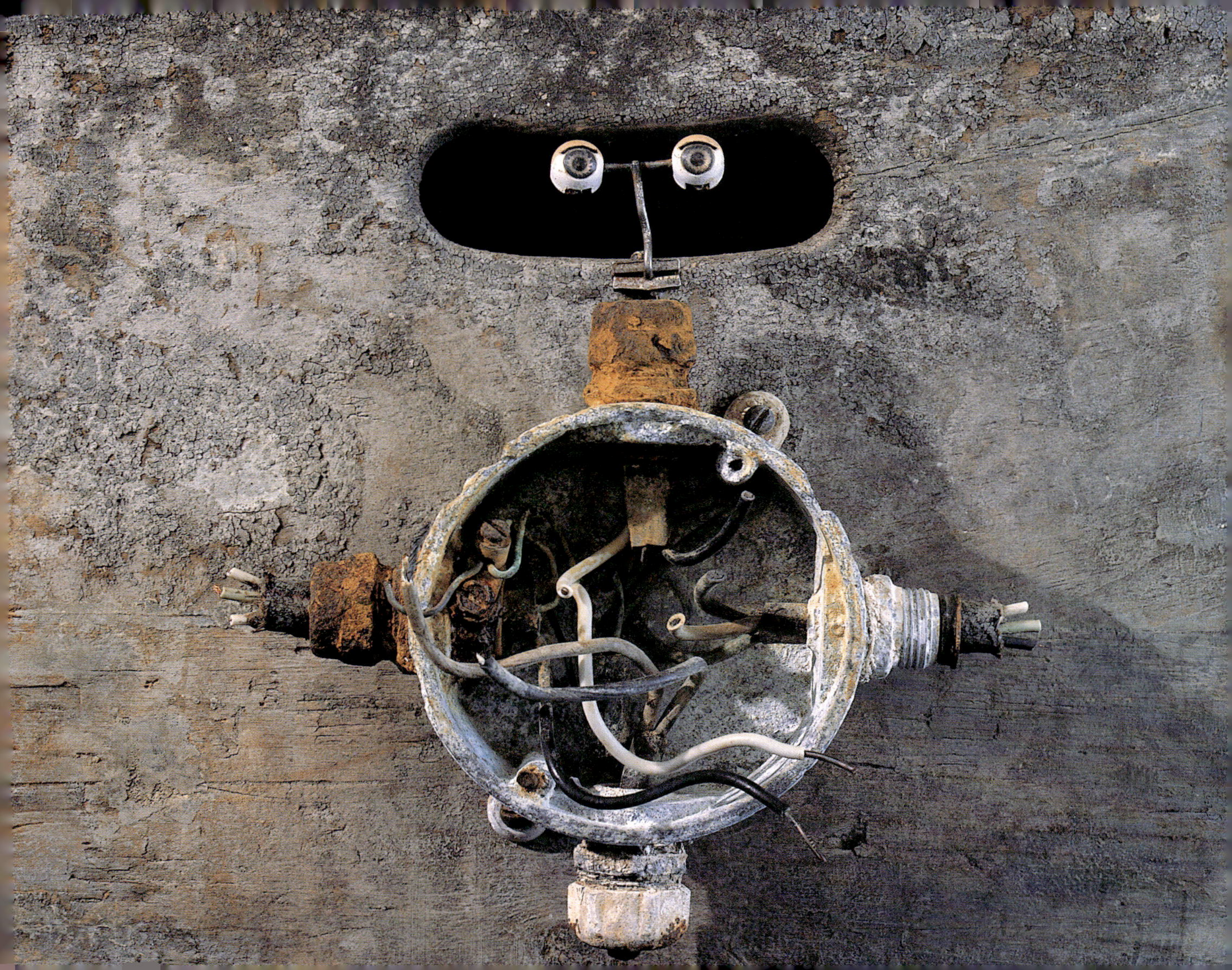

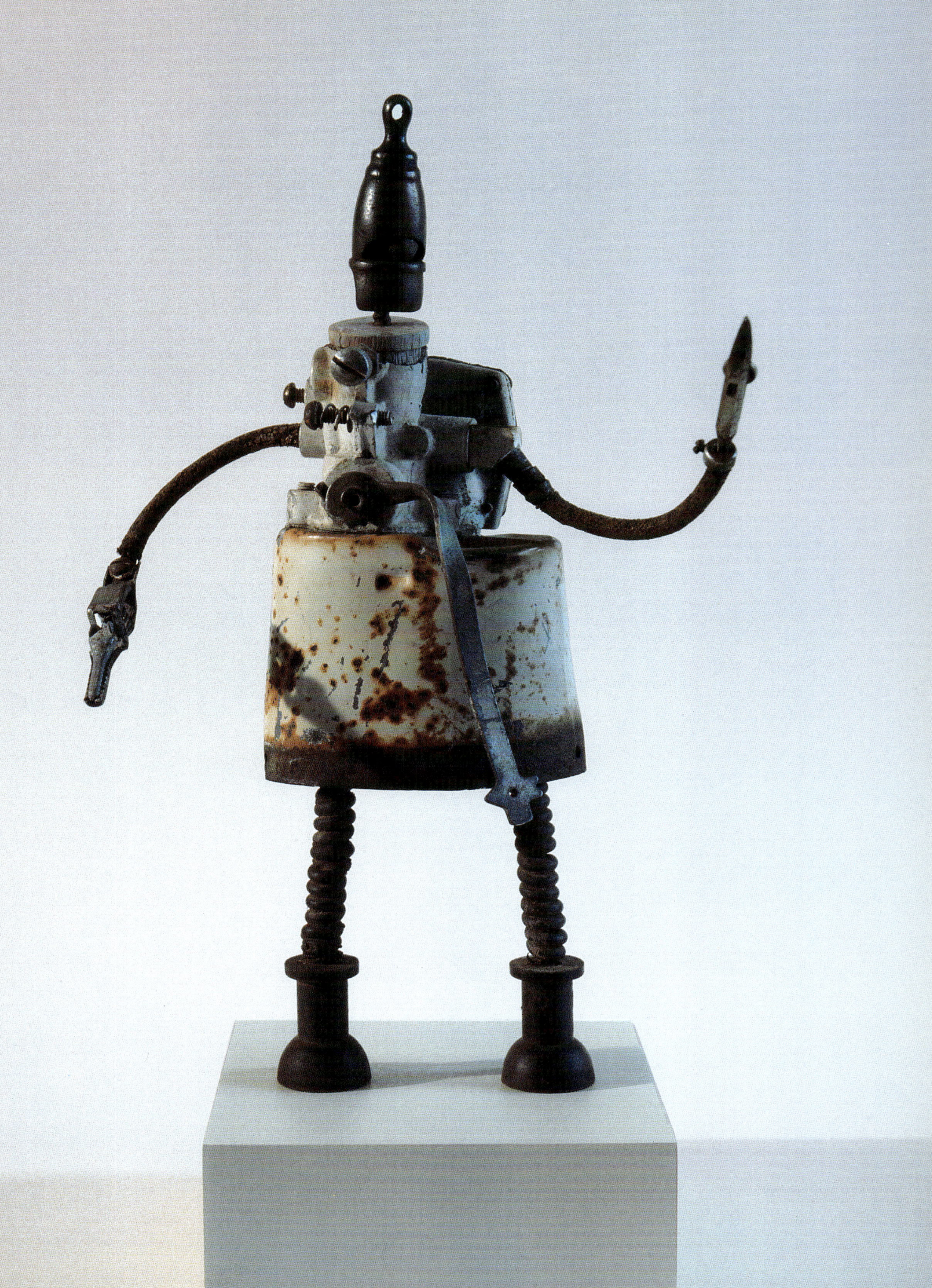

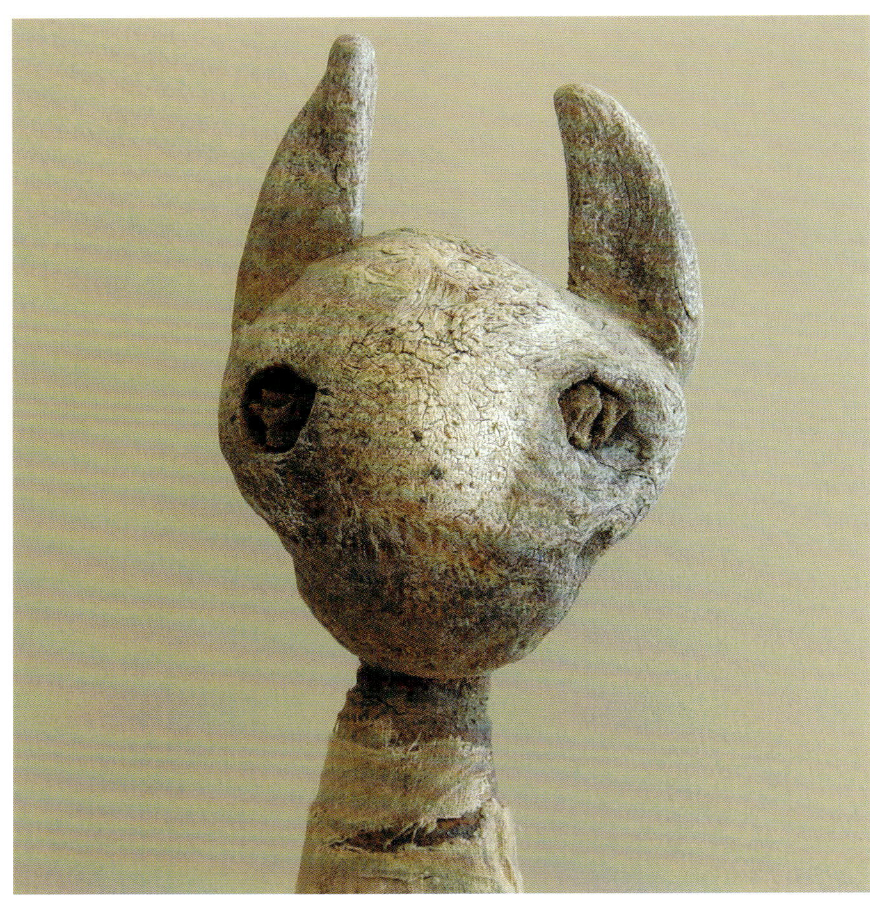

Family (and detail), 1994, mixed materials, h. 14 ¾"

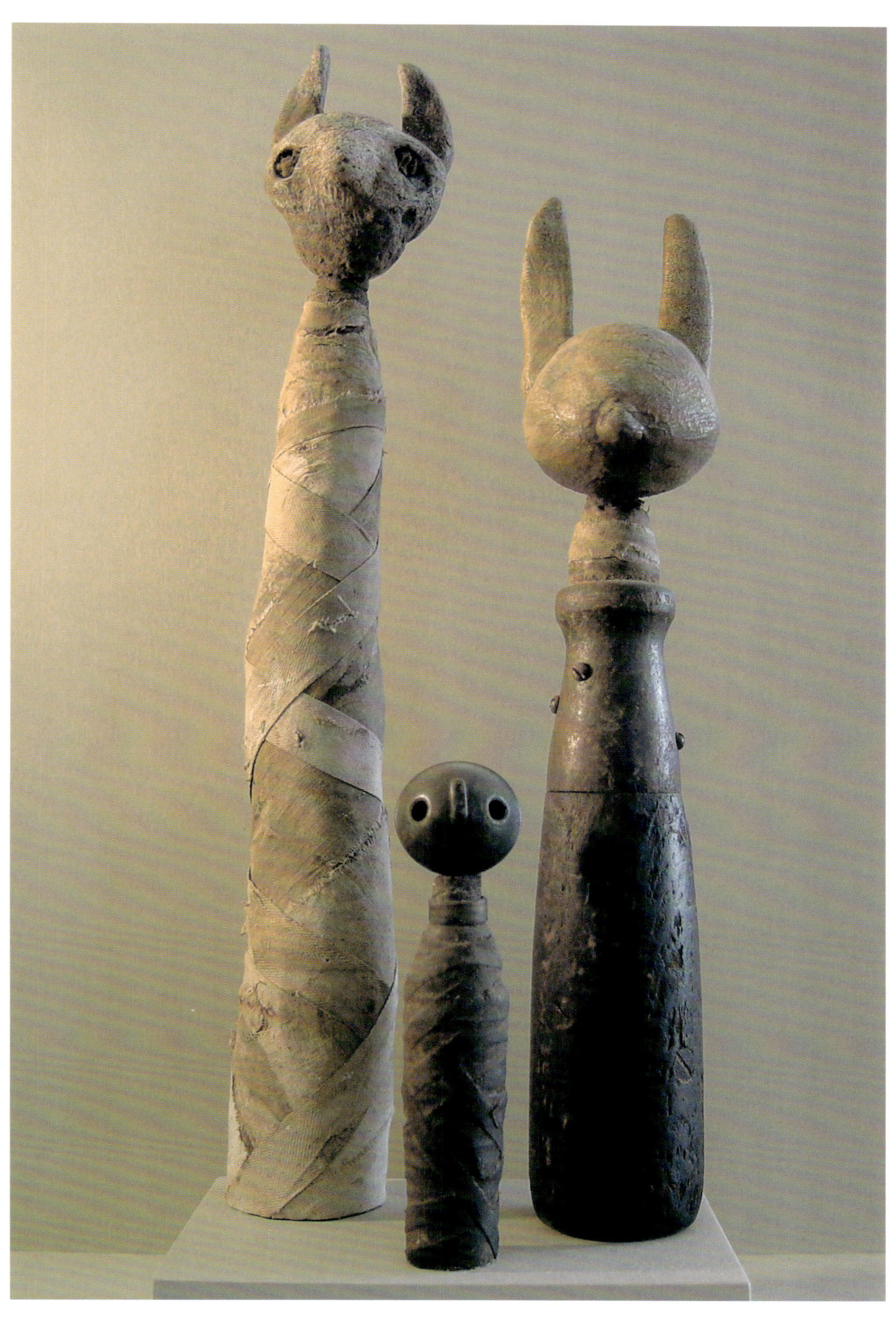

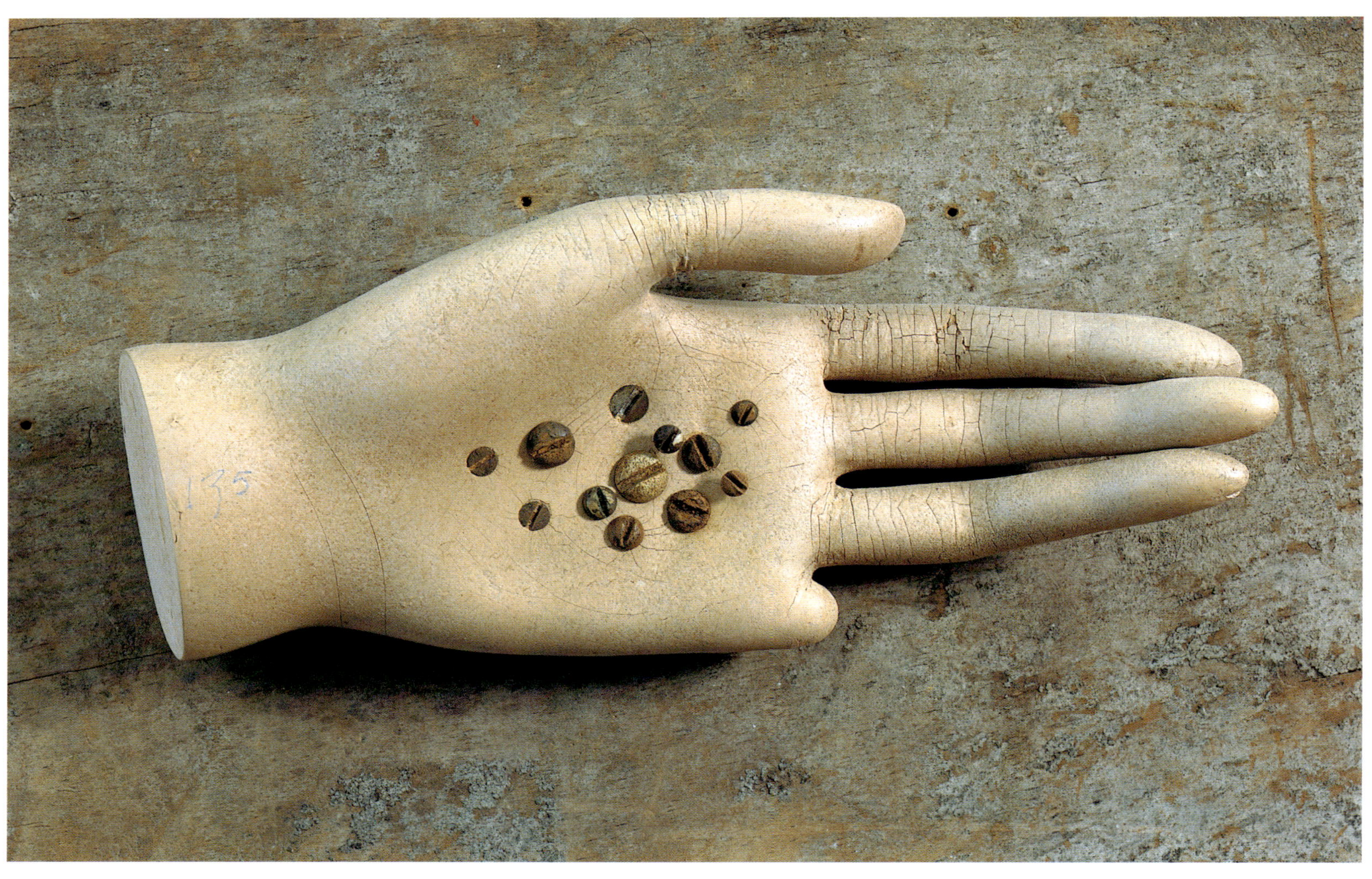

Penalty (For Carl Theodore Dreyer), 1994, mixed materials, 7 ½ x 13 x 4"

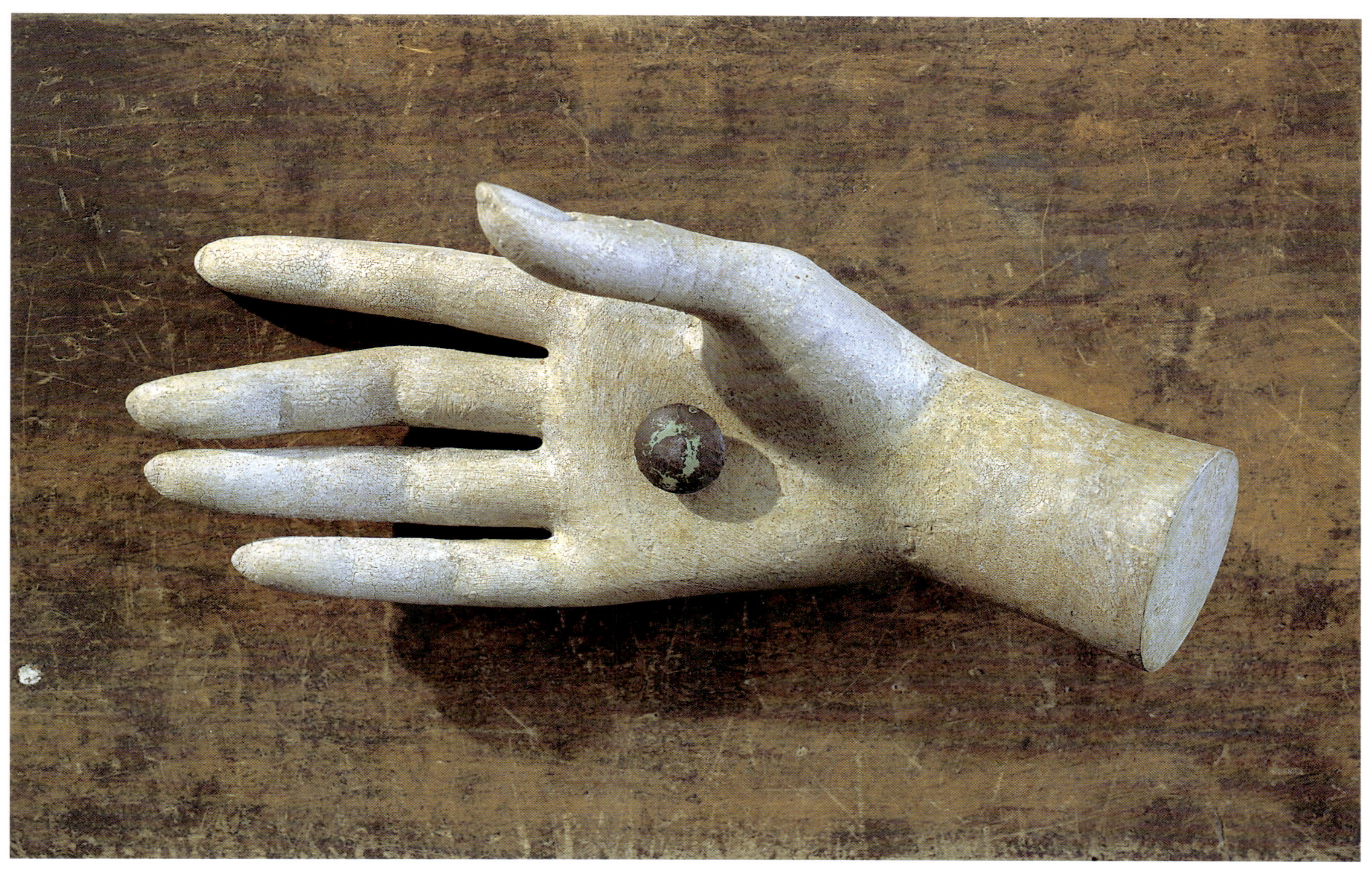

Sign, 1994, mixed materials, 7 x 13 x 3"

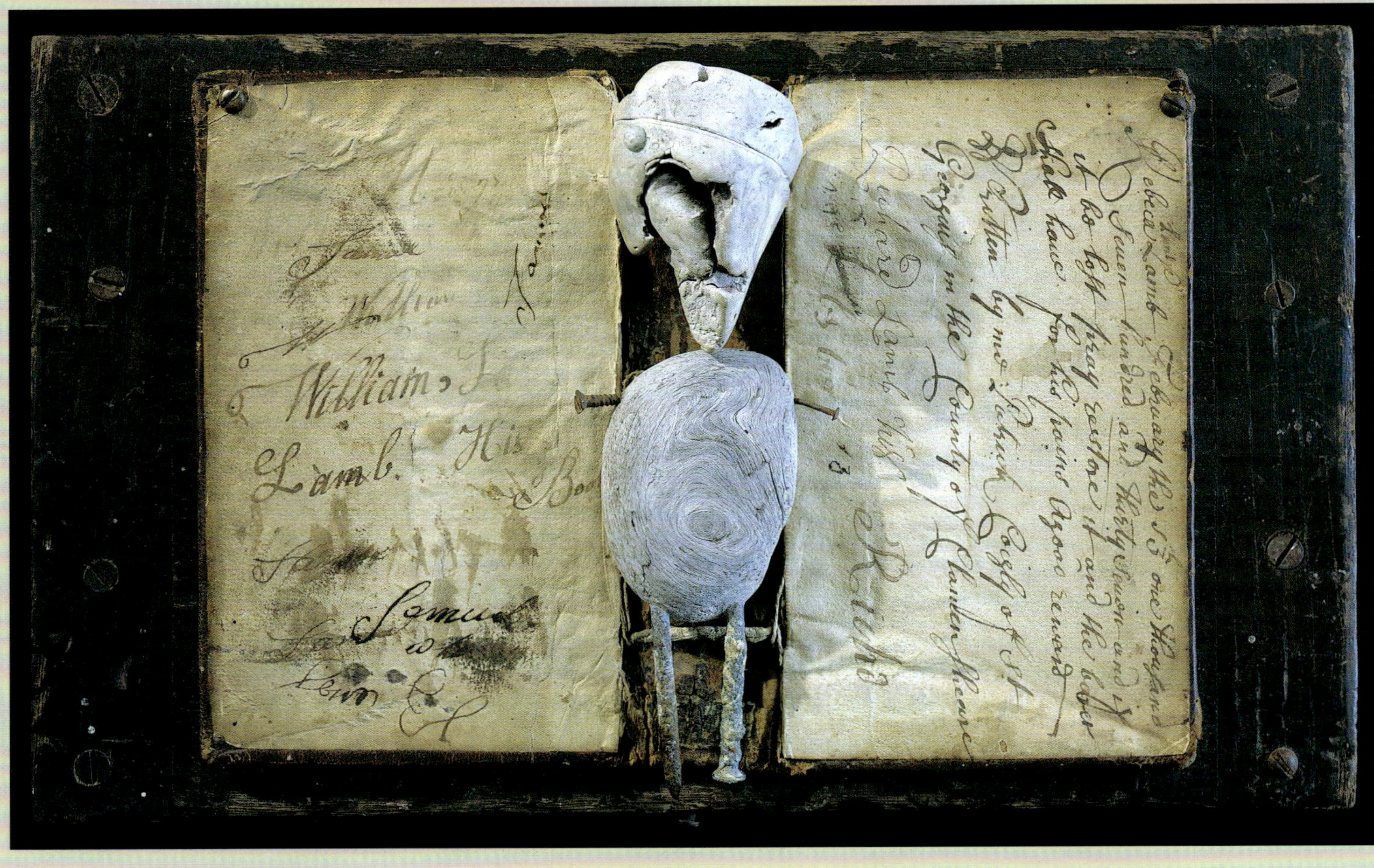

Der Dichter, 1994, mixed materials, 6 ½ x 10 ½ x 3"

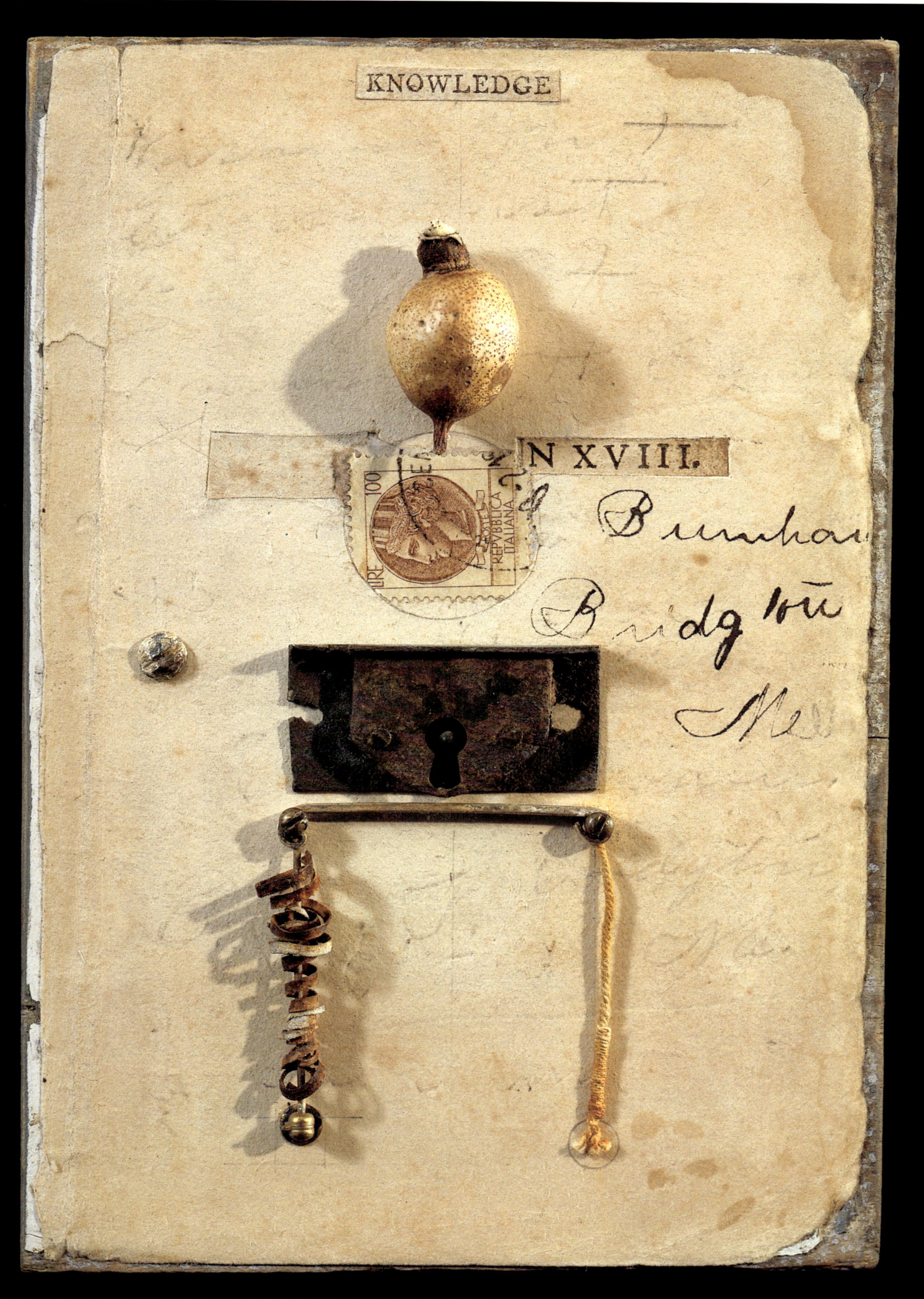

Knowledge, 1994, mixed materials, 8 ½ x 6 ½ x 2"

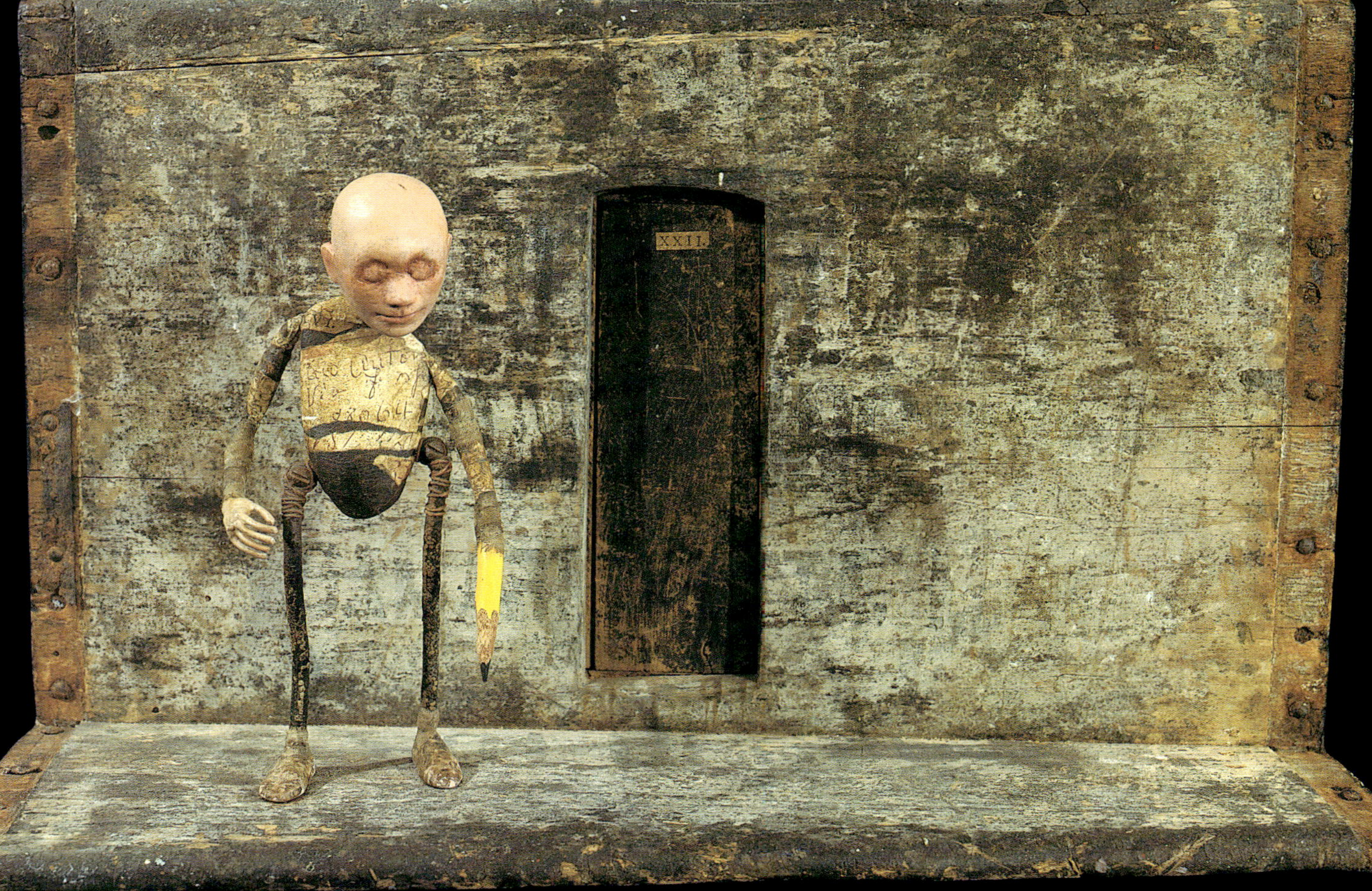
XXII.

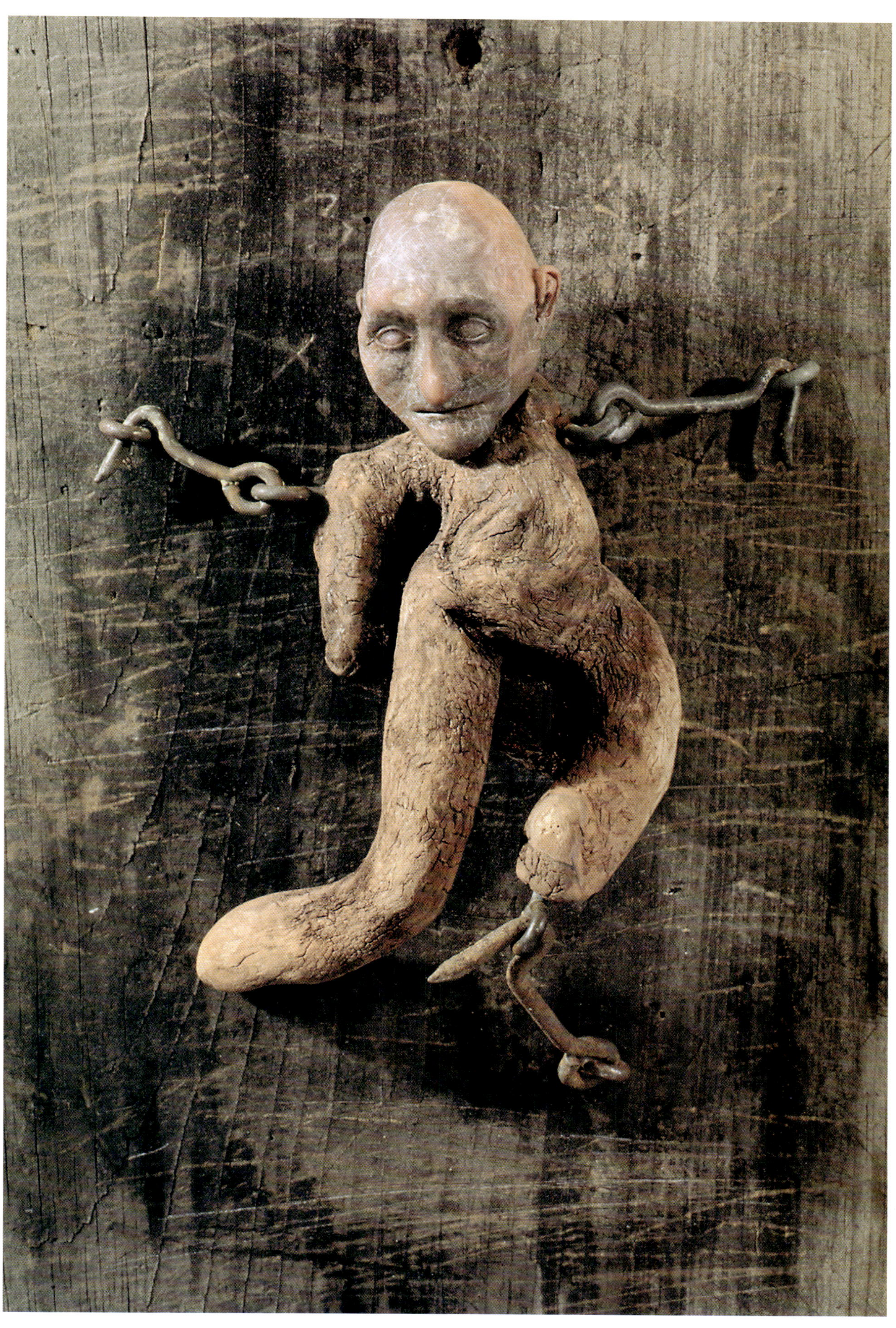

Dissent, 1994, mixed materials, 14 x 9 x 3 ½"

ARCHIVE MONOTYPES

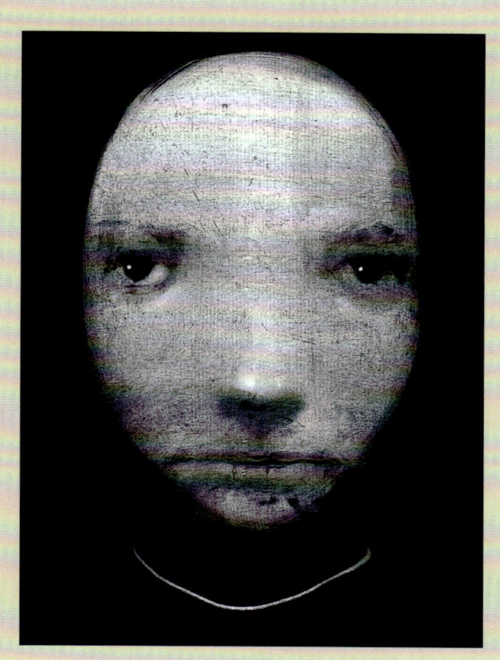

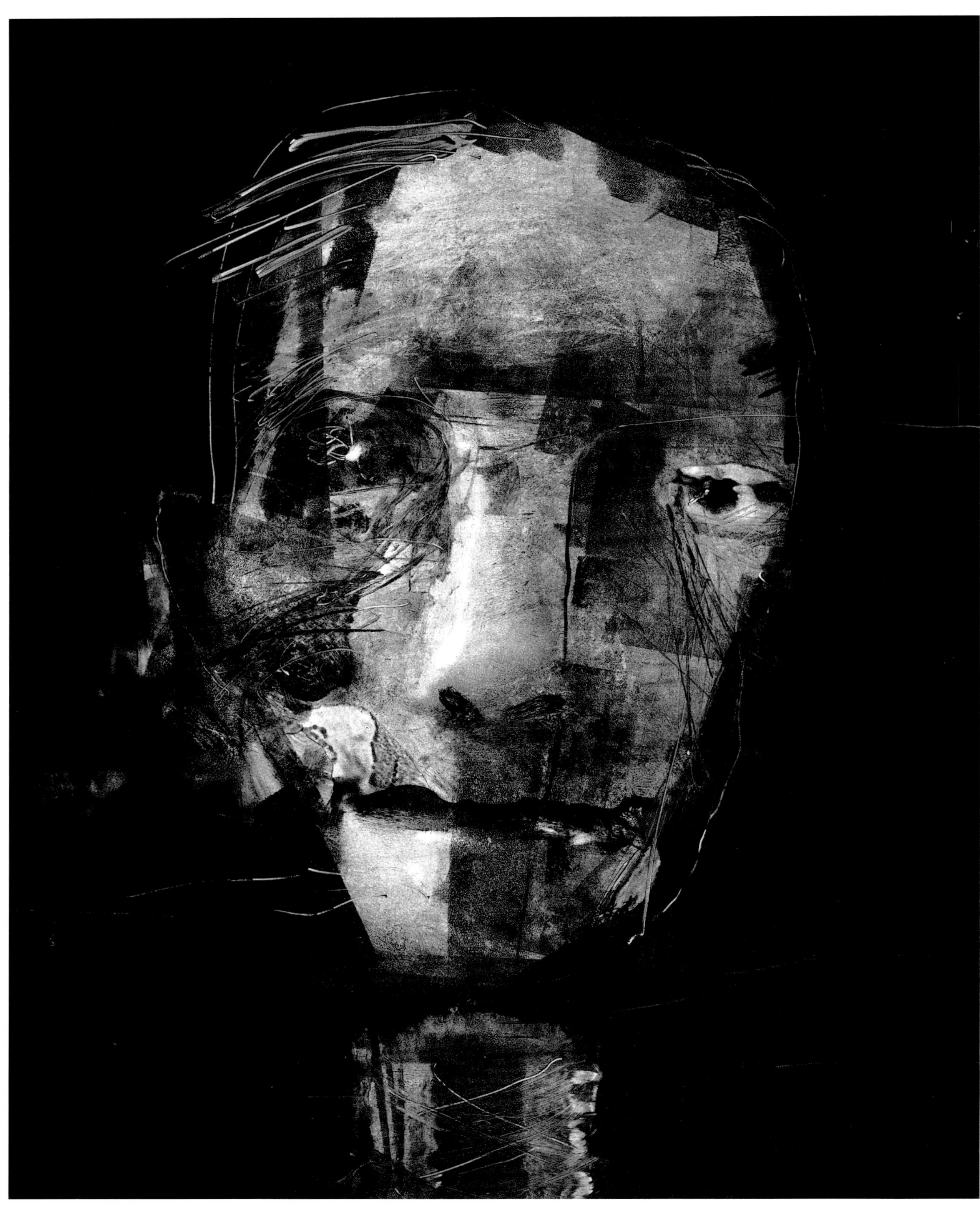

◁ *J'Accuse,* 1990, monotype, 24 x 18"
Mirror, 1990, monotype, 14 x 11"

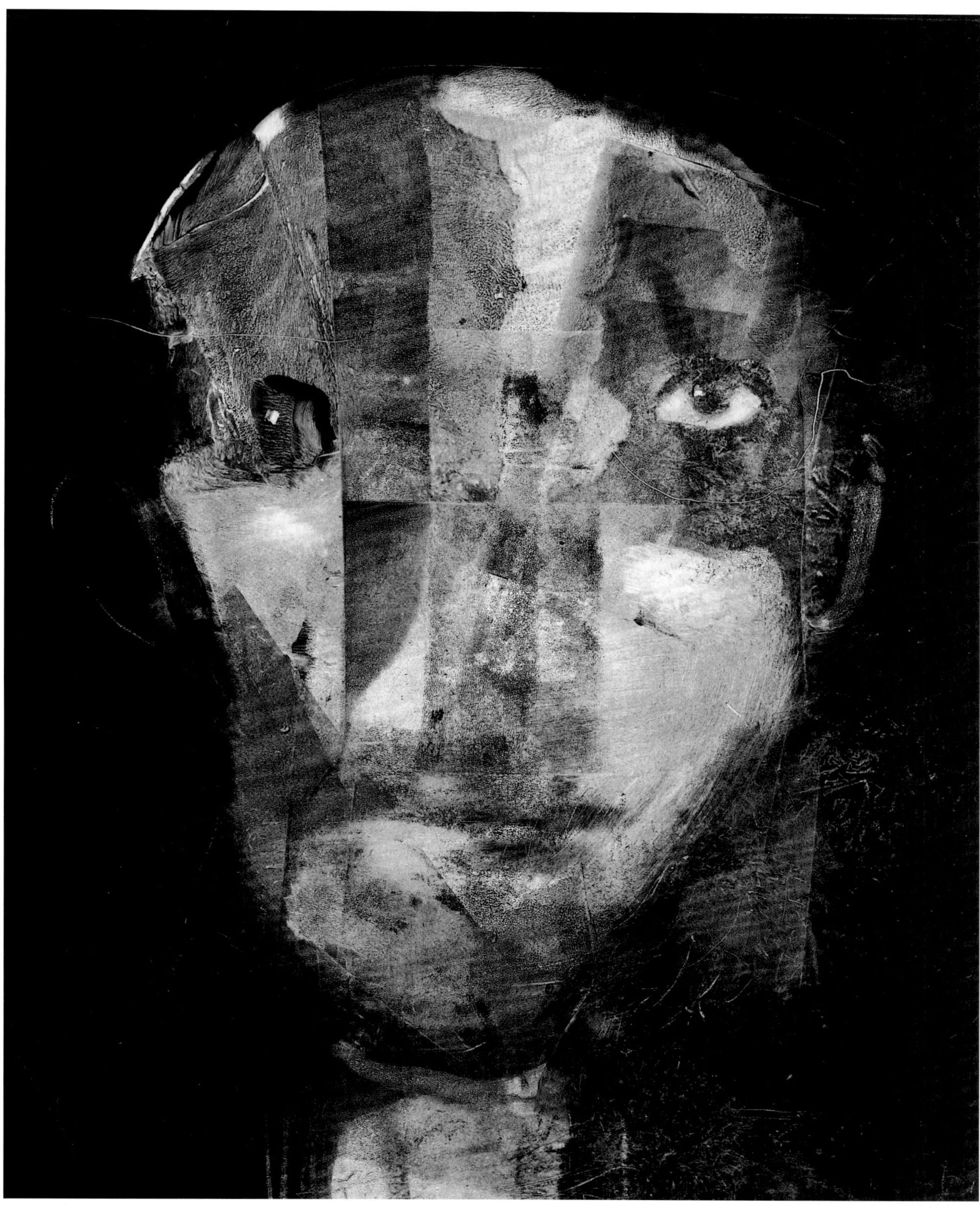

Tumultus, 1990, monotype, 14 x 11"

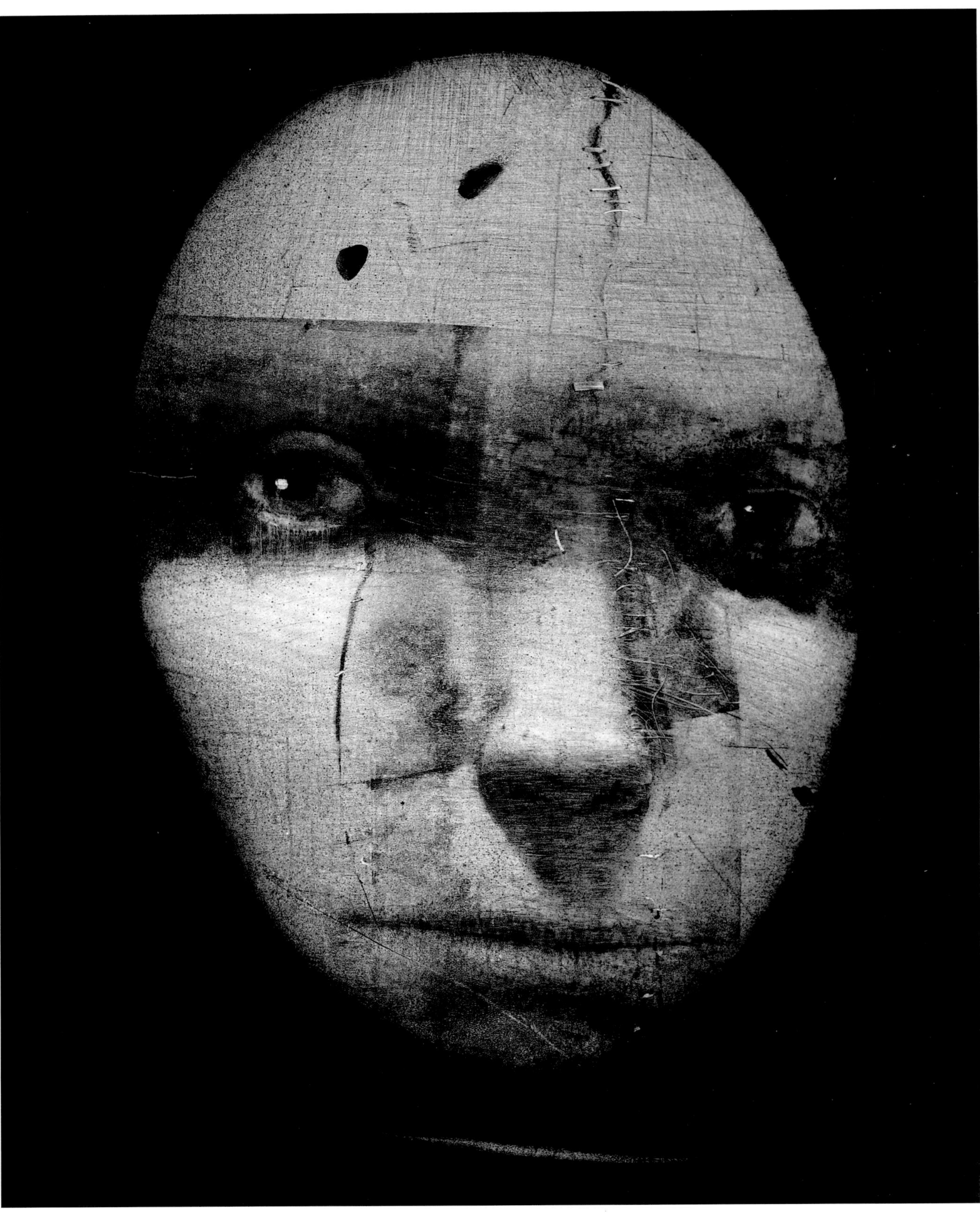

Horizon, 1995, monotype, 14 x 11"

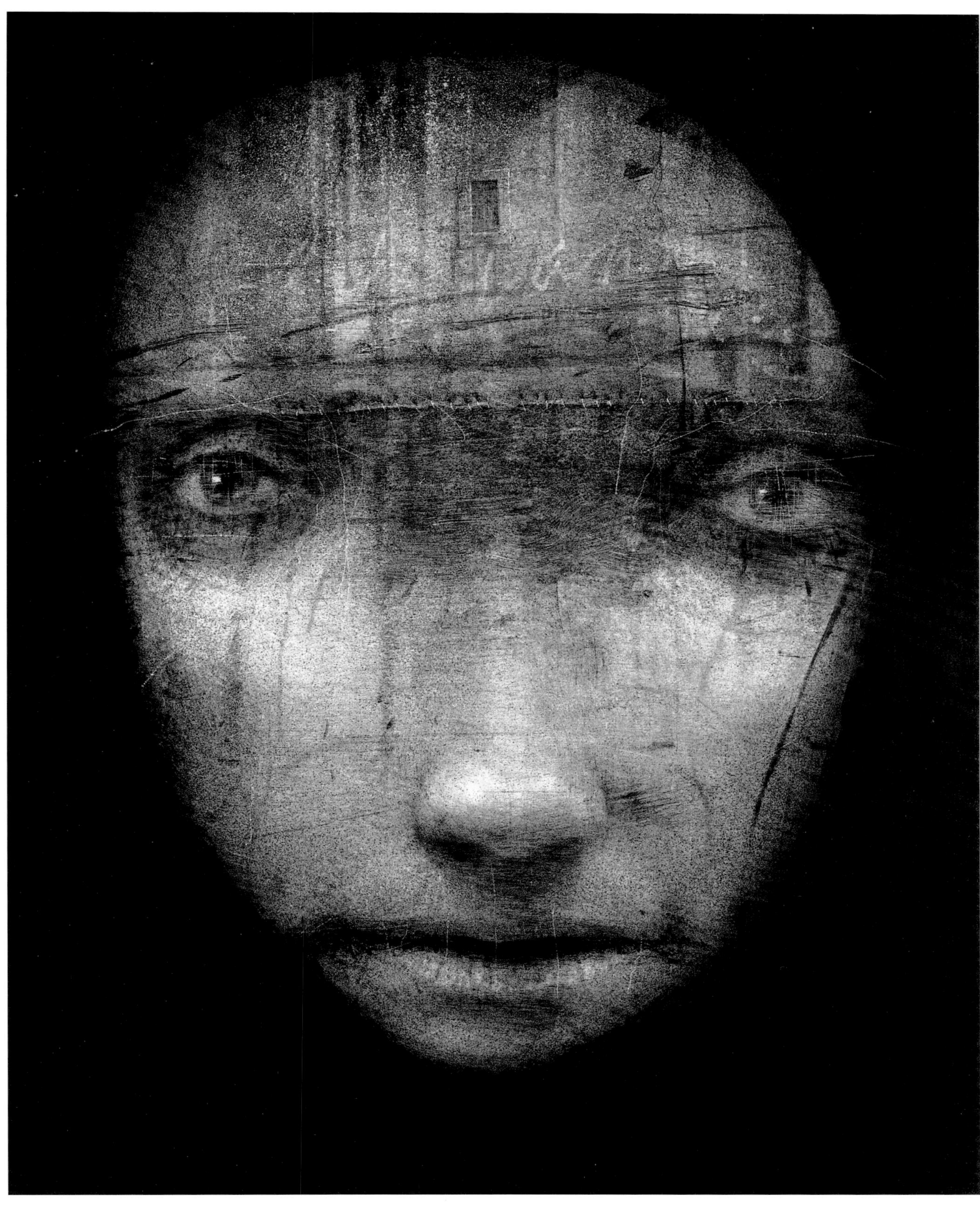

A European Education, 1995, monotype, 14 x 11"

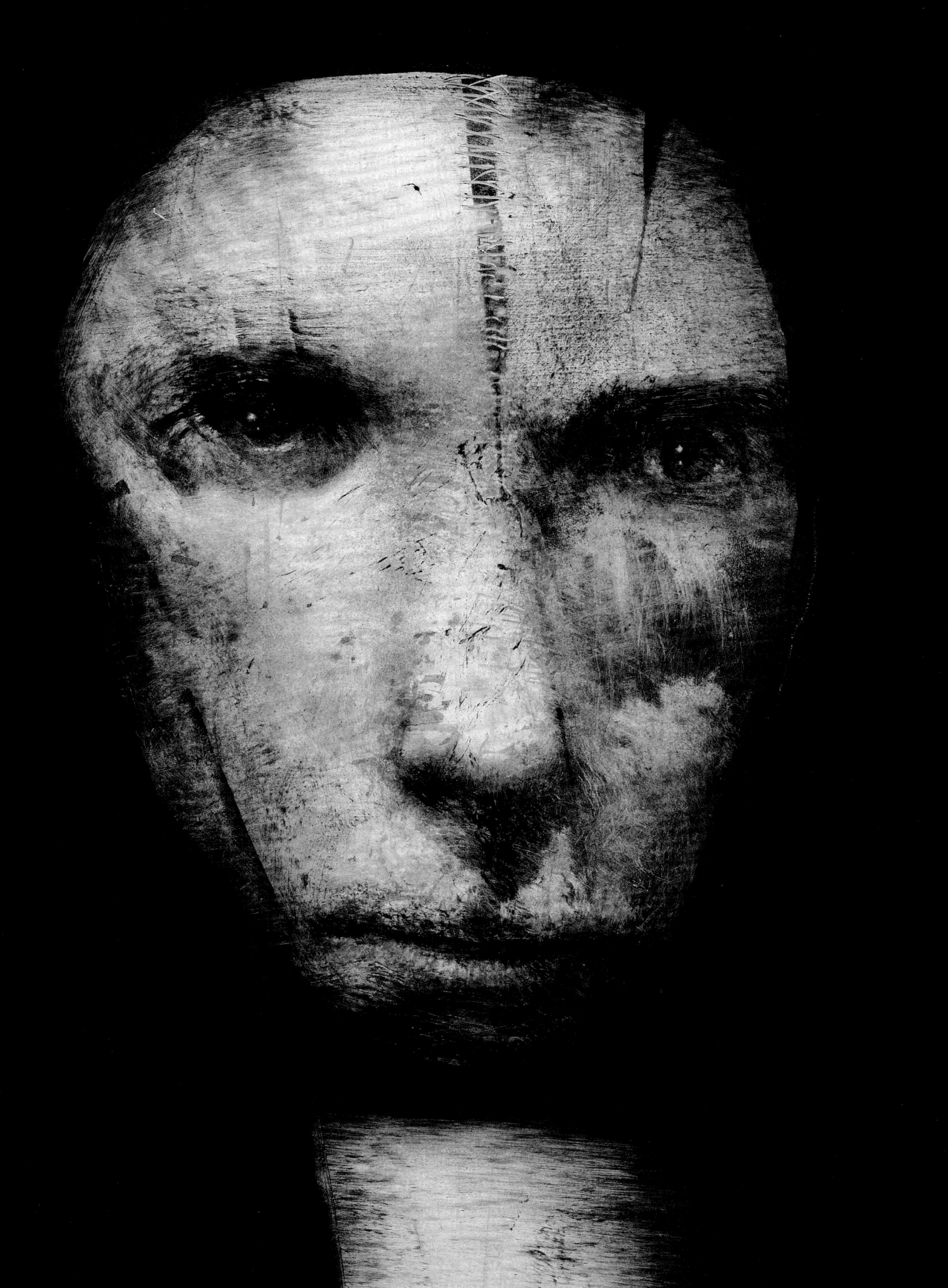

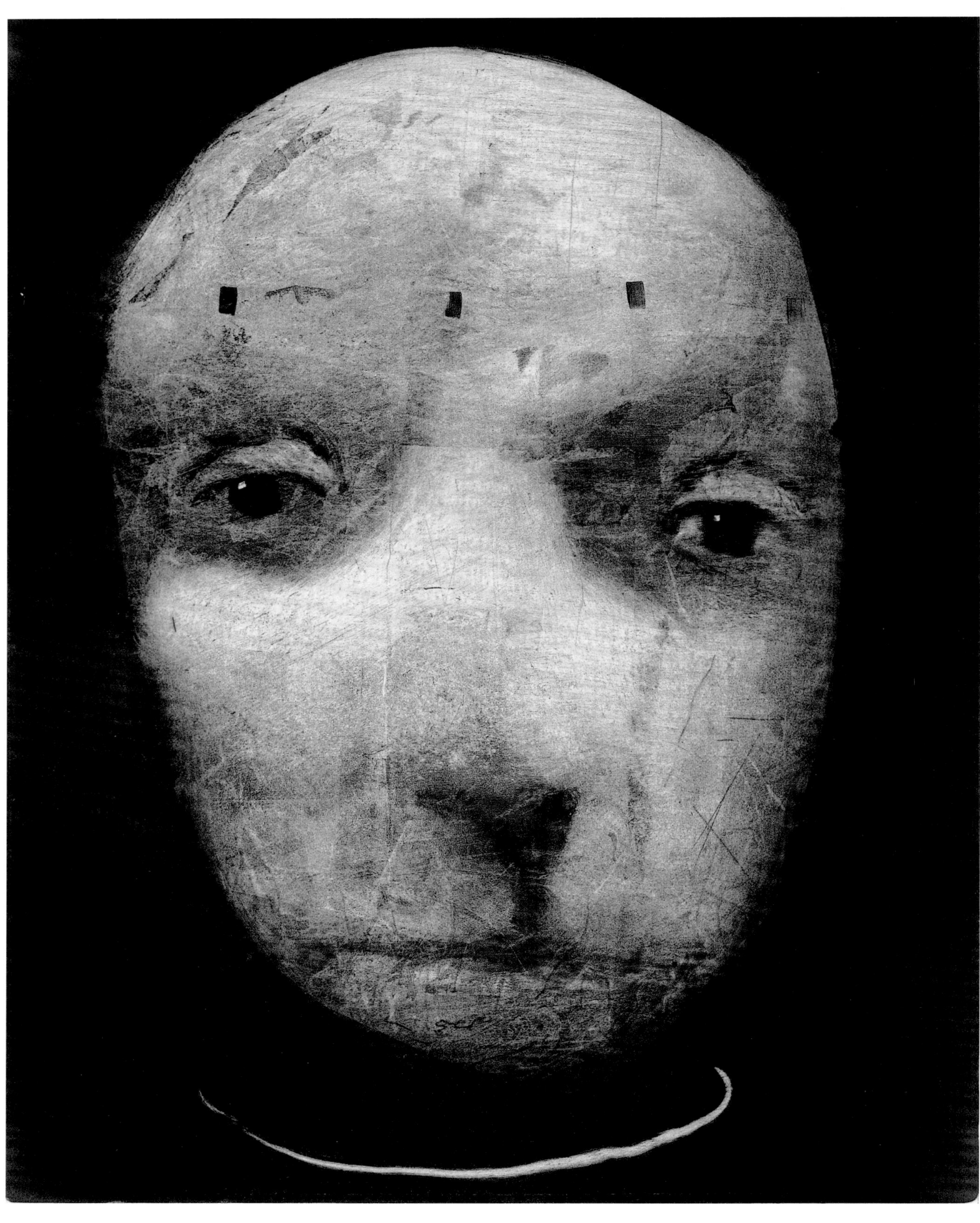

◁ *Wound*, 1995, monotype, 14 x 11"
Memoir, 1995, monotype, 14 x 11"

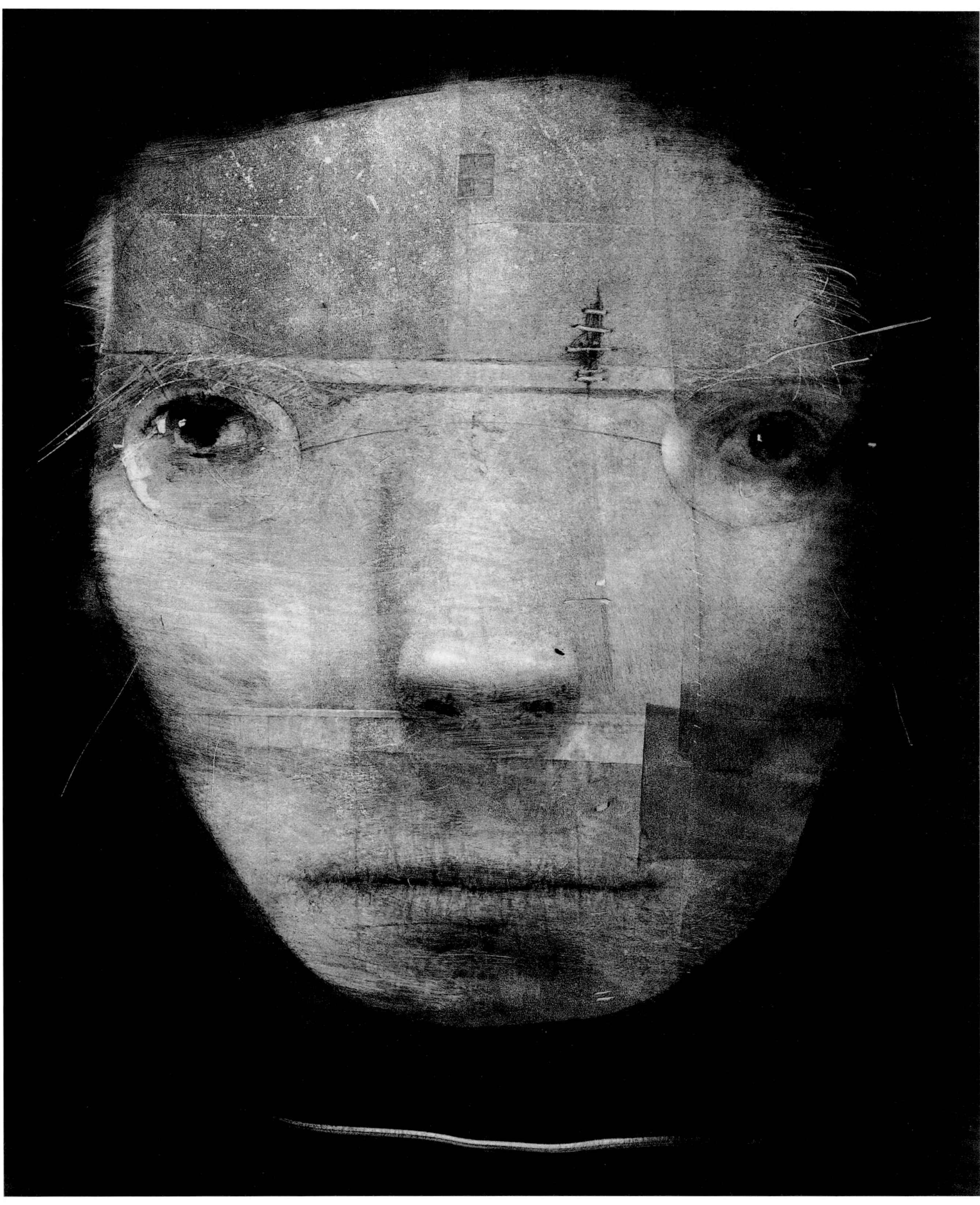

Archive, 1995, monotype, 14 x 11"

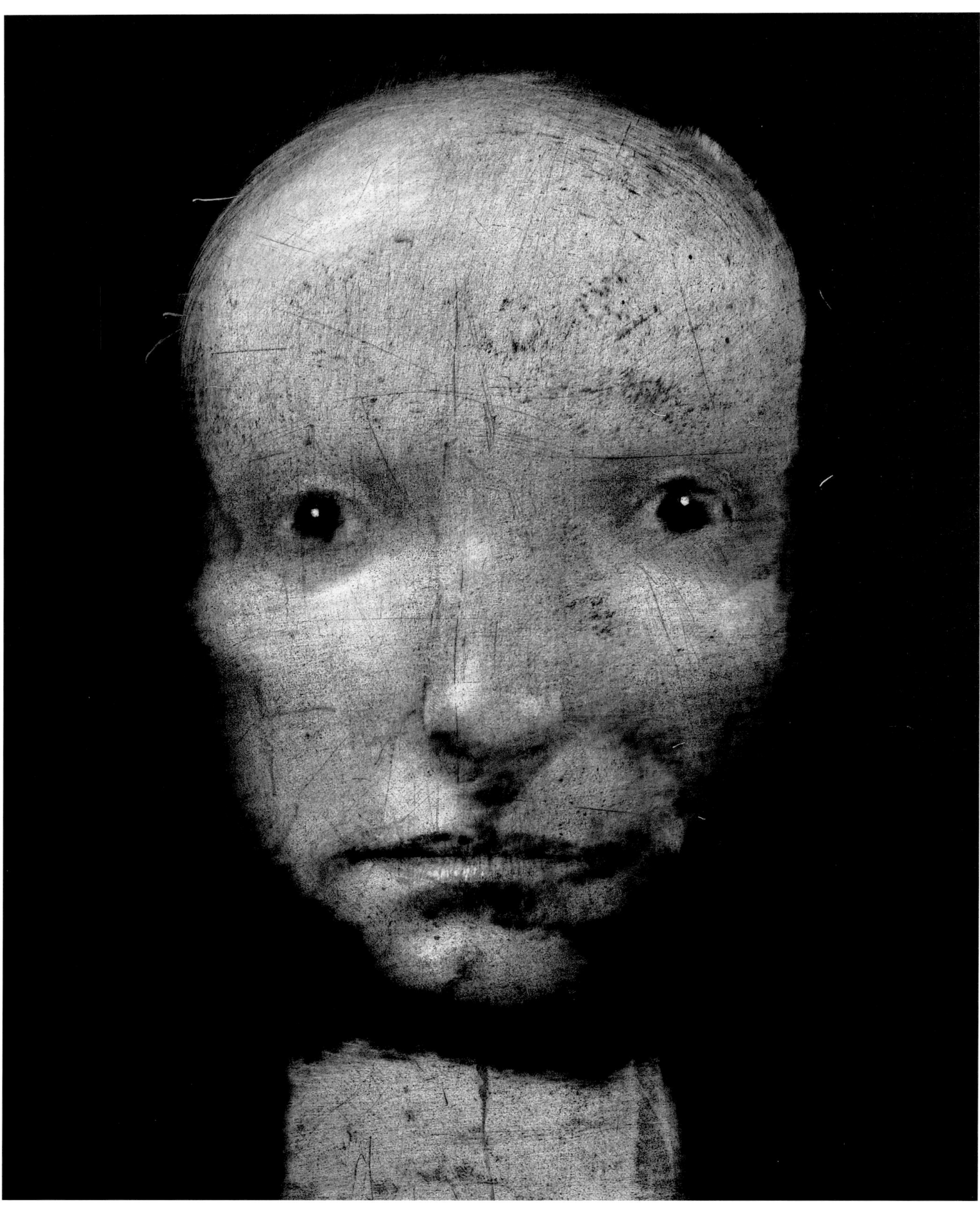

The Hemispheres, 1992, monotype, 20 x 15 ¾"

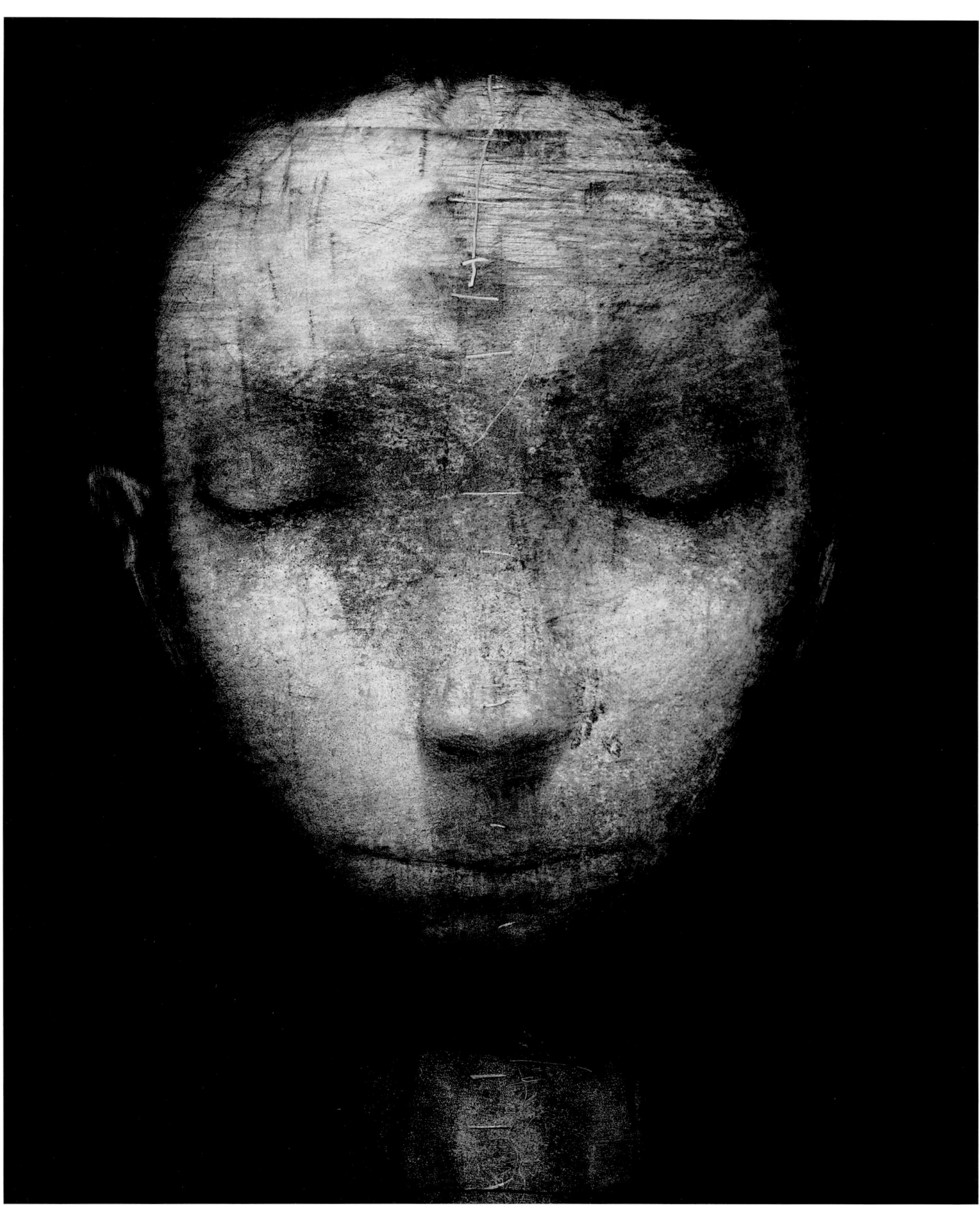

Sabi (Rust), 1995, monotype, 14 x 11"

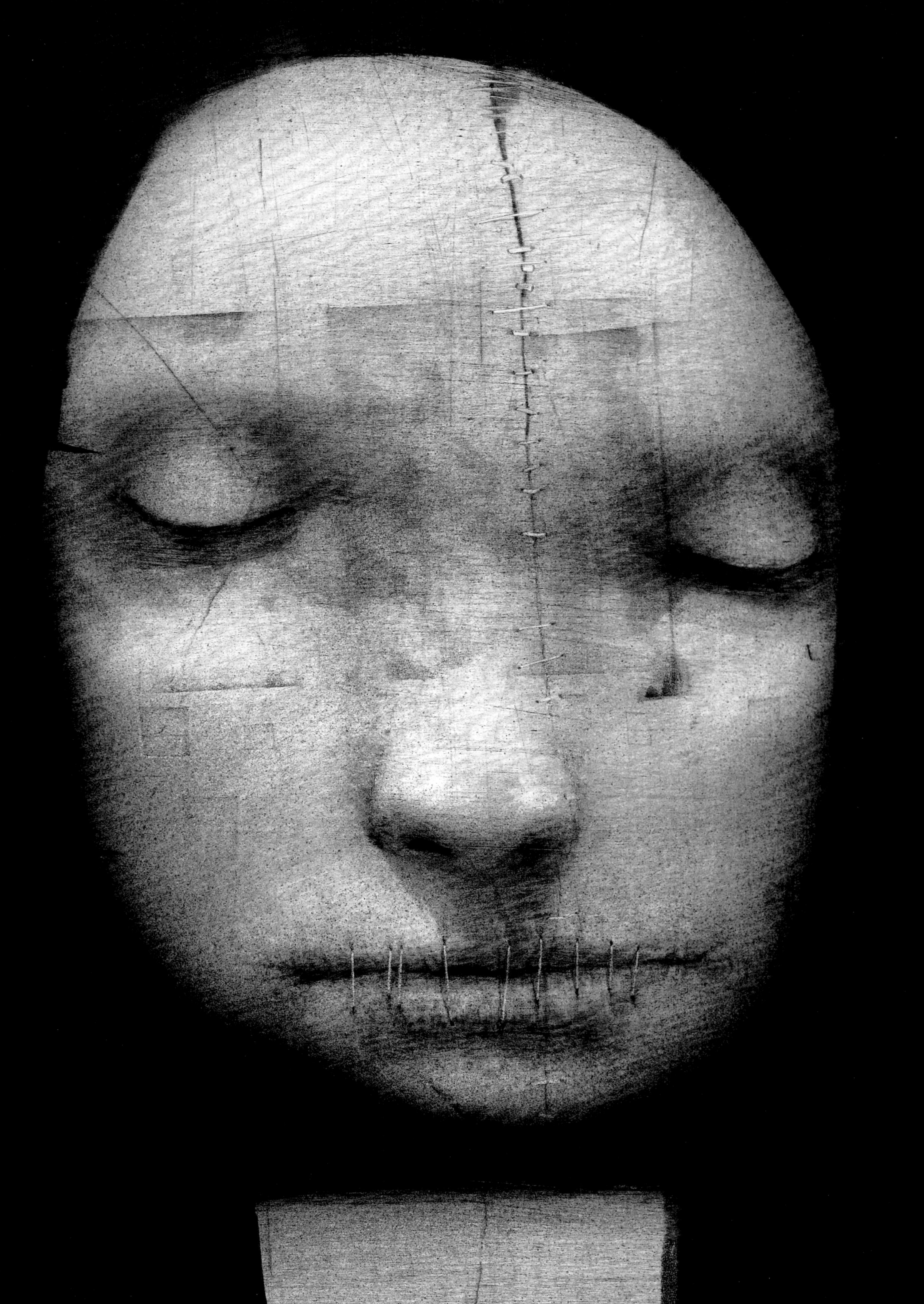

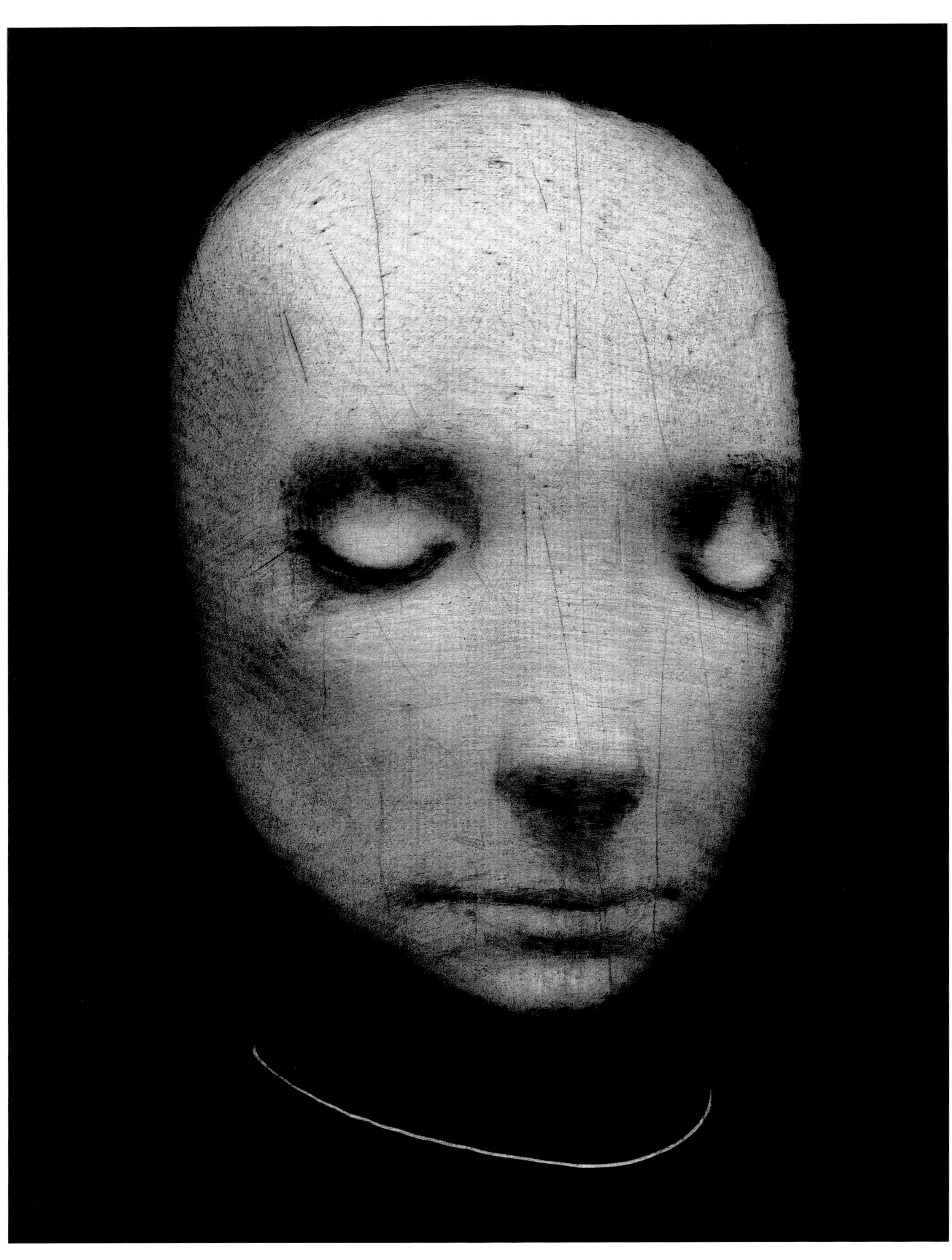

◁ *Silence*, 1995, monotype, 14 x 11"
Trauerarbeit, 1990, monotype, 24 x 18"

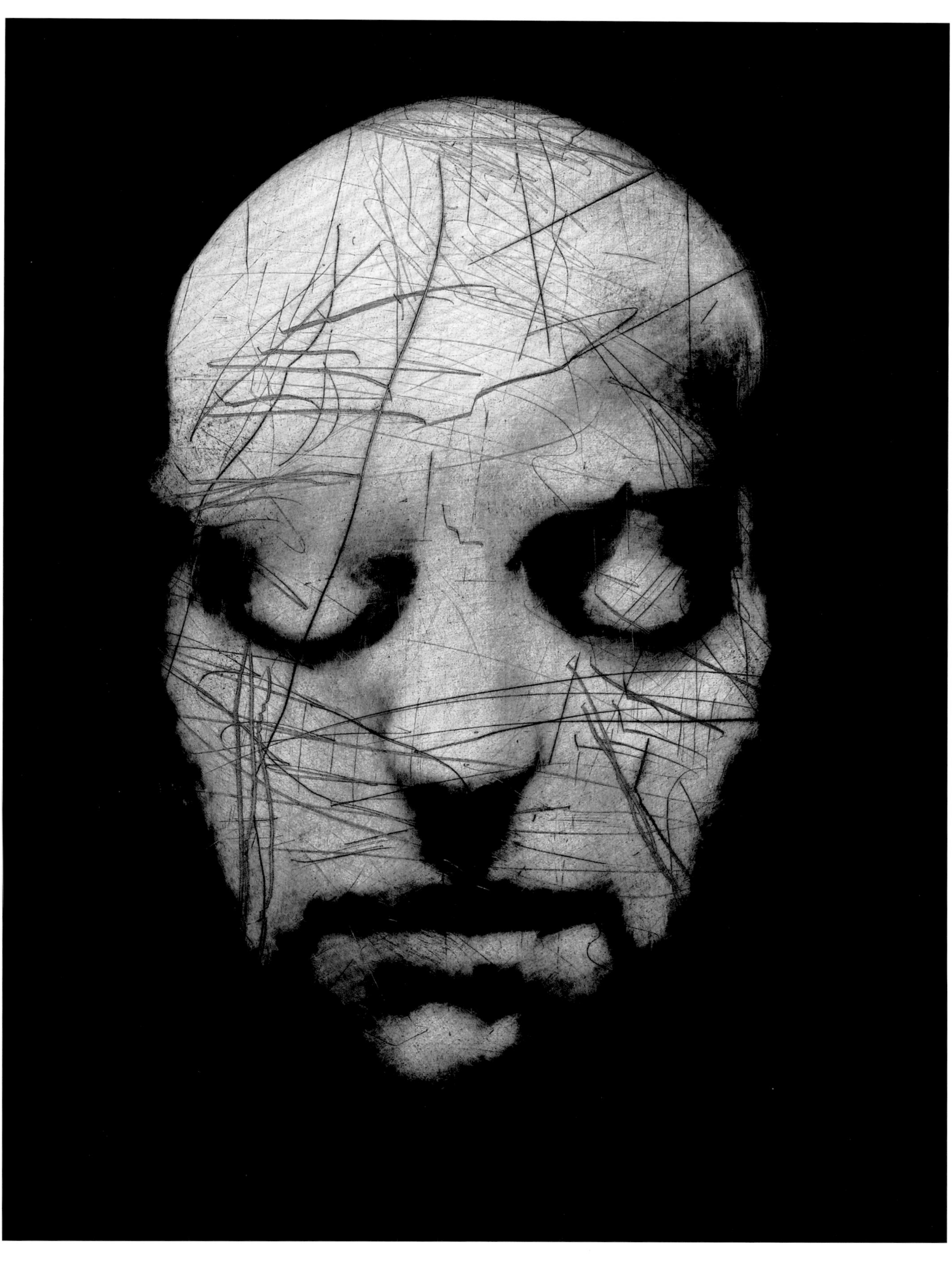

Weather, 1992, monotype, 24 x 18"
Cracks, 1990, monotype, 24 x 18" ▷

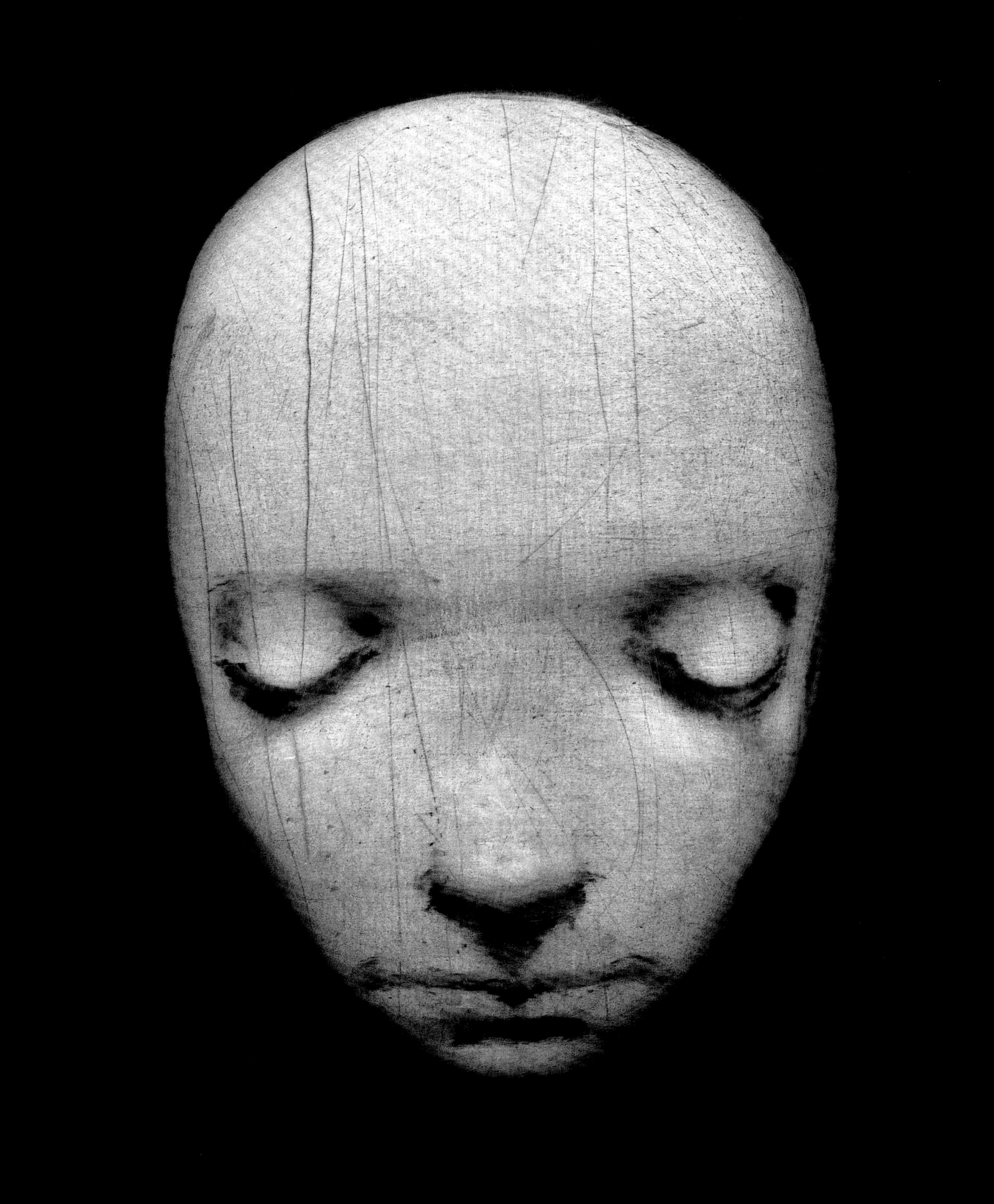

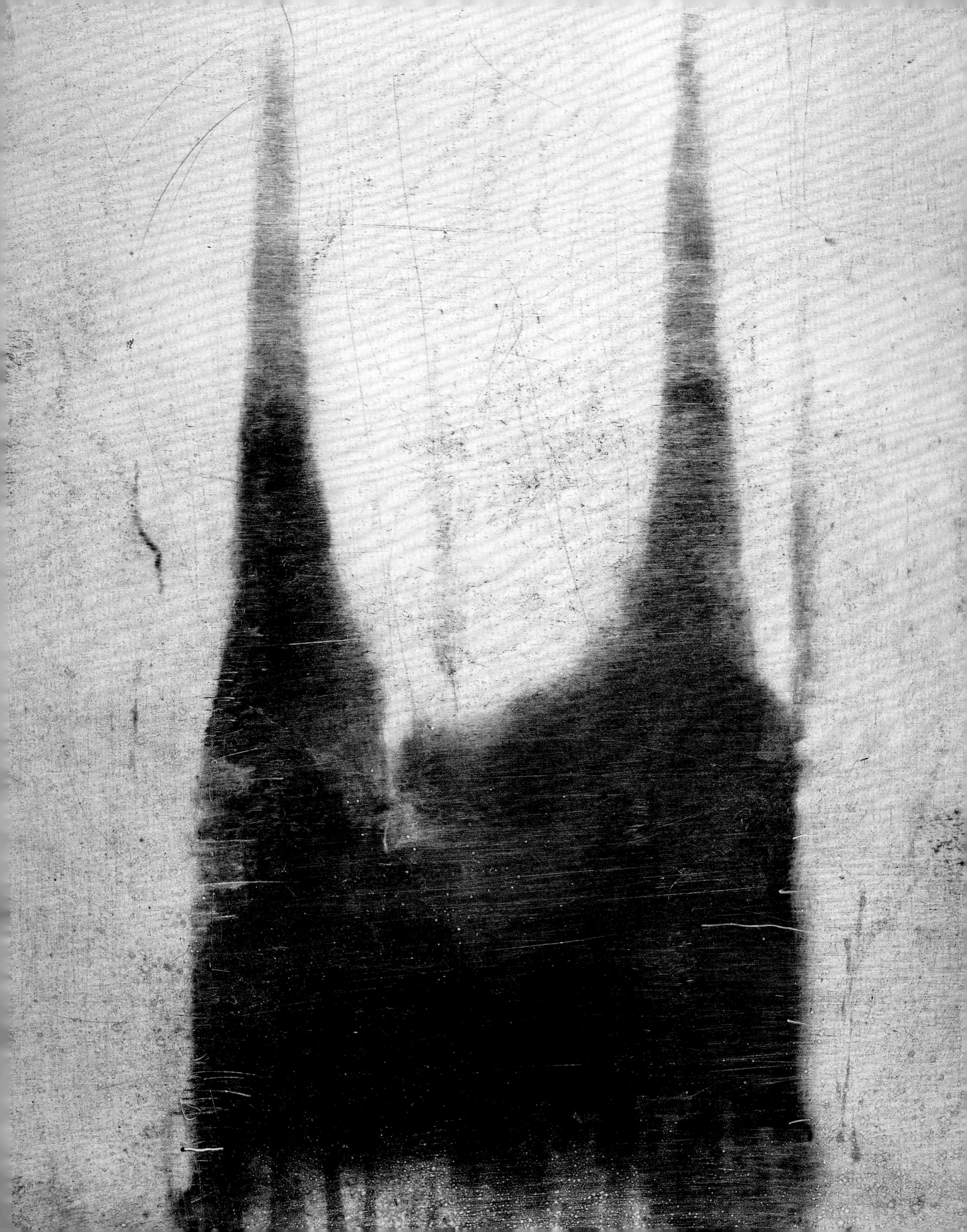

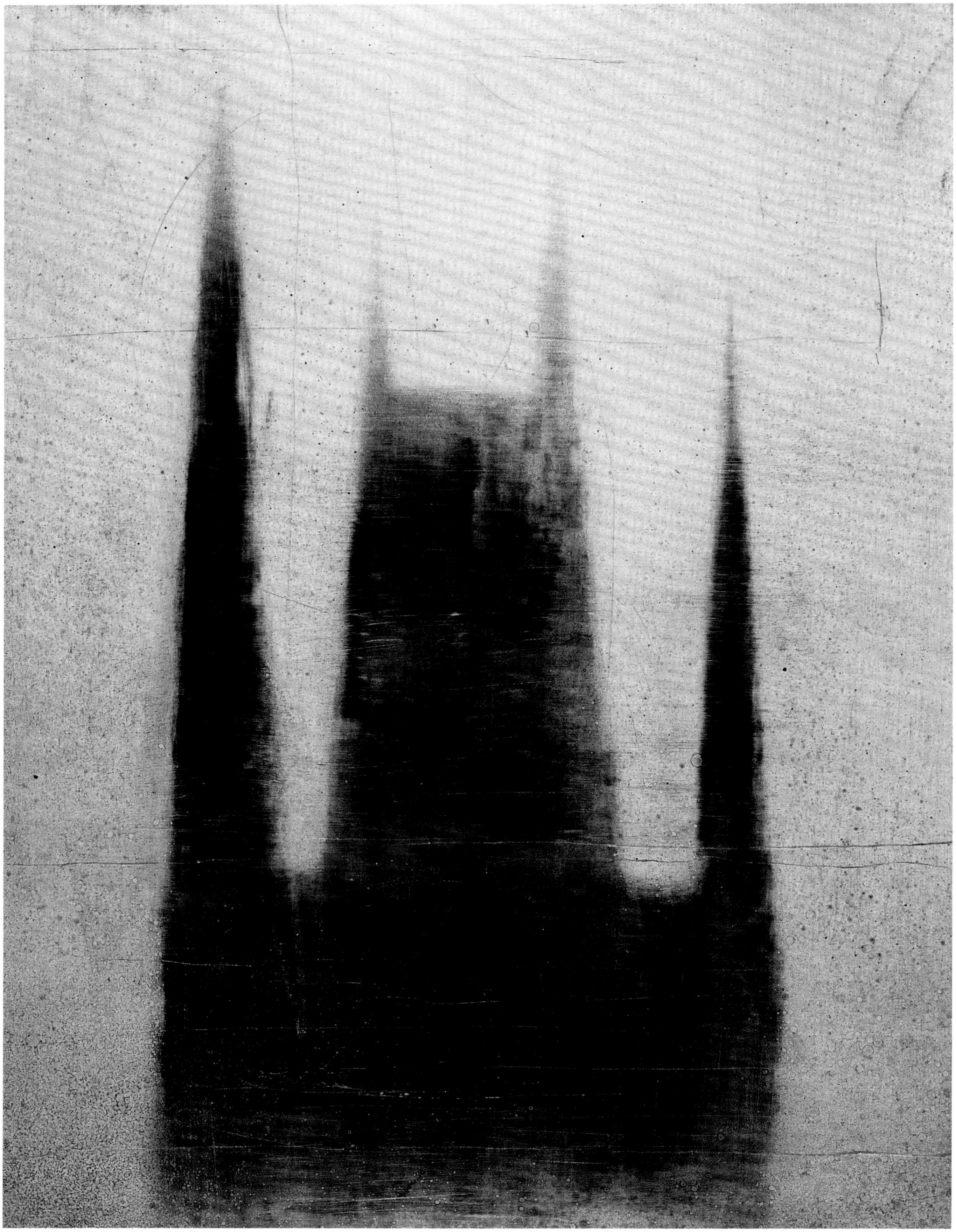

◁ *Spires*, 1990, monotype, 24 x 18"
Altstadt, 1992, monotype, 24 x 18"

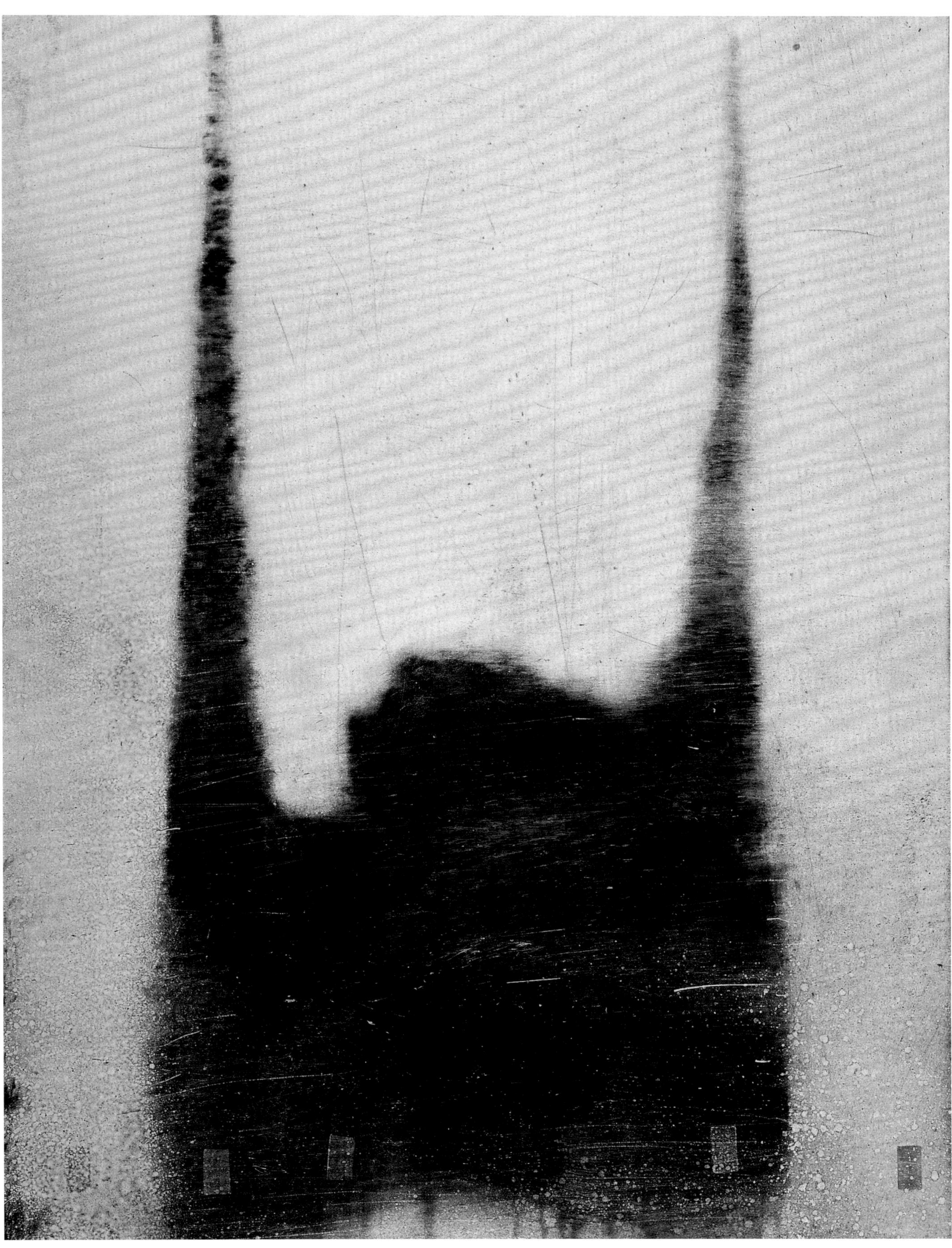

Five Windows, 1990, monotype, 24 x 18"

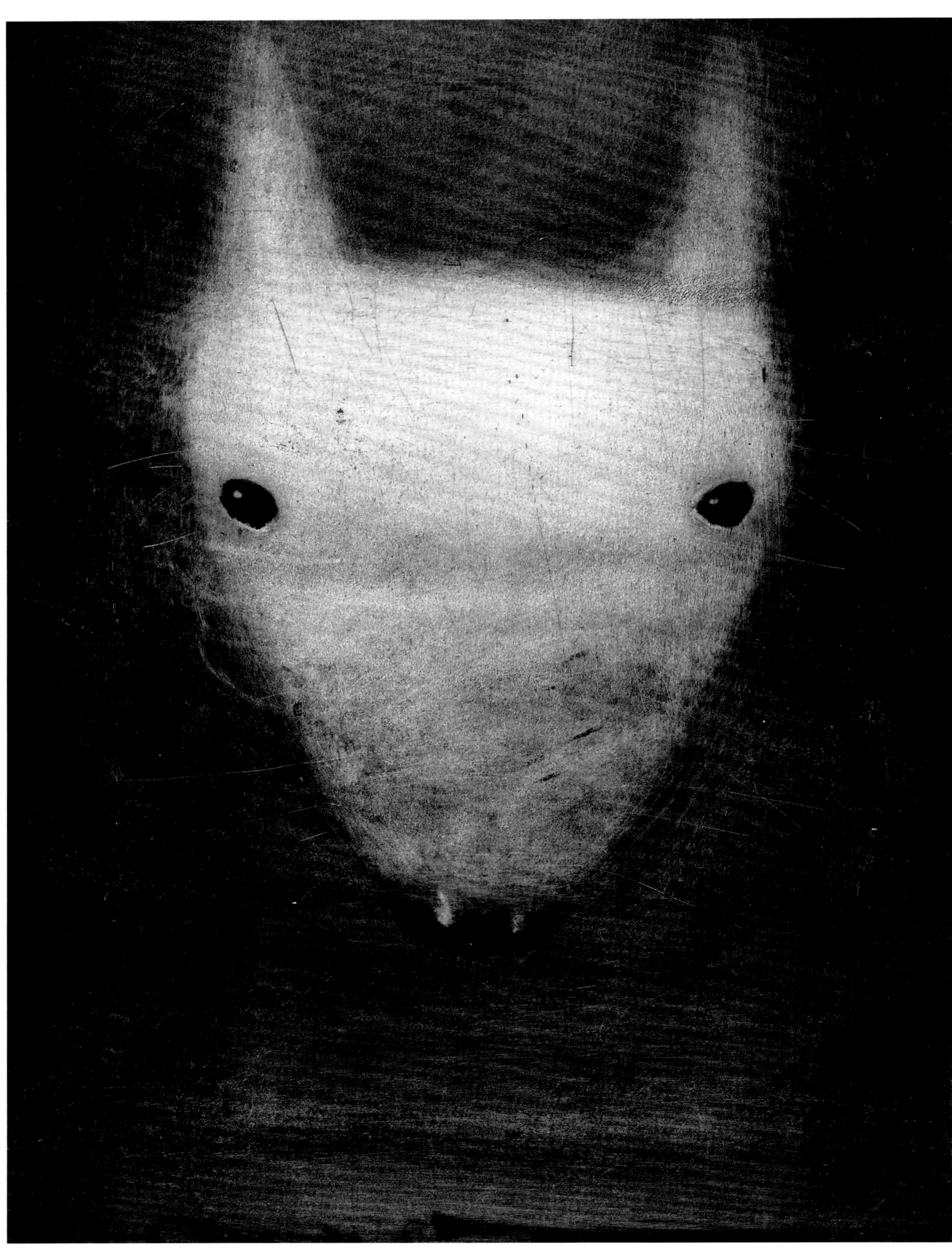

The Animals, 1994, monotype, 24 x 18"

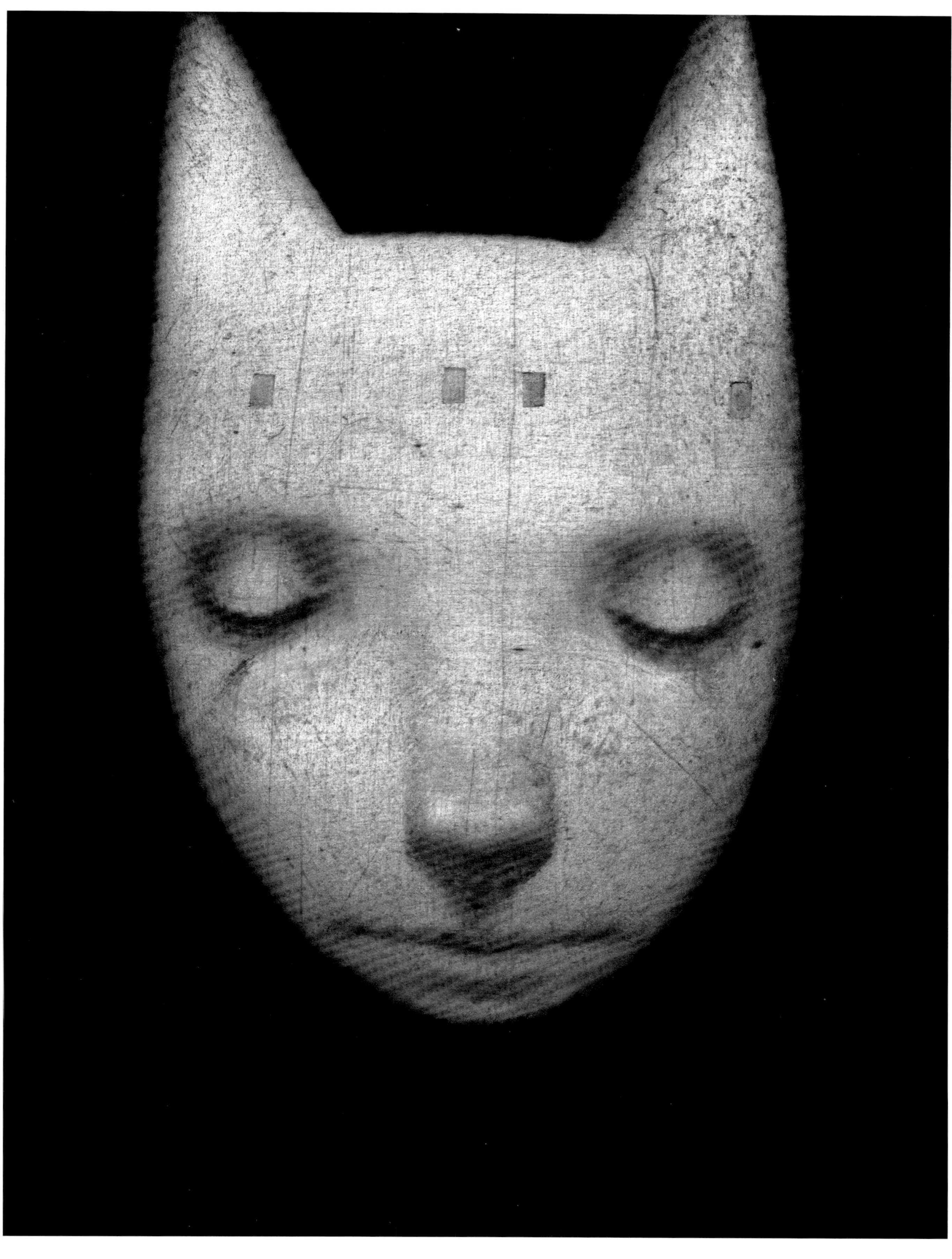

Spirit, 1990, monotype, 18 x 12"

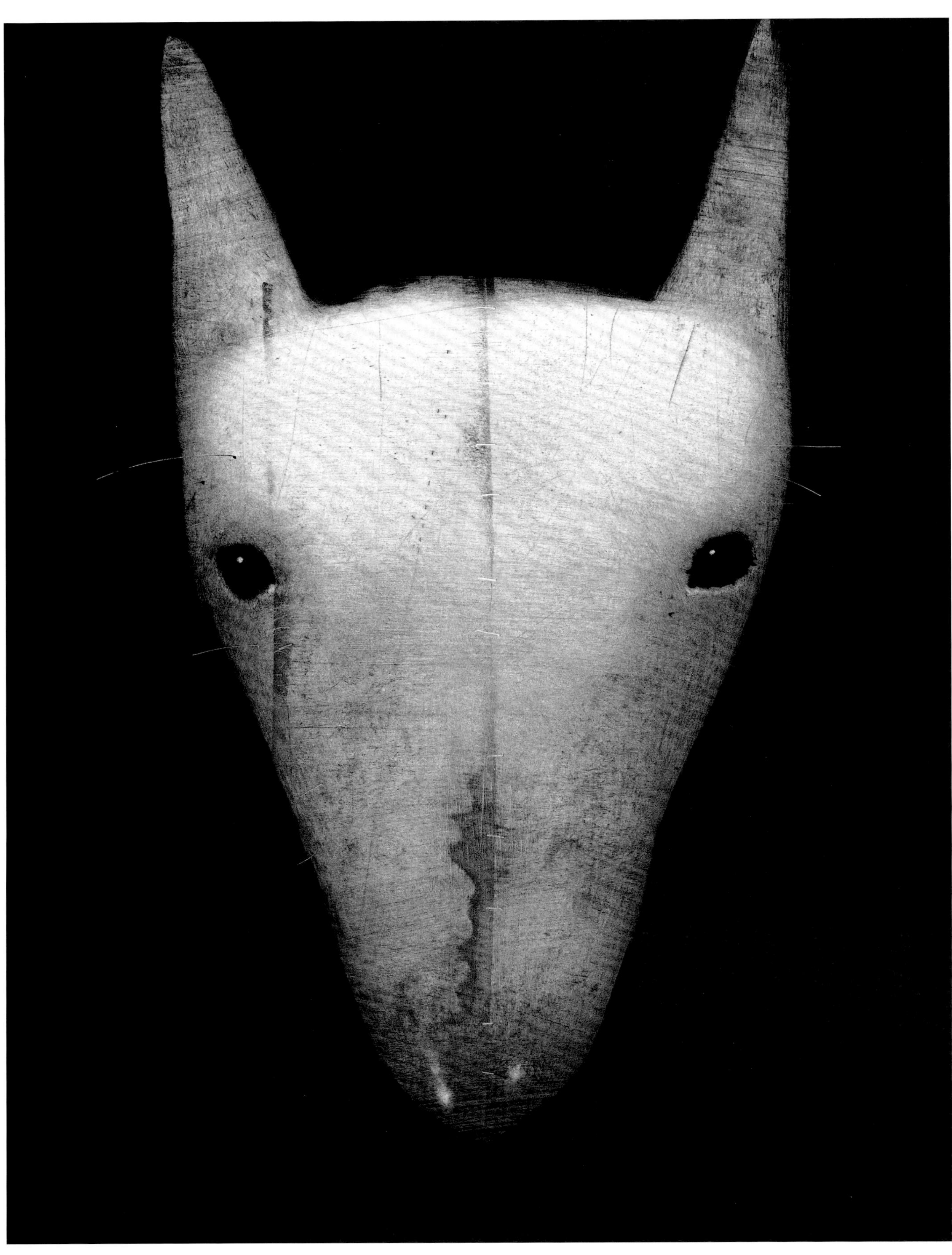

Art Thou Not a Man Like Me?, 1990, monotype, 24 x 18"

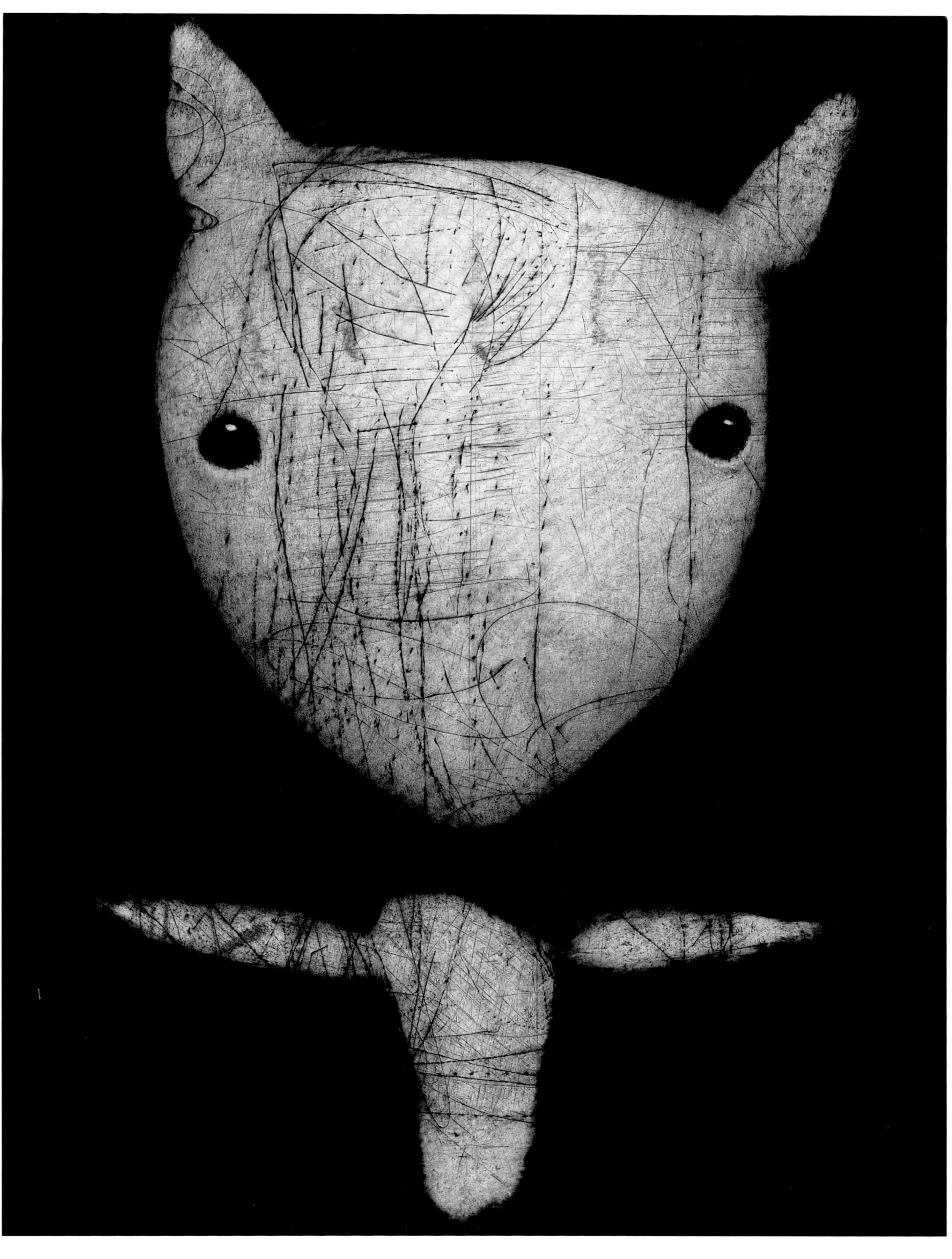

Companion, 1992, monotype, 24 x 18"

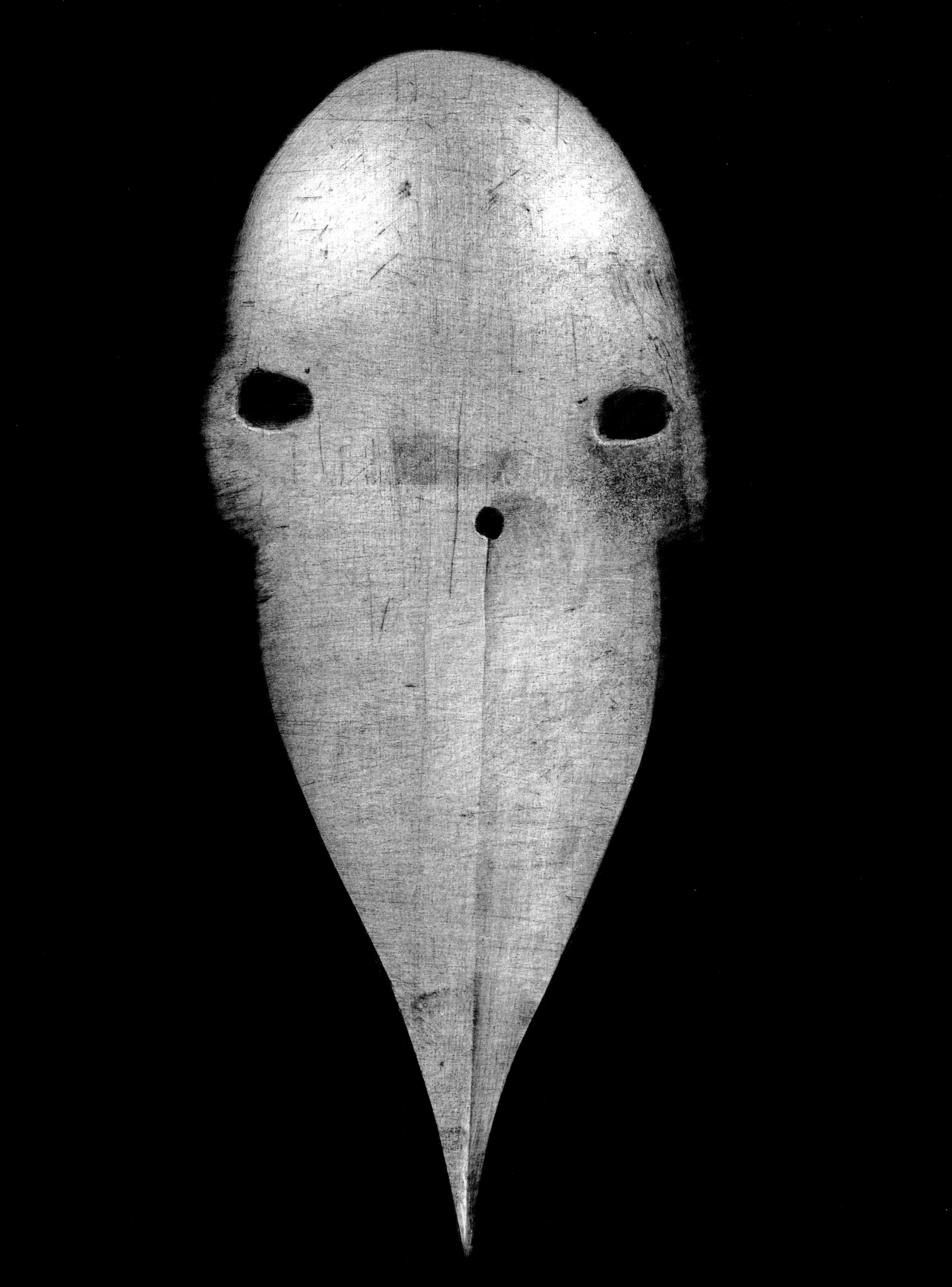

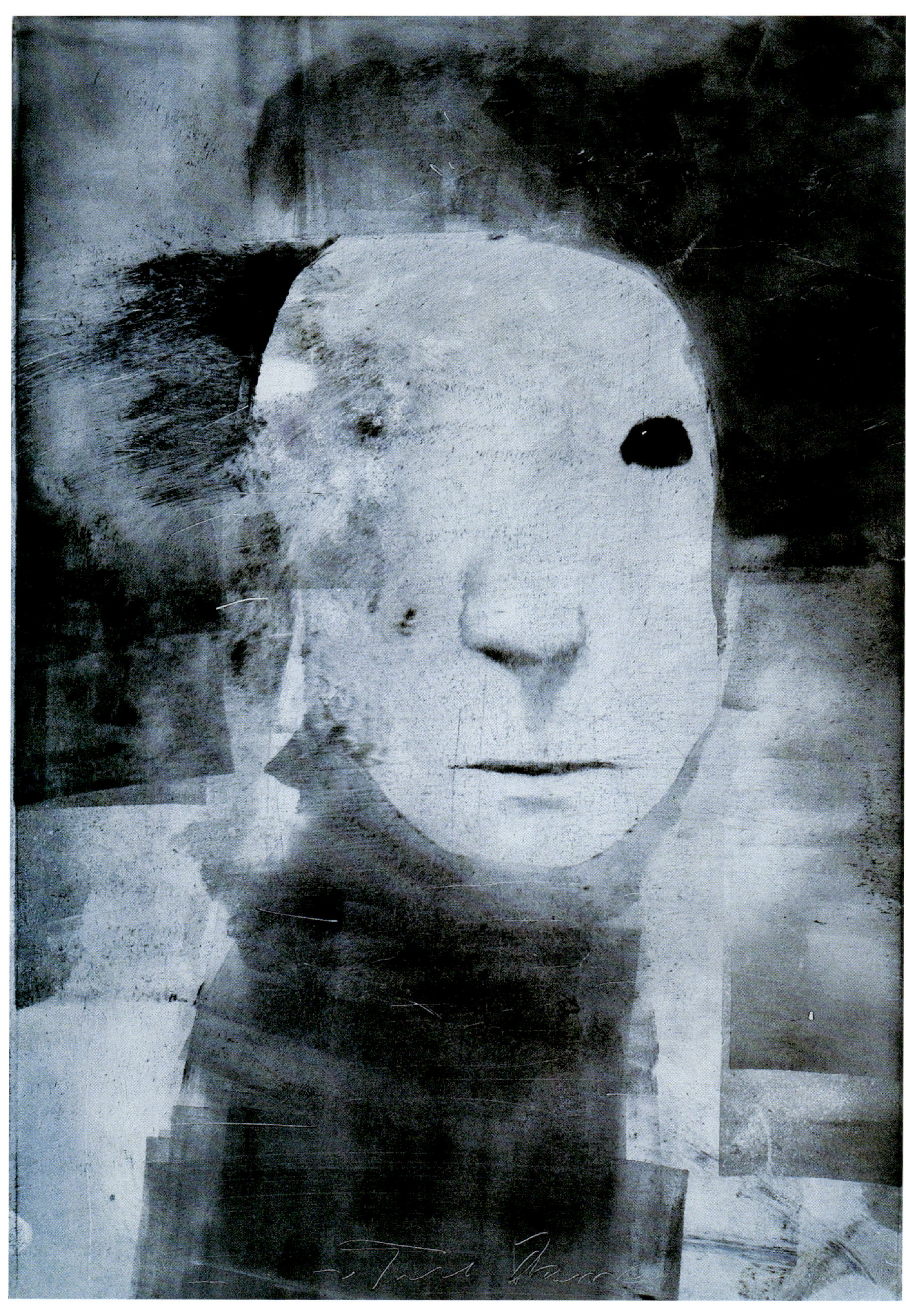

◁ *Writer's Mask*, 1990, monotype, 18 x 12"
Wind, 1992, monotype, 18 x 12"

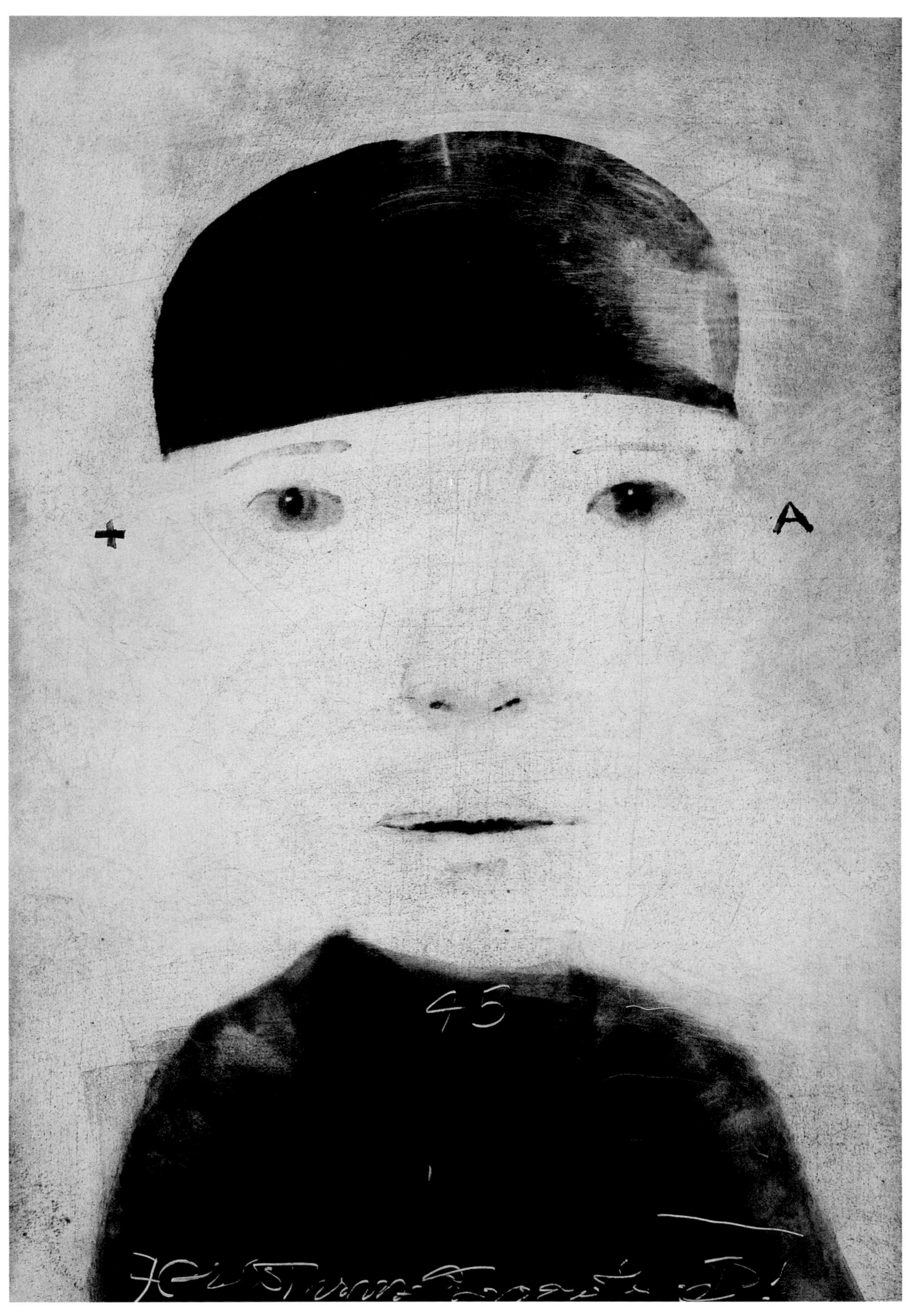

The Calling, 1992, monotype, 18 x 12"

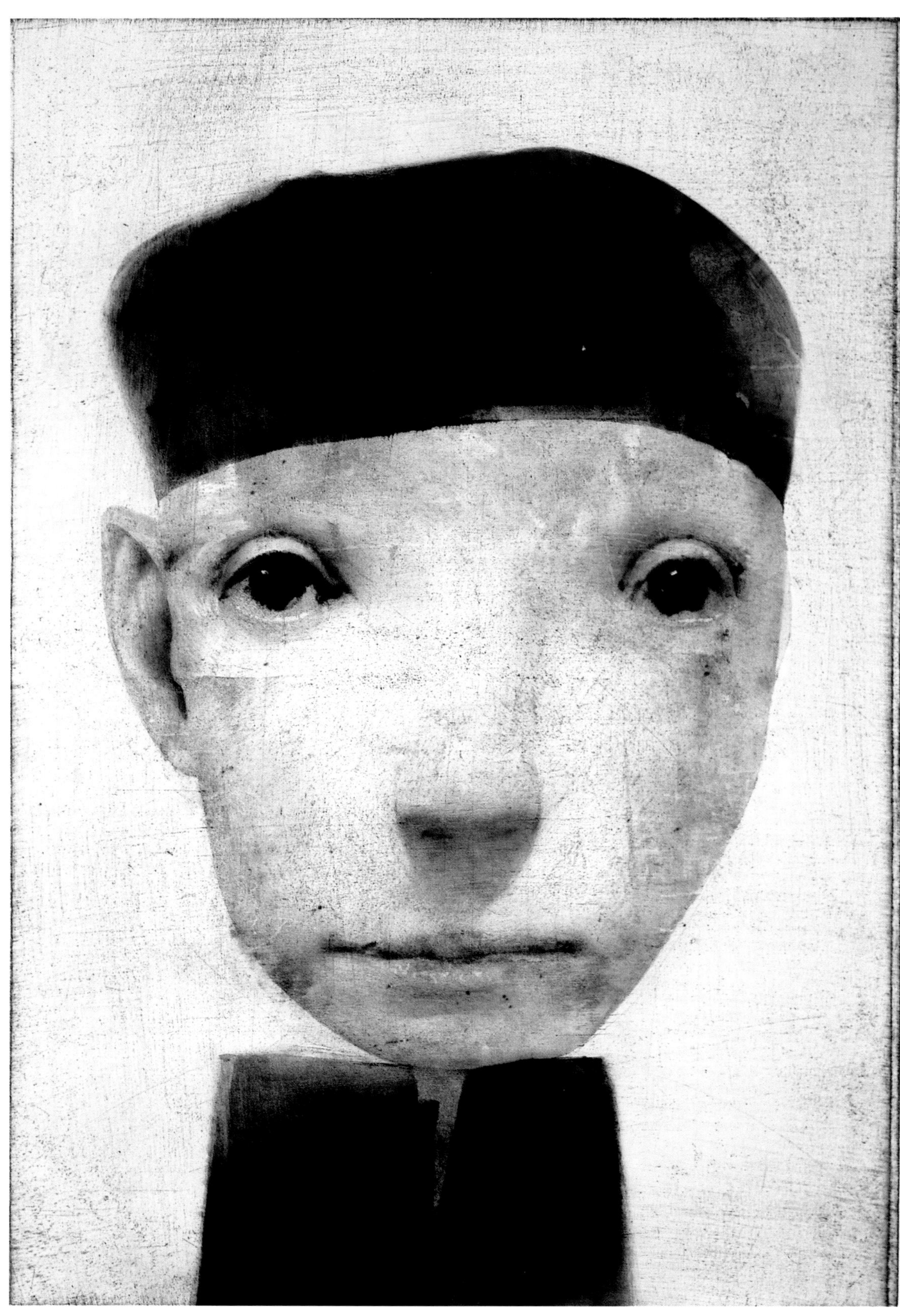

Prelude, 1992, monotype, 18 x 12"

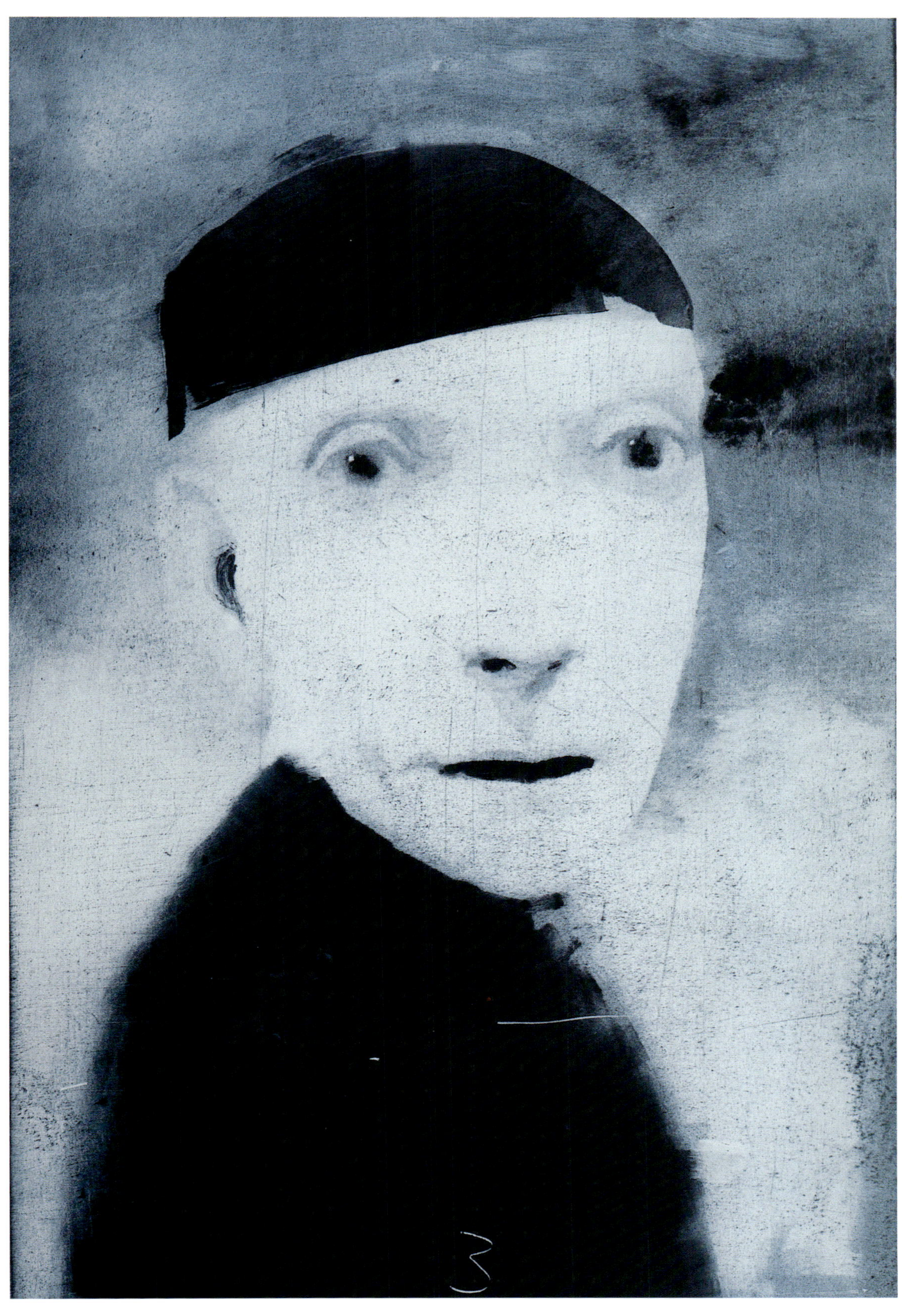

Dialogue of Comfort, 1992, monotype, 18 x 12"

GLOSSARY AND NOTES

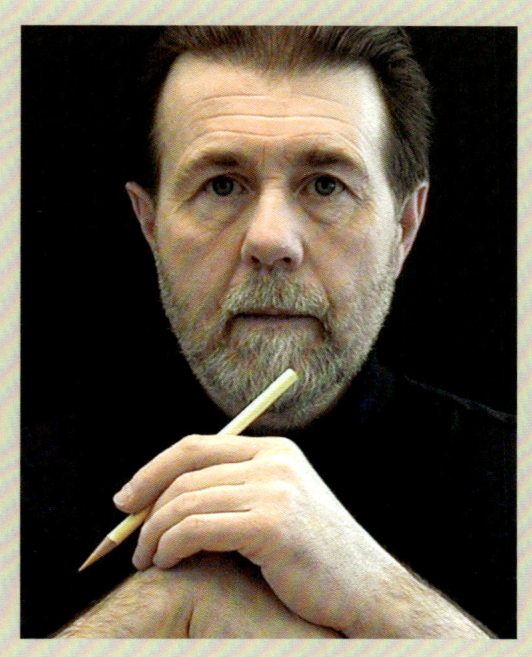

NOTES ON SELECTED TITLES AND REFERENCES:

Albinus, Bernard Siegfried (1697-1770)
German anatomist (worked in the Netherlands)
Albinus is the author of the compendium of human anatomy, *Tabulae Sceleti et Musculorum Corpus Humani*, published in Leiden, the Netherlands, in 1747. The book, illustrated with engravings by Jan Wandelaar (who spent 19 years on the 40 plates), was a monumental achievement in the field of scientific illustration; it established new standards for the illustrated anatomical atlas. My painting, *The Young Albinus*, contains a re-drawing of one of my own "anatomical studies" made at around age 5.

Altstadt, *n.* [German] the old city, the historic city center—often occupying the space within an original city wall.

Art Thou Not a Man Like Me? The title is borrowed from William Blake's poem, "The Fly."

Benjamin, Walter (1892-1940)
German essayist and Marxist literary critic
Walter Benjamin was not well known during his lifetime, but his works are now regarded as prescient. His essays, including "The Work of Art in the Age of Mechanical Reproduction" (1936), are frequently cited by contemporary art writers and post-modern theorists. Along with his friend Bertolt Brecht, he is remembered as an articulate opponent of totalitarianism. Benjamin committed suicide after an unsuccessful attempt to escape Nazi-occupied France via the Spanish border in September, 1940.
Throughout his life, Benjamin retained a child-like curiosity. He studied toys from Mexico and Russia, liked to examine debris from construction sites, and loved to wander the boulevards, arcades, and back streets of Paris. *Walter Benjamin in Paris*, focuses on the playful, innocent side of the formidable thinker. See Hannah Arendt's book, *Men in Dark Times* (1968), for short biographies of Walter Benjamin and his contemporaries.

Cairn (*Little Cairn*), A cairn [Scottish, from the Gaelic, Carn] is a pile, or heap, of stones. "certain piles of stones ... erected by the early inhabitants of the British Isles, apparently as sepulchral monuments." (Webster)

Catena, *n.* a chain, a chain of linked ideas, a series of contingent premises in theology.

Dialogue of Comfort, The title is borrowed from Thomas More's, *Dialogue of Comfort Against Tribulation* (1557), a book More wrote while imprisoned and awaiting execution. The fictional dialogue offers insight and advice on a wide range of human dilemmas.

Der Dichter, *n.* [German] the poet, a writer with high literary ambition or merit. See Elias Canetti's essay, "The Writer's Profession" from the collection, *The Conscience of Words* (1979). (This essay was a catalyst for the creation of my assemblage, *Der Dichter*).

Dreyer, Carl Theodor (1889-1968)
Danish filmmaker
Dreyer made a number of inspired, visually stunning films which address the plight of the visionary and the outsider. His *Day of Wrath* (which portrays the trial and execution of a 17th century herbalist accused of witchcraft) made a powerful impression on me during my student years. I have occasionally made reference to the film in my own work.
My assemblage, *Penalty*, alludes to Dreyer's understanding of the price of dissent, and also to his apparent empathy toward the countless historic injustices borne by women. See Dreyer's, *Day of Wrath* (1943), *The Passion of Joan of Arc* (1928), *Ordet* (1955), and *Gertrud* (1964).

Gowin, Emmet (1941-)
American photographer
(*Mesa Blanca, for Emmet Gowin*) This montage is a tribute to my friend Emmet Gowin. Emmet became well known in the 1970s for his enigmatic photographs of his wife, Edith, his children and extended family. In 1980 he began to photograph, mostly from the air, the scarred landscape left by the eruption of Mount St. Helens. Since then he has been working on a series of aerial images that record the toolmarks of human activity on the land. Some of Gowin's photographs depict man-made devastation: abandoned missile silos in the American West, the remains of Hanford Nuclear Reservation, and strip mining sites in Eastern Europe.
Mesa Blanca is a teasing reference to Emmet's aerial work. I made my "mesa" from a horse's mandible which was sent to me by a Texas rancher, and which I have always imagined as a miniature Southwestern landscape. I photographed the little flying machine at a toy museum in London.
See Gowin, Emmet, *Changing the Earth, Aerial Photographs*, Yale University Press, (2002)

Höch, Hannah (1889-1978)
German collagist and painter
(*Portrait of Hannah Höch*)
In the early 1980s my imagery began to change in response to my growing social and political concerns. During that time I made several extended trips to Europe to search out art and artists with whom I hoped to find a sense of concordance and perspective on my recent work.
The strongest single impression from those travels was my discovery of the collages of German Dadaist Hannah Höch. I was moved by the powerful, elemental faces she assembled in the 1920s, like her *Children* and *The Melancholic*, both from 1925. I found her collages more compelling—and more subversive—than those of her better-known contemporaries Raoul Hausmann and George Grosz. Her work also seemed to foreshadow, more than the overtly political works of the period, the tragic events Europe would face in the decades to come.

J'Accuse, [French] "I accuse"
The title of my monotype is borrowed from the anti-war film by French director Abel Gance, *J'Accuse* (1938) in which millions of dead soldiers from the first World War rise from their graves and march the earth in condemnation of war.
(*J'Accuse*, 1894, is also the title of a book by Emil Zola in which the author denounces the imprisonment of Army Captain Alfred Dreyfus, falsely accused of espionage in France in 1893 and banished to Devil's Island until his reprieve in 1906. Zola's book was an indictment of the prevailing anti-Semitism and official corruption in late 19th-century France).

Kafka, Franz (1883-1924)
Czech writer (wrote in German)
My portrait of Kafka—and my sense of Kafka—was shaped more by the writer's poignant diaries than by his novels. The *Diaries* reveal a complex man—highly capable and dedicated in his daytime work (insurance law), reticent and uncommonly polite in his personal interactions. Kafka was able, in the late-night hours which he claimed as his own, to tap a hidden universe of dark, prophetic imagination. His brilliant use of parable and symbolism was never academic nor, from his own accounts, premeditated. His novels and stories seem to have sprung almost involuntarily from his restless, agitated sensitivity.
The frail, skeletal body in my portrait makes reference to Kafka's hypochondria, which tormented him throughout his short adult life. (Kafka died of tuberculosis at the age of 42.) The background for the portrait is the black and white monotype, *Altstadt* (see entry above), that I made after a trip to Prague in 1988.

Kleine Pinakothek, *n.* [German]
The Alte (Old) Pinakothek, and the Neue (New) Pinakothek are two great art museums in Munich. Both museums' collections are treasures for anyone who appreciates the art of representational painting.
My painting, *Kleine Pinakothek*, could be seen as a little museum, with its gallery of postage-stamp paintings and miniature, industrial sculpture.

The Land of Ancestors is a chapter heading in Carl Jung's *Memories, Dreams, Reflections (Erinnerungen, Träume, Gedanken, 1961)*. The title of my painting is borrowed from that heading. Jung looked at tribal cultures in formulating his ideas about all cultures and the "collective unconscious" of individuals.

Lopez-Garcia, Antonio (1936-)
Spanish realist painter
Most of the representational painters I know place Lopez-Garcia at the top of their lists of influences. His paintings, the products of intense observation and extraordinary skill, possess an irresistible gravity. A feature film, *Dream of Light*, (1990) directed by Victor Erice, documents Lopez-Garcia's working methods as the artist paints a single quince tree in his Madrid studio backyard.

Luftpost, *n.* [German] air mail
The painting makes a references to my appreciation for German Art, from Dürer to Hannah Höch, and beyond.

Memling, Hans (c. 1440-1494)
German/Flemish painter
Hans Memling, a student of the Flemish master Rogier van der Weiden, produced some of the most beautifully designed and finely crafted portraits of the Northern European Renaissance. His best work projects a sense of transcendent calm and clarity unique among the paintings of his day. *The Lost Memling* is my re-painting of a lost Memling portrait (documented only through a remaining black and white catalog photograph. The painting was stolen from the Uffizi during the Nazi evacuation of Italy in 1944.

Mimesis, *n.* imitation, representation, mimicry of aspects of the world in literature and art.

Number 22 Alchemist's Street, This is the address of a little house in Prague that was owned by Kafka's sister, Ottla. Kafka borrowed the house for a brief period as a retreat for writing. Today the house, on the Alchemist's Street, or Golden Lane, is a literary tourist attraction.
My small sculpture was made after a visit to Prague and to the revered "Kafka House."

Numen, *n.* a presiding spirit, a phenomenon, or experience, that embodies an aura of divinity.
In his book, *The Idea of the Holy* (1923), German theolological scholar, Rudolph Otto, uses the words "numen" and "numinous" to explain "the thrill of awe or reverence" that can result from clear-sighted observation of the physical world. Some of Otto's ideas have been helpful in reinforcing my thoughts about the value of heightened attention to familiar places or objects.

Owen, Wilfred (1893-1918)
British Poet
Portrait of Wilfred Owen
Wilfred Owen's poems, stark and powerful descriptions of life and death in the trenches of France, convey a profound empathy with the soldier and a fierce indignation toward the greed and profiteering that fueled the war. Owen produced virtually all of his war poems in a single year, between August 1917 and September 1918. He was killed on the Western Front on November 4, 1918.

Paleographia, *n.* the study and interpretation of ancient forms of writing.

Palimpsestos, *n.* [Greek, English form, Palimpsest] "rubbed again," a parchment or tablet which has been written on and erased repeatedly, and which still bears the traces of previous marks.

Quay Brothers (1947-)
American animators and filmmakers (living in London)
The Quay Brothers were classmates of mine at The Philadelphia College of Art in the late 1960s. We were students in the illustration department where many young artists with a talent for representational painting ended up in those days. Even then the Quay's work was remarkable—the darkly eccentric drawings that they brought to class already hinting at the extraordinary animated films to come. As students, they found inspiration in the Polish poster (particularly in the works of Roman Cieslewicz and Franciszek Starowieyski), in the films of Luis Buñuel and Carl Theodor Dreyer, and the music of Leoš Janáček.
The Quays give credit to a wide range of esoteric sources, and are the first to honor their precursors and contemporaries, but their achievement, in my view, towers above the best of these. The sheer aesthetic force of a Quay film convinces us that we are experiencing something startlingly new.

Roth, Ed "Big Daddy" (1932-2001)
American custom car designer and artist.
The eccentric, iconoclastic Ed Roth was a hero to 15-year-old boys from Southern California to New England in the late 1950s. Although Roth abhored the values of the flower children, his influence on the emerging counterculture, its attitudes and its art, is certainly equal to that of Lenny Bruce, or the Bay Area poets.
Despite the intentional tackiness of his public persona, Roth was a sculptural visionary and a master craftsman. His cars, the *Outlaw*, and *Beatnik Bandit* are four-wheeled masterpieces. Watching Roth at work—airbrushing stylized monsters onto white sweatshirts for fans at the Philadelphia Custom Car Show—made me want to be an artist.

School Figures, in dance, practice patterns, fundamental patterns of movement that establish the basic structures of a particular dance.

Sabi, *n.* [Japanese] rust, patina.
In Japanese culture, the qualities of age and patina are highly valued.

Samizdat, *n.* [Russian] "a system by which manuscripts denied official publication in the Soviet Union [and throughout Central Europe under the former regimes] are circulated clandestinely in typescript or in mimeograph form, or are smuggled out for publication." (Webster)
A number of books that survived suppression in Central Europe have helped to shape my understanding of literature, and of all art. Bohumil Hrabal's *I Served the King of England*, and *Closely Watched Trains*, along with Josef Škvorecký's, *The Cowards*, *Miss Silver's Past*, and *The Bass Saxophone*, demonstrate, among other things, that even the most serious subjects can be handled playfully, and may indeed gain force through understatement. The idea of the Samizdat publication also has great appeal to me in its example of art's resilience through times and places inhospitable to it.
My painting, *Samizdat*, is a tribute to the art and literature of Prague—to the animator Jan Švankmajer, the collagist Jiří Kolár, the writers Bohumil Hrabal and Josef Škvorecký. The painting contains references to these artists while alluding to that quality of disillusioned child's play so characteristic of Czech art.

Selbstbildnis, *n.* [German]
self-portrait

Sommer, Frederick (1905-1999)
American Photographer
Sommer's disturbingly surreal, aesthetically beautiful photographs have had a far reaching, if somewhat hidden, influence on many of today's best-known fine art photographers. I was introduced to his work through Emmet Gowin who has been Sommer's close friend and enthusiastic advocate for many years.
Portrait of Frederick Sommer makes reference to Sommer's love and knowledge of the Italian Renaissance, as well as to his photograph, *Virgin and Child with Saint Anne and the Infant Saint John*. (That title was borrowed by Sommer from Leonardo Da Vinci's magnificent cartoon for the painting, *Madonna of the Rocks*. I used the Da Vinci cartoon as a background.) The figure of Sommer in my montage was made from a piece of molten aluminum picked up from the site of a house fire.

Stoss, Veit (c.1447-1533)
German sculptor and woodcarver, active in Nuremberg and Cracow.
My first encounter with the work of the Nuremberg sculptor, Veit Stoss, was in 1986 when his powerful *Crucifix* of 1505 was on temporary display at the Metropolitan Museum of Art in New York. I stood spellbound before the piece. Stoss' sublimely crafted vision of the crucifixion seemed to hold within it a living presence—a profound embodiment of the universal story of the visionary and reformer and of his destiny. A number of Stoss' major works can be seen in Nuremberg at St. Lorenz Church, and at the Nürnberg Germanisches Nationalmuseum.
While working on the *Portrait of Veit Stoss* I remembered a biographical detail about the sculptor that I had read years before; he was convicted of forging a promissory note in 1503, was imprisoned, and branded on both cheeks as punishment.

Švankmajer, Jan (1934-)
Czech animator, filmmaker and graphic artist
Jan Švankmajer is the creator of some of the world's most aesthetically brilliant and politically barbed animated and live action films. Anthony Lane, in his *New Yorker* review of Švankmajer's *Faust* writes,"The moviegoing world is split into two unequal camps: those who have never heard of Jan Švankmajer, and those who happen upon his work and know that they have come face to face with genius." I agree with Mr. Lane.
I wanted to depict Švankmajer as the feisty, irreverent Punch—a salute to his artistic courage and militancy. (Švankmajer's films contain many allusions to the traditional Eastern European and Russian puppet theater, where apparent mischief and child's play have carried the weight of dangerous political messages.)
In Portrait of Jan Švankmajer, the Prague facade becomes a miniature cinema, with an etching by Švankmajer (in the manner of Arcimbaldo) on the screen.

Tarkovsky, Andrei (1932-1986)
Russian filmmaker
Tarkovsky's films are characterized by their powerful symbolic imagery, by their unconventional narrative structures, and by a rigorous sense of human responsibility. His seven feature films, while engendering bewilderment for some viewers, have now received acclaim from audiences and critics around the world.
Tarkovsky believed that art itself is a spiritual practice and that the self-conscious ironies and critical games characteristic of late modernism represent a cultural "wrong turn." Like Tolstoy, he insisted that genuine art charted man's spiritual progress—that it marked the threshold of mankind's slowly-evolving capacity for kindness and humanity.
In his extraordinary book, *Sculpting in Time*, (one of the best books I know about the practice of art by an artist) Tarkovsky writes:
"The allotted function of art is not, as is often assumed, to put across ideas, to propagate thoughts, to serve as example. The aim of art is to prepare a person for death, to plough and harrow his soul, rendering it capable of turning to good."

Trabajadora, *n.* [Spanish, fem.]
the worker, laborer

Trauerarbeit, *n.* [German]
"work of mourning"
The title of my monotype is taken from the work of the German psychologists, Alexander and Margarete Mitscherlich. The Mitscherlichs identified the collective, psychological denial of the Nazi years by its participants as creating a "mass melancholia" in German society. This collective silence, according to the Mitscherlich's study, *The Inability to Mourn* (1967), was particularly harmful to children of the war generation. The Mitscherlichs proposed that Trauerarbeit was essential to cultural healing after the Nazi years. (See Susan Sontag's preface to Hans Jürgen Syberberg's screenplay, *Hitler, A Film from Germany*, Farrar, Straus & Giroux, 1982).
Trauerarbeit, for me, offers a valuable example to American culture as well. My monotype, *Trauerarbeit*, belongs to a series that I began in the months before the 1991 Gulf War bombing. The Iraqi civilians killed in that action and its aftermath remain largely unacknowledged and unmourned.

Tucholsky, Kurt (1890-1935)
German essayist, satirist, and novelist
Kurt Tucholsky, in his short satirical essays of the early 1930s for the literary magazine, *Die Schaubühne* (The Stage), kept up a relentless attack on the complacency of Berliners toward the rise of Nazism. Tucholsky was one of the great practitioners of the famous *Berliner Schnauze*, or Berlin wit, which will be remembered (in English equivalents) from the films and offhand remarks of Billy Wilder.
Some of Tucholsky's short works are collected in the book, *Deutschland, Deutschland (Germany, Germany, 1929)*. Originally published as a collaboration with political photomontagist, John Heartfield, the collaborative edition, in German, is still in print.
My collage, *Paperwork, for Kurt Tucholsky*, refers to the often-cited multitude of small, banal, public acts of complicity without which a corrupt regime cannot exist.

Tumultus is the Latin root of Tumult, meaning commotion, disturbance, surging up; from the Latin verb-tumere: to swell.

Zazen, *n.* a meditation practiced in Zen Buddhism [from Japanese, za: to sit down, and zen: silent meditation]

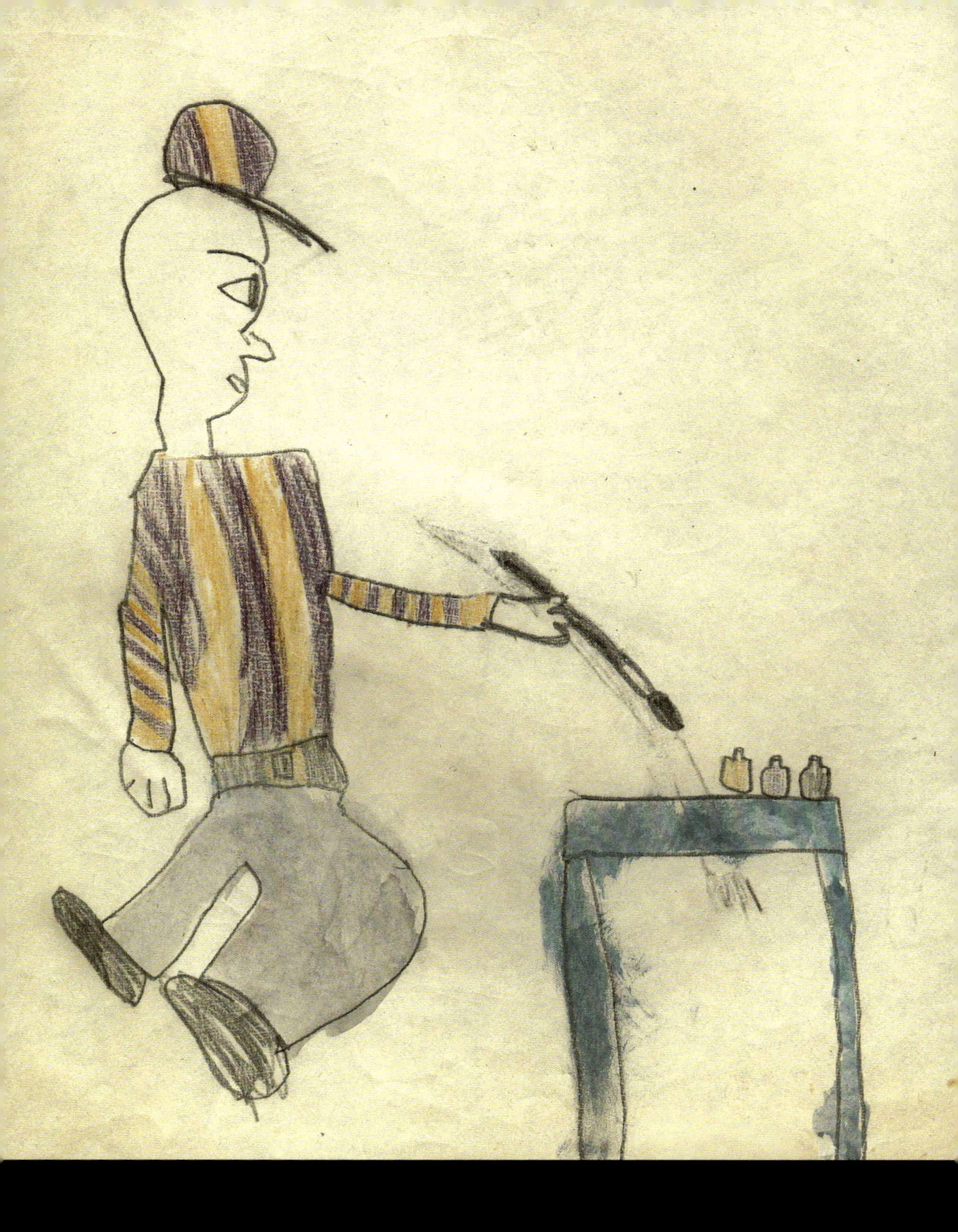

Self Portrait, 195[illegible], watercolor, colored pencil and graphite on paper, 10 ¾ x 8 ½"

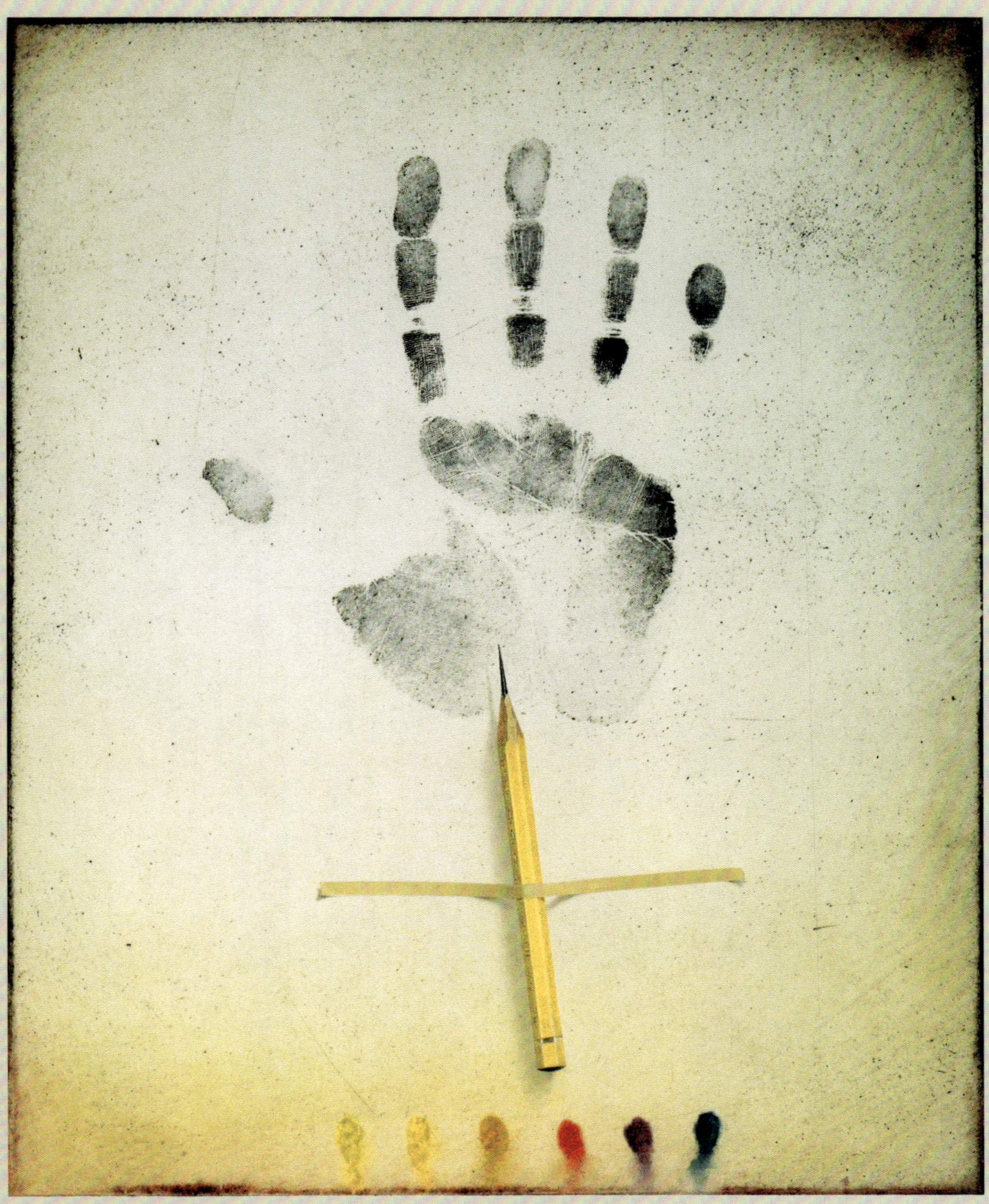

Selbstbildnis, 1993, acrylic and watercolor over monotype, 14 x 11"

SELECTED ONE-PERSON EXHIBITIONS:

2003 Forum Gallery, New York, NY
2003 James A. Michener Art Museum, Bucks County, PA
2002 Forum Gallery, Los Angeles, CA
2002 Portland Museum of Art, Portland, ME
2001 Atrium Gallery, University of Southern Maine at Lewiston-Auburn
2001 The Art Gallery, University of New Hampshire at Durham
2000 Berlin Philharmonie, *Alan Magee, Monotypes*, Berlin, Germany
2000 Hollis Taggart Galleries, NY, NY
1998 Edith Caldwell Gallery, San Francisco, CA
1998 OP Photogallery, Hong Kong, *Alan Magee, Literacy and Fiction in Portraiture*
1997 Edith Caldwell Gallery, San Francisco, CA
1996 Edith Caldwell Gallery, San Francisco, CA
1995 Edith Caldwell Gallery, San Francisco, CA
1994 Carnegie Hall, University of Maine at Orono
1993 Edith Caldwell Gallery, San Francisco, CA
1992 Edith Caldwell Gallery, San Francisco, CA
1992 Cheekwood Museum of Art, Nashville, TN
1992 Kodak's Center for Creative Imaging, Camden, ME
1992 Selby Gallery, Ringling School of Art & Design, Sarasota, FL
1991 Farnsworth Art Museum, *Alan Magee, A Ten Year Survey*, Rockland, ME
1991 James A. Michener Art Museum, *A Ten Year Survey*, Bucks County, PA
1990 Staempfli Gallery, New York, NY
1990 Kipp Gallery, Indiana University of Pennsylvania
1990 Joan Whitney Payson Gallery, Westbrook College, Portland, ME
1989 Schmidt Bingham Gallery, New York, NY
1989 Allport Gallery, San Francisco, CA
1988 Gallerie Gérard Gustau, Paris, France
1988 Clark Gallery, Lincoln, MA
1986 Schmidt Bingham Gallery, New York, NY
1986 Meckler Gallery, Los Angeles, CA
1985 Fresno Art Center, Fresno, CA
1984 Farnsworth Art Museum, Rockland, ME
1984 Newport Art Museum, Newport, RI
1984 Allport Gallery, San Francisco, CA
1983 San Jose Museum of Art, San Jose, CA
1983 Norton Gallery and School of Art, W. Palm Beach, FL
1983 FIAC Grand Palais, Paris, France
1982 Staempfli Gallery, New York, NY
1981 Allport Gallery, San Francisco, CA
1980 Staempfli Gallery, New York, NY
1979 Clark Gallery, Lincoln, MA
1978 Allport Gallery, Larkspur, CA

SELECTED GROUP SHOWS, *(since 1995):*

2002 Center for Maine Contemporary Arts, *Fiftieth Anniversary Exhibition*
2002 Naples Art Museum, Naples FL, *Photorealism, The Liff Collection*
2001 Arkansas Art Center, *Magic Vision*
2001 Ringling School of Art, *Real(ist) Men*
2001 Center for Maine Contemporary Arts, *Print Portfolios*
2001 Forum Gallery, New York, NY
2000 Hunt Institute for Botanical Documentation, *Gifts of Winter*
2000 Memorial Art Gallery, University of Rochester, *New Realism for a New Millennium*
2000 Katonah Museum of Art, *Déjà Vu: Revisioning the Past*
1999 Art Institute of Chicago, *Contemporary American Realist Drawings*
1998 Hollis Taggart Gallery, New York, NY
1998 Hackett Freedman Gallery, San Francisco, CA
1998 New York Armory, New York, NY, *Works on Paper*
1997 Portland Museum of Art, Portland, ME, *A Legacy for Maine*
1997 New York Armory, New York, NY, *Works on Paper*
1997 National Museum of American Art, Washington, DC, *The Monotype in America*
1996 New York Armory, New York, NY, *Works on Paper*
1996 Forum Gallery, New York, NY, *Exactitude*
1995 Philadelphia Museum of Art, *Rolywholyover, A Circus*, John Cage, Curator

BOOKS BY THE ARTIST:

2000 *Archive: Alan Magee Monotypes* (Spectrum Concerts Berlin and Darkwood Press), essay by Maureen Mullarkey
1991 *Alan Magee 1981-1991* (The Farnsworth Art Museum) essay by Carl Little, interview with Alan Magee conducted by Beth Critchlow
1987 *Stones and Other Works by Alan Magee* (Harry N. Abrams) foreword by Theodore F. Wolff and essay by Alan Magee

AWARDS:

2001 *CA (Communication Arts)* Award of Excellence
1992 The Maine Arts Commission Fellowship for Film
1990 National Academy of Design, The Leo Meissner Prize
1983 *Communication Arts*, Award of Excellence
1982 The National Book Award
1981 American Academy and Institute of Arts and Letters, Richard & Hinda Rosenthal Foundation Award
1977 *Communication Arts*, Award of Excellence, client: *Playboy*

1977	*Playboy Magazine*, Annual Editorial Award, Best Nonfiction Illustration
1977	The New York Art Director's Club Award
1974	Art Directors Club of Los Angeles Award

SELECTED MUSEUM COLLECTIONS:

Achenbach Foundation
San Francisco, CA
Arizona State University Art Museum,
Tempe, AZ
Arkansas Art Center,
Little Rock, AK
Art Institute of Chicago, Davidson Collection
of American Realist Drawings,
Chicago, IL
Columbus Museum of Art,
Columbus, OH
DeCordova Museum and Sculpture Park,
Lincoln, MA
Farnsworth Art Museum,
Rockland, ME
Hunt Institute for Botanical Documentation,
Pittsburgh, PA
James A. Michener Art Museum
Bucks County, PA
Josolyn Art Museum,
Omaha, NB
Newark Museum,
Newark, NJ
Norton Gallery & School of Art,
West Palm Beach, FL
Portland Museum of Art,
Portland, ME
Zimmerli Art Museum,
New Brunswick, NJ

SELECTED PRIVATE COLLECTIONS:

American Hospital Supply Co.
Atlantic Richfield Co.
Bank of Japan
Nicholas Cage Collection
Sammy Cahn Collection
Cargill Corp.
Johnny Carson Collection
Chermayeff & Geismar Inc.
Richard Cohen Collection
Continental Grain Co.
Jalane and Richard Davidson Collection
Deloitte, Haskins, and Sells
Henry Fonda Collection
Janss Collection
Lucasfilm, Inc.
Burton & Deedee McMurtry Collection
Mobil Oil
Morley Safer Collection
Mike Nichols & Diane Sawyer
Signet Banking Corp.
Union Trust Bank
Billy Wilder Collection

GUEST LECTURES:

American Academy in Berlin,
with John Harbison and Robert Helps
Boston College of Art
Bowdoin College
Cheekwood Museum of Art
Chewonki Foundation
Colby College
Connecticut College
Emporia State University
Farnsworth Art Museum
Indiana University of Pennsylvania
Philadelphia College of Art
Portland Museum of Art (Maine)
Rhode Island School of Design
Ringling School of Art and Design
University of Maine
University of New Hampshire
Utah State University

TELEVISION AND VIDEO:

2002	UMVA/Maine PBS *Alan Magee: Maine Master*
1993	Maine PBS *Made in Maine, Center for Creative Imaging*
1992	Maine PBS *Three Maine Artists*
1991	Suburban Cable, Bucks County, PA *Alan Magee: 1981-1991*
1988	Maine PBS *Alan Magee, Visions of Darkness and Light*
1983	KGO San Francisco, CA, Channel 7

RADIO:

2000	Utah Public Radio
1993	KPFA, (Pacifica Radio) Berkeley, CA, Interview
1991	WHYY, Philadelphia, ARTSCAPE Interview
1989	Voice of America Interview with Larry Freund
1987	Monitor Radio Interview, National Public Radio
1986	Voice of America Interview with Larry Freund
1985	Maine Public Radio Interview

SELECTED COMMISSIONS:

Portrait of Senate Majority leader George Mitchell,
commissioned by the U.S. Senate
Mural, Maine State House Complex,
Burton M. Cross Building, 2001
Mural, Bryand Global Sciences Center,
University of Maine, 1997
Tapestry, Riverview Psychiatric Center,
Augusta, ME
Atlantic Magazine, article, 5/87
Atlantic Magazine, article, 5/90
New York Magazine, cover, 12/24/73
The New York Times Sunday Magazine, cover, 9/16/73
Time Magazine covers, 2/20/78, 4/23/79, 3/9/81,
2/15/82, 4/15/85

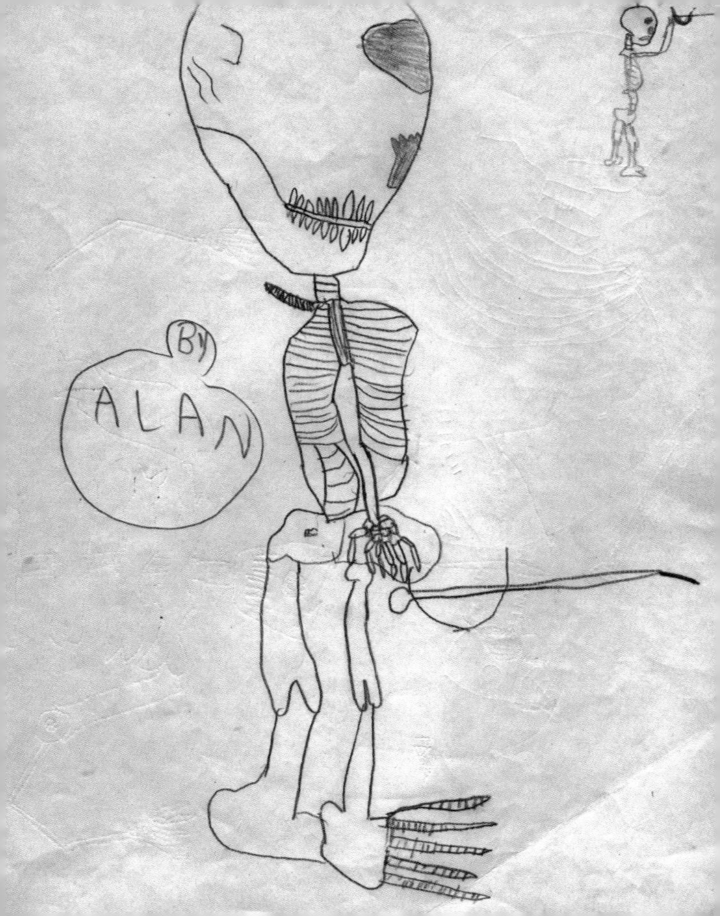
BY
ALAN

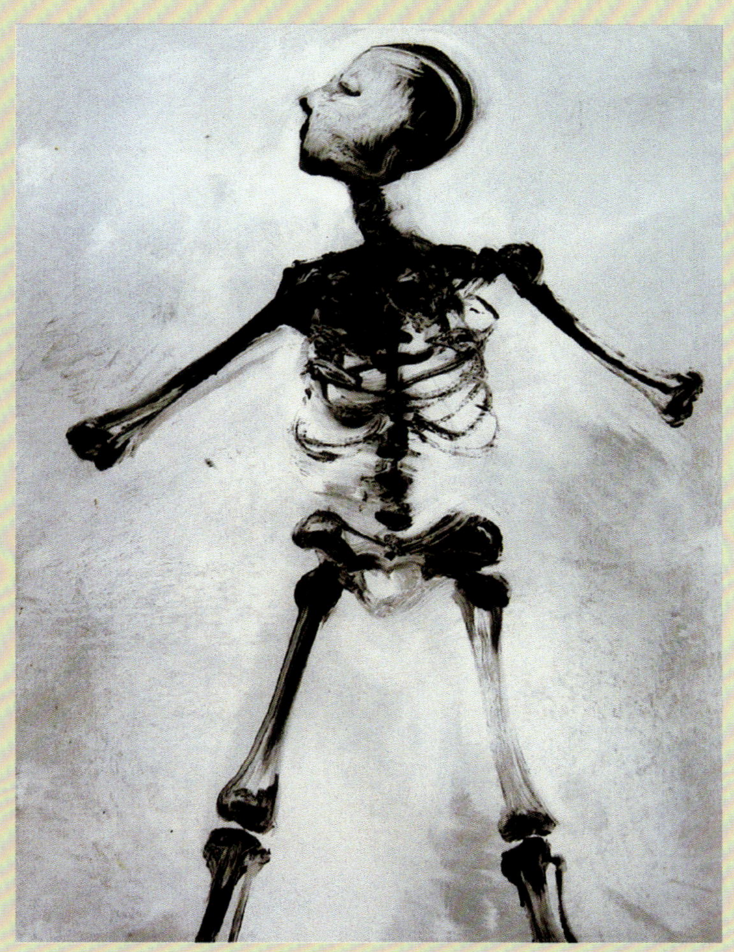

Skeleton, 1991, monotype, 24 x 18"

SELECTED BIBLIOGRAPHY

BOOKS

Beem, Edgar Allen III. *Maine Art Now*, with essay, "Alan Magee and His Perfect Stones." The Dog Ear Press, 1990, pp. 69-73.

Fine, Ruth; Hernández-Duran, Raymond; Pascale, Mark. *Contemporary American Realist Drawings, The Jalane and Richard Davidson Collection*. The Art Institute of Chicago, 1999, pp. 14-15, 111, 125.

Little, Carl; Critchlow, Beth; Magee, Alan. *Alan Magee 1981-1991, A Ten Year Survey*. Farnsworth Art Museum, 1991.

Moser, Joann. *Singular Impressions, The Monotype in America*. The National Museum of American Art, Smithsonian Institution Press, 1997, pp. 153-154.

Mullarkey, Maureen; Magee, Alan. *Archive, Alan Magee Monotypes*. Spectrum Concerts Berlin and Darkwood Press, 2000.

Wolff, Theodore F.; Magee, Alan. *Alan Magee, Stones and Other Works*. Harry N. Abrams, 1987.

CATALOGS

Bloemink, Barbara J. PhD. *Déjà Vu: Reworking the Past*. Katonah Museum of Art, January 16, 2000.

Brown, Bruce. *Alan Magee, Undercurrents*. University of Southern Maine, April 30, 2001.

Canaday, John. *Alan Magee, Recent Paintings and Drawings*. Staempfli Gallery, October 12, 1982.

Chase, Linda. *Photorealism, The Liff Collection*. Naples Museum of Art, 2001, pp. 3, 35.

Cohen, Ronny H. *Meticulous Realist Drawing*. Squibb Gallery, May/June 1989

Fishko, Robert. *Alan Magee*. Forum Gallery, March 2002.

Little, Carl. *Alan Magee and the Mystery of Form*. Hollis Taggart Gallery, April 2001.

Lopez, Barry. *Alan Magee Inlets*. Joan Whitney Payson Gallery of Art, April 7, 1990.

Magee, Alan. *Alan Magee, Recent Paintings and Drawings*. Staempfli Gallery, September 16, 1980.

Magee, Alan; et al. *Sols, Peintures Sculptures Installations*. Fondation Nationale des Arts Graphiques et Plastiques, Paris, France, 1984.

Magee, Alan. *Alan Magee, Stones and Other Works*. Schmidt Bingham Gallery, October 8, 1986.

Magee, Alan. *Digital Imaging Here and Now*. International Photography, Number One, 1993.

Magee, Alan. *West/Art and the Law, 15th Annual Exhibition*. West Publishing Company, 1990, pp. 68-69.

Magee, Alan. *West/Art and the Law, 14th Annual Exhibition*. West Publishing Company, 1989, pp. 50-53.

Milovich, Rose. *The Allure of Illusionism: Trompe l'Oeil in Contemporary American Painting*. Nora Eccles Harrison Museum of Art, October 7, 1992.

Ringling School of Art and Design. *Twenty-three Artists in Residence at Ringling School of Art and Design*. 1999.

Staempfli, George. *Alan Magee*. Staempfli Gallery, November 13, 1990.

Taggart, Hollis. *Works on Paper*. Hollis Taggart Galleries, March 13, 1999.

Wolfe, Townsend. *Magic Vision*. Arkansas Arts Center, 2001, p. 54.

Wolff, Theodore F. *On the Edge, 40 Years of Maine Painting 1952-1992*. Maine Coast Artists, 1992, p.79.

VIDEOS

Passerman, Harriet. *Alan Magee, Visions of Darkness and Light*. Maine PBS, 1988.

Shetterly, Robert; Vendetti, Deb. *Alan Magee, Maine Master*. Union of Maine Visual Artists, Maine PBS, 2002.

SELECTED ARTICLES

Altabe, Joan. "No Stone Unturned, While Studying Rocks, Alan Magee Uncovered the Human Condition." *Sarasota Herald-Tribune*, January 12, 1992, pp. G1-3.

Barry, William David. "An Art Book from Maine Stone Age." *Maine Sunday Telegram*, May 3, 1987.

Beem, Edgar Allen III. "A Painting Should Not Mean, But Be." *Maine Times*, May 25, 1984, p. 33.

Beem, Edgar Allen III. "Alan Magee." *Art Voices*, July/August 1981, p. 59.

Beem, Edgar Allen III. "Alan Magee." *Arts Magazine*, October 1986, p. 108.

Beem, Edgar Allen III. "Alan Magee & Allison Hildreth in Pursuit of Depth." *Maine Times*, April 13, 1990.

Beem, Edgar Allen III. "Alan Magee and His Perfect Stones." *Maine Times*, February 6, 1981, pp. 14-17.

Beem, Edgar Allen III. "Alan Magee in the Unknown World." *Maine Times*, July 5, 1991, pp. 24-25.

Beem, Edgar Allen III. "Image is Everything, Alan Magee and His Creative Images." *Maine Times*, June 19, 1992, pp. 13-15.

Beem, Edgar Allen III. "Magee's Images Go Beyond the Real." *Maine Times*, July 18, 1986, p. 29.

Beem, Edgar Allen III. "What is the Maine Drawing Biennial?" *Maine Times*, January 13, 1984, p. 25.

Burkhart, Dorothy. "Painter Draws on Reality and Dabbles in Abstractions." *San Jose Mercury News*, January 6, 1983.

Canaday, John. "A Dazzling New Realist Painter." *Saturday Review Magazine*, December 1980, pp. 86-87.

Canaday, John. "A New Realist." *Dialogue Magazine*, Summer 1981.

Caponigro, John Paul. "Alan Magee, Intensity and Realism." *Preview!*, July 12, 1991, pp. 8-9.

Caponigro, John Paul. "Travels to India, England Infuse Two Artists' New Work." *Preview!*, May 4-25, 1990, p. 14.

Carlock, Marty. "Latest Clark Exhibit Explores 'The Dark Side.'" *Lincoln Journal*, November 9, 1989.

Cherol, John A. "Alan Magee." *Cheekwood TN Botanical Gardens and Fine Arts Center*, March/April 1992, p. 9.

Cohen, Ronny H. "Alan Magee-Magic and Real." *Arts Magazine*, November 1982, pp. 106-107.

Cohen, Ronny H. "Drawing the Meticulous Realist Way." *Drawing Magazine*, March 1982, pp. 121-125.

Cooper, James F. "Magee Excites With Texture, Composition, Detail." *New York City Tribune*, October 17, 1986.

Cremin, Ann. "L'Expo des Expos: A Show of the Shows That Were." *The Magazine of Paris*, October 1983, p. 30.

Dempsey, Susan Carey. "*Time* Illustrator Draws on His Successes." *Bucks County Courier Times*, June 9, 1987, p. B18.

Der Tagesspiegel (Berlin). "Gezeichnet vom Krieg" (Drawn from War). November 22, 2000.

Dodd, Ivy. "Cushing Artist Being Honored." *The Courier Gazette*, January 25, 1990.

Dodd, Ivy. "Magee Series Shows in Portland." The Courier Gazette, April 12, 1990.

Edwards, Owen. "The Very Last 'Is it Art' Article, A Little Art to Art Talk." *American Photographer*, February 1981, pp. 36-38.

Ernest, Dagney C. "About Face, Alan Magee." *The Courier Gazette*, April 18, 2002, p. C1.

Fauntleroy, Gussie. "Delicate Tragedy and Vulnerability of Life. Mixed-Media

Show at Lambert." *Pasa Tiempo*, April 15-21, 1994, p. 25.

Gold, Donna. "Artist Sets Aside His Realism for the More Disturbing." *Maine Times*, April 18, 2002.

Gold, Donna. "Eye of the Beholder." *Maine Times*, March 30, 2000, pp. 22-23.

Gold, Donna. "Stone to Soul." *Maine Times*, October 28, 1994.

Gold, Donna. "The Artwork of Alan Magee." *Kennebec Journal*, October 22-23, 1994, pp. M1-2.

Grandchamp, Catherine. "FIAC PARIS." *Art World*, November 1983.

Harper's Magazine. "Readings: Insider, Gold Card, and Tenure by Alan Magee." July 1990, p. 35.

Hurlburt, Roger. "Magee's Fine Observations in Line With Definition of New Realism." *Fort Lauderdale News and Sun Sentinel*, March 27, 1983.

Isaacson, Phillip. "A Fine Artist Emerges at the Farnsworth." *Maine Sunday Telegram*, June 10, 1984, p. A44.

Isaacson, Phillip. "Exhibit Shows an Artist Taking Control of His Technique." *Maine Sunday Telegram*, July 7, 1991, p. G4.

Isaacson, Phillip. "Journeys of Introspection and Fantasy." *Maine Sunday Telegram*, April 29, 1990.

Kernan, Sean. "Alan Magee: Works and Days." *Graphis*, March/April 2001.

Kinnicutt, Michael. "Cover Artist, Alan Magee." *Down East Magazine*, February 1981, p. 29.

Kohen, Helen. "Norton Director Makes His Art Choices with Care." *The Miami Herald*, August 21, 1983, p. L5.

Lake Worth Herald. "Works by Alan Magee on View at the Norton." March 3, 1983.

Lambert, Carol S. "Alan Magee: Anatomy of Illusion and Allusion." *The Camden Herald*, August 21, 2002, pp. B1-2.

Little, Carl. "Alan Magee." *Maine Boats and Harbors*, February/March 2002, pp. 76-80.

Little, Carl. "Art at Your Fingertips. The Internet Provides a New Venue for Maine Artists." *Maine Times*, November 9, 2000, p. 20.

Magee, Alan. "Bread, Butter and Fine Art." *The York Weekly*, June 10, 1992, p. 13.

Magee, Alan. "Read Any Good Books Lately? King, Chute, van de Wettering et al. Offer Some Suggestions." *Maine Times*, February 1, 1985, pp. 16-17.

Marxsen, Patti M. "Alan Magee: The Man, His Art and Change." *The Camden Herald*, August 1, 1991, pp. 10, 20.

Marxsen, Patti M. "Foskett and Magee Exhibit in Memorable Show at CCI." *The Camden Herald*, July 23, 1992, p. 16.

McKenna, Kristina. "The Exquisite Forms Depicted…" *Los Angeles Times*, March 14, 1986.

Mullarkey, Maureen. "Alan Magee, The Mystery of Form." *Review, the Critical State of Visual Art in New York*, April 15, 2000, p. 32.

Nudelman, Stuart. "Artists' Renderings." *York County Coast Star*, May 2, 2002, p. C3.

Ouellette, Larry E. "Artist Alan Magee: Striking a Chord." *Portland Press Herald*, May 26, 1984, p. 17.

Palm Beach Daily News. "Realist Alan Magee's Art Showing at Norton." March 6, 1983.

Pantalone, John. "What's Really There." *Newport: This Week*, August 23, 1984, p. 21.

Publishers Weekly. "Stones and Other Works." March 13, 1987.

Raynor, Vivian. "Precision for Precision's Sake in a Show by Virtuoso Realists." *The New York Times*, May 21, 1989.

Raynor, Vivian. "The Art of Drawing II." *The New York Times*, June 26,1981, p. C26.

Richter, Nikola. "Ikonen aus dem Jenseits" (Icons from the Beyond). *Berliner Morgenpost*, November 14, 2000.

Russell, John. "Alan Magee." *The New York Times*, October 22, 1982.

Russell, John. "New York Contemporary Realists." *The New York Times*, February 14, 1986.

Schiferl, Ellen. "Alan Magee." *Art New England*, July/August 1984.

Schwan, Gary. "Realist-Illusionist Magee Captures the Essence of Objects." *The Palm Beach Post*, March 6, 1983, pp. G1, G7.

Schwan, Gary. "Unusual Media Used to Explore 'Chinks in the Armor of Reality.'" *The Palm Beach Post*, January 12, 1986, p. E8.

Shere, Charles. "Two Visions of Life in San Jose." *San Jose Tribune*, 1983.

Shultes, Anne. "No Stone Left Unturned." *The Courier Times*, Bucks County, PA, September 17, 1991, p. B4.

Sozanski, Edward J. "Magee Exhibit in Doylestown." *The Philadelphia Inquirer*, October 10, 1991, p. D5.

Stapen, Nancy. "Salons Put on a Show." *The Boston Herald*, December 26, 1985, p. 50.

Stump, Susan. "Magee's Farnsworth Show." *The Camden Herald*, May 17, 1984, p. 8.

Terwoman, Beverly. "A Simple, Delicately Balanced Show." *Independent Journal*, San Rafael, CA, January 22, 1981.

The Advance of Bucks County. "Alan Magee: Illustrator Turned Fine Artist; Major Exhibition of Newtown Native's Work at Michener Center." August 15, 1991, p. 3.

Thompson, Chris. "Dead Center, Dulce et Decorum: Alan Magee's Archive at PMA." *The Portland Phoenix*, April 5, 2002, p. 16.

University of Maine at Orono. "Magee's exhibit hailed as highlight of UMO season." *UMO Campus Newspaper*, November 1985.

Walker, David. "The Universe According to Paint—Artist Alan Magee." *The Camden Herald*, November 14, 1985, pp. 1, 10.

Weston, Suzanne L. "Forms of Logic, Art by Alan Magee." *The Philadelphia Inquirer Magazine*, May 1, 1994, pp. 18-21.

Wolfe, Millie. "Ordinary Objects Have Caught the Eye of Imaginative Artist." *Palm Beach Daily News*, March 2, 1983, p. 2.

Wolff, Theodore F. "…Flash and Dazzle are Hyped while Wisdom and Maturity are Ignored." *The Christian Science Monitor*, May 6, 1985, p. 37.

Wolff, Theodore F. "Drawing is Back in Style." *The Christian Science Monitor*, June 15, 1981, p. 19.

Wolff, Theodore F. "Emergence of a Gifted Artist." *The Christian Science Monitor*, October 26, 1982, p. 19.

Wolff, Theodore F. "Exuberance Under Control." *The Christian Science Monitor*, December 16, 1985, p. 25.

Wolff, Theodore F. "Painting in the Late '80s." *The Christian Science Monitor*, November 24, 1986.

Wolff, Theodore F. "Profound or Provincial, American Realism Searches for Meaning." *The Christian Science Monitor*, December 12, 1985, pp. 22-23.

Wolff, Theodore F. "The Many Masks of Modern Art: A Breeze Makes the Picture." *The Christian Science Monitor*, August 14, 1986.

Wolff, Theodore F. "The Many Masks of Modern Art: Small, Unassuming, Profound." *The Christian Science Monitor*, July 5, 1984, p. 34.

Wolff, Theodore F. "The Many Masks of Modern Art: There's a Form of Realist Art Emerging Today …" *The Christian Science Monitor*, December 9, 1982, p. 20.

Wolff, Theodore F. "The Many Masks of Modern Art: We've Entered a Most Fascinating Time …" *The Christian Science Monitor*, March 10, 1981, pp. 20-21.

Wolff, Theodore F. "Today's Challenge to Art Critics: Be Willing to Sort out the 'Junk.'" *The Christian Science Monitor*, June 18, 1984, p. 23.

Alan Magee, born in 1947 in Newtown, Pennsylvania, attended art school in Philadelphia and, in 1968, began working as an editorial and book illustrator in New York. Among his regular clients were *Time*, *Atlantic*, *Playboy*, *New York Magazine*, *The New York Times*, and Bantam, Ballantine and Simon and Schuster Books. In the late 1970s Magee began to concentrate on his personal paintings and in 1980 had his first solo exhibition in New York at Staempfli Gallery. Since that time he has had annual one-person shows throughout the United States and Europe. Books of Magee's paintings include *Stones and Other Works*, published by Harry N. Abrams in 1986, *Alan Magee 1981-1991*, published by the Farnsworth Art Museum in 1991, and *Archive, Alan Magee Monotypes*, published by Darkwood Press and Spectrum Concerts Berlin in 2000. Magee has received awards for his painting from the American Academy of Arts and Letters and the National Academy of Design and received a National Book Award in 1982. Several television documentaries have been made about his work including the Maine PBS and UMVA productions, *Alan Magee, Visions of Darkness and Light*, and *Alan Magee, Maine Master*. His works are in many private and public collections.

Barry Lopez was born in 1945 in Port Chester, New York. He grew up in Southern California and New York City and attended college in the Midwest before moving to Oregon, where he has lived since 1968. He is an essayist, author and short story writer, and has traveled extensively in remote parts of the world. Recent trips have taken him to Argentina, Cuba, Greenland, and Antarctica. He is the author of *Arctic Dreams*, for which he received the National Book Award, *Of Wolves and Men*, for which he received the John Burroughs Medal, and eight works of fiction including *Light Action in the Caribbean* and *Field Notes*. Mr. Lopez was the recipient of the Award in Literature from the Academy of Arts and Letters, the John Hay Medal, Guggenheim and National Science Foundation Fellowships, a Lannan Foundation Award, and Pushcart Prizes in fiction and nonfiction, among many other honors.

Jonathan Weiner is an independent writer. His latest book (working title: *His Brother's Keeper*) will be published by Ecco Press in the fall of 2004. His previous book, *Time, Love, Memory*, won a National Book Critics Circle Award in 2000. His book *The Beak of the Finch* won a Los Angeles Times Book Prize in 1994, and a Pulitzer Prize in 1995. His books have been supported by grants from NASA and the Alfred P. Sloan Foundation, and have been translated into more than a dozen languages, while his articles and essays have appeared in many newspapers and magazines, including *Time*, *The New Republic*, *The New York Times Magazine*, and *The New Yorker*. He Lives in Bucks County, Pennsylvania with his wife, Deborah Heiligman, who writes children's books. They have two sons, Aaron and Benjamin.

Richard V. West, a native of Prague, Czechoslovakia, graduated with highest honors from the University of California, Santa Barbara in 1961, going on to studies at the Academy of Fine Arts in Vienna and the University of California, Berkeley, where he undertook graduate work in art history. West is currently director of the Frye Art Museum (Seattle, Washington) and previously directed the Newport Art Museum (Rhode Island), the Santa Barbara Museum of Art, the Crocker Art Museum (Sacramento, California), and the Bowdoin College Museum of Art (Brunswick, Maine).

Active in many professional arenas, West has written and lectured extensively on the life and work of the American painter Rockwell Kent, and is currently preparing a book on that artist. Keenly involved with issues of modern and contemporary representational art, West has organized exhibitions on a wide range of subjects from *Standing the Tempest: Painters of the Hungarian Avant-Garde, 1908-1930* to *Representing LA: Pictorial Currents in Contemporary Southern California Art*.

ACKNOWLEDGEMENTS

I am grateful to many colleagues and friends who have helped and advised on this book: Walter Bernard, Byron Dobel, David Farmer, Sean Kernan, Robert Stanton, Michael Putnam, Ken Gaulin, Ana Pearson, Christopher and Rosalee Glass, Frank Dodge, Emmet Gowin, Edith Caldwell, John Collier, Stacey, Joel and Elly Glassman, Eileen Roth, the Quay Brothers, and my Forum Gallery representatives Robert and Cheryl Fishko and Niccolo Brooker.

Special thanks are due to artist and designer Lance Hidy, who conceived of this book and set the course for its content and design. Thanks to B. Martin Pedersen, to my editor Michael Porciello, and to designers Lauren Prigozen, Nicole Recchia and Luis Diaz. I appreciate the help of Christopher Crosman and Helen Fisher at the Farnsworth Art Museum, Bruce Katsiff at the James A. Michener Art Museum, and Gary Edson and Denise Newsome at the Museum of Texas Tech University. Special thanks to Richard West, Director of the Frye Art Museum, for his support and for contributing the Foreword. I am grateful, also, to Bill Tydeman, David Marshall, Sue Barr and Alice Olson at the Southwest Collection/Special Collections Library at Texas Tech, for their assistance in facilitating and transcribing the Barry Lopez/Alan Magee conversation.

Finally, I thank my wife and partner, Monika Magee for generously extending her wide range of skills to every aspect of this project.

Burrow, 2000, monotype, 14 x 11"▷

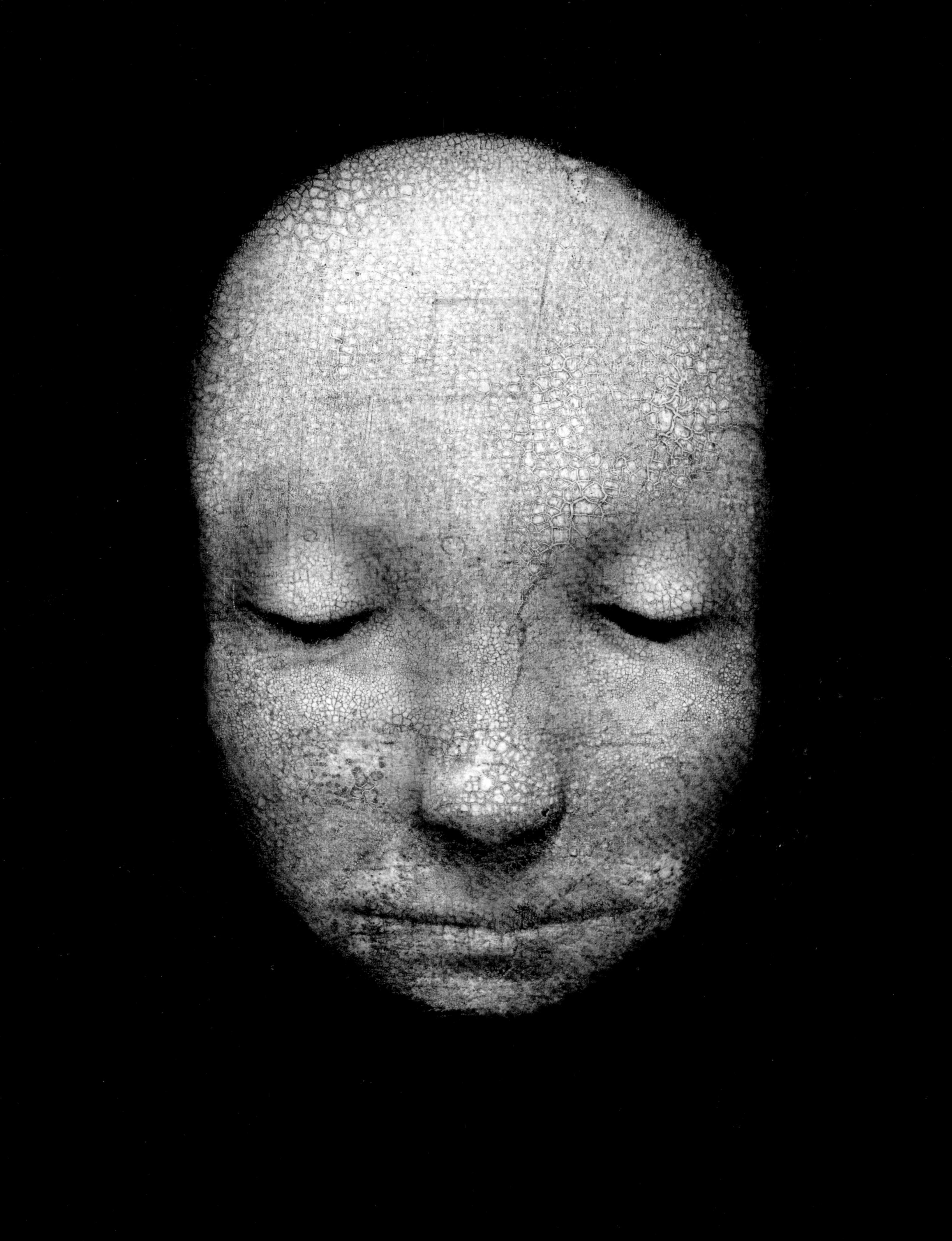